HOW TO BE A GARDENER

Alan Titchmarsh

HOW TO BE A GARDENER

Photographs by Jonathan Buckley

HYLAS
PUBLISHING

HYLAS
PUBLISHING

Hylas Publishing
Publisher: Sean Moore
Creative Director: Karen Prince
Designer: Gus Yoo
Editor: Ray Rogers

Published in the United States by
Hylas Publishing
129 Main Street, Irvington,
New York 10533

Copyright © BBC Worldwide 2003

First published by BBC Worldwide Ltd,
Woodlands, 80 Wood Lane, London W12 0TT

First American Edition published in 2003
02 03 04 05 10 9 8 7 6 5 4 3 2 1

ISBN 1-59258-036-X

Set in Akzidenz Grotesk and Sabon
Printed and bound by Tien Wah Press,
Singapore
Color origination by Radstock Reproductions Ltd,
Midsomer Norton

Distributed by St. Martin's Press

This book is published to accompany the BBC
television series titled *How To Be A Gardener*.

The series was produced by BBC Bristol.
Executive produce: Dick Colthurst
Producer: Kath Moore

First published by BBC Worldwide Ltd,
Woodlands, 80 Wood Lane, London W12 0TT

Text copyright © Alan Titchmarsh 2002-2003
The moral right of the author has been asserted.

Commissioning editor: Nicky Copeland
Project editor: Helena Caldon
Copy editor: Lin Hawthorne
Art director and designer: Isobel Gillan
Picure researcher: Susannah Parker
Artist: Amanda Patton
Production Manager: John Martin

CONTENTS

Introduction to Part One

I've been entranced by gardening for as long as I can remember, but I know that for many people it's a baffling world out there. What makes plants grow? Is there such a thing as a green thumb? Why do plants suddenly die for no apparent reason? Will I ever become a gardener when everything I touch seems to shrivel?

This book aims to answer all these questions. It will not only tell you *how* to garden, it will also tell you *why* certain techniques work better than others. Oh, you might not want to be bothered with the "why," but if you can find the patience to stick with it, the background information can be fascinating and just as rewarding as the results of the craft itself.

Gardening is, in part, instinctive, but so many people have lost touch with that "earthy" side of their nature in this technological age. They no longer rely on their instincts and intuitions – it's a great pity, since these are often the basic tools of the trade. *How to be a Gardener* will, I hope, put that right. I want you to get a *feel* for gardening as much as anything... to use all your senses – touch, taste, smell, sight, and hearing – and, above all, to bring that common sense to bear that will make you a good gardener.

Traditionally, such skills have been handed down from generation to generation but, with so many people into other interests, such as surfing the tide and surfing the net, there's a real danger that such skills will be lost. How, then, do you acquire the necessary skills?

It's simple. Just getting to know your plants, your soil, and your situation will make you a better gardener. It might also give you a different outlook on life and encourage you to do your bit for the environment, which, more than ever, depends on you for its very survival. A sound organic approach, backed up by a knowledge of science is, I reckon, the secret of success. We need gardens, and we need wise gardeners who can make sure that all forms of wildlife continue to thrive.

Part One of *How to be a Gardener* starts with the basics to help you understand what a plant is, how it grows, and what it needs to develop successfully. I have explained what gardening is and how the language works and, on a practical level, where and how to get started. Each chapter takes you through what you need to know to garden successfully, learning how to assess your site and soil, choose healthy plants, plan your borders, and plant things properly. I want to show how the seasons affect what you do in the garden, and highlight routine gardening jobs – identifying what they are as well as how and why we do them. There's lots of useful information to help you identify, eliminate, and prevent weeds and pests – always a big concern, I know! – and a whole chapter on your lawn.

There are practical, step-by-step instructions in my "How to…" features, and plenty of boxes and charts to highlight some of the more essential information or summarize things for you. I've also used "side stories" in the margins to include extra bits of interesting information that I thought you might find interesting and enjoy.

There's no great mystery to being a successful gardener – most of it is just plain common sense – but an appreciation of the natural world at work in our gardens helps. Part One of *How to be a Gardener* aims to encourage this appreciation and help the first-time gardener get started, as well as enhance the understanding of the more experienced gardener. Part Two (starting on page 260) builds on that knowledge and experience to explore planting and design further and to provide you with a complete reference manual for your garden. It's not all hard work and earnest endeavor, I promise. There are sublime pleasures to be had from growing plants successfully and producing crops with a bumper harvest. As I hope this book will show you, it's not nearly as complicated or as difficult as you might think… whatever the weather may throw at you!

1 GARDENING BASICS

What is gardening?

As a rule, I'm a fan of dictionaries, but the one thing they lack is any kind of passion. Look up gardening, and you'll discover that it is "the activity of tending and cultivating a garden as a pastime," which sounds to me just a bit casual. If you ask a gardener why he or she gardens you might just as well ask why they breathe – it's because they can't imagine life without it. Gardening is part art and part science, but more than anything else it's a craft that is fueled by subterranean passion. It's all about nurturing and achieving, triumphing over nature and harmonizing with it. It panders to our primitive hunter-gatherer instincts. It can be incredibly satisfying and also very humbling; it can also be frustrating, annoying, and, let's be honest, disappointing. But one thing I promise you is that once you get started and have the thrill of seeing your first seedlings flower, or your first new border bloom, you'll be hooked for life.

Formal gardens, like this one at Hatfield House in Hertfordshire, England, were especially popular in the 17th and 18th centuries. They still appeal today to lovers of straight lines and balanced proportions.

What are gardens for?

Today's garden, for the vast majority of us, is cultivated for pleasure and fun. More than ever before it's used like an outdoor living room – weather permitting – but it's also a place where you can pursue your own particular interest. If you are an avid plantsperson, you can use it to collect and cultivate your favorite flowers; for creative souls, the garden makes a good outlet for design talents. Families need somewhere for children and pets to play safely, while, for a lot of people, the garden is a place for relaxation – a place to sit, cook, and eat in the open or to entertain friends.

But that isn't the way gardens have always been used. In the past, there was a huge distinction between the gardens of the rich and poor. The rich used their grand gardens and landscapes as status symbols – they were there to impress and were filled with expensive features such as mazes, fountains, and statues. Massive borders, shrubberies, and lawns were maintained by a large staff. You can still see this type of garden when you visit stately homes – fascinating to look at, but not the sort of thing you can hope to recreate at home in a small space. (And anyway, good-quality staff is very nearly impossible to find!) The gardens of ordinary people were not only smaller, they were on-the-spot survival kits in the days when there wasn't a handy corner store or supermarket down the road.

Self-sufficiency

Up until a century ago, the average garden was there for one thing only – to produce food. If you'd gardened then, you'd have kept animals and grown vegetables and herbs, not just for immediate use, but to store for the winter. You'd also have grown the ingredients of do-it-yourself medicines, cleaning products, fabric dyes, and virtually anything else you wanted to use around the house. Even weeds were put to good use – horsetail (*Equisetum arvense*) makes a great scouring pad. It's all a long way removed from how we live today, but the way our gardens look still reflects the way they are used.

The first "real" gardens were probably enclosures, made by settlers and homesteaders around their homemade hovels to prevent livestock from wandering off. As people became better off financially over the centuries, and with the rise of suburbs, gardens became less utilitarian and more ornamental.

Traditionally, the working garden was at the back of the house, where there'd be the pigsty and poultry house, vegetable plot and fruit trees, and a well or pump providing the domestic water supply.

The "cottage garden" effect appeals to anyone with a nostalgic or sentimental streak.

However humble, a basket full of home-grown produce is always deeply satisfying.

At the front was a pretty flower garden, where you might have kept hives of bees for honey that could be used for sweetening. Bee-attracting plants were a must!

Until as recently as the end of World War II, home gardens still enabled some of their owners to be virtually self-sufficient; even today, country gardeners earn pin-money by selling honey, eggs, and cut flowers at the roadside, as they would have done a hundred years ago or more.

Anyone who's ever sown a packet of seeds knows that one of the pleasures of gardening is the satisfaction of seeing the end result – serving up home-grown produce, cutting flowers for the house, and raising plants for ourselves and friends, just as gardeners have done throughout history.

Decoration

The first garden flowers were useful plants, such as herbs, and what grew naturally – wildflowers – particularly the prettier variations with unusual colors or double flowers, which early gardeners dug up from hedgerow and field to plant in their patches. Today, we're more conservation-conscious; many wildflowers are protected, which means that cultivated specimens must be bought in nurseries or raised from seed.

New plants brought from abroad by early traders, explorers, or invaders meant that gardeners gradually had a greater variety to choose from. In England, for example, the biggest influxes of imported plants came in with the Romans, with knights returning from the Crusades, and by Elizabethan explorers and the Victorian plant hunters sent out by wealthy patrons. Such new plants always went to the owners of grand houses first, since they were the only ones who could afford them – ordinary people got the throw-outs via gardener's boys who lived in the village and passed them "over the garden wall." But plants also came back in Uncle Bill's kitbag when he returned from the Napoleonic wars or other early campaigns.

By the 16th century, plants were being grown for their beauty alone, rather than simply for medicinal or culinary value. Naturally, it was the well-to-do who had the space, inclination, and staff to grow such plants, but the idea rubbed off on the common folk who were, in spite of their lack of breeding, not insensitive to beauty!

In the 17th and 18th centuries, hobbyists bred and exhibited specially developed plants that became known as "florists' flowers" – they included laced pinks and gold-laced polyanthus, some of which are still collected by enthusiasts today. Since then, plant breeders have added an enormous range of flowers to our gardens that have never been seen in the wild, and, today, they are available to anyone who will hand over a dollar or two for a packet of seeds.

Entertainment

Now that we don't need a garden as a do-it-yourself supermarket, modern gardens can be all about having fun. For some people, it's the plants and design that matter most, but, increasingly for others, the garden is used as an outdoor living room. The different ways we use gardens today is one reason why there are now so many styles of garden to choose from.

Gardens provide a creative outlet that is often lacking in modern life; you can practice arts and crafts, go organic, or experiment with "interior" decorating outdoors. A garden is one of the few places in life where you can do what you like – a haven of peace where you can pull up the drawbridge after a hard day's work and indulge yourself.

Even a rooftop is today valued as an outdoor room for relaxation and for entertaining.

The garden environment

There's no getting away from it: a garden is a totally artificial environment. If you don't believe me, just leave a patch of ground alone for a year and see what comes up naturally – weeds, brambles, and tree seedlings, for starters. The natural vegetation of North America, historians tell us, was once mostly vast forests and grasslands that were cleared to provide lumber for housing, shipbuilding, and domestic enclosures, and of course vast acreage for agriculture. Leave your garden to its own devices, and a century from now it will be well on the way to becoming a wild wood. If we left our gardens alone now, in one hundred year's time, wild plants would have erupted from our gardens through our network of highways and all but destroyed them. It's a thought I always find heartening.

A world of plants under one roof

North America might not have an enormous range of exciting native plants compared to places like the Amazon rainforest, but we have one huge advantage – our range of climates. Without violent extremes of heat or cold, somewhere on the continent we can grow probably the widest range of plants from all over the world. Even an unassuming garden might hold maples from Japan, peonies from China, tulips from Iran, hardy cyclamen from Turkey, and potatoes from South America.

How plants cope in a hostile environment

Wild plants have spent many thousands of years perfecting their survival techniques, and some have adapted to living in rather hostile conditions. In the garden, this means there are plants you can choose that will enjoy "problem spots" where more ordinary and less suitable plants often fail.

In dry regions, leaves may be very narrow or have silver, gray, or furry coverings to reduce water loss – plants such as artemisia, *Stachys byzantina*, and pinks. Desert plants, such as cacti, have dispensed with their leaves altogether and just have fat, water-storing stems instead.

In tropical rainforests, where the humidity is high and plants are sheltered from drying winds by an overhead "umbrella" of trees, they grow large, thin leaves that are the best sort for gathering low light. This is why they make good houseplants.

In boggy ground, plants don't need to conserve water, so they tend to have big leaves like giant solar panels. Where the ground is short of nutrients, some plants, such as sundew and Venus flytrap, are carnivorous and obtain their nutrition by digesting insects.

Escapologists

Some imported plants have escaped from gardens to become naturalized nuisance weeds. Japanese knotweed (above) was imported by a botanist who thought it would make a good plant for his herbaceous border. It did – his and everybody else's. Many other plants taken from their native lands eventualy became pests - kudzu, multiflora rose, buckthorn, lantana, eucalyptus, Tatarian honeysuckle, tree of heaven, English ivy, garlic mustard, and purple loosestrife, to name a few.

Climbers have 'learned' that they don't need to go to all the bother of growing rigid stems to get their leaves up to the light, because they can just scramble up somebody else's instead. They have developed all sorts of ways to hold on to other plants, from rose thorns that act like grappling hooks on twiggy stems, to the twining honeysuckle that corkscrews its way up anything upright.

Bulbous plants go into suspended animation when growing conditions get tough – a bulb is actually a complete plant in a time capsule. Some types, such as tulips, go dormant in summer to survive a long, hot, dry spell, while summer-flowering dahlias have tubers that are dormant in winter when it's too cold to sustain growth.

Many plants that live where there's lots of competition have learned to spread fast and swamp their neighbors. That explains the success of weeds, such as greater bindweed and quackgrass.

Plants cope with their environments in various ways. The white furry covering on the leaves of *Stachys lanata* (*left*) helps conserve moisture in the sun-baked environment where the plant originated. The lush leaves of the banana (*center*) are large so as to absorb as much sunlight as possible in a tropical rainforest, and *Rodgersia* (*right*) grows in boggy ground and has access to plenty of water to support its large, fingered leaves.

What this means for the gardener

Because most gardens contain a wide range of plants that don't grow there naturally, we need to match the varied needs of each plant to the actual growing conditions, which change slightly all around the garden. Because plants can't choose where they grow, we need to provide them with what they need – whether it's food and water, shelter, or something to climb up. We also need to make them behave, which might mean pruning, restricting their roots, or deadheading to prevent aggressive self-seeders from taking over. It's all part of the taming of nature that we call gardening.

The tropics are all very well, but one of the greatest pleasures of gardening is to observe the effect of the changing seasons on the familiar patch of land around the house. Instead of everything staying the same all the time, you can see small changes taking place from one week to the next – new flowers coming out and new leaf tones developing. That's what makes walking around your own garden continually interesting, however well you know it.

Temperate gardens have one big advantage over their tropical counterparts – an ability to change the view through the seasons. Here, (*from the top, down*) white birch trunks, red stems of *Cornus sanguinea* 'Midwinter Fire', and drifts of snowdrops, *Galanthus* 'Atkinsii', provide interest in late winter and early spring. Daffodils, *Fritillaria meleagris,* and spears of iris foliage arrive later. In summer, the lush foliage of blue hostas and green ostrich ferns, *Matteuccia struthiopteris,* as well as pink astrantias and feathery, pale green astilbe plumes give the border its full-blown glory. By autumn, the tints and contrasting shapes in the foliage still remaining from the herbaceous plants and the brown seedheads of astilbe, with the turning cornus leaves, are still providing color and vibrancy in the garden.

Seasonal plants

Nothing ever stands still in the garden. Herbaceous plants (see page 28) die down for the winter and pop up again next spring; bulbs grow, flower and then die down again at different times of year – there are spring-, summer- and autumn-flowering bulbs, each with their own separate schedule.

Deciduous trees (see page 29) come into leaf in the spring and, during the summer, you'll gradually notice the leaf color change from fresh lime-green to duller shades. Finally, the leaves fade or, in some cases, take on brilliant autumn tints before falling, to leave the bare shapes of trunks and stems visible in winter. Shrubs flower and some go on to produce colorful berries or fruits.

Some flowers bloom strongly all summer, while others stop early or go on to produce architectural seed heads that attract birds to feed. There are also short-lived seasonal flowers – annuals, or bedding plants – that are planted to provide a patch of color for one particular season, in the garden or in containers, before being pulled out and replaced with something else for the next season.

Oh, I know that some gardeners can't keep up with this and feel that they can never get the garden "sorted." But once you stop thinking of the garden as ever being "finished," you'll begin to enjoy the fact that it is always "work in progress."

Seasonal work

It's not just plants that are affected by the changing seasons. A lot of gardening activities are triggered at particular times of year and by the effects the seasonal weather has on plants.

Spring is the traditional start of the gardening season. It's the busiest time in the garden (see pages 124–26), when the warmer weather brings the spring flush of weeds, aphids, and other pests, and there's a lot of sowing and planting to be done. It's a good time for putting in perennials and, if you grow vegetables, there's a lot to do in the edible garden. You'll feel a bit like the circus performer who spins plates on tall sticks – sooner or later, some of them are bound to fall off. But don't worry – you can always pick them up again.

As the weather continues to improve, the big date in a gardener's calendar is that of the last frost. Once that has passed, it is safe to plant out frost-tender bedding plants, such as pelargoniums and fuchsias (see page 127) and that's when you start to see colorful summer displays in hanging baskets and tubs around front doors and on patios.

Summer is the most colorful season for flowers, when roses, perennial plants (see pages 28 and 128), and bedding are at their best, but, since most of the main jobs have been done, it's just a case of keeping on top of routine jobs, such as weeding, mowing grass, and

Wait until the danger of late spring frosts has passed, and then you can safely plant out summer bedding.

hedge clipping (see pages 127 and 129). For goodness sake, train yourself to relax at this time of year. Too many gardeners are incapable of sitting down. I know, I'm one of them – but I *am* in therapy!

Autumn is the end of the gardening season, when perennials, roses, and bedding plants finish flowering and the garden is made ready for winter. It's a good time for planting fruit trees and bushes and ornamental trees and shrubs (see pages 130–34), since the wet weather means you won't need to do a lot of watering. The first frost of autumn means that cold-tender plants need to be brought under cover if you want to keep them for next year. I like this time of year – I can move faster than the garden and once more get on top of things.

From November to February or March, gardeners try to do all their garden planning, soil preparation, and construction jobs (see page 135), because the lack of routine chores means there's more time to spare. It's also the time when a lot of pruning is done – particularly clematis, grape vines, and standard fruit trees – though other plants are pruned at various times during the growing season.

Looked at in this way, the garden seems a pretty demanding beast. But if you can learn to look at it in a more relaxed way, you'll appreciate it for what it is – a miracle of survival in an ever more demanding world.

The growing season

Gardeners talk about "the growing season" (see pages 114–21), by which they mean that part of the year when plants are growing actively – from spring to late autumn. The rest of the year, from late autumn to spring, is the dormant season, which is when deciduous trees and shrubs have lost their leaves and most plants are resting. The length of the growing season varies according to where you live. Generally, if you live in the far north or at high altitudes, the climate is colder and the growing season can be several weeks shorter than further south or at lower altitudes.

One thing you need to know when you start gardening: the expected dates of the last spring frost and the first autumn frost in your area. This tells you when you can safely plant out frost-tender plants in early summer and when you need to move them under cover in autumn. Because the climate varies so much around the country and the weather changes from year to year, it's impossible to give an exact date. Don't gamble – ask the locals – the veteran gardeners and people in a garden club. The average last frost date in general is later the farther north you live, but there are many exceptions. Also, areas within your own garden may be slightly warmer or colder and less or more protected than others. Learn to recognize these microclimates and use them to your advantage.

What is a plant?

Plants are more like us than you might think. We have blood that flows through veins. They have veins through which flows a fluid called sap, which, like blood, also transports nutrients and other active ingredients. Plants breathe, and their lives are ruled by hormones and (admittedly basic) "nervous systems." They can reproduce themselves and even move. Sounds scary? Not really. I know a few people who are not such good company as a potted palm!

If you look back far enough into the past, it seems very likely that we once had a common ancestor. It may come as a surprise to you that we share half the same DNA as a banana and that our blood is almost identical to a plant's green pigment (chlorophyll) – except that blood contains a molecule of iron, whereas chlorophyll contains one of magnesium. OK, so it's stretching a point, but it makes you think.

Look at a traditional herbaceous border at the height of summer, and you'll see plants at the peak of their performance.

Parts of a plant

To you and me, a chrysanthemum looks quite different from a pear tree, which in turn is nothing like a dandelion. But strip them down to their component parts, and you find that all flowering plants have the same basic structure and work in exactly the same way.

Roots (1)

There are two sorts of roots. The big ones that you can see when you take a plant out of its pot, or dig it up, are there to anchor it in the ground. Most plants have branching roots that spread over a wide area, but some have taproots that just go straight down. Seedlings grow taproots first, to penetrate the ground, then they branch out later. Thick taproots, such as carrots, are used for storing starches that the plant uses to fuel its flowering next year. None of these big roots take in water. That is done by the microscopic root hairs concentrated around the very tips of the main roots. Besides water, the root hairs take in dissolved nutrients – plants can't take in solid food; they suck up a mineral "soup" that is drawn up through the plant by the pull exerted by water evaporating from the leaves.

Stems (2)

Stems stiffen the plant so that it doesn't fall over, and they hold leaves, flowers, and fruit in the most advantageous positions for them to do their work. Some long-lived plants have thick stems, in which part of the tissue turns to wood. This gives them an even stronger framework, which is vital in the case of trees that are big and have a lot of weight to carry.

Ringing in the years

Lignin (wood) in trees is laid down in distinct layers during each growing season, making the tree's characteristic rings. You can tell the age of a tree by counting the rings. The width of the rings shows which years were good or bad growing seasons, because, in a good year, a tree lays down more lignin, creating wider rings.

Parts of a plant:
1 Roots absorb water from the soil, and taproots, like this carrot, store food in the form of starch.
2 Stems are the pipes that transport food and water to the parts of the plant where it is needed. The stem here has adapted and formed hairs to help prevent water loss in windy conditions.
3 Leaves and fronds – such as this tree fern – act like giant solar panels and factories, converting sunlight into food.

Stems also contain special tissue, called xylem, that transports water and minerals all around the plant, and phloem that takes starches and other things the plant has manufactured to wherever it's needed – usually to the roots, where it can be stored.

Leaves (3)

Leaves are the powerhouse of the plant. Think of them as super-efficient solar panels with added technology. They absorb sunlight and, via the chemical wizardry of the green pigment, chlorophyll, use the sun's energy to transform carbon dioxide from the air and water from the soil into starches. Starches are ultimately used for building more plant parts, or for hoarding in underground parts, such as taproots or tubers – think of carrots and potatoes. As a by-product of this process, known as photosynthesis, plants "breathe out" oxygen – they are the lungs of the planet.

Flowers and seeds

Flowers are the way plants reproduce themselves. Male pollen from one flower is transferred to another of the same species, so that the female part of the flower is fertilized and can then produce a fruit or pod containing seeds, which eventually ripen and are shed to produce the next generation.

Each flower is made up of several parts. The petals act rather like a neon sign to attract pollinating insects. The stamens are the male part, made up of a stem (filament) with pollen-bearing anthers at the tip. The female part of the flower is the pistil, composed of a stigma (the sticky tip that traps the pollen), a tubular stem (the style), and an ovary deep in the flower, where the seeds form and which ultimately becomes a fruit or seed-pod.

Just like children, seeds need to leave home; otherwise, the parent plant would be swamped with lively offspring competing for light, water, and nutrients. For this reason, they have evolved all sorts of ingenious ways of traveling. Winged seeds, such as those of maples, literally fly away. Seeds inside hooked fruit, like burdock, latch on to passing animals for a free ride. Coconuts float on the sea for up to a year, traveling between islands without a thought of *mal-de-mer*. Seeds inside tasty fruits, such as blackberries, rely on animals or birds eating them and, later, depositing the seed elsewhere.

Most plants have flowers with both male and female parts, but some, such as birch and hazel, have separate male and female flowers on the same plant (monoecious plants). Others, like hollies, have male and female flowers on separate plants (dioecious plants). With these you need to grow a male and female plant close together to produce berries on the female. The sex life of plants makes our own look tediously straightforward in comparison.

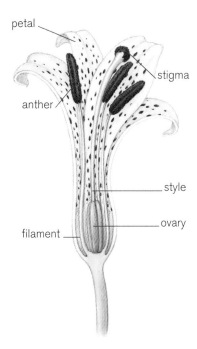

The stamen (male part) of the flower is made up of the filament and anther. The pistil (female part) includes the stigma, style, and ovary.

Doing the business

Some flowering plants are pollinated by insects and produce large, colorful, scented, or nectar-rich flowers to attract bees and other pollinating insects. Others, such as grasses and catkin-bearing trees, are wind pollinated and don't have colorful flowers because they don't need them. But some flowers are pollinated by creatures, such as bats, hummingbirds, flies or even, in the case of the aspidistra, by slugs. But then I've always thought the aspidistra a particularly desperate plant.

Different types of flower:
1 Daisy-like flower: rudbeckia.
2 Spike: lavender.
3 Raceme: verbascum.
4 Panicle: gypsophila.
5 Corymb: achillea.
6 Umbel: dill.

Types of flower

Flowers come in all shapes and sizes as well as colors. There are proper names for the various ways in which they are arranged on their stems. It helps to know them, because that's the way they are often described on seed packets and in books. Knowing a bit of basic botany means you can picture the flower shape when there isn't a photo. There are several types apart from the solitary flower, like the tulip, which has a single flower at the end of each stem.

Daisy-like flower (**1**) The classic daisy flower is actually a mass of tiny disk florets surrounded by ray florets; together they make up a single flowerhead.

Spike (**2**) A spike is a straight stem with lots of single, stalkless flowers evenly spaced out along it, as in lavender.

Raceme (**3**) Racemes are like spikes, except that each flower grows on a short stalk instead of straight from the main stem, as they do in verbascums. With me so far?

Panicle (4) Panicles are like racemes, except that each flower stalk is branched, so instead of one flower on the end of it, there is a whole bunch of them, as in gypsophila.

Corymb (5) A corymb is like a raceme, but the flower stalks are longer at the bottom than at the top of the stem, making a flat-topped flower, like those of achilleas.

Umbel (6) In an umbel, there are lots of florets on stalks radiating from the stem tip in a very geometrical pattern, like the spokes of an umbrella with flowers at the tips. Dill is a good example of this. And, if this seems a lot to remember, don't worry – you can look it up!

Plant names

There are a heck of a lot of plants out there. No one knows for sure quite how many because, even today, new ones are being discovered in remote areas but, at the last count, there were almost 300,000 different species. That isn't the total by any means – each species may include several wild varieties with different characteristics, such as flower color. And it doesn't include the manmade forms (cultivars) that have been bred in cultivation.

What's in a name?
Even the most expert gardeners are familiar with only a fraction of the whole plant kingdom, but, with so many to talk about, it's essential that we all use the same system of plant naming. The one used by botanists and gardeners the world over is based on that invented by the Swedish botanist, Carl von Linne (Linnaeus), in 1753. Once you get used to using the plants' Latin names, they are no more difficult to remember than your friends' first and last (family) names. This doesn't prevent you from calling them by their nicknames or common names.

Plants have their last name first, so all roses are called *Rosa*. The second name – equivalent to a first name – tells you which species it is, for example, *Rosa rugosa* (Latin names are always italicized). Wild forms of *Rosa rugosa* include several different color forms, so you have a third name, such as *Rosa rugosa alba*, which tells you that it has white flowers – the lower case, italicized last name tells you that it occurs in the wild. Any variant of *Rosa rugosa* discovered or bred in captivity has the third name (the cultivar) in Roman type and single quotes and always begin with a capital letter, thus *Rosa rugosa* 'Scabrosa'. Some plants are so interbred that nobody knows their precise parentage, so most modern roses are just known, for example, as *Rosa* 'Peace'. But you can still quite correctly call it a rose!

Infinite variety

The average garden center or nusery probably stocks about 1000 different plants, which is a tiny fraction of the total number of plants available (roses alone number in the thousands). Plant societies can help you locate a particular plant, and there are source directories available at book stores. Perhaps the most accessible and comprehensive resource, however, is the Internet - type a name into a search engine, and voila!

Family trees

If you really go into plant names in detail, you can get a complete "family tree" that shows you which plants are related to which others and share similar botanical characteristics, which means they are more likely to share similar needs in cultivation. This is what the family tree of two common roses looks like.

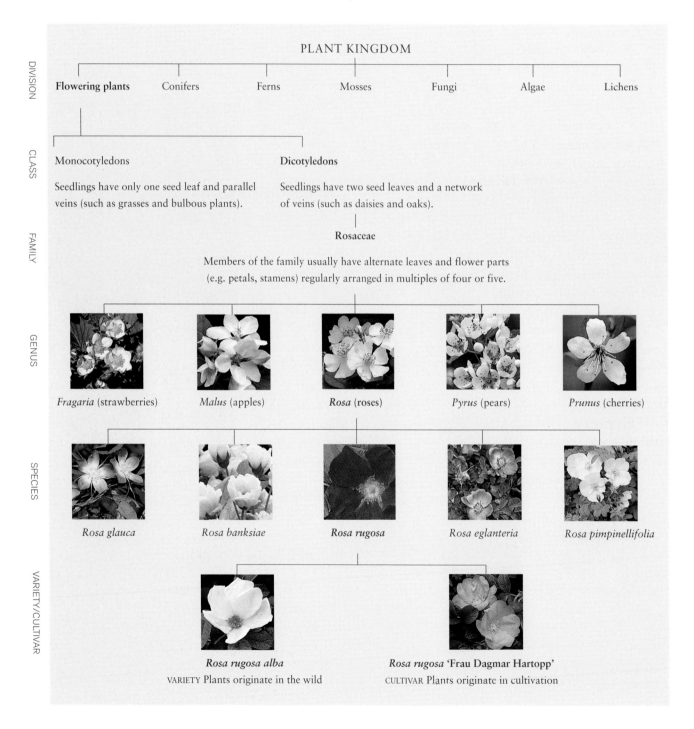

DIVISION

PLANT KINGDOM

Flowering plants   Conifers   Ferns   Mosses   Fungi   Algae   Lichens

CLASS

Monocotyledons

Seedlings have only one seed leaf and parallel veins (such as grasses and bulbous plants).

Dicotyledons

Seedlings have two seed leaves and a network of veins (such as daisies and oaks).

FAMILY

Rosaceae

Members of the family usually have alternate leaves and flower parts (e.g. petals, stamens) regularly arranged in multiples of four or five.

GENUS

Fragaria (strawberries)   *Malus* (apples)   **Rosa** (roses)   *Pyrus* (pears)   *Prunus* (cherries)

SPECIES

Rosa glauca   *Rosa banksiae*   **Rosa rugosa**   *Rosa eglanteria*   *Rosa pimpinellifolia*

VARIETY/CULTIVAR

Rosa rugosa alba
VARIETY Plants originate in the wild

Rosa rugosa 'Frau Dagmar Hartopp'
CULTIVAR Plants originate in cultivation

Plant behavior

Although plants don't "behave" in the sense that animals do (but they can be just as tricky), they can do enough to take care of their own interests. In the wild, plants exist to reproduce themselves as quickly as possible and, if conditions are tough, they'll sacrifice leaves and other non-essentials in their effort to set (produce) seed. They'll stop flowering as soon as enough seed has been set, expending their energies on swelling and ripening the seed ready for distribution. Wild plants will also spread to colonize new areas for themselves and eliminate potential competition from other plants wherever possible.

In the garden, plants exist because the gardener wants them to be decorative; we want plants that keep flowering for as long as possible, with healthy, attractive foliage. We are not usually bothered about gathering any seeds, but we do want plants to share the space happily with others. Gardening is all about making plants conform to what we want them to do, instead of letting them have their own way all the time.

Movement

Plants can't run around quite like animals, but some get quite close. To save water, the prayer plant (*Maranta*) folds its leaves up at night, when it's not using them to photosynthesize. *Mimosa pudica* has ferny leaves that collapse at a touch as a defense against predators.

Many plants show movement by opening and closing their petals in response to outside stimuli (though others keep their flowers open all the time once they start to bloom). Crocus flowers open when the air is warm enough, which makes sense, since early spring flowers stand a risk of being damaged by cold. Gazania and mesembryanthemum flowers only open when the sun is on them, and the evening primrose only opens at night – they are all responding to light intensity.

Family likenesses

You might be surprised to learn that plants as different as strawberries, roses, and pears are related, but just take a close look at their flowers and you'll see that the similarity is evident (see page 24).

Plants move in different ways. An evening primrose flower (*left*) opens at the end of the day; a dandelion (*center*) moves by dispersing its seeds; and a strawberry plant (*right*) sends out long stems, known as runners, on which grow small plants with roots to enable the parent plant to reestablish itself elsewhere.

Plants can move by sending out runners, like strawberry plants, or invasive roots, as with goutweed and nettles. But the way most plants move physically to a distant location is by shedding seed that is carried by the wind, or by animals, to a new site where the next generation can colonize. Think of dandelion heads, which blow away as individual seeds on parachutes; maple seeds, which have built-in "propellers"; explosive seeds like impatiens, which are fired off a short distance, or blackberries, which are eaten by birds and then dropped with a built-in portion of nourishing manure, ready to grow into new plants. Garden weeds are particularly good at doing this. But then that's why they've become weeds – wild plants growing where we don't want them.

Response to light

We all know about houseplants that lean over to face the light, which is why it's recommended that you give them a quarter turn every few days to keep them growing symmetrically. But if you plant your clematis up a tree on the north side of the garden hoping their flowers will brighten up your view, you'll be disappointed because the plant will grow toward the light in the south and the flowers will turn to face it. The odds are that your next-door neighbor will have a much better view of them than you do. The plants are only following their basic instinct and responding to light. Roots do the reverse, growing away from the light to ensure that they grow down into the soil.

Response to gravity

Have you noticed how, if a potted plant falls over and remains in that postion for a while, the tip of the stem very soon bends upward again? It's because it is responding to gravity – you can tell that it's gravity and not sunlight, because they'll do it even in the dark. Some plants don't have such a strong anti-gravity response, and these are the plants that naturally grow out along the ground or trail down.

Response to daylength

Some plants (such as chrysanthemums) are triggered to flower when the daylength shortens in autumn, while others flower in summer when the days are long. Commercial growers deliberately exploit this tendency in order to grow flower crops out of season, either by putting plants under artificial lights to lengthen the days, or by covering them with black cloth to give them shorter days. This is how growers get poinsettias to flower in time for Christmas – if left to their own devices, poinsettias would flower around Easter, when the days and nights are roughly equal in length.

Learning the language

You don't need to learn a lot of gardening jargon to get growing, but the right word can say what might otherwise take a couple of sentences to explain. It's particularly handy to know the terms used on plant labels and in catalogues to categorize particular types of plants, as they tell you a lot of things you need to know at a glance.

Annuals

These are plants that last for one season only. They either die after flowering and setting seed or, like bedding plants, are thrown away at the end of their first year. There are two sorts of annuals:

Hardy annuals stand some cold, so you can sow them outdoors in spring: March or April are the usual times. They'll germinate as soon as the soil is warm enough and can flower several weeks earlier than half-hardy annuals. Examples are sweet peas (*Lathyrus odoratus*), sunflowers (*Helianthus annuus*), and nasturtiums (*Tropaeolum majus*).

Half-hardy annuals are killed by frost but are also severely checked by cold. You can't plant them out until after the last frost, but then they keep growing until they are killed by the first frost of autumn. They include marigolds (*Tagetes*), flowering tobacco (*Nicotiana*), impatiens, zinnias, and petunias.

This really will be the scene 10 or 12 weeks after the seeds of hardy annual flowers are sown. Their life cycle is completed in a single growing season.

The foxglove *(Digitalis purpurea)* is a biennial. Seeds sown in one year grow into plants that flower in the second year, after which the plant will normally die.

Biennials

Not so widely grown these days, biennials are plants that are sown one year and flower the next – such as wallflowers (*Erysimum cheiri*), sweet Williams (*Dianthus barbatus*), and foxgloves (*Digitalis purpurea*). Many are actually short-lived perennials – just to confuse matters – and may live for several years. But they are usually pulled out after they have finished flowering for the sake of garden neatness or to make room for something else.

Perennials

Perennials are plants that die down to an overwintering rootstock each autumn and grow up again the following spring, like daylilies and irises. Years ago, we called them herbaceous plants and grew them in herbaceous borders. It's true that some perennials don't actually die down in winter – the evergreen kinds like hellebores, heuchera, and bergenia – but they are used in the same way in the garden and so they are conveniently lumped in the same category.

Hardy perennials are the ones you leave in the ground all year round (where they can tolerate the cold), like hostas and phlox. In fact, you can usually leave them for three to five years before they need digging up and dividing (see pages 195–96).

Half-hardy (or tender) perennials sound similar, but they differ in one major way. They include plants like pelargoniums, and woody ones, such as fuchsias, that live for years but won't survive the cold in your area. These are plants that need to be kept under cover, such as taken into a heated greenhouse or indoors, for the winter. (Yes, I know some fuchsias are hardy, but many of the large-flowered kinds are not. Gardening has exceptions to every rule, mainly to prevent the likes of me from becoming too confident.)

Bedding plants

Bedding plants are any that are planted temporarily in beds, containers, or in odd gaps around the garden. These days, people usually mean half-hardy annuals or half-hardy perennials when they talk about bedding plants, but you can use bulbs and even shrubs as bedding plants if, for instance, you grow them for temporary color in the border or in patio containers.

Woody plants

This is a shorthand way of referring to plants that have a permanent structure of woody stems and branches above the ground, and they include trees, shrubs, and climbers. A tree always has a trunk, even if it is only a short one with branches starting quite low down. A shrub has branches, but no trunk. Climbers and wall shrubs often cause a bit of confusion. Climbers have several stems where they leave the ground and scramble or climb naturally, but wall shrubs are normal free-standing shrubs that have been specially trained to grow flat against a wall, often because they are a tad too tender (fragile) to do well in the open, and they'll usually have only one stem where they leave the ground.

Deciduous and evergreen plants

Deciduous plants are those that lose their leaves every year in the autumn and replace them in spring, while evergreens keep theirs all year round – well, not quite. They do shed old leaves a few at a time throughout the year – often quite a lot of them in summer, in the case of holly and evergreen oaks (*Quercus*) – but with most plants you'd hardly notice. Plants described as semi-evergreen, such as *Cotoneaster horizontalis*, can't make up their minds. They'll keep their leaves in a mild winter or a sheltered location, but shed them in cold winters or in exposed sites.

Most garden borders combine different types of planting, as found in this one:

1 Deciduous shrubs: *Physocarpus opulifolius* 'Diabolo' and
2 *Cornus alba* 'Elegantissima'.
3 Deciduous tree: *Gleditisia triacanthos* 'Sunburst'.
4 Perennial grass: *Miscanthus sinensis* 'Zebrinus'.
5 Perennial: hosta.

Bulbs

Lots of plants have storage organs, and there are several different kinds – true bulbs, corms, tubers, and rhizomes – all with minor botanical differences that aren't of much practical interest to the gardener, so we usually lump them under the general term "bulbs."

A bulb (1) is a modified shoot; if you cut one in half vertically, you'll see it is made up of scale leaves (true leaves in embryonic form) and a bud joined to a circular base plate, as in tulips and daffodils.

A corm (2) is an enlarged stem base and is replaced every year by a new corm that grows from a bud on the original one. Crocus and gladiolus are examples of corms.

Tubers (3) are modified stems or roots, enlarged for storage. Examples are potato (stem tuber – the shoots or "eyes" all over its surface are the giveaway) and dahlia (root tuber – the shoots occur only at the top of the tuber).

Rhizomes (4) are creeping, horizontal, underground stems that produce roots. Examples are bearded iris and waterlilies.

Types of "bulb":
1 The daffodil is a true bulb.
2 The cyclamen is a corm.
3 The dahlia grows from a root tuber.
4 The bearded iris grows from a rhizome.

What plants need

Considering they can't get up and move around, plants are surprisingly sophisticated. They are like living factories; they manufacture some very complicated products – starches, fats, and proteins, plus all their own colorings, hormones, and enzymes – which is pretty good going when you think that they only have air, sunlight, water and soil to start with.

Every time you go around with the watering can, or a bag of fertilizer, you're helping to keep plants topped up with things they need, but how often do you really think about what you are doing? As in a real factory, plants need to be constantly supplied with all their various ingredients to work at peak efficiency; there's a very delicate interaction between ingredients. If one runs short, growth slows or stops until the shortage is made up. That's why commercial growers take such pains to manage the temperature, watering, and fertilizing in their greenhouses so precisely – they may even add the carbon dioxide needed for photosynthesis to the air. Not at all surprising when you consider that it's their living.

At home we grow plants for fun, so it doesn't really matter if they don't work at peak potential all the time, though naturally we want them to grow well so that we have a garden that looks good. Even though we can't control the weather, keeping plants supplied with everything else they need is the secret of creating good growing conditions.

In the wild, plants grow in a natural situation that provides them with all they need – the rich woodland soil suits English bluebells down to the ground.

Water

Plants are made up of over 80% water, but most of the water inside a plant isn't stored – it's in transit. Water is "sucked in" through the root hairs (see page 20) and drawn up through the plant by the "suction" created by evaporation through the leaves. A plant is just like a giant wick. On a hot summer's day, a really big plant, such as a mature oak tree, might lose up to 66 gallons (300 liters) of water through its 700,000 leaves, all of which comes from the soil.

Water is the carrier for all the things that move around inside a plant. Oxygen and carbon dioxide gases are dissolved in it; so are mineral nutrients taken in from the soil. As any gardener knows, the faster a plant grows, the more water it needs. That's because the hotter and drier the air is, the faster the plant loses water through the pores (stomata) beneath its leaves. But there comes a point when the plant can't move enough water through itself to keep pace with demand, either because conditions are too hot or because there isn't enough water at the roots, so it craftily closes the whole system down by shutting its pores. This happens automatically when the water pressure drops inside special guard cells around the stomata, which shrink like deflating balloons, blocking the opening. Once the crisis is past and the temperature drops, or the plants are watered, the pressure returns to normal and the guard cells plump up again, which opens the pores.

Now, that might just sound like a bit of useless information, but it explains why a lot of pot plants run into problems on hot, sunny windowsills, or in a greenhouse in summer. Every time the soil in a pot dries out, or your greenhouse overheats in the sun, the plants stop growing until conditions return to normal. And if conditions just keep getting worse the plants lose more water and start to wilt. Wilting is what happens when all the cells – not just those around the pores – lose their water pressure. And if plants wilt badly enough or for long enough, even cooler temperatures and more water aren't enough to start the flow of water through the plant running again, and then there's nothing you can do to save it. Desiccation sets in and it dies. Crispy plants will not revive.

So if you didn't already know it, wilting plants need urgent attention, but it's much better to prevent them from wilting in the first place. That's why I'm always going on about fertilizing and watering plants in containers, and ventilating your greenhouse or conservatory. Shading helps, too, in summer. The idea is to keep the temperature below 85°F (30°C), because that is the point at which virtually all plants stop growing temporarily until things get a bit cooler.

Water moves up through a plant and transpires through pores (stomata) on the undersides of the leaves. When its dry and hot, the plant cannot transport water fast enough, so its water pressure drops, closing the pores, and the wilting process begins.

This water-loss business is also why newly planted bedding plants, vegetables, and even woody plants, such as trees, shrubs and climbers, need watering until they get established. Until new roots can grow out into the soil to find moisture, new plants can easily lose more water through their leaves than they take in through the roots. And in windy weather, they lose water even faster.

Nutrients

Plants might look pretty solid, but most of their bulk is made up of oxygen, carbon, and hydrogen, obtained from air and water and transmuted into solid form during photosynthesis. The rest consists of around 30 chemical elements taken up from the soil, which are needed in different quantities and must be replaced regularly as they grow. Yes, I know all this is getting a bit scientific, but stick with me – it will all make sense in the end.

Domestic science

You can easily prove to yourself how much of a plant is water. Next time you cut a bunch of herbs to dry, weigh them as soon as you have cut them, then again after drying them in a warm oven until they are crisp. The difference is all water. Don't think of it as a scientific experiment – although it is – because you can still rub the leaves from the dry stems and store them in jars, ready to use.

Major nutrients	Deficiency symptoms	Natural sources
Nitrogen promotes leafy growth	Slow growth, upper leaves pale green and lower leaves yellow	Rain, nitrogen-fixing nodules on the roots of leguminous plants, (like clover, peas, and beans); compost and manure; nitrogen-fixing bacteria in soil containing plenty of organic matter
Phosphorus encourages root development	Stunted plants with very dark leaves with red or purple tinges; leaves tend to fall early	Some rocks and soils
Potassium promotes fruit and flower production	Tips and edges of older leaves near the base of the plant turn yellow and then die and turn brown	Some rocks and soils, especially clay soils, with sandy soil most likely to be deficient
Minor elements		
Magnesium		Dolomitic limestone
Sulfur		Air pollution
Calcium		Limestone, eggshells, shellfish shells, hard tapwater, bonemeal, calcified seaweed, superphosphate
Vital trace elements		
Iron, manganese, molybdenum, zinc, copper, and **boron**		Bulky organic matter, seaweed products

Optional extras used by some plants: chlorine, sodium, cobalt, aluminum, bromine, iodine, vanadium, and silicon

A tomato leaf (*left*) showing signs of magnesium deficiency, and a tomato plant (*right*) with healthy green leaves.

There are three main elements that are vital to plant growth – nitrogen (N), phosphorus (P), and potassium (K). Think of them as the proteins and carbohydrates of the plant's diet – the meat and two vegetables. Then there are several minor elements and 20 or so trace elements that are needed only in minute amounts. Think of these as the vitamins that plants need. They are all present in most garden soils, especially those that contain plenty of organic matter, but you can't keep taking material out of the garden – whether it is vegetables, cut flowers, lawn mowings, or fruit tree prunings – without putting something back (see pages 49–51).

Although you sometimes find plants suffering from a shortage of one particular mineral – tomatoes, for example, are very prone to magnesium deficiency – it is much more common to find them short of a whole range of nutrients because they are generally underfertilized. That is where fertilizers come in (see pages 52–53). But don't panic! If you improve the soil and use fertilizers properly, you'll rarely see deficiency symptoms.

Air

We take air very much for granted because it's all around us. Most gardeners think of air in terms of greenhouse ventilation. My old boss at the municipal nursery talked about "putting on a crack of air" when he wanted the greenhouse vents opened only slightly. But there's much more to it than that.

Air provides plants with the oxygen and carbon that, with sunlight acting as the energy source and water providing hydrogen (it's H_2O, remember?), are the ingredients needed for photosynthesis, the process by which plants make sugars and starches (see pages 35–36). They don't stop there. Those sugars are converted into everything else plants need by more complicated chemical processes, using other elements taken up from the soil.

The air is also a source of nitrogen, one of the "big three" plant nutrients, which gets into the soil in several ways. Some of it is dissolved in the rainwater every time there is a thunderstorm. You can almost smell it. Nitrogen is also "fixed" in the soil by bacteria in the nodules of the roots of leguminous plants, such as clover, peas and beans, and by the soil bacteria that are found in healthy soils where there is lots of organic matter.

Light

Photosynthesis – the process that kick-starts a plant's entire internal factory – happens only in light, so it figures that if plants don't get enough of it, they can't work at full potential.

But some plants need more light than others. Some are adapted to work in low light – ferns, hostas, and the tropical plants we grow as houseplants that live naturally under tiers of trees. That's why they are so happy indoors. Living room conditions (apart from central heating, which can really dry out the air) are virtually identical in terms of shade and temperature to those of a tropical jungle. Just think of that next time you plan an exotic holiday!

You can usually tell a plant that is used to shady conditions by its large, light-gathering leaves, which will be quite thin if it also likes moist soil or humid air. If you give shade lovers sunny conditions, some – such as hostas – will be all right provided they have enough moisture at the roots, so they don't dehydrate. But often, shade lovers, such as ferns, will "scorch" in bright sunlight. The leaves just dry out and go brown, lacking the ability to absorb sufficient moisture to combat the drying effects of the sun, and then the plant dies.

Photosynthesis enables plants to use sunlight (1), carbon dioxide (2) and water (3) to produce oxygen (4) and vital energy (5) with which to grow.

Plants, such as ferns, have adapted over millions of years to make use of the low light intensity in shady spots – so much so that in full sunlight their leaves can be scorched.

True sun-lovers need a lot of direct sunlight on their leaves; otherwise, they grow weak and spindly trying to reach the light. What's more, if they don't have enough light, they won't flower. Plants that are naturally adapted to life in really hot, bright sun have developed their own defenses – their reflective silvery coats or furry or waxy surfaces are designed to protect them from overheating and prevent them from losing too much water.

In the wild, plants can "choose" where they grow. The parent scatters seeds, which will end up in all sorts of places, and it's only the ones that land in the right set of growing conditions that survive. In the garden, plants need to put up with where we put them, so that's why it pays to do a bit of homework and find out what conditions they need, so we can give them a place where they'll do well.

The plants growing in this gravel garden enjoy brilliant sunlight and good drainage at the roots, which mirrors their natural environment.

Warmth

Plants grow over virtually the whole surface of the planet Earth, including under the sea, and there are even a few that survive in deserts and areas of permafrost. But because the climates vary so much between the equator and the poles, the same plants don't grow everywhere – different plants have evolved to suit different temperature regimes.

The trouble is, we want to grow all of them – well, okay, a lot of them – in our gardens. Sometimes, we need the help of a greenhouse or conservatory to grow tender or exotic species, but, in many cases, we expect plants from all over the world to grow happily side-by-side in the garden. That's why it's useful to know what they are used to in the wild.

Plants that live in cold regions, or at very high altitudes, we usually refer to as alpines. They are adapted to life in harsh environments, with a short growing season between snow melt and snow fall and must get their growing, flowering, and seed distribution over with quickly. Many have their own built-in, cellular "anti-freeze" to keep them alive.

In hot areas, plants need to adapt to particular cycles of heat and cold, often with alternate wet and dry seasons that can be quite extreme. Tulips are a good example. They come from hot countries, such as Turkey and Iran, and grow in winter when the weather is mild and wet, flower in spring as the weather warms up, then duck underground to sit out the hot, dry summer as dormant bulbs safely insulated by a thick layer of soil.

Even in temperate zones you can experience different degrees of cold in winter and warmth in summer depending on latitude, and the plants that will grow happily in one place don't always survive in another. So it pays to know your own garden climate and how to pick the plants that will be happy in it (more later, on pages 115–21).

Soil

Soil has been created by nature from a strange mixture of ingredients. Most of it is rock that has taken millions of years to be turned into mineral dust. Sometimes this happened when glaciers picked up boulders and moved them slowly over bedrock, grinding up pebbles on the way. Chalk formed under water from the shells of trillions of tiny marine animals that lived and died millions of years ago. When the earth's crust buckled, it pushed the chalk up into cliffs – think of England's White Cliffs of Dover – and sun, wind, and rain continually battered the outer layers of soft rock into dust. It's still going on now. The same kind of things happened to weather other types of rock, from sandstone to granite, into soil, which is why soil types vary so much. They all depend on the kind of parent rock.

The chemical elements found in soil also depend on the rocks it was made from – in Australia, soils are often very short of phosphorus because the parent rocks don't contain much. In some parts of the world, soil is composed largely of ash from volcanoes – it is rich in a huge range of plant nutrients and very fertile. The Indonesians never use fertilizer, yet produce enormous crops of rice and vegetables on their rich volcanic soil.

Soil also contains a proportion of organic matter, made from the natural decay of animal and plant matter, which is particularly high in woodland, where large numbers of fallen branches and leaves die and decay, enriching the soil. In the world's wetlands, there are areas of highly organic soil; in the fens and bogs, there are big peat

Well-nourished soil produces well-nourished plants. Most of them will thrive in organically rich soil that is nevertheless well drained. You can almost see this lily-of-the-valley growing.

deposits that formed when prehistoric plants that died and were consumed by bogs could not decompose completely because of the high acidity and lack of oxygen.

But the soil you see on the surface of your garden is only the tip of the iceberg – if you dig down about a 3ft (meter), you'll probably find things look quite different underneath (see pages 48 and 242–45). If you can stand the slave labor this is quite a good thing to do, because what's underneath may have a considerable bearing on common garden problems. You'll often find there's a layer of solid clay beneath a layer of good topsoil, which prevents plants from rooting down deeply, or causes waterlogging in winter. Or you might find a band of sand that explains why plants dry out so badly in summer. Digging a hole, as well as doing a soil test to check the pH (the measure of acidity or alkalinity, see pages 90–94) is always a good first move when you take on a new garden.

From a plant's point of view, soil is the foundation of their home. It provides several things their roots need – nutrients, water, and air, as well as a means of holding themselves upright.

Soil nutrients

Strange as it sounds, you *can* grow plants without soil. It's a technique called hydroponics, and commercial growers use it all the time for some types of crops – tomatoes and orchids are often grown in rockwool. At home people sometimes grow hyacinths in jars of water, or houseplants in containers filled with clay granules.

But if you grow plants without soil, you need to find other ways of providing them with the nutrients they'd normally get from it. Growing in soil is much easier, because plants take up what they want and leave what they don't want – the nutrient reserves in the soil act as a natural buffer against hard times, and you don't get these in artificial growing media or in peat-based growing mixes.

Soil, if it's healthy, actually generates a lot of its own plant food – naturally occurring micro-organisms all work away, making nutrients out of atmospheric nitrogen or organic matter, and there are special fungi that cohabit with plant cells to help create a root-friendly feeding environment. Oh, soil might *look* brown and dreary but, as ever, you shouldn't be fooled by appearances.

Soil air

You never really think of roots needing air, but they do; they need oxygen to "breathe" in order to function. They get it from tiny air spaces between soil particles. Soil is naturally porous, or should be.

Sandy soil is made up of large particles with correspondingly large air spaces in between them – that's why sandy soil dries out so quickly, because there's lots of room for water to run through it.

Clay and silty soils, on the other hand, are made up of very tiny particles with equally tiny air spaces in between, so water can't run through them easily. That's why clay soils tend to become water-logged in persistent wet weather. Plants can literally die by drowning if the soil is waterlogged.

You can begin to see now why organic matter is so important. It is spongy, so it actually improves both types of soil. On sand, it helps bind the particles together to fill some of the gaps, and its spongy nature helps the soil hold water. On clay, it binds tiny particles together to create bigger ones, which helps form drainage channels. Organic matter also encourages earthworms, which improve the drainage by making tunnels. Adding gritty sand is even better for opening up the texture of clay soil.

Look at a fallen tree, and you'll see that most of its roots spread outward from the trunk rather than going straight down. This is so that the fine feeding root tips reach the perimeter of the umbrella-like canopy, where they can better absorb rainwater and nutrients.

Soil anchorage

The thing that's easily overlooked about soil is the way it provides support and anchorage for roots. Roots grow out into the soil to keep the plant upright. It's easy to imagine big trees having roots like guy ropes to hold them upright, but that's not always so, as we saw when the Great Hurricane of 1987 blew so many big trees over in England. Looking at the trees that came down around my garden at Barleywood, I wondered how most of them had remained upright for so long. There was just a circle of roots fanning out round the bottom of the trunk, with nothing going down to any depth at all.

Since only the tiny roots at the very tip of the beefier ones actually take in water, this is pretty smart of trees. It means that all the water-absorbing roots are arranged round the dripline – the circle of soil under the very edge of the canopy of branches where they'll find most of the water that runs off the foliage as if from a giant umbrella. But it also explains why if you have a huge tree in your garden nothing much grows underneath it – the soil is full of surface roots that take up all the available moisture and nutrients.

What plants need	Why they need it
Water	To prevent stems from wilting and leaves drying out
Nutrients	To prevent slowing or stunting of growth and unhealthy changes in leaf color (fading, yellowing, or purple tinging)
Air, light, and warmth	To enable them to photosynthesize properly and convert energy to food in order to grow
Soil	As a source of nutrients, water, and air, and as support and protection for the root system

What you need

Clean your tools occasionally (*opposite*) – it's really quite therapeutic – and sharpen them regularly.

My shed is groaning with gardening gear. I have special tools for everything from digging ditches to thinning grapes, but I never use them – they just decorate the walls. You could count the ones I use regularly on the fingers of two hands, and you'd know right away which ones they were because they are propped up just inside the door. They are usually dirty, either because I've just finished using them, or because I am just about to pick them up again, so they get cleaned properly only in winter.

The initial outlay

Considering that the spade I use belonged to my grandfather and was used by him on his Yorkshire allotment and by my dad (the plumber) for mixing concrete, it's actually doing very well in spite of the apparent mistreatment. But it just goes to show, if you've never done any gardening before, you don't actually need all that much to get started. Most people begin with a few old tools handed down from a parent or grandparent who has upgraded. Don't spurn these beauties. They'll be broken in for you – with silky smooth handles and well-honed blades. With luck! If you don't have a relative with an overflowing shed, then I'd suggest buying just the essentials from the economy ranges of any of the well-known garden tool manufacturers – you'll have no trouble finding them in most good garden centers. There's no need to spend a fortune. You can always add to your basic tool kit later, but for starters these are the things you'll really need.

The handles of spades and forks come in different styles – here a 'T' and a 'D' shape. Choose whichever you find most comfortable to use.

Spade and fork

These are the basic digging implements. A spade is better for digging sandy or loamy soil. Some people find a fork is best on clay soil, since it makes it easier to smash up the clods. A spade tends to get clogged if the ground is a bit stodgy, but a fork is definitely better on soil that contains stones because the prongs go between them, whereas a spade would just come to a grinding halt midstroke. A fork is also handy for moving manure or compost from a pile into a wheelbarrow and then spreading it around.

I reckon the fork is the most valuable implement in the garden. I use it even for final breaking down of soil on the vegetable plot. Hold it horizontally and bring it down at an angle on the soil, knocking the clods to shatter them. Using a rake to break soil down produces too fine a tilth that "cakes" in a shower of rain. A rake is for final leveling – nothing else.

With spades and forks some people prefer a T-handle and others swear by a D-handle (or none at all; see the next paragraph), so try out all options before buying. Tempered steel blades are perfectly adequate. If you fancy stainless steel, be prepared to pay more, but beware of the cheaper models – they can be brittle and short-lived.

Tall people, or those with dodgy backs, might also find it worth trying the long-handled, typical American-style digging shovel, the sort you see gold miners using in old black-and-white films. They are said to be much less of a strain. Personally I'll stick to my grandad's old spade; it's like a family heirloom now.

Hoe

Garden tool catalogs are awash with fancy varieties of hoe, but they all do the same basic job: weeding. One is enough to start with, but hoes are something you tend to acquire as you find new models that you enjoy using just that little bit more. There are two basic types.

Draw hoes, or chop hoes, have the head at right angles to the handle; they are used with a chopping action and are best for hacking down big weeds, as you will need to do if you are clearing an overgrown vegetable patch. Short-handled versions with arched, "swan" necks are known as onion hoes, and they are excellent for weeding between rows of any vegetables, on your hands and knees, where you need a bit more precision.

Push hoes, or Dutch hoes, are better for smaller weeds in borders, where the plants don't grow in rows. To use these, you just glide the blade forward through the soil. Some of the newer designs work on both the push and the pull strokes, so in theory you get double the work for your efforts. In practice, you can end up chopping off a lot of plants, too, if you aren't careful. Try several before buying, even if the other customers in the shop think you are a bit odd practicing your hoe-swings out on the floor.

Remember, when using a hoe, skim it just below the surface of the soil so that weeds are cut off at their stocking tops – where the shoot meets the roots. Hoe too deeply, and the weed will be dug up and can easily reroot after a shower of rain.

Hoes are most effective at controlling weed seedlings and annual weeds – things like crabgrass and chickweed (see page 141). They can weaken perennial weeds, such as goutweed (see page 146), and repeated hoeing can eventually wipe them out, but it takes a long time. Thick-rooted perennial weeds (such as thistles and pokeweed) are always best forked or dug out completely.

Rake

The ordinary garden rake, with short parallel teeth, is meant for leveling soil to make an even surface ready for sowing or planting. When used properly, the idea is to gather up large stones, bits of root, and other rubbish behind it, which can be easily picked up and removed – you shouldn't end up with a great pile of soil as well. If you do, have another go. The idea is to redistribute the soil as you rake, and gather up only unwanted surface material. Don't over-rake, and don't remove too many stones. Plants' roots have no problem getting around them, and you'll only need to find a way to dispose of them.

The sort of rake with a wide fan of springy wire or rubber tines is meant for raking leaves off the lawn or smoothing out footprints from gravel paths.

Trowel or hand fork

You need one or other of these for weeding, planting bedding plants and small perennials, and for fiddling about in pots on the patio. I like to use a hand fork for scuffling over the soil between plants to neaten up after planting a bed; it's just a habit, I suppose, but it does stop the soil from looking like a game field. But if you are going to have only one of these implements, choose a trowel – one that feels comfortable in your hand.

When you use it, don't hold it like a flour scoop. Position the handle so that the end of it sits right in the palm of your hand with the concave side of the blade facing you. A hole is excavated by pushing the trowel into the soil and pulling the soil toward you – rather like a primitive claw. Stainless steel trowels and hand forks are a good buy. They are relatively inexpensive but last for years, unlike cheap hand tools, which have a nasty habit of bending double or snapping off just when you've gotten used to them. I love old trowels, which can often be bought for next to nothing and have blades that are razor sharp.

Various tools are needed for jobs around the garden. The push hoe (*left*), or Dutch hoe, is great for cutting off annual weeds, but keep it sharpened with a file so that it works efficiently. A stainless steel trowel (*center*) is comfortable to use for digging and very long lasting, and a rake (*right*) should be thought of as a leveling tool, not as a way of turning soil into dust.

Wheel barrow

Get a decent builder's barrow if you have some serious shifting to do. If you don't, then get a garden hamper – a plastic tub with two handles. It's all you really need for carting weeds to the compost pile, or for spreading soil improvers and mulches around the garden.

Watering can

A watering can is very handy for watering containers on the patio, and it's difficult to use liquid fertilizers without one. But if you want to use a watering can for liquid weedkillers, then I'd have a separate one clearly marked: WEEDKILLER. However well you rinse it out, there is always the risk that a trace will remain, and that's often all it takes to kill susceptible plants. Tomatoes are notoriously sensitive to hormone weedkillers – even months after they were used in a can. Buy cans in two different colors, so there's no confusion.

If you have a big garden, or a lot of things to water, then it's worth getting a hose, but then you really need to have an outdoor faucet plumbed in – you'll soon get fed up feeding the end through the kitchen window. Liquid-fertilizer dilutors, which make sure that the right strength of fertilizer is dispensed, can be bought to fit onto hoses.

Pruners are a vital pruning tool, so keep them well oiled and rub the blades with sandpaper to remove any dried sap, which can make them stick.

Pruners

Even in a brand-new, or labor-saving garden, you'll need to prune a rose or cut back an overgrown shrub sooner or later. There's no need to spend a fortune on professional-quality pruners. An inexpensive pair will do very well to start with; then, when you graduate to a better pair later, you'll have an old pair to use for all the rough jobs.

Some people prefer the parrot-beak type of pruners – the ones with two sharp blades that bypass each other like scissors – while others go for the anvil type, which have one sharp blade that cuts down onto a flattened base. It's entirely up to you – I'm a bypass man myself. A good pair, which may be guaranteed for life, can cost a reasonable sum, but it's money well spent. Choose pruners with bright red handles, because they will then show up well when you put them down somewhere.

Normal, short-handled pruners will cut through stems up to ½–¾ in (15–20mm) thick. For thicker stems, a pair of long-handled loppers is handy – they have wider jaws and longer handles that give you more leverage. If you need to cut back climbers or tall trees, you can get long-reach pruners, which are like pruners on a pole with a trigger handle at your end.

Where to start

Before you can start any serious garden-making, the ground nearly always needs clearing. You might have inherited a jungle of weeds and overgrown shrubs from a previous owner that needs clearing completely, or you might just want to turn a patch of grass into beds and borders. Even if you start with what looks like a virgin site on a new housing development, you might find the ground has been badly churned up by heavy machinery and needs a bit of sorting out before you can grow things in it.

I know it's very tempting to get some plants in right away and worry about the weeds or the dreadful soil later. Everyone does it at some time, because they are so eager to start seeing some flowers. But if you don't tackle the serious problems first, you'll be struggling with bindweed or wondering why nothing wants to grow for years – and it can cost a fortune in failed plants. Soil improvement is vital too, so, at the risk of sounding like a killjoy, make sure you do the groundwork first.

Second-hand gardens

When you inherit someone else's old garden, you never know what you are going to find. There might be some real treasures, or entire borders that are basically okay apart from being a bit overgrown with weeds. On the other hand, you might be faced with an overgrown tangle that you just want to clear away so that you can start again from scratch. If there are only a few plants worth saving, it's probably easier to dig them out and put them in pots to keep them safe while you tackle the undergrowth.

Digging weeds out by hand is the safest way to clear them when they are growing close to plants that you want to keep. If you are razing entire beds to the ground, it is much quicker to burn them off with a flame gun, though that won't kill perennial roots, and you'll probably need to do it several times to kill the regrowth if the ground is very weedy.

If you don't mind using chemicals, then weedkiller is often the easy answer if the "jungle" contains a lot of persistent perennial weeds, such as bindweed and goutweed (see pages 145 and 146). Even though I don't usually use chemicals, this is one situation in which I'd seriously suggest using a glyphosate-based product to eradicate them, because it kills them roots and all. The residue of glyphosate is nonpersistent and safe to pets and wildlife, once dry. One or two doses, about six weeks apart, applied at any time the

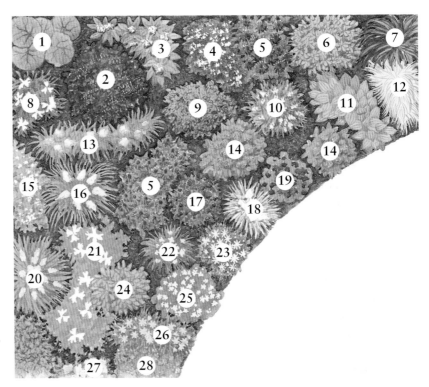

Revive an old bed (*above*) by keeping some established plants to provide structure and adding new plants around them. A simple, or detailed, planting plan (*right*) can help you envisage the finished border (*below*). The plan shows plants at their peak, and not all of them can be seen here.

weeds are growing strongly, is usually all it takes to do the job, unless there is a very serious infestation (see pages 153–54). You can garden without chemicals from then on.

Real organic fans will sometimes opt for the old carpet method, which involves smothering weeds out under a complete layer of old carpet or black plastic. This starves the weeds by depriving them of light, but it takes about two years to work (see pages 155–56).

Whatever you do, don't just plow the lot with a rototiller. If there are perennial weed roots, all you'll do is chop them up and propagate them. Each piece turns into a root cutting that grows into a new plant.

If you need to get rid of entire trees or tree stumps, hire a qualified person who knows what they are doing. An arborist ("tree surgeon") will cut the branches off a big tree and then reduce the trunk in stages, which is much safer than chopping it down in one go, especially if it's close to buildings. Tree stumps can sometimes be winched out if there is room for the equipment; otherwise, bring in a contractor with a stump grinder. It looks like a rototiller and chews the stump to sawdust; then you shovel out the remains. If you refill the hole with topsoil, you can plant something else later the same day.

Lawn conversions

Maybe you have an existing garden and fancy digging up a patch of the lawn to make a new bed. If so, don't just rorotill or dig it in, or you'll have grass growing up as weeds in your new bed forever. Either kill off the grass with glyphosate and dig it in after four to six weeks, or strip the grass right off to leave bare soil. You can skim off the grass to about 1in (2.5cm) deep with the back of a spade – unless you feel like hiring a mechanical sod stripper. Use the sod to resod a new piece of ground, or stack it up in a pile somewhere out of the way, grass side down, for a year. By then it will have decomposed and turned into good topsoil that is handy for topping up a bed.

Ground that has been under grass for several years usually has a very good structure. The old roots provide fiber and the worms will have worked through it. But on the downside, it'll have a high population of soil pests just waiting to nibble off the roots of any plants you put in. Turf and grassland are the preferred habitats of such root-eating pests as wireworms (click beetle larvae) and a variety of white grubs, including Japanese beetles. If you don't want to use a soil pesticide, then it's best to turn the soil over several times during the season. This exposes the soil-dwelling beasts to hungry birds, who'll be happy to deal with them for you.

Key to the plants chosen for the border (*left*):

 1 *Darmera peltata*.
 2 *Cotinus* 'Grace'.
 3 *Verbascum* 'Raspberry Ripple'.
 4 *Cimicifuga simplex* var. *simplex* Atropurpurea group.
 5 *Echinacea purpurea*.
 6 *Skimmia fortunei*.
 7 *Phormium* 'Maori Queen'.
 8 *Lilium regale*.
 9 *Weigela florida* 'Foliis Purpureis'.
10 *Penstemon* cultivar (white).
11 *Hosta* 'Halcyon'.
12 *Hakonechloa macra* 'Aureola'.
13 *Eremurus* hybrids (mixed).
14 *Sedum spectabile* 'Indian Chief'.
15 *Cimicifuga simplex*.
16 *Cortaderia selloana* 'Sunningdale Silver'.
17 *Rosa* 'Indigo'.
18 *Sisyrinchium striatum* 'Aunt May'.
19 *Geranium sanguineum*.
20 *Kniphofia* 'Yellow Cheer'.
21 *Melianthus major*.
22 *Sisyrinchium striatum*.
23 *Osteospermum* 'Buttermilk'.
24 *Rhododendron yakushimanum*.
25 *Geranium sanuineum* 'Album'.
26 *Gazania* cultivar (yellow).
27 *Trollius x cultorum* 'Lemon Queen'.
28 *Geranium* 'Johnson's Blue'.

First-time gardens

If you've just moved into a brand-new house, don't assume you'll have good soil all ready to garden on. You might be lucky… but take a good look around. New houses often have piles of builders' rubble left around outside, or ground that has had the life squashed out of it by heavy vehicles. Sometimes there are oil spillages or, most frequently, infertile subsoil has just been dumped and spread out, so the ground needs quite a bit of work to get it back in good shape before anything much will grow. It's a soul-destroying process, but later on you'll be glad you sorted things out at the beginning.

A worm's-eye view

The cross section of any soil is known as a soil profile – a sort of worm's-eye view of the different layers within the ground. On the surface, just below any living vegetation, will be a layer of rotting and rotted organic matter. It is a vital source of soil improvement when dragged under the surface by worms. It enriches the topmost layer of earth known, not surprisingly, as topsoil. This is where most plant roots grow. Beneath it is subsoil – it may be clay or gravel or sand. It is usually lacking in nutrients and not nearly so hospitable to root growth as the richer topsoil. Below the subsoil will be a layer of fragmented rock and, eventually, a layer of bedrock. The depth at which these layers occur varies from garden to garden, but the deeper the layer of topsoil, the better the conditions will be for plant growth.

The first thing to do is to rent a dumpster and get rid of all the old cinder blocks and bricks (well, okay, save a few if you think you'll need them – they're often handy for odd jobs) and any baddies, such as lumps of concrete, or piles of building sand. Bright yellow builders' sand is no good for the garden – it's very fine and contains a lot of lime, unlike horticultural sand, which is grittier and lime-free.

If the soil has set in big, hard lumps, is yellow or blue in color, or forms a glutinous mess in wet weather, then take a spade and dig down to see if there's something better underneath. The odds are that you've had a heap of subsoil dumped on your property, and the original topsoil may be several inches down. You can improve subsoil, but it takes years of work. Frankly, you are much better ditching it, loosening the ground underneath with a fork to repair the compaction, and buying some decent topsoil to spread on top. Builders! Don't ya just love 'em?

Soil improvement

Unless you are lucky and have naturally good ground, it'll need improving. The time to do this is when you are first making a new bed or border, because that's usually the only time the ground is completely clear and at its most "get-at-able." There are two ways of improving the soil – one is by digging in bulky organic matter, such as manure or compost, and the other is by adding fertilizers. People often confuse the two substances, or they imagine you can use one *or* the other, but don't need both. Actually, you *do* need both because they each have a different job to do. The task of digging them in also helps to improve the soil.

At Barleywood, where I reckon to be about 95 percent organic, my standard soil improvement technique consists of digging in lots of organic matter (on newly cultivated soil), or mulching the surface of the soil (on established beds) in winter. I use masses of well-rotted stable manure and homemade compost. I fork in a good sprinkling of a general organic fertilizer just before sowing or planting, and established borders get the same treatment in early spring. Avid vegetable growers often add seaweed meal to their vegetable plots in the belief that the extra trace elements make everything taste better.

At Barleywood, I use manure and compost as a surface mulch on established beds and borders – it keeps down weeds and helps retain soil moisture, while the worms slowly drag the mulch material beneath the surface, enriching the soil.

Organic matter

Bulky organic matter is "roughage" – it improves the structure of the soil and, as it breaks down, releases small amounts of nutrients when worked over by soil bacteria. That's what organic gardeners are talking about when they say "feed the soil, not the plant." But though organic matter is a good source of trace elements, the quantities of major nutrients released in this way aren't enough for serious gardening, so, along with organic matter, you need to use fertilizer as well (see pages 52–53).

For most people, the cheapest and most convenient form of bulky organic matter is compost (see page 51). You can make it yourself and it costs you nothing. In rural areas, manure is often available cheaply through small ads in the local paper – some horse owners give it away free at their yards just to get rid of it.

There are also various soil improvers that you can buy in bags at the garden center, and mushroom compost or spent hops are sometimes available locally. They all have their pros and cons (see pages 51–53). When in doubt, go for whatever you can get most of at the price you can afford. But don't miss out on your own free soil improver – make a compost pile, if you don't have one already.

Manure (1) varies in quality according to the type of animals and farming system used. Manure from racehorse stables, for instance, tends to be much better quality than that from intensive cattle farms where little bedding is used. Avid organic gardeners prefer to use manure from nonintensive systems on the grounds of animal welfare.

Fresh manure of any kind needs stacking for six months so that it rots down before use – if it is used fresh, it releases a lot of ammonia that can scorch or even kill plants. But manure needs to be bought with care. If it has been stacked in a weed-infested corner of a field, it is often full of weed seeds or roots, and it's easy to find you have imported something nasty, such as bindweed, to your garden, along with a load of muck. If manure has been stacked for too long, then most of the nutrients will have been washed out by the rain and run away into the soil beneath the pile, so, though you benefit from the roughage, you miss out on the trace elements that your garden should benefit from.

Leaf mold (2) is something you'll get only if you have a patch of woodland in your own garden, or if you can gather a lot of dead leaves to rot down and make your own. Don't, whatever you do, go digging leaf mold out of forestry land or woods – it's illegal and you're likely to get arrested! It's really too precious to use for general soil improvement, but, if you are making a shady bed for choice woodland plants, then it's the best thing to use.

Mushroom compost (3), these days, is usually based on peat rather than rotted manure, as it once was, and tends to be alkaline due to the chalk used in the casing material. But if you live in a mushroom-growing area, then it's a useful source of organic matter.

Chipped bark (4) is good for mulching, but composted bark is the next best thing to leaf mold, and most garden centers sell it. It holds moisture but doesn't go boggy in very wet conditions as peat does.

Compost (5) is potentially a much richer source of nutrients than other forms of bulky organic matter, especially if you use a good mixture of ingredients to make it. Use kitchen waste, such as tea leaves, orange peels, potato peelings, crushed eggshells, and vegetable waste, as well as lawn clippings and weeds. It's really worthwhile to build a bin and recycle all this waste that would otherwise just be thrown away (see pages 204–7).

Peat (6) used to be the gardener's first choice for improving the soil, but now that we realize how damaging peat-extraction is to wetland habitats, it's best avoided. Peat doesn't contain any nutrients, so other forms of organic matter are a much better bet.

Types of organic matter:
1 Stable manure needs to be stacked for six months before being used on the garden.
2 Leaf mold needs at least a year to rot down to a brown and crumbly texture.
3 Mushroom compost, which contains bits of chalk, is especially useful on acidic soils (see page 93).
4 Chipped bark is a good mulch, but composted bark is more useful for soil enrichment.
5 Compost is one of the best soil conditioners of all...
6 ... and peat the most overrated – to be avoided for conservation reasons, also.

Recycled materials are increasingly being investigated since peat has been off the soil-improvement shopping list. Manufacturers have experimented with all sorts of alternatives, based on everything from municipal waste to composted bank notes – no, there's no chance of finding the odd, half-digested fiver; they've all been carefully shredded first. Ask your local authority for details of their own recycling progams, and keep an eye on what's offered by garden centers.

Fertilizers

Fertilizers are concentrated plant foods. They come in two types, organic and the other sort – inorganic. In gardening terms, "organic" means those that come from natural sources, such as plants, animals, or naturally occurring rock (see pages 53 and 164–66), instead of manufactured "chemical" fertilizers, but plants can't tell the difference. So long as they get what they need in a way they can use it, they really don't mind. Organic fertilizers have the advantage in that they keep soil bacteria busy breaking them down into a form absorbable for plants, and busy bacteria are happy bacteria.

The thing you need to do is look at the label to see what you are getting. Fertilizer packages must, by law, be printed with a declaration that lets you know the amount of each of the three main elements, N:P:K.

N (nitrogen) is good for promoting leafy growth, P (phosphorus, or phosphate) helps the roots, and K (kalium, the ancient name for potassium, or potash) is vital for producing flowers and fruit. If the declaration on the package is 6:4:4, it means that in every 100 pounds of the fertilizer you get 6 pounds of nitrogen and 4 pounds each of phosphorus and potassium (the rest is bulking agent). This tells you right away which applications the product is best for – a product high in N but low in P and K is a high-nitrogen fertilizer for encouraging leafy growth – the sort of thing you'd put on the lawn in spring. Nowadays, you usually don't need to bother working it out for yourself, because it usually tells you on the label what it's for – when in doubt, read the small print. But there are various types of fertilizers for use in different situations.

Granular or powdered fertilizers are the kind to use on the open garden when you are first preparing the soil ready for planting. You can also use them to replenish the nutrients in spring at the start of each new growing season. With heavy-bearing plants, such as roses and vegetables, it's a good idea to sprinkle some more fertilizer around the plants during the summer and water it in, or use it to pep up the ground on the vegetable patch between crops.

Fertilizers are an essential supplement to bulky manures and are much easier to apply.

General-purpose fertilizer, available in many formulations and brands, is good for preparing soil before planting or sowing, and it's also good for fertilizing all around the garden. If you want to buy only one kind of fertilizer, this is it. The three main nutrients are present in roughly equal quantities, making this a 'balanced' fertilizer – the plants' answer to a good square meal. General-purpose fertilizers are also handy to use as a de-icer for steps and sidewalks in winter in areas where snow and ice are problems. Their contents are much friendlier to plants than the sodium chloride (salt) that is the only or the primary constituent of most commercially available de-icers.

Rose fertilizer contains more potassium and magnesium than a general-purpose fertilizer and, though not essential, it's good to have if you grow a lot of roses. Fork this into the ground before planting, sprinkle it all around the plants, and fork it in in spring, then again in summer, just after the first flush of flowers. The fact that plants can't read means that you can also use rose fertilizer on other flowering shrubs and perennials, since they'll all enjoy the same blend of nutrients, and it saves your using two different products.

Single fertilizers contain just one of the main nutrients: ammonium sulfate supplies nitrogen; superphosphate supplies phosphorus, and potassium sulfate supplies potassium. Use them if you know what you are doing. An onion grower, for instance, would use super-phosphate for preparing the bed for his prize-winning exhibits. But for most gardeners – me included – balanced fertilizers that contain all the main nutrients are best for most everyday uses, since they contain a bit of everything plants need.

Organic fertilizers, such as dried blood, bonemeal, or crab shells. provide an unbalanced mix of nutrients – dried blood is a fast-acting nitrogen fertilizer, while crab shells slowly release nitrogen and other nutrients. Bonemeal is a very slow-acting, high-phosphate fertilizer that is traditionally used when planting trees or shrubs, especially in autumn and late winter. In reality, most of the phosphates are "locked up" by the soil, which is why I have stopped using bonemeal and prefer to use bulky manure at planting time instead – the improvement of soil structure is, I reckon, more conducive to root establishment than the addition of fertilizers. It's rather like giving an invalid chicken soup instead of filet mignon.

Seaweed meal is a particularly good source of trace elements, though it doesn't provide the main nutrients in worthwhile quantities. Think of it always as a supplement that helps provide a balanced diet.

Most plants need fertilizer if they are to grow to their full potential – vegetables are especially greedy, due to their rapid growth rate.

Digging

"Why bother?" is the reaction you hear from a lot of new gardeners to this most traditional of gardening jobs. There are several good reasons for digging and, even with no-dig techniques, you still need to prepare the ground by digging it in the first place – it's just that from then on you don't need to dig it again.

Digging controls weeds by burying them. By turning them in on the spot, instead of composting them first, you cut out an extra job. This works only if you are turning in annual weeds before they form ("set") seed. If you bury ripe seedheads, the seeds will grow. And if you dig in roots of perennial weeds, you are simply spreading them, too. Even with annual weeds, if you let them grow big, there is too much leafy growth to bury properly.

Digging fluffs up the soil, aerating ground that has been squashed down (compacted) by being walked on or by heavy rainfall. Loose soil has bigger spaces between the soil particles for air to move through and for surplus water to drain away. It also makes it easier for roots to penetrate, so plants grow better, and, because the soil is soft, it makes sowing and planting much easier.

But the main reason gardeners dig is to incorporate organic matter, which improves the soil structure and adds nutrients before planting. Years ago you were always told to double-dig the ground to make a new bed. Frankly, that's incredibly hard work and you just don't need to do it, unless you want to grow award-winning parsnips or giant dahlias. And if your garden has a thin layer of decent topsoil over stones or a layer of nasty yellow or blue clay subsoil, then the last thing you want to do is bring that lot up to the surface. For most people, single digging is quite enough.

The no-dig technique

With the no-dig technique, as used on the deep beds that are very popular with organic vegetable gardeners, you do need to dig – deeply – when you prepare the beds in the first place. But from then on, you add new organic matter by mulching thickly on the surface (see pages 154–55) with well-rotted manure or compost whenever the soil is vacant between crops. You then simply wait for the worms to pull the mulch down into the soil and do the digging for you.

You can achieve the same result without digging by making a raised bed. Use low walls of boards to outline the bed and fill it with well-rotted compost laid on top of the existing soil.

Bear in mind that the no-dig technique works only if you avoid walking on the soil; otherwisel, it quickly becomes too compacted.

How to... single dig

If you want to get the ground ready to plant trees, shrubs, or perennials with well-established roots, this is all you need to do. If you want to sow seeds or grow small plants, such as annuals or vegetable seedlings, then you need to dig it over, then rake the ground lightly to reduce the surface layer to what gardeners call a "fine tilth" – a fine-textured surface that looks more like cake crumbs.

Don't overdo the digging – if you aren't used to it, it can be hard work. Divide the area into several parts, and do it in easy stages. If you are working in autumn, you can leave the ground roughly dug for the weather to work on. Birds will ferret out a lot of soil pests for you. If you are adding only a thin layer of organic matter to previously worked beds, it's easiest just to spread it over the ground and turn it in as you dig, instead of actually burying it in the trench.

> ### What you need
>
> • *digging fork*
> • *sharp spade*
> • *organic matter*
> • *wheelbarrow*

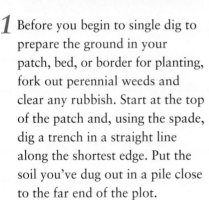

1 Before you begin to single dig to prepare the ground in your patch, bed, or border for planting, fork out perennial weeds and clear any rubbish. Start at the top of the patch and, using the spade, dig a trench in a straight line along the shortest edge. Put the soil you've dug out in a pile close to the far end of the plot.

2 Spread organic matter along the bottom of the trench with a spade or fork. If you are making a new bed on previously unworked ground, add a 3–4-in (7–10-cm) layer of organic matter to give it a really good start. On ground that has been dug over before, a thinner layer of organic matter is perfectly OK.

3 Dig a second trench alongside the original one, throwing over each spadeful of soil, so it lands upside down in the first trench. That'll bury any small annual weeds and cover the organic matter. Remove any perennial weed roots as you work, and bash down any large earth clods with the fork into walnut-sized lumps. When you get to the end of the row, the first trench will be full and you'll have created a second one about 9in (23cm) farther down the plot. Keep doing this until you've dug the entire area, and use the original soil pile to fill in the final trench.

2 GROWING AND PLANTING

How plants grow

Producing seeds is the ultimate goal of most plants, and seedheads, such as the round heads of *Echinops*, the bluish *Perovskia*, and the golden *Stipa gigantea* in the background, can be a valuable addition to the autumn garden.

Just like us, plants pass through several distinct phases of life. In their natural state, they begin as seeds that germinate and become seedlings. They pass through a nonflowering, juvenile phase before reaching the mature, adult stage, when they flower and produce seed to complete the cycle. They'll sometimes have a short senile phase, when they don't bear much fruit, as in the case of old apple trees, for instance, but with a lot of plants, such as annuals, producing the next generation leaves them exhausted. I have two daughters. I know how plants feel.

Seeds

When you think about it, seeds are pretty amazing things. The tiny acorn in the palm of your hand might not look like an embryo oak tree, but that's exactly what it is. Like a bird's egg, it contains everything the new life inside it needs to get growing. It just needs something to trigger it into 'hatching'. But, unlike birds' eggs, which are very fragile and need intensive care, seeds are very rugged and are designed by nature to withstand adverse conditions. They'll lie dormant until conditions are right for them to spring into life.

What seeds need is air, a suitable temperature, and moisture. They don't even need nutrients to germinate, because they have their own supply stored in the seed leaves (cotyledons) packed inside them, which is enough to last until they have formed roots. The bigger the seed, the more food reserves it contains. In the wild, seeds must take their chances. Lots of them never germinate at all because they land in unsuitable places. A fair percentage will be eaten by animals, and there's a high mortality rate among the seedlings that do make it. Life is tough from the outset, and that's why most plants produce and shed huge quantities of seed to allow for natural wastage.

But in the garden at home, when you are paying for seeds by the packet, you want as many to reach maturity as possible, which is why the germinating seeds and small seedlings are normally treated very carefully. If you've never tried growing plants from seed, give it a go. It's about the most rewarding gardening activity of all.

Seed packets

Virtually every kind of seed has its own ideal set of conditions for germination, and the closer you match them, the better your results. Don't just guess. Seeds can be expensive, and there are a limited number in the packet, so do your homework – read the instructions!

Lots of useful information gets thrown away along with the seed packet, so write a plant's name on a plant label to stick into the pot or at the end of the row when you sow. Copy useful details, such as height, what type of plant it is (hardy annual, half-hardy bedding plant), sowing date, and so on, onto the back of the label to act as a reminder. A seed packet stabbed onto a stick rots or blows away.

The small print

Name: you might be given the full botanical name or just the variety name, depending on the supplier; with vegetable seeds, you'll usually be given the type of vegetable and variety name only.

Description: designed to whet your appetite. Allow seed merchants a bit of leeway… they're not quite real-estate agents, but they can sometimes get a bit overly enthusiastic.

Height: lots of popular old varieties, such as flowering tobacco, are being bred in ultra-compact versions nowadays, so make sure you're buying what you need for the place you have in mind.

Sowing information: gives times and places for sowing indoors and/or outdoors, and a required temperature range for fast, even germination.

Spacing: the distance apart to thin out seedlings or plant out young plants, allowing them to grow to full size without competition from neighbors.

When you buy seeds from a garden center, the packet usually has a picture on the front and instructions on the back. If you buy direct from the seed companies' catalogs, you'll have a bigger choice of varieties, but the seeds are often sent out in plain packets with few or no instructions – just the name. You can look up the description or photo in the catalog, but there's usually little growing information. Some firms supply a booklet with detailed germination requirements for different types of seed; if not, you'll need to look up advice in a good plant dictionary or encyclopedia.

Seed diversity

Seeds range in size, from coconuts to specks of dust and, in shape, from long, thin quills, as in marigolds, to winged maple seeds. The reasons for their odd shapes and sizes are mainly to do with the way the seed is dispersed naturally: on the wind, by hitching a lift with animals or birds, by firing from an explosive capsule, or by being shaken from pepper-pot-style pods. Seeds also have some elaborate survival tricks up their pods. Think what would happen if seeds all grew as soon as they were shed. You'd have some coming up just as winter was around the corner, when seedlings would stand no chance of survival. The seed's internal chemistry makes sure it remains dormant until there's the right combination of warmth, light, and moisture, but some won't grow until they've experienced a particular set of conditions.

Eucalyptus seeds, for instance, only germinate after a bush fire, so to help them germinate you need to simulate one. Australian growers buy smoke pellets to imitate the chemicals released by burning wood; at home you'll get eucalyptus seeds to germinate quicker by pouring a splash of boiling water over the soil mix in which they've been sown. Many woody plants from temperate regions must experience a cold period before they can germinate.

Unless you know about such special needs in advance, seed raising with certain plants can be a bit slow. But even a "normal" seed needs special care as it's coming up. The critical time in any germinating seed's life is the 12 to 24 hours during which the seed coat cracks open and the first tiny shoot starts to emerge. If it dries out or becomes chilled or waterlogged, then the seed will just die, and you don't get a second chance.

Golden rules for good germination

Germination is a seed's first stage of growth, when the first root and shoot emerge. Different types of seeds need to be sown in different ways to ensure they germinate properly. (See pages 64-67 for step-by-step instructions on sowing seeds and pricking them out.)

Storing seeds

Ideally, don't! It's much better to buy the seed you need and use it the same year. The percentage of seeds that will germinate drops the longer they are stored, even in good conditions. Don't leave packets of seed lying around in the greenhouse – keep them at a low, steady temperature somewhere out of the sun. If you really want to store partly used packets for future years, tape them shut and put them in a screw-top jar in the salad compartment of the refrigeator. They'll become a delightful source of family disputes.

1

2

3
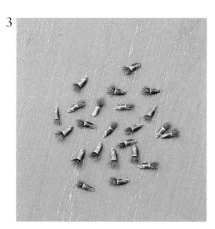

Seeds come in all shapes and sizes and produce plants of different habits:

1 These sweet pea seeds will produce clambering plants with lots of delicate flowers.

2 The sunflower seeds give tall stems with big, bold, yellow flowers.

3 And the cornflower seeds produce shorter plants with small flowers in mixed colors.

Big seeds (e.g. peas and beans)

To start the germination process, seeds must first soak up moisture. The bigger the seed, the more moisture it needs, which is why it's worth soaking pea and bean seeds for 12 hours before you sow them. Don't soak them for longer, though, because that's as long as seeds can go without air; after that they'll literally drown. As a rule of thumb, when sowing large seeds, cover them with their own depth of sowing medium. Large seeds are so easy to handle that you can space them out in the seed tray or sow them in individual pots, which saves pricking out seedlings later.

Medium-sized seeds (e.g. French marigold)

These are seeds from apple-seed size down to large pinhead size. They are usually sown by scattering them thinly over the surface of the sowing medium in a seed tray or pot, so that they rest about ¼in (5mm) apart. They are then covered with more medium until they *just* disappear from view. To get a really fine, even layer of medium, shake it through a sieve. Never bury seeds too deeply – they are not moles.

Very small seeds (e.g. begonia, impatiens)

Very small to dustlike seeds won't germinate if they are covered with sowing medium. Scatter them on to the gently firmed, level surface of medium in a pot or tray. To moisten, stand the pot in about an inch (a few centimeters) of water for about 10 minutes until you can just see moisture glistening on the medium's surface. Watering with a can just washes the seeds to one end of the tray. Then cover the top of the pot with plastic wrap or slip it into a loosely tied plastic bag, to keep the humidity high and prevent the seeds from drying out.

Hard seeds (e.g. canna, strelitzia, sweet peas)

Built like ball-bearings, these seeds won't germinate until the outer casing has decomposed enough to let water in to start the germination process. To speed things up, chip a hole in the seed coat. Use a sharp knife to carefully pare away a sliver of the seed coat, so you can *just* see the greenish or white layer of live seed inside.

Chipping seed is a pretty risky business, but you can play it safe and just rub one side of the seed with fine sandpaper instead. Don't do the whole seed – you need to do only a tiny patch, and just enough to get a glimpse of the live seed inside.

Seeds needing cold treatment

Some trees, shrubs, and many alpines won't germinate until they have experienced one or more periods of very cold weather. Sow

Sweet peas germinate faster if their tough seed coats are chipped with a sharp knife, but watch your fingers!

them in pots or trays in the autumn, as for ordinary seeds, and cover the tops with fine-mesh wire netting to protect them from birds, mice, and squirrels. Stand them out in an open cold frame, or in a safe place in the open garden, for the winter. If they don't come up next spring, keep them watered all summer and leave them out again next winter. Be patient – some kinds can take three years to come up.

Alternatively, you can give slow-germinating seeds an artificial winter in your refrigerator. Sow in pots and water them in as usual, then place them in the salad drawer for six weeks. Bring them out into a temperature of 60–70°F (15–21°C). If they don't come up within 12 weeks, put them back into the refrigerator for another six weeks – some will actually germinate there. Seedlings raised by the "refrigerator method" are often not as robust as outdoor-grown seedlings, so it's best to prick them out and grow them on under cover until they are well established.

Moisture-loving plant seeds (e.g. candelabra primroses)
Sow these seeds thinly on the surface of sowing medium in pots and, to keep them moist, stand the pots in a dish or tray containing 1in (2.5cm) of water. Keep it regularly topped up until the seedlings are pricked out. Don't try this trick with anything except real moisture-lovers – other types of seed won't appreciate standing in water.

Seeds with wings or tails (e.g. clematis, maple)
Sow very thinly, so the wings or tails don't overlap with their neighbors, then cover them with a thin layer of fine grit, which weighs them down so they can't blow away. Or break off the tails and wings and just sow the seeds as usual – but that's a pretty fussy job.

Primrose seeds need light to germinate, and moisture-loving candelabra primroses (shown here) need very damp sowing medium, too.

How to... **sow seed indoors**

The most reliable way to sow seeds is under cover, where you can control the conditions. Avid seed raisers use a cold frame or greenhouse, ideally with a heated propagator. If you don't have special facilities, then small numbers of seedlings can be raised on a bright windowsill indoors, as long as it is out of direct sunlight. Check the temperature needed for germination and sow all the seeds that need the same temperature at the same time, especially if they are sharing a heated propagator (a closed case). It sounds obvious, but you'd be surprised how often people don't bother with heating a propagator, and it can make all the difference to your success rate.

You won't often need to use a whole packet of seed, but sow in a tray if you do need lots of plants. Sowing too thickly will encourage fatal fungal infection. Check your "nursery" daily. If the medium starts to dry out, water again by the dunking method (see step 3). When the first seedlings germinate, remove the plastic cover, or open the vent in the propagator lid, to give them fresh air. If any seedlings keel over, or grow fluffy gray mold, remove them with tweezers to avoid contaminating healthy seedlings.

1 Loosely fill a pot or tray with sowing medium. Spread it evenly and use the base of another clean pot/tray to firm the medium down gently – don't steamroll it. Write the plant name and sowing date onto the label so that it can be pushed into the pot after sowing.

2 Tip the seeds onto the palm of one hand. Hold it 4in (10cm) above the medium and tap it with the other hand, so the seeds are dislodged onto the medium. Move your hand from side to side to get a thin, even distribution over the surface of the medium.

3 Cover the seed thinly with sieved medium. If it's very fine seed, leave it uncovered, and stretch plastic wrap over the top of the pot. Stand the pots in tepid water until moisture has soaked up to the surface of the medium. Let all excess water drain away, then place the pots inside a large, loose plastic bag or in a heated propagator. A germination temperature of 65–70°F (18–21°C) suits most seeds.

Pricking out

Once most of the seedlings have opened out the first true leaf (and before they become tall and spindly), they are ready for spacing out – or "pricking out," as gardeners call it. True leaves look like miniature versions of adult ones, as opposed to the small, rounded cotyledonssss ("seed leaves") that are the first to emerge on germination (see pages 59 and 60–63). To avoid passing on fungal infections, never reuse sowing medium from the original pot of seedlings – put it on the garden and use fresh sowing medium here. Pricking out is easiest if the medium is slightly on the dry side; don't water the seedlings just beforehand unless the medium is dry.

Keep seedlings carefully watered while they are growing into young plants, but don't overdo it. They need to be evenly moist, not waterlogged. From now on, the seedlings will need bright light; shade only from hot, direct sun, which can scorch or shrivel the leaves. The sowing medium contains all the nutrients they need for the first six weeks, but, after that, begin fertilizing them once a week with general-purpose liquid fertilizer, diluted to the correct strength. By the time the pots or trays are full of roots, the young plants will be ready for planting out or potting up into larger pots.

4 Fill a clean seed tray with fresh sowing medium, then bang the tray gently on the work surface to level it off. Firm it gently. Use a dibber to gently loosen clumps of seedlings and separate their roots from excess medium. Don't handle seedlings by their stems or true leaves; the slightest bruise can become infected by gray mold, which usually proves fatal.

5 Lift each seedling by a seed leaf and lower it into a finger-sized hole in the new medium. If necessary, coil the roots around the bottom of the hole, so that the seed leaves rest just above the surface of the medium. Don't leave long stems sticking out, or you'll end up with weak, leggy seedlings. Nudge medium around the seedling to fill the hole and cover the roots.

6 Space the seedlings about 1½in (3.5cm) apart. You will get between 28 (seven rows of four) and 48 (eight rows of six) seedlings in a standard-sized seed tray. Water them in, either by standing the tray in water or by using a fine nozzle on a watering can. If you want only a few plants, you can either use a half-sized seed tray (a half-tray), or individual 3½-in (9-cm) pots.

How to... **sow seed outdoors**

What you need

- *digging fork*
- *general balanced fertilizer*
- *rake*
- *soft sand*
- *garden line or a length of bamboo stake*
- *packets of seed*
- *plant labels and soft pencil*
- *twiggy pea-sticks*
- *watering can with a fine nozzle*
- *hand trowel or fork*

This is the best method to use for hardy annuals and vegetables. You can also use it for seeds of perennial and biennial flowers in early summer. Don't bother trying this method with half-hardy plants, since you can't sow them outside until after frost: there won't be any flowers until late summer, when the season is nearly over.

You don't need any special equipment, but, because you can't control the growing conditions, it's essential to pick your moment. Even hardy annuals won't germinate if conditions are very cold in spring, and, if the soil is also too wet, many seeds, such as peas and beans, will rot before they have chance to germinate. It is always best to wait until the weather improves. If you are impatient, place a row of cloches (mini-greenhouses) or plastic sheeting over the soil for a couple of weeks to dry and warm it slightly first.

The other big thing to watch out for is weeds. If your ground is full of weed seeds, sow seeds in rows: yes, even annual flowers. It makes weeding much easier, because you can see clearly which are weed seedlings and which are sown ones. If necessary, you can always move them to their flowering positions later.

1 To produce a colorful border like the one shown on page 67, you first need to make a fine seedbed by forking over the soil to loosen it. Remove any weeds, then sprinkle general fertilizer evenly over the surface and rake it lightly in, leaving a fine, cake-crumblike tilth. Hardy annuals are usually sown in "drifts" – mark these out with a trickle of sand. A different variety is then sown in each area.

2 When sowing in drifts, a garden stake can be pressed into the soil at 3–4-in (7.5–10-cm) intervals to make shallow furrows or drills. On the vegetable plot, mark out a row with garden line and make a furrow with the corner of a rake, about ½in (1cm) deep, alongside it. Scatter small seeds thinly along the row, or "space sow" larger seeds, setting them out individually one to four finger widths apart.

3 Cover to roughly their own depth. Remove the garden line, if sowing vegetables, and push a plant label in at the end of the row or drift, marked with the plant name and sowing date. Cover with twiggy pea-sticks to protect from digging cats. Water well with a can fitted with a fine nozzle or a sprinkler bar. If no rain is forthcoming, water again (carefully) before the soil dries out.

4 Start thinning out the seedlings as soon as they are large enough to handle. It's a good idea to do this in several stages as the seedlings get bigger.

5 Aim to leave the strongest ones growing about 1–2in (2.5–5cm) apart. Thin again as the plants grow larger, so that the remainder are about 7–10cm (3–4in) apart. If the plants are to be left in the same row they were sown in throughout their lives, they'll need a further thinning to leave them at their final spacing.

6 To transplant plants to a different position, prepare their new bed beforehand by forking over the soil and removing all weeds. Dig up each plant carefully with a good ball of roots and soil. Set them out at the correct distance apart and dig a planting hole for each. Pop them in at the same depth at which they were originally growing. Firm gently and water thoroughly.

A sight that most of us remember from school, when we would germinate bean seeds inside a jar against a sheet of damp blotting paper. The root pushes down first, and then the shoot emerges into the light.

The developing plant

It's not often you get the chance to watch a seed germinating, but think back to the "bean in a jar" experiment at school. Remember the seeds sandwiched between damp blotting paper and the side of the glass jar? You could almost see the seed growing daily. The seed would swell, then the first root (the radicle) would push downward. The first shoot (plumule) would uncurl from between the fat seed leaves (cotyledons) and push up to the light, while the fine root hairs started reaching out in all directions, exploring for moisture and food.

When a seed germinates, the resulting young plant is very basic, with just one or two leaves and a short stalk. Monocotyledons (plants with one seed leaf, such as palms and grasses) live up to their name. They produce one spearlike seed leaf, followed closely by further leaves, one at a time, which look very similar to the original seed leaf. Dicotyledons have a pair of seed leaves. As the two seed leaves open out at the tip of the emerging stem, one on each side, you can often recognize them as being the two halves of the seed that has burst out of its surrounding coat. They look nothing like the plant's true leaves, which appear later from between the seed leaves. When seedlings have one or two true leaves, that's the best time to prick them out, as they are just about big enough to handle at this stage, but the root system is small enough to move without damage. The nutrients from the seed leaves are absorbed as the seedling develops, and these eventually dry out and drop off – which is why you use them as handles when picking up seedlings (instead of the more vulnerable stems). It won't matter if you bruise a seed leaf slightly, because it's dispensable, but a damaged stem is unlikely to recover.

Once they have been given more room, seedlings really put on a growth spurt and quickly turn into young plants. By the time they have been potted up or planted out in the garden, they are really in high gear and have begun to develop mature characteristics – a bit like us giving up rented apartments and clubbing after a while, in favor of settling into paying the mortgage and putting down some more permanent roots. Some plants go on to produce entirely different leaves at maturity; for example, many eucalyptus have sickle-shaped adult leaves, while the juvenile ones are disk-shaped.

While they are settling into grown-up life, it's important for maturing plants to gather as many resources as possible – water, food, light, and space – ready to produce a family. Although most plants are content to jostle for space in a border, there is one type of plant that always seems to want more than its fair share, and that's the climber.

Clingers and climbers

Climbing plants produce fast-growing stems fitted with all sorts of nifty devices for getting a leg up on whatever comes in its path – other plants, fences, or a trellis – and some can even attach themselves to the sheer face of a wall. Their aim is to leapfrog over the heads of competitors and hog the light, and some of them aren't worried about the trouble they cause on the way. If you are planting climbers, it's a good idea to know their little ways: it helps to understand the climbing techniques that they use to further their own ends.

Thorns on plants, such as climbing roses, are curved backward like hooked claws. As stems grow longer, thorns act like grappling irons, grabbing hold of branches to help the rose scramble over other plants. The more strongly curved the thorns, the harder it is to pull the stems down, because you are pulling in the opposite direction to hundreds of hooks. If you want to pull out a stem you've just cut off a climbing rose, do so from the tip and it'll slide out quite easily. But unless you grow them through a tree, you need to treat climbing roses like wall shrubs and tie their main stems in to some form of support to keep them in place. Thorns are hopeless at clinging to flat surfaces like walls.

Tendrils are stems or leaves that have been modified for climbing. Plants like sweet peas and grape vines use tendrils for "straphanging" from branches, netting, twiggy pea-sticks, or a trellis. Clematis don't have tendrils, but the leaf stalks twine around branches or a trellis in much the same way, so they, too, hold on without harming anything. Tendril plants are among the most docile climbers for garden use, but, though you need to give them something to climb up, there's no need to tie them in once they get going.

Roses (*left*) climb and scramble through other plants using their thorns as grappling hooks, while plants like this grape (*right*), use tendrils to clamber upward.

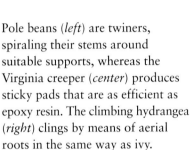

Pole beans (*left*) are twiners, spiraling their stems around suitable supports, whereas the Virginia creeper (*center*) produces sticky pads that are as efficient as epoxy resin. The climbing hydrangea (*right*) clings by means of aerial roots in the same way as ivy.

Twining stems are used by a lot of plants, including honeysuckle, wisteria, and pole beans, which climb by sending their stems out in a spiral motion. Instead of growing straight, they wind themselves around anything they touch, which might be another plant, a stake, twiggy stems, or a trellis. Some twiners follow the direction of the sun and twine clockwise, while others do the opposite. If you are winding bean plants around stakes to help them get started, observe which way they want to go, because if you try to go against their natural inclinations they'll just unwind themselves and flop on the ground. Big twiners, such as wisteria, need watching. Don't let them wrap themselves around gutters or downspouts, because the thin shoots fatten with age and will eventually wrench the pipework off the wall.

Sticky pads on Virginia creeper (*Parthenocissus quinquefolia*) and its cousins enable them to hang on to bare walls. The sticky pads are rather like the rubber suckers on the tips of toy arrows, but they hold on tighter and for longer, so they can damage less-than-perfect masonry. They are fine for a sound surface, such as a concrete block wall, or if you want to cover a hideous old outbuilding in a hurry, and they are magnificent let loose over a pergola, a steep bank, or up a big tree.

Aerial roots are used by ivies and climbing hydrangea to cling to bare walls or tree trunks. First, short, bristly roots grow out from the stems when they touch something solid, then aerial roots reach out to penetrate cracks, thickening out to wedge themselves into place. If the surface is an old brick wall, they can enlarge cracks and make the surface crumble. Again, sound surfaces, or structures that don't matter, are the best places for this type of climber.

Flowers and pollination

It's only when plants reach maturity that they will flower, which explains why it sometimes takes plants such as passionflower several years to bloom if you grow them from seed. From the plant's point of view, flowers aren't just there for decoration; they are a vital step towards their final goal – producing seed to ensure the species' survival.

Pollination is how plants reproduce, transferring pollen from the male anther onto the female stigma (see diagram page 21) in order to produce seeds. Not all plants bother with fancy flowers. Grasses, bamboos, and some trees, such as willows (*Salix*), have just greenish tufts or catkins – a sure sign of a plant whose flowers are pollinated by the wind. Plants that use the wind to pollinate usually give out vast clouds of pollen to make sure there's a sporting chance of at least some of it reaching a mate. It's a numbers game.

Plants that have elaborate and colorful flowers do so in order to attract the right sort of creature to pollinate them. This means that the flowers don't need to produce so much pollen, but they'll often have scent to attract helpers, with a supply of nectar as a reward. Most flowers are pollinated by insects, such as bees or hoverflies. Those that open only at dusk may be pollinated by night-flying moths. At home, if you want your melon plant to produce melons (known as "setting" in the trade), and there are not many bees about, you simply cheat and take a small artist's paintbrush to do the job by hand – dusting the pollen from male anther to female stigma.

Bright flowers are produced for a reason – to attract pollinating insects. This leads to seed production and ensures the plant's survival for another generation.

In some parts of the world, flowers may be pollinated by bats or hummingbirds, and some have evolved into special shapes so that they can only be pollinated by one particular species. Flowers that are pollinated by hummingbirds, for instance, have elongated throats the same length as the bird's beak. As the bird drinks the nectar, pollen sticks to the top of its head and is transferred to the next flower it visits: a neat trick for accomplishing pollination.

In the interests of beautiful gardens, we've done plenty of cheating on nature. In the wild state, most plants have single flowers, which come complete with a full set of sexual organs. By selecting accidental mutations or freaks, or by deliberate plant breeding, we've managed to increase the number of petals for our own enjoyment. But, in most cases, it is the reproductive parts of the flower that have been converted into extra petals, so double flowers rarely produce any seed. The extra petals can take the place of scent-producing organs, which is why some sumptuously double flowers are lacking in fragrance. And, since they don't yield seed, you need to divide them (see pages 195–96) or take cuttings to get more plants from such sterile varieties. Crude genetic engineering has been going on for centuries, but, in such instances as these, the engineering is allowed by nature.

Why cross-pollinate?

Unlike cuttings, which are clones with exactly the same genetic makeup as their one parent, seed-raised plants have two parents, each contributing half their genes. All of the offspring have a slightly different genetic mix. Although still recognizably the same type of plant as the parents, they have tiny differences – maybe bigger leaves, different-colored flowers, or more drought resistance – which may give them the edge in the survival game.

In the wild, cross-pollination gives a species the ability to adapt to changing conditions. It's such a good, long-term survival strategy that some plants have built-in mechanisms to prevent self-pollination. Most hollies have male and female flowers on separate trees, so the females must be pollinated by another, male, plant. Slipper orchids (*Cypripedium*) have a complex one-way system for bees to negotiate through, which ensures that their own flower's pollen never reaches their own female parts.

In cultivation, plant breeders make use of cross-pollination to produce desirable new varieties, known as hybrids, like this *Rosa* 'Graham Thomas'. By crossing two parent plants with the required characteristics, they can create a super strain with bigger leaves, more flowers, or tastier fruit. This is all accomplished with no artificial genetic engineering, which involves introducing genes from unrelated plants, or even things like jellyfish, that could never have gotten it together naturally.

For this apple tree, the reproductive cycle and natural progression of plant growth(in a single season) is:

1 The bursting of shoots.

2 The production of flowers, which will be pollinated.

3 Developing fruitlets, which turn into...

4 ... the full-sized fruit, bearing seeds inside.

Fruit and seed

Once pollination – the transference of pollen from the male anther to the female stigma – has resulted in the flower being fertilized, the petals drop and the ovary at the base of the flower begins to swell and turn into a pod, berry, or fruit full of seeds. At this stage, a short-lived plant, feeling its job is nearly over, starts to shut up shop. The first thing it does is stop producing any more flowers, concentrating its energies instead on swelling and ripening the seeds.

Unfortunately, that doesn't always suit us, since we don't want our border plants to give up after the first flush of flowers and produce a load of ratty old seedheads. So we deadhead them, picking off the dying flowers. The plant's immmediate response is to form some new flower buds in its effort to set seed. The same thing happens with peppers – pick them green, and the plant promptly grows some more. But if you allow them to ripen and turn red, the plant thinks it has done its job and stops producing new flowers, so you don't get such a big crop. It's the same story with sweet peas and zucchini. These also need harvesting regularly to prevent them from feeling their work is finished.

Choosing and planting

Some plants are just not practical to raise yourself. Maybe they need nursery facilities, complicated production techniques, or take a long time to reach planting size, so there's a lot to be said for buying already-grown plants. Visiting nurseries or garden centers also introduces you to new plants you might not meet otherwise, and it's the obvious answer if you want instant results.

When and where to buy

Years ago, you could buy trees and shrubs that had been dug up from a nursery field only in autumn, once they had lost their leaves. You ordered them during summer, they were delivered after leaf fall in autumn or before bud-burst in spring, and you planted them right away, if only temporarily (known as "heeling them in").

Garden centers changed all that by selling their plants in pots. Because there's less root disturbance, you can plant them at any time of year the ground is not frozen, even when in full flower – provided that the soil is in reasonable condition, and that you plant them properly and keep them watered until established. Opening up all or most ot the year for plant sales paved the way for garden centers to grow into one-stop garden stores. Now, as well as providing essential garden tools and products, they also sell anything you can think of for the garden – and much else besides.

Nowadays, nurseries tend to specialize in particular types of plants – perhaps unusual shrubs, old-fashioned cottage-garden plants, trendy perennials, cacti, or conservatory climbers – especially the less common ones that you won't find so readily in garden centers. Because such nurseries are often out in the sticks, you may need to be prepared to travel some distance, but the best place to find them and their plants is at flower shows and plant fairs.

Busy people increasingly buy plants by mail order, or from Internet gardening sites, but here it pays to know your supplier, because you can't see what you are getting until it arrives. You are relying on somebody else to pick out good plants, pack them carefully, and see that they are sent out by a speedy delivery system. If a specialty nursery runs a mail-order business, you can usually be sure that the plants will be healthy and carefully packed. Such businesses are, by their very nature, run by enthusiasts and can usually be relied on when it comes to quality of plant and speed of dispatch. Mail order is an especially popular way of buying young plants and plugs, which, being small, are easy to pack and relatively cheap to send to the buyer.

Check plants over carefully before adding them to your cart.

Choosing healthy plants

You can usually tell a good nursery or garden center because it's busy. If the plants were of poor quality, people wouldn't keep going back. One of the reasons plants tend to be good at busy outlets is precisely because the turnover of stock is rapid, which allows you to buy plants in nursery-fresh condition. Few garden centers grow their own stock these days, but many nurseries do and are always worth patronizing. Word of mouth is the best recommendation for nurseries that are a bit off the beaten track. They are worth the traveling time, because many supply a specialized selection of plants that are unobtainable elsewhere. But wherever you shop for plants, get into the habit of checking them over before adding them to your cart, to make sure you are buying the best.

What to look for when buying plants

Flowers	Leaves	Stems and branches	Soil mix	Roots
Should match the picture or description on the label.	Should be healthy, unblemished, and free of signs of pests or diseases.	Should be sturdy and evenly spread around a central stem.	Should have a surface free of moss and liverworts – signs of overwatering and nutrient shortage.	Should be plentiful. By the time they are offered for sale, most plants have filled their pots with roots.
If not, the plant may be wrongly labeled – it happens in even the best-run nurseries (often because customers stuff labels back into the wrong pots!).	Leaves (unless they are meant to be golden or variegated) should be a rich shade of green, not pale and pasty. Why trouble yourself with extra fertilizing and pest control when you can choose a perfect specimen?	Standard plants and trees should have strong, straight stems, with well-branched heads at the top.

Avoid lopsided or broken plants, and trees whose leader (main central shoot) is missing or broken. | Some weeds spread, so weed them out, but don't reject an otherwise healthy plant just because of a few weeds.

Avoid plants where soil mix has shrunk from the pot sides due to drying out. | Roots through the pot's bottom are not a problem; standing pots on a damp sand bed for a long time encourages the roots to wander. If the plant is healthy, buy it and cut the pot off carefully. |

How to... plant

What you need

- *bucketful of water, if needed*
- *digging spade and fork*
- *well-rotted organic matter*
- *general balanced fertilizer*
- *mulching material (bark chips or well-rotted manure)*

There's an old gardening saying that goes "dig a five-dollar hole for a fifty-cent plant". Some people will happily spend a small fortune on a tree then just dig a hole and shove it in without any preparation at all – and very indignant they are when it dies. A barrowload of organic matter (compost), from a couple of handfuls for a small plant to about two bucketfuls for a large tree, and sufficient water would have made all the difference.

The same basic planting technique works for almost anything, from a semi-mature tree to a tiny alpine, though there are a few small variations on the theme that are worth knowing for particular plants (see pages 77–79). And, after planting, keep new plants well watered if the weather is dry, so that the roots are encouraged to grow out into the surrounding soil.

1 If the plant's soil mix is bone dry, stand the pot in a bucket of water until it's thoroughly moist. On well-prepared soil, dig a hole twice the diameter of the pot, then fork a bucketful of organic matter into the bottom of the hole. If planting in spring, when you want to encourage growth, fork in a sprinkling of general fertilizer, too. If you are planting a tree in grass, or on ground that hasn't been cultivated for a long time, make the hole about four or five times the diameter of the pot and add correspondingly more organic matter.

2 Remove the plant from its pot. If it is potbound, tease a few of the biggest roots out from the bottom and sides of the rootball. Some gardeners bash the rootball to break up the cylindrical shape. This is advisable with conifers and other tough-rooted trees and shrubs that are excessively pot-bound, but with fleshy-rooted plants, such as magnolias, it can set them back years. In this case, leave them alone. Stand the rootball in place in the hole. If the plant has a best side, make sure it faces the direction from which you'll normally view it.

3 Check that the top of the rootball is level with the surrounding soil and that the plant is standing upright. Mix more organic matter with the excavated soil, then shovel the mixture back around the rootball, firming it gently with your foot. When you have filled the hole, neaten up and level the area, then water thoroughly. Spread an 3-in (8-cm) layer of mulching material, such as manure or bark chips, over the cultivated area, and that's it – the job's done.

Variations on the planting theme

While most plants respond well to the basic planting technique (see page 76), there are a few variations on the theme that are used to guarantee success with more specialized plant groups.

Alpines

Most rock plants need very good drainage, and rosette-formers, such as hen and chicks (*Sempervivum*), need especially good drainage around their "necks" (where the stem meets the roots)' otherwise, they rot off at soil level. When planting alpines, set the top of the rootball ½in (1cm) above the soil surface, and then spread a layer of gravel, granite chips, or slivers of slate around the plant neck and all over the soil surface as a top dressing. Besides setting the plants off well, it prevents mud splash, improves surface drainage, and lets air circulate beneath the rosettes.

Bulbs

Bulbs generally need planting a lot deeper than you'd think. The rule of thumb is at least three times their own depth, so for a daffodil bulb that is, say, 2½in (6cm) long from top to toe, you'd be looking at making a hole 7in (18cm) deep. Yes, really. Deep planting places bulbs safely below cultivation depth, so you won't accidentally chop them up with a hoe or spear them with a fork when you're weeding. It also ensures they have good supplies of moisture. It's not disastrous if you get the depth wrong, because most bulbs can winch themselves down into the ground using special, contractile roots – it takes time, but they get there eventually. If you're planting bulbs on rather heavy soil, put a shovelful of coarse sand in the bottom of the hole first to ensure good drainage.

Alpines must have good drainage, which is why they grow well in shallow sinks – with the plug left out!

Plant daffodils and snowdrops (*below left*) deeper than you might think. When planting spring-flowering bulbs, your rule of thumb is to plant them at least three times the depth of the bulb (*below*).
1 crocus.
2 snowdrop.
3 tulip species.
4 Dutch iris.
5 tulip.
6 hyacinth.
7 daffodil.

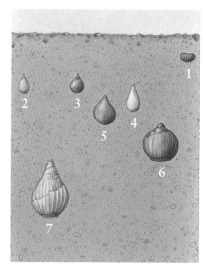

A few bulbs prefer shallow planting, so put Madonna lilies (*Lilium candidum*) in with their "noses" (the tip of the bulb) just showing above ground. In the case of crown imperials (*Fritillaria imperialis*), which have hollow-centered bulbs, lay them on their sides so that water can't gather in the hollow and promote rot.

If mice or squirrels are in the habit of stealing your bulbs, plant them with a layer of small-mesh wire netting or lots of holly leaves over the top to put them off.

Clematis

Clematis are the major exception to the normal rule about planting depth; they need deep planting. The top of the rootball should be buried 4–6in (10–15cm) below the surface of the soil. The usual reason given for deep planting is so that clematis can recover if they are attacked by clematis wilt. This disease affects new plants in particular, first making the plant droop as if it were short of water before it dies down to ground level. Deep planting means there is sufficient stem from which new growth buds can develop, so you don't lose the plant, and it's not long before new shoots appear. Deep planting also helps keep clematis roots cool and moist (they love this), and if you do happen to go a bit wild with the hoe or nylon-line trimmer, a butchered plant can still regrow.

Plant clematis deeper than normal to ensure recovery after an attack by clematis wilt and to keep the roots cool.

Evergreens

Planting evergreens is pretty standard (see page 76); it's the after-care that you might need to vary a bit. Evergreens are very big on turning brown if they dry out after planting, so it's especially important to keep the soil moist. Severe scorching can kill a young plant completely, and conifers may end up with permanently brown patches, since the browned-off bits never regrow.

It's not only dry soil at the roots that causes scorching – strong winds and hot sun can do it, too. Scorching happens when the leaves lose water faster than the roots can take it up, and, on new plants, the full complement of roots has not yet developed. If you live in an exposed area, protect newly planted evergreens and conifers by hammering in a circle of poles and tacking windbreak fabric around them. It's not an object of great beauty, it's true, but it'll be for only a few months. Oh, yes, wandering neighborhood dogs cocking their legs can have a similar damaging effect.

Grafted plants

Quite a few garden plants – such as fruit trees, some ornamental trees, roses, and the more expensive shrubs, such as Japanese maples – are grafted, or joined together. Grafting is done because it's the most convenient way to raise named varieties that can't be grown from seed or that are very slow or difficult to root from cuttings. What you are buying is actually two plants in one: the roots of a reliable grower (the rootstock) and the named variety on top, which is known as the scion. The point where the two have been joined by grafting is called the graft union. It can usually be identified by a pronounced bulge in the stem.

With ornamental trees and fruit trees, where the eventual size of the tree is controlled by the vigor of the rootstock, you don't want the scion to take root, so it's essential to plant with the graft union about 4in (10cm) above ground. When you buy grafted shrubs growing in pots, they will already be planted at the right depth, so just plant with the top of the rootball flush with the ground. The same is obviously true with a few trees, such as some weeping, ornamental cherries, that are top-grafted at the head of a long, straight stem.

Roses are different. They are generally budded on to rootstocks for reasons of cheapness and efficiency of production; one to several buds of one variety are used to make each bush, and the vigor of the rootstock is not the main reason for grafting. With roses, you might as well encourage the scion to root for additional stability, so plant bushes with the union about 1in (2.5cm) underground, even if they were riding higher in their pots.

When planting most grafted plants, make sure the graft union is kept above the soil line.

Trees

It's a good idea to stake any new tree in excess of 6ft (2m) tall through its early life, while it's getting properly rooted in. The tree experts have changed their views lately about a lot of things we once regarded as holy writ. Now there's no need to use tall stakes and tie the trunk in two places, unless you are planting a variety with a notoriously feeble root system or a very well-developed crown. All you need is a 3–4-ft (100–120-cm) stake that is hammered in at an angle of 45 degrees a short distance from the rootball. The top end of the stake should point in the direction of the prevailing wind. Use a proper tree tie to attach the trunk to the stake about 12in (30cm) from the ground – the buckle of the tie should rest against the stake, not the tree.

By holding the base of the tree firmly in this way, the roots can't rock loose in the wind, while the top is free to sway. This movement encourages the trunk to strengthen, so that when you remove the stake, the tree can stand up on its own. You can usually take the stake out after two years. In the "bad old days" it was quite common to find that apparently established trees fell over the minute their "crutch" rotted.

In a garden afflicted with rabbits, slip a spiral tree guard around the trunk after planting to prevent the bark from being chewed off. It's normally in winter, when food is short, that this happens, and, if the bark is ringed right around, the tree will die.

Tall trees need staking. To do this, use a single short stake at an angle of 45 degrees, and fasten the trunk to the stake with a commercial tie.

Moving

If you are thinking of moving plants with you to a new garden, think again: unless you have formally agreed with the new owners exactly what you are taking, you can land yourself in legal hot water. Garden plants are often considered part of the fixtures, just like the bathtub and kitchen units. Although you can take plants growing in patio pots and tubs, don't roll up the lawn or walk off with the newly planted hedge. If you know you are going to be moving, gather seeds and take cuttings well beforehand – or else just regard the new garden as a blank canvas, where you can start again with a completely new collection of plants.

Moving existing plants

Sometimes it's necessary to move established plants – maybe because you've redesigned part of the garden, or something has outgrown it's space, or you just think it will look better elsewhere.

Moving perennials

Border perennials present no problem, since they are regularly dug up and divided anyway. Spring is the best time for dividing or moving most perennials, but there are a few exceptions: bearded irises should be split and shifted about six weeks after flowering; move primroses immediately after flowering. Autumn suits tougher plants, like New England aster (*Aster novi-belgii*), and, on light soils, many robust perennials are happily moved at this time.

A few perennials, such as hellebores, never really move well. Look out for self-sown seedlings around the original, then transplant them in spring. Peonies move perfectly well if you do the job in spring instead of autumn, contrary to popular belief. The secret is to dig up a good rootball and not to bury it too deeply – the tuberous roots should rest just beneath the surface of the soil.

You can move spring bulbs at any time during summer, when they are dormant. You can also dig them up as soon as they finish flowering and move them "in the green." This is certainly the best time to move snowdrops and winter aconites (*Eranthis hyemalis*), which don't transplant at all well if the bulbs are allowed to dry out.

Moving existing shrubs

Most shrubs will move with no trouble at all, provided that they have not been growing in place for more than a few years. Shallow-rooted kinds, such as rhododendrons, which form tight, fibrous rootballs, move very easily. Evergreens move best in early autumn or early spring. Spray evergreens with an antitranspirant just before moving them, and again two weeks later, to reduce water loss. Move deciduous shrubs when they are not in leaf, which means any time between autumn and early spring when the soil is not frozen.

Whichever the shrub you are transplanting, take it up with as large a ball of roots as possible. Shift it straight to a new, well-prepared planting hole, with lots of organic matter forked into the bottom, and get the roots tucked in quickly. Make sure that the shrub is replanted at the same depth as it was growing before, and ensure that a big plant faces the same direction as previously. Water it in well, and keep it watered during dry spells.

Before moving a large plant, plan ahead. It's advisable to dig right around it, during the spring before you want to move it. By doing this you'll sever some of the big thick roots, and this encourages the plant to make lots of new fibrous roots, which form a dense rootball that transplants better. By the time you move it, six months or a year later, the plant will have girded its loins for the disturbance.

It just isn't worth the risk of moving some shrubs, unless you absolutely have to, because they rarely recover – magnolias, for instance. And, frankly, it's not worth moving established roses. Damaging their roots usually means they produce a forest of suckers from the rootstock, and damaged roots are often more susceptible to soil-borne diseases. Roses are usually past their best after 10 years anyway, so it's better to buy new plants.

Moving existing trees

Trees will move happily if they have been planted for only a year or two, provided that they are shifted in the dormant season. Otherwise, many will have developed a deep or extensive system that simply doesn't transplant well. The only exception is if you are buying semi-mature trees from a nursery. Such big trees will have undergone a special process of preparation before they are offered for sale. They are grown in what I can only describe as underground cages – giant mesh containers filled with good, fertile soil. The root system is regularly undercut as they grow, so they never get the chance to develop taproots, and the container becomes filled with fibrous roots that transplant perfectly.

They are harder to establish than a younger, smaller tree, and, since they are expensive, you'll need to look after them well. Have the planting hole ready with lots of organic matter worked in, so the tree can be swung straight into it from the crane. To make sure that the tree establishes well, keep it very well watered in dry spells for the first two years. Guy ropes or short, thick staking will be necessary for stability. Expensive? Yes, but at least you can have a tree in your garden instantly that looks as if it's been there for years.

Planting time

You can plant container-grown trees and shrubs at any time of year except when the ground is really difficult to cultivate (i.e. if it's waterlogged, frozen solid, or set really hard), but the best time is at the beginning or end of the growing season.

Autumn is the best planting season if you garden on lightish soil, since the soil stays warm, and rains help new roots to get established without you having to do any watering. Spring is better if you garden on cold, wet clay soil, as plants still have time to get going before the weather turns hot and dry, and there's no risk of new roots rotting because of poor conditions over the winter.

Summer is fine, too, but if the weather's dry, you will need to keep the new plants watered through the dry weather – all season, if necessary.

Foolproof planting checklist

Location	Preparation and planting	Aftercare
Check soil type (see pages 90–91)	Dig soil and improve it (see pages 49–55)	Water
Check site: is it sunny, shady, boggy, dry?(see pages 86–88)	Water plant while in pot	Stake if necessary (see page 79)
Check situation: is it affected by geographical location and exposure? (see page 89)	Prepare hole (see pages 76–79)	Mulch
	Plant and water in	Check for signs of pests and disease (see pages 32–33 and 221)

3 PLANNING AND MAKING BORDERS

Making a start

The golden rules with gardening are (first) don't take on too much at once and (second) never expect your garden to be completed. A garden evolves – it doesn't stand still, and it's always changing. You're not going to rush into the house one day and say "That's it, Mildred, it's finished."

I still haven't "finished" my garden at Barleywood, and I've been here 20 years. But planning and planting up an individual bed or border is a different matter entirely. If it's properly sorted out in advance, you can usually reckon to complete a new border (or make over an old one) in a single weekend, instead of the job trailing on for weeks, with you feeling that you're getting nowhere fast.

The list of preparatory tasks seems daunting – far more than a weekend's work. But work out the basics first and enjoy doing so, and the job itself will be more straightforward.

You'll be surprised at what you can achieve in a short time if you get your act together. This hardy annual border, planned (*right*) and sown in spring (*above*), is in full bloom by midsummer (*opposite*).

1 *Agrostemma githago* 'Milas'.
2 *Amaranthus caudatus*.
3 *Nigella damascena* 'Miss Jekyll'.
4 *Nicotiana* (white).
5 *Tropaeolum majus* 'Alaska Mixed'.
6 *Convolvulus tricolor* 'Blue Ensign'.
7 *Cosmos* 'Seashells Mixed'.
8 *Calendula officinalis* 'Pacific Apricot'.
9 *Limnanthes douglasii*.

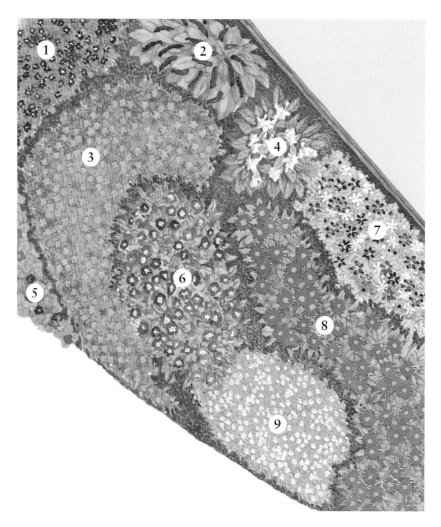

Order of working

We are about to deal with all this in detail but, in a nutshell, when you start to work in the garden, there is a basic order of working through the jobs that need doing. First assess your site to check your soil type and the site location in terms of which way it faces and how it is affected by sun and shade. This vital information helps you plan your design on paper. Bear in mind color, height, and spread of plants suitable to your site. Marking out the border shape on the ground is important to ensure it's where you want it, and weed and rubbish clearance, as well as soil preparation and improvement, must be done before you plant. Place your plants in position – and judge the overall effect – before planting the major trees and/or shrubs and evergreens to create a framework. You can then add your perennials and fill the gaps with annuals while you wait for the shrubs to grow and fill in the space. You'll then need to fork the soil over lightly and mulch it well to give your plants a really good start.

Assessing the site

Step into David Attenborough's shoes for a moment, and look at your garden as a series of mini-habitats. Each area provides different growing conditions that make one place more suitable than another for particular plants.

Before planting anything, check out the amount of light, shelter, and soil type so that you know the facilities that are present at the spot where you want to make your bed. Once you know which cards you are holding, it's a heck of a lot easier to start dealing with plants. If you've set your heart on growing shade lovers in a hot, sunny garden, or drought lovers on wet clay soil, there's a certain amount you can do to make the growing conditions more suitable. These are things to tackle before you start planting, but, to avoid future disappointment, it's important to accept that there is a limit.

From early morning to late evening, the sun moves across the garden (*below*). Take time to sit in your garden on a sunny day and see just which areas get the most sunlight, and which stay in the shade.

Light

Lie in a hammock on a sunny summer's day and watch what happens as the shadows move around the garden. Resist rude remarks from the family. They may suggest you are just lazing around, when you are actually engaged in valuable research. What

you are looking for are areas that are in shade all the time, those that are shaded for about half the day, and those that remain in full sun throughout the day. Are the shady areas in deep shade – can you see to read a book easily? If not, then it's too dark to grow even shade-loving plants, unless you do something to improve matters.

Light shade beneath a canopy of trees produces an attractive dappled effect, where it is very pleasant to sit and enjoy a cold drink. Both shade-loving plants and choice woodland species will enjoy it too, as long as there is some shelter from cold or strong winds. Once you know your garden well, taking account of light and dark corners becomes second nature, but, in a new garden, mark them on a sketch plan of the garden to help you work out what to plant where.

While you're enjoying the sun, don't forget that, in winter, the picture will have changed quite a bit. Deciduous trees will have shed their leaves, so some areas will be a lot brighter. The winter sun is lower in the sky and shadows are longer, so some previously sunny places may now be in shade for some of the time. You probably won't want to wait and see through the whole gardening year before going ahead with your plans, but at least be aware of the way the light levels change as the year rolls around. But what if your light levels don't tally with what you want to grow?

Creating shade

It's very easy to introduce shade into a sunny garden. You can plant trees with a light canopy: birches (*Betula*) and crabapples (*Malus*) cast enough shade to cool things down without blotting out the sun entirely. For additional summer shade, you can plant a screen of tall grasses, such as *Miscanthus*, which you could then cut down in winter, when they turn brown, to let in more light. And arches, pillars and pergolas will introduce a nice bit of dappling.

Let there be light!

If the garden is too shady, you can often increase the amount of light it receives. Every little bit helps! So, prune overgrown shrubs and remove trees and shrubs that don't contribute much to the garden. Ask an arborist to thin out the overly dense canopies of big trees or to remove the bottom branches to "lift" the crowns. You can also paint walls in pale, pastel colors, or use mirrors or water to reflect all available light and add some sparkle to shady areas.

Shade lovers will enjoy areas beneath shade-casting shrubs, while sun lovers will prefer full light at some distance from the shrub's canopy.

Exposure

The direction a garden faces has the most significant bearing on the amount of light it receives. It figures that a garden with a south-facing exposure is going to be sunny, while one that faces north gets little, if any, direct sun – although it won't necessarily be gloomy. As long as it has a wide-open horizon around it, a north-facing garden may enjoy quite reasonable light levels, and the lack of direct sun can make it ideal for those delicate plants that are easily scorched.

A garden's exposure can lead to problems that are not easily foreseen. For example, it's not a good idea to plant early-flowering plants in an east-facing garden, because the petals can scorch if early morning sun hits them while they are still frozen by the previous night's frost. It's bad enough having all your camellias ruined, but if you grow fruit trees in an east-facing garden, this is probably why you don't get very good crops. If late frost coincides with flowering time, it "burns' the petals and scorches the pollen-bearing anthers, so it's curtains for that year's crop of fruit.

On the other hand, a west-facing garden receives late afternoon and evening sun, so as well as being safe for early spring flowers, it's a fine place for sitting after work. A west-facing niche is a really good site for your favorite fragrant plants, and you can enjoy them in warmth and comfort.

Locality

Gardening conditions are also affected by geographical location. A high-altitude garden, or one surrounded by wide-open country-side, is likely to be very windy. If it's on a cliff top, or close to the ocean, the odds are that the garden will also be exposed to the abrasive action of blown sand or the burning action of salt spray. In these situations, you need to decide whether you want a conventional garden, in which case you'll need to put lots of shelter around it first, or whether you'd prefer to keep the wonderful views and settle for a more natural effect, using plants that can rough it a bit.

If your garden is next to a busy road, you can expect to have dust blown over it on a regular basis, so you might want to settle for a design that includes lots of glossy-leaved evergreens that are easier to keep clean. You might also need to consider taking a few basic security precautions: avoid putting containers or garden ornaments where they can be seen or easily carried away. And make the most of plants that are naturally prickly to make screens or hedges around a garden that needs protection from intruders, vandals, or animals.

In a seaside garden, use plants that are resistant to wind and salt spray.

Assessing your soil type

To most people soil is just dirt, but, to a plant, it's life or death. It's not hard to identify your soil type, given a bit of basic detective work. Whether you garden on clay, sand, chalk, or on the perfect loam soil, it affects what will grow well. Loam is generally regarded as the best garden soil, and traditional soil improvement is designed to turn whatever soil you inherit into something as much like loam as possible. You don't need to take that route – if the soil is particularly extreme, it can often be easier to design a garden that uses plants that are naturally at home in such conditions. But first you need to assess what you have before you can make the best of it.

Simple soil analysis
You can discover a lot about your soil just by looking at the garden shortly after it's rained, then by rubbing a handful of soil between your fingers.

Sandy or gravelly soil (**1**) feels gritty when rubbed between your fingers and won't hold together if you try to form it into a ball. After rain, surface puddles drain away in next to no time.

Different types of soil:
1 Sandy soil is free-draining but often lacking in nutrients.
2 Clay soil is fiendishly difficult to work and slow to drain.
3 Chalky soil will not suit acid lovers such as rhododendrons.
4 Loamy soil is everybody's dream.
5 Peaty soil is rich in organic matter.

Clay soil (2) feels smooth and takes a surface polish when rubbed between your fingers. If you roll a ball of clay into a sausage shape, it will hold together without crumbling and allow you to shape it into a ring without breaking. Clay soils turn rapidly into sticky mud after rain, and long-lasting surface puddles form easily. But when clay soil is dry, it sets like concrete and may crack.

Chalky soil (3) is usually pale in color, and white chunks of chalk are often visible, especially if the chalk rock is close to the surface – chalk hills or outcrops nearby usually give the game away. Chalk soils drain very freely, so puddles don't last long after rain.

Loamy soil (4) is dark brown in color and holds moisture quite well, but excess water drains away after heavy rain, so puddles don't last more than a few hours. If you roll it into a sausage, it will hold its shape, but it will break when you bend it into a ring.

Peaty soil (5) is almost black when moist, being composed almost entirely of partially decomposed organic matter, such as moss or sedge from bogs or fens. It crumbles if rubbed between the fingers and, after rain, glistens with moisture. It absorbs water like a sponge, so surface water forms puddles only if the soil is totally saturated.

Elementary chemistry

There's also a very simple test you can do. Take half a handful of soil and stir it into a clear glass jar full of water. Allow the mess to settle, then take a look after a couple of hours.

Sandy or gravelly soil will have sunk to the bottom, forming a distinctly gritty layer with slightly dirty water above it.

Clay soil is full of very fine particles that don't settle out quickly, so the solution will still look very cloudy with only a thin layer of fine muddy material sitting on the bottom of the jar.

Chalky soil makes the water turn a pale grayish color, and there will be a layer of gritty white fragments at the bottom of the jar.

A good loam settles slowly into fairly even layers, with the biggest particles at the bottom and smaller particles on top. This is as it should be, because a good loam contains some clay, some sandy particles, and plenty of organic matter.

Naturally peaty soil contains a large amount of floating material suspended in dirty water.

Improving the soil

Well-rotted organic matter is the closest you will get to a universal panacea in soil-improvement terms, and it comes in many forms (see pages 50–51). If you have sandy, chalky, or gravelly soil, you can improve it by digging in organic matter in spring and autumn, mulching heavily where you can't dig. But this type of ground is very fast-draining and "hungry," absorbing organic matter quickly, so you'll need to add organic matter on a regular basis – as part of your annual garden routine. If your patch is also hot and sunny, I'd recommend you make a Mediterranean or seaside-style garden and save yourself the hard labor.

Clay soil turns into good, fertile earth if you add plenty of organic matter and dig in enough "roughage" to open it up. Use horticultural grit, coarse sharp sand, or fine river-washed gravel. Don't use builder's sand, which contains too much lime, or gravel dredged up from the ocean, because it is too salty for plants. Dig in at least a bucketful of grit per square yard/meter, or sprinkle it on as a mulch along with some well-rotted organic matter. Then let the worms do the work.

Good loamy soil needs occasional helpings of organic matter to keep it in good condition, especially if you crop it heavily, but it takes a heck of a lot of the hard work out of gardening if the soil is on your side to start with.

Peaty soils, though moisture-retentive and free-draining, are very short of nutrients and very acidic. Organic matter provides a range of essential trace elements and adds "body" to a thin, peaty soil. Excessive acidity can be countered by applying lime (see page 95) and you will also need to use a general-purpose fertilizer regularly, especially for vegetable crops (see pages 52–53). But many gardeners positively yearn for soils like this – it's perfect for a huge range of choice, lime-hating plants, such as rhododendrons and azaleas.

A Mediterranean-style garden is a good choice on hot, sunny sites, particularly if your soil is very free-draining.

Acidity and alkalinity

If you have chalky soil, it's almost certainly going to be alkaline, and you can usually guess you have acidic soil if your neighbors can grow wonderful rhododendrons. But the safest way to tell for sure is to do a pH test, the accurate measure of acidity and alkalinity. You can buy a soil-testing kit from any good garden center.

Doing a soil test

First take your soil sample. It's no good just grabbing the first handful of soil you find and expecting it to tell you about the soil all over the garden. You need to test a sample that is typical of the entire area, avoiding those places where you have (for example) mixed cement, which might affect the result.

Use a trowel to dig several cores of soil from different areas around the garden. Carefully remove the top 1in (2.5cm) of soil from the core, so that you are testing soil from just below the surface. Mix the samples together well, and use a small portion to do the test.

If your garden clearly has several different types of soil within it, then do a separate test for each area, again mixing several soil samples from within each area to ensure truly representative results.

Spread the sample out on a clean glass dish to dry, then follow the instructions in the soil-test kit. The box contains almost everything you need: a test tube, pH indicator fluid, and a color chart. You will also need some distilled water (from a car accessory shop or pharmacist).

After mixing the soil sample, put some in the test tube, adding the chemical and the distilled water, shake it up well, and allow it to stand. When the soil has settled at the bottom of the test tube, it leaves a layer of colored liquid above it. Compare the color of the liquid with the colors on the chart, thenread off the pH value (see below).

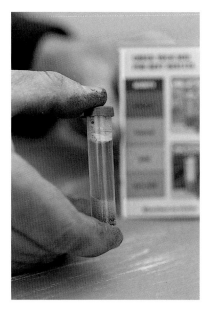

Simple soil-test kits tell you in a matter of minutes whether your soil is acidic or alkaline – something that affects the types of plant you can grow in it.

Soil acidity and alkalinity

The result of the test tells you the pH of your soil, which shows how acid or alkaline it is. If the pH is 7.0, you have neutral soil, which means most plants will grow happily and you can safely skip reading the next bit altogether because you don't need to do anything about your pH.

Most garden soils are in the pH range 6–8; that is, slightly acidic to slightly alkaline. Most plants grow in such soils without problems, except for real acid lovers, such as rhododendrons and most heathers. For all intents and purposes, the soil pH is controlled by its calcium content. If the pH reading is 7.5 or more, then the soil is alkaline. The higher the number, the more alkaline it is and the more calcium it contains – mostly in the form of lime (calcium carbonate). At pH9 or more, the soil would be seriously limy.

Stone fruits like plums and cherries do well on alkaline soils, since they need calcium to make their stones. Encrusted saxifrages will get all the calcium they need to make the silvery, limescale encrustations that are such a feature of their leaves. Plants such as clematis, pinks (*Dianthus*), and scabiosa will be very happy, although they also grow in less alkaline soils. They are natives of chalk soils (chalk being a form of calcium carbonate).

A pH reading below 7 means your soil is acidic; the lower the number, the more acidic it is and the less lime it contains. Soils of pH3 are so acidic, you'd find them only in truly boggy areas, where a limited range of very specialized plants grow, such as cotton grass (*Eriophorum*) and cranberries (*Vaccinium*). In a slightly acidic soil, you can grow plants such as camellias, rhododendrons, and heathers, and also more choice lime haters, such as *Crinodendron* and *Berberidopsis*. The terms "lime haters" and "acid lovers," by the way, mean exactly the same thing.

In alkaline (chalky) soil, encrusted saxifrages can happily produce the white powdery deposit on their leaf rosettes.

Why is soil pH important?

The big problem with soils that are very acidic or very alkaline is that certain nutrients are chemically "locked up" and so are unavailable to plants – that's when you may see deficiency symptoms showing up on the leaves or other plant parts.

On alkaline soil, iron and some trace elements are locked up. That's why, if you try to grow rhododendrons on limy soil, their leaves turn yellow – it's a symptom of iron deficiency. On the plus side, earthworms, nitrogen-fixing bacteria, and the soil bacteria that break down organic matter are more active in alkaline soils, which is good news for organic gardeners. Vegetables, especially the cabbage family, are usually happier on slightly alkaline soils, since the nutrients they need are more available in those conditions. Clubroot disease is less of a problem – it was once a tradition to lime gardens to prevent its occurrence. Potatoes, however, are more likely to be affected by scab on limy soil, so the potato patch was always left unlimed.

On acidic soil, phosphates are locked up, and some trace elements, such as aluminum, are unlocked and are toxic to plants in large quantities. Some plants, particularly ericaceous, or acid-loving types, like rhododendrons, camellias and most heathers, grow happily only on acidic soil. Most conifers and a few other plants prefer it, though they'll also grow in neutral or slightly alkaline soil.

Altering the pH

If you have extremely acidic or alkaline soil, it's expensive and difficult to make drastic changes to the pH, and "cures" are rarely permanent. You might make a special effort to alter a small patch, perhaps, but for a whole garden… forget it. Although it's relatively easy to raise the pH by adding lime, it's important not to overdo it, or you'll just scorch the plants. Don't try to make a big change in the pH all at once; it's safer to use enough lime each autumn to alter the pH one point at a time. Test again a year later and then add more if necessary.

The amount of lime you need to add depends on your soil type – clay soil needs more than sandy soil. As a rough guide, it takes about one pound per sq.yd (500g of lime per 1sq.m) of soil to raise the pH by one point. You'd need half that amount on sandy soil, but half again as much on clay. Never use lime at the same time as organic matter or fertilizers, because they react with each other and spoil the effect. The usual system is to put lime on in early autumn, dig organic matter in during late autumn, then put the fertilizer on in spring when you are ready to plant.

If you have chalky soil and you want to make it acidic enough to grow lime haters, you'll have a difficult job on your hands. You can dig in acidic forms of organic matter, such as well-rotted pine needles or leaf mold, but it will make only a tiny difference. Once upon a time, moss peat would have been used to make an acidic peat bed, but this is rightly frowned on these days, due to the need to conserve our fast-disappearing peat bogs. One alternative is to dig in sulfur chips and fertilize lime-hating plants in spring with chelated iron (sold as sequestered iron), but you need to apply both regularly, and they are too expensive to use in anything but a small area.

So, if you pine to grow rhododendrons or other lime-hating plants when you are saddled with chalky soil, the best way is to grow them in containers, using a lime-free (ericaceous) soil mix. There are several peat-free brands available.

Liming

Years ago vegetable growers used to lime their gardens the way they took baths, whether they needed to or not, in order to avoid diseases like clubroot. It's far better to be a bit scientific about it and do a soil pH test, then apply lime if the results indicate that it is needed. The sort of lime to use on the garden is sold as garden lime or hydrated lime. Lime doesn't last in the soil for very long, so undertake a soil test every year and reapply (or not) depending on what the test tells you. Although it supplies calcium, lime isn't really a fertilizer, but, by reducing the acidity of the soil, it releases nutrients that have been chemically locked up, so in a way it acts like one.

If your soil is badly drained, make a bog garden – go along with nature rather than fighting her.

Moisture levels

Some gardens are naturally wet and some are very dry for most of the year due to a combination of site and soil type. However, you can have problem pockets within an otherwise fairly normal garden, so it's worth taking a look around.

Gardens on heavy clay tend to be boggy in spring and during prolonged rain. Elsewhere, wet soil can be caused by natural springs or a high water table. The water table is the level below which the ground is saturated with water. You can easily check the height of the water table in your own garden just by digging a hole. Make it about 2ft (60cm) deep, and watch it over a couple of days. In winter in low-lying areas, the water table can be very close to the surface, which is no good at all for the roots of those plants – such as many Mediterranean natives – that must have well-drained conditions.

Wet soil can be drained, but it means burying porous pipes to take the water away. This can be a very costly undertaking and, in any case, works only if you have somewhere for the water to run to, so it's no good for flat sites. Under such circumstances, it's much better to turn the conditions to your advantage by making a bog garden. Where there's a high water table, it's usually only high around winter, so grow tough plants that won't mind wet winters and drier summers. Springs can be turned into a natural water feature, perhaps surrounded by outcrops of rock, or they can be piped away underground (at more expense). Make raised beds for treasured rock plants, herbs, and Mediterranean plants that hate having wet feet.

It's usually chalky, sandy, or gravelly soils that are prone to drought. This type of very light, fast-draining soil can be improved by adding organic matter, but it decomposes so quickly in these conditions that you need to apply it twice a year, in spring and autumn. I'd rather make the most of the superb drainage by making a gravel garden and planting it with drought-lovers. If you want to make the odd "conventional" flower bed, dig in plenty of coarse or incompletely rotted organic matter, and work in some of the water-retaining gel crystals sold for hanging baskets. Do the same where you want to grow vegetables, which are also a problem to grow if they keep drying out.

As a general rule, whenever you are faced with "problem" places, my advice is: don't try to fight the conditions, but make the most of plants that like to grow naturally in the given circumstances. It's cheaper and much less labo r-intensive, and you'll enjoy your garden much more if you don't turn it into a battleground, fighting your soil all the time.

Designing a bed

I'm not going to tell you about designing a complete garden here. Instead I'll concentrate on individual beds and borders. There are several different planting styles and types of border, and the ones you choose will help create your garden's character.

Planting styles

The style of planting you choose makes a big difference to the overall "feel" of your garden. Style is largely a matter of taste and personal preference, but each of the different planting styles has its own advantages.

Traditional herbaceous borders are the sort you see in the grounds of stately homes and at public gardens, ablaze with midsummer flowers, such as daylilies, coneflowers, delphiniums, and lupines, often set against a yew or a beech hedge. Such borders can be a lot of work, because the hedge may harbor weeds and pests, and the tall plants that form the back row often need staking. Sadly, once the summer display is over, there is nothing much to see.

The traditional herbaceous border offers wonderful form and color and is at its best in high summer. Choose plants such as:
1 *Alchemilla mollis*.
2 delphiniums.
3 achillea.
4 nepeta.

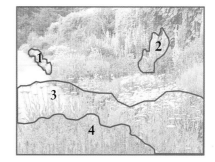

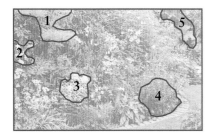

In a huge garden, that doesn't matter much, because other seasonal hotspots can become the center of attention. In a small garden it isn't so great, and you'll probably be better off planting a mixed border, perhaps in an island bed (see page 101) so that perennials are shown off by a backbone of small trees, shrubs, and bulbs. There's less work involved in this kind of planting design, and everything is within easy reach.

Mixed borders are the best choice for most gardens. For example, this border has:
1 *Gleditsia triacanthos* 'Sunburst' (tree).
2 *Gladiolus callianthus* 'Murieliae' (bulb).
3 *Phlox paniculata* 'Norah Leigh' (perennial).
4 anthemis (perennial).
5 *Gunnera manicata* (perennial).

Mixed borders include a bit of everything. The great advantage of a mixed border is that there is something to see during most of the year. These areas of your garden are the original pick 'n' mix selection, and you can choose your own blend of components to fill a mixed border.

You can include trees and shrubs to give the border height and bulk and to give it some interest during winter. Bulbs will provide a spring and/or summer show to brighten up the bed, and perennials will add most of the summer color. Bedding plants can then fill any seasonal gaps you find you have.

Contemporary areas (1) are easy to care for; they include plenty of open space, interesting surfaces (such as pebbles, cobblestones, or decking), and dramatic clumps of "architectural" plants, such as phormiums and bamboos, grouped together to make eye-catching features. Quite unlike a traditional bed, the effect is more like living architecture.

The cottage garden (2) style is an easy-going one, created by planting beds of self-seeding annuals and perennials that will spread without needing regular digging up and dividing. But modern cottage gardeners are often plant addicts who use this style as an excuse to house their ever-expanding collections. In this case, it's a good idea to keep invasive plants in beds of their own, so that they can't smother slower-growing treasures.

Prairie planting (3) is a stylish and fashionable form of perennial planting. Here, you can forget about lawns and beds and, instead, have a solid carpet of low-maintenance perennials and ornamental grasses that you walk between on winding bark or gravel paths. It's quite easy to look after, as long as you don't have masses of perennial weeds in your soil.

Various planting styles:
1 Gardeners who like a minimalist approach will position carefully chosen plants alongside stones, lumber, and ornaments.
2 Traditionalists will probably prefer the cottage garden approach with its show of old-fashioned flowers.
3 The prairie garden uses a mixture of grasses and wild-looking plants for a natural, "untamed" effect.

1

2

3

Border types

Traditionally, a border is the type of wide bed that runs around the edge of the garden, though you might have a narrow one that runs along the edge of a path or patio. Borders often have straight edges, which gives them a formal style. For softer, more informal effects, create borders with generously curving edges. But beware! Make your curves broad and sweeping – lots of tight bends tend to make a garden look fussy and are a real pain when it comes to mowing. And make your borders as wide as you can so that you have room to plant with lots of interesting variation in height without cramping an individual plant's style.

There are several variations on the theme that you can use to get away from the "ribbon-development" effect – if that's what you want:

The wider the border, the more dramatic the effect and the more room plants will have to grow. Straight-sided borders have a clean, formal feel.

Island beds are the sort that are sited within the garden, to form planted "islands" surrounded by lawn, gravel, or paving. They usually have informal, curving outlines and may be, for example, teardrop- or kidney-shaped. Island beds look particularly good when landscaped to fit into existing hollows, perhaps in a sloping lawn, to give them a natural appearance. Again, tight curves and sharp angles are best avoided.

Raised beds are much more artificial creations. They are made with brick, lumber, or drystone walls and filled with soil. Raised beds might be specially built to bring the garden up to easy working level – ideal for gardeners who are becoming a bit creaky in the back! In this case, it's a good idea to build a wide top edge that doubles as a seat.

They are often built to create better drainage for plants that hate wet feet – Mediterranean plants and most alpines, for example. If so, you'll need to put lots of drainage material at the bottom (it's a good place to get rid of all your old bricks) and fill the beds with a mixture of soil and horticultural grit or very coarse sand. One of their other big advantages is that your favorite plants are brought much closer to eye (and nose) level.

Borders sculpted in sweeping curves have a more natural, relaxed look.

Where plants need really good drainage (or when you reach that time of life when bending becomes more difficult!), raised beds are a good idea.

Creating planting plans

The plan becomes reality – the mapped out "winter interest" border (*below*), will also look great in summer (*right*).

1 *Corylus avellana* 'Contorta'.
2 *Carex fraseri* 'Frosted Curls'.
3 *Cornus sanguinea* 'Midwinter Fire'.
4 *Erica x darleyensis* 'Silberschmelze'.
5 *Mahonia aquifolium* 'Smaragd'.
6 *Erica x darleyensis* 'Kramer's Rote'.
7 *Bergenia* 'Sunningdale'.
8 *Eleagnus x ebbingei* 'Limelight'.
9 *Pennisetum alopecuroides* 'Hameln'.
10 *Hamamelis x intermedia* 'Westerstede'.
11 *Mahonia japonica* 'Hivernant'.

Once you've worked out a shape and decided on a style for your bed, make a planting plan that shows you which plants to put where. Why not just go to the garden center and buy whatever takes your fancy? Well, the trouble is, impulse buying is fun at the time, but you'll probably pick plants that look great on the day. When they've finished flowering, it may be ages before they "peak" again. It's impossible to resist the most eye-catching plants, but they don't always make good neighbors – they may not even enjoy the same growing conditions. No, we need to be just a bit methodical – sorry!

Do your research

One of the best ways to plan your bed or border is to take a sheet of paper and write at the top the theme of your bed – say a mixed border, prairie bed, exotic island bed, or whatever. Make a note of the soil type, site, and exposure – hot, sunny, and sandy, or cool, wet, and shady maybe – and start jotting down the names of plants

that will grow well in such circumstances. Where to look?
Plant reference books contain useful lists of plants for particular
situations, and if they have illustrations, so much the better.
It may be worth buying a book that covers gardening on clay or
chalky soil, if that's your particular situation, because it will
contain far greater detail about plants that grow best there. If you
belong to a gardening club, other members often have pertinent
advice to offer.

Try spending a fact-finding morning in a garden center. Some
centers group plants for particular situations together, or they may
make special display gardens. Even if the plants are arranged in
alphabetical order, you'll still find vital information on the labels
attached to individual plants.

But the most enjoyable way of undertaking research is to visit
other gardens looking for inspiration. If you live in a problem
area, maybe near the water, then visit gardens close to home with
similar conditions. Look out for open gardens with features you
admire, such as bog or gravel gardens, or particular planting
styles. Take a notebook and camera and, when you see a planting
design you like, take notes or take a picture of the plants to act as
a reminder later.

Labels in the garden

*If you don't like to see your
plant labels, save them and file
them in an old shoe box. If you
think you won't remember
what's where, draw a map and
mark the positions and names
of your plants on it.*

*If you like to keep your
plants labeled, I'd still remove
the plastic pictorial tags – they
quickly fade, get buried, or
break off and blow away. Copy
vital information, such as name
and pruning instructions, onto a
metal label to push down into
the soil by a clump of plants or
bulbs, or tie it discreetly to an
inner branch of a tree or shrub,
where you can still find it.*

Read the plant label

This is the type of basic information you should find on a good plant label in a garden center or nursery.

Name: Latin and common names.

Height and spread: average size after five years. Don't expect plants to follow this to the letter; actual size varies according to growing conditions.

Flowering time: may be represented by a number that corresponds to the month (or months).

Hieroglyphics: symbols representing sun, partial shade, shade, etc.

Special instructions: pruning instructions or other critical information.

Arranging shapes

Choosing plants that enjoy the growing conditions in your garden is only half the battle. It's the way you put them together that really gives your planting design star quality. When you analyze what makes a border successful, you'll see that there are several basic plant shapes: tall and upright, low and spreading, spiky, domed, rounded, and foamy "filler." Forget about plant names for now; the best way to start designing is just by arranging the shapes on paper.

It's a good idea to cut out different-sized triangles of paper, sketch in rough plant shapes – spiky, weeping, upright, domed, and so on – and put them together to get an idea of the finished effect. Then arrange them on your plan. By working in black and white, you can see instantly which contrasting shapes have dramatic effects when positioned beside each other.

Don't try to tackle an entire bed at once. Start with small units and then put them together. The units that work best for me are triangles or pyramids. A typical triangle might contain an upright tree, a rounded shrub and a low, spreading plant. These will work well together if you just want a free-standing trio of plants to form a small contemporary feature, surrounded by a carpet of gravel, perhaps with a single large stone for dramatic focus.

A traditional, plant-filled border works in exactly the same way – there's just a lot more of it. Go about it in the same way, and keep putting triangles together until you've filled the entire area. Use different-sized triangles: large ones for upright tree shapes, rounded shrubs, and low, spreading perennials, and smaller triangles for evergreen herbs, perennials, and bulbs.

You can use triangles to fill any shape, from a long, narrow border with the tallest plants along the back row, to an irregular island bed in which the tallest plants are grouped along the "backbone" so that you can see everything as you walk around the margins. Above all, try to avoid making your planting design look like a plate of buns.

Think in triangles, and your beds and borders will end up having an interesting and flowing shape.

Adding color

Different color combinations:
1 The contrasting green *Paris polyphylla* and red *Lobelia* 'Fan Scharlach'.
2 Purple *Verbena bonariensis* and yellow *Patrinia scabiosifolia*.
3 Blue agapanthus against a background of orange crocosmia.
4 A multicolored confection of electric blue *Eryngium x oliveranum*, scarlet *Crocosmia* 'Lucifer', yellow *Coreopsis verticillata*, and magenta *Lychnis coronaria*. Stunning!

This is the point where I feel a quick watercolor coming on, but you don't need to be at all artistic to have a go for yourself. Start filling in the triangles using splotches of color. The effect will be more Picasso after a wild night out than Gainsborough doing a detailed landscape. There's no need to be realistic in terms of shape or detail, because what you want is just an impression of which color goes where, and how they go together.

If you're making a traditional border, you'll probably want to include a lot of different colors. To prevent them all from clashing and looking artlessly garish, it makes sense to have a preponderance of green – provided by evergreens and foliage plants – with blobs of color sprinkled throughout. Avoid placing colors that shriek right next to each other. You could be very coordinated and stick to shades of purple, mauve, and pink, or blues, pinks, and whites; or go for hot and trendy using red, yellow, and orange. A word of advice though: don't mix these two color ranges, or the result will be like an explosion in a paint shop. Oh, and don't worry that you still haven't put any plant names in, or thought about how to keep color in the border throughout the seasons, because that comes later (see pages 122–34 and 197–99).

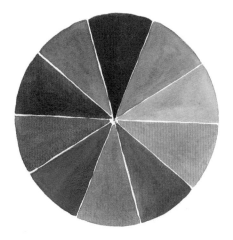

Use this color wheel to work out the color scheme of your planting. Adjacent colors harmonize; those opposite one another on the wheel, such as red and green, will make dramatic contrasts.

The color wheel

Artists have some of the most expertly color coordinated gardens, even if they don't know all that much about plants. They instinctively apply the same color theory for putting plants together as they do when they are painting.

An artist's color wheel shows immediately the relationships colors have to each other. Imagine a rainbow bent around into a complete circle. Red – orange – yellow – green – blue – indigo – violet. That's a color wheel. Any time you are planning a color scheme, you can use it to see at a glance which colors combine together well.

They say opposites attract, and that's certainly true with colors. Some of the most striking combinations are the contrasting colors that lie immediately opposite each other on the color wheel, such as red and green, purple and yellow, orange and blue. Three-way combinations make slightly more subtle contrasts. The most successful are based on three colors that are spaced at equal distances around the color wheel – red, blue, and pale yellow, or purple, green, and orange-yellow.

Instead of choosing contrasting colors, you can make harmonious effects by using three colors that lie next to each other in the color wheel. You might choose yellow, orange, and red, or

mauve, purple, and violet; it's exactly this technique that works so well at the world-famous Sissinghurst Castle in Kent, England.

I find it really helps me to paint my plan for a garden or border to assess how the colors will come together. Remember, there are more than just pure colors that you can put together; colors come in all sorts of variations, and flowers come in all sorts of tints and tones. Their foliage, also, has an almost infinite number of variations in color – yellow-greens, bluish greens and soft grays, right through to deep bottle green, burnt copper, and almost black.

Crimson *Astrantia* 'Hadspen Blood' (foreground), the ruddy pokers of *Sanguisorba menziesii*, and the rose 'Dusky Maiden' combine to make a hot, monochromatic scheme.

Monochromatic color schemes

If you want a monochromatic color scheme, you can go about it by putting together the colors from one segment of the color wheel only but, for that to work in a garden, you must also think laterally. Vita Sackville-West's famous white garden at Sissinghurst Castle actually contains lots of gray, silver, and glaucous blue foliage, plenty of gold- and silver-variegated leaves, and a few lilac flowers. The variety gives it depth and brings it to life. White gardens planted with white flowers alone would look flat and dull.

The only colors that don't appear on the color wheel are black and white. White is off the scale at one end, since there is no color at all. Black would be a single spot in the center of the wheel, because black is what you get when all the colors are present. To the gardener, black and white are neutral and go with everything, though they are not colors to use in large quantities. Remember, above all else, that green is the most important color of all, because it complements all the others and acts as a buffer between flowers of different shades. What's more, leaves are interesting for a greater part of the year than flowers.

Putting it all together

Once you have designed the shape and size of the bed, worked out which plant shapes and which colors to put where, it's simply a matter of putting plant names to the specifications and making sure that they'll all be right for your soil and situation.

Plantspeople with a bit of past experience in putting plants together often cut out the formal planning process and do the job by eye in the garden center or nursery. They pick out several groups of plants with contrasting shapes that look good together, then experiment by arranging the groups in various combinations to see how they might work best as a team.

Large plants, such as trees, shrubs, and evergreens, are relatively easy to position, but smaller plants, such as alpines and perennial flowers, are not always so simple to sort out. The secret is to go for trios of contrasting shapes that have something in common – maybe color – then put the various trios together until they fill the area.

Timing

Remember that however carefully you plan your design, it is going to change with the seasons and as it matures over the years. Start by planning for the main summer effect, and then try to stretch the season of interest by adding evergreens and spring bulbs, for example. I never said it was going to be easy. Just easier!

Professional planting

If you still don't feel very confident about putting groups of plants together, try organizing them with a common theme running through the area. This is a valuable concept garden designers call "unity." In the case of a rock garden, for example, you might use a mulch of stone chips to tie the design together. In a border, you could repeat groups of one particular "filler" flower throughout, or use skeins of silver foliage running through a whole flower border to "pull" trios of more individually striking flowers together and prevent them from clashing.

The do's and don'ts of planting designs

Do...	Don't...
Choose plants that suit your soil, exposure, and situation	Go for plants with widely varying growth rates, or the strong ones will smother their weak neighbors
Place plants in threes so that they create triangles and form a clump	Choose plants with identical shapes, or you'll end up with a very tedious effect. Lots of variety is needed
Think about colors that will go together well or contrast well	
Have a theme of some sort running through a bed, whether it's a color scheme, a regularly repeated flower, or rustic accessories	Make beds with lots of sharp bends and acute angles, since they are a pain to mow around

A basic framework of shrubs and perennials can be thinned out in an established garden, and new plants added to refresh the design.

Renovating or restoring an old bed

It's all very well planning a completely new bed from scratch, but, if you want to make over an existing bed, you'll need a slightly different approach, since you aren't starting with a clean slate.

First, you need to work out what's already there. Make a plan of the border with the plants marked in, then decide what you think you'd be better off without. Maybe the bed has been there a long time and is a bit overgrown, or you might have been inspired by something you've seen on TV and feel like giving an old border a new look. It's a great opportunity to weed out some of the old plants you've lost interest in and to replace them with something more exciting. And, while you're at it, take the opportunity to replenish the soil now there are gaps in the border. After digging out the unwanted plants, work some well-rotted compost and a dressing of general fertilizer into the ground.

When deciding what else to plant, if you draw a plan, it's quite easy to get an impression of the effect when the surplus ingredients have been erased. You can then sketch in new plants that will look good against the existing background, in just the same way as if you were planning a completely new border from scratch.

Unplanned arrivals

Very often, what happens is that you've had a very good day out at a show or a nursery, gone mad with the credit card, and come back with the car full of new plants. We've all done it and, frankly, it's part of the fun, but the trouble with buying on impulse is that you usually have no idea where you are going to plant your exciting new finds.

A lot of people try to accommodate their new plants by making new beds or enlarging existing beds and borders. This is fine if you happen to have a rambling, informal cottage garden, or a natural, prairie-style one. But in a formal or a contemporary garden, you can find you've lost the entire thrust of your design if you clutter the clean lines with extraneous matter that wasn't part of the original plan.

I find that the best way of working new plants into an established design is to leave them in their pots and just stand them in gaps all around the garden. That way, you can move them around until you find the best combination of plants and gaps before finally deciding where to plant them.

But don't go worrying about it too much; the great thing about plants is that, if you decide you don't really like the result later, you can always dig them up and move them again – it's a lot easier than moving to a new town.

How to... **remove unwanted old shrubs**

When you are renovating an old border, you need to remove the items you don't want (or that are diseased) without disturbing or damaging the plants that you have chosen to keep. There is a simple way to do this, but it's hard labor, so take care of your back when you're doing it. Some of the more "macho" gardeners prefer to work bare-handed, but I'd advise wearing a pair of sturdy gloves to protect your hands and help you keep a good grip.

Old tree stumps can be quite a feature in the wilder type of garden and, if you have to need a tree taken down, it's often a good idea to leave a fairly tall stump and train climbers over it. The best way to remove an unwanted stump is to have it winched out, provided that there's room to get the equipment into the garden. Otherwise, bring in a stump-chipping service. The stump chipper is a machine that looks rather like a rototiller; it chews up the stump, roots and all, to sawdust. Just shovel out the sawdust and refill the hole with new topsoil. You can replant once the ground has settled.

What you need

- *pruners or loppers*
- *spade*
- *flat-bladed pick (mattock)*

1 Cut the stems back to about 2ft (60cm) above ground level with pruners or loppers. These stems can be used as a lever when you dig out the roots, making the plant less unwieldy, and so reducing the risk of damage to nearby plants and yourself. Beware of the cut ends – it's very easy to give yourself a nasty poke in the eye as you bend over the butchered shrub.

2 Dig around the stump with a spade to reveal the roots, then chop through them bit by bit with the spade or one of those flat-bladed picks that we call a "beck" in my part of Hampshire. In other areas, it is known as a mattock. The secret is to tackle the main roots individually.

3 Use the remaining stems to lever the rootball back and forth. This will reveal any remaining roots. Continue chopping through them, and, eventually, you will be able to remove the whole thing. Fill the hole with fresh soil. After a bit of a breather, you're ready to replant.

4 FROM SEASON TO SEASON

The growing season

One phrase that crops up all the time in gardening parlance is "the growing season" – that time between spring and autumn when plants are actively growing. In many areas for the rest of the time – winter – most outdoor plants are dormant and barely ticking, a bit like hibernating animals.

For us, the start and finish of the growing season are the signals that trigger the changing routines of the gardening year. There are particular jobs that need to be done either when plants are just starting to grow – such as seed sowing and repotting – or when they are safely dormant – such as moving deciduous shrubs or pruning grape vines. Life would be so easy if you could just look at the calendar and say, "Right, March 15th, prune the roses," and know you should do the same thing on the same day each year.

At the height of the growing season plants produce lots of lush growth. Some grow so quickly you notice the difference daily.

Unfortunately, it doesn't work out quite like that. The climate varies widely around the country, and the weather means that each year's growing season is different. You need to know your local climate and observe natural signs that show when plants are starting or stopping for the year.

Deciduous plants are the big giveaway. They detect subtle changes of light and temperature, which start the sap flowing and hormone levels surging. When their growth buds start swelling and bursting open, that's the start of the growing season and, when they lose their leaves in the autumn, that's the end of it… regardless of the precise date on the calendar.

Climate

It's easy to confuse climate and weather. It's probably a tad un-scientific, but the way I think of it is that climate is created by major geographic features that affect local conditions on a permanent basis, and weather is the stuff that changes from day to day.

If your garden is close to the ocean, or at high altitude, or in the far north or south of the country, or in the middle of a large city, you're probably well aware that you have a rather different climate from the standard conditions of nearby larger areas, which are the places targeted by anyone giving gardening advice in general or many region-specific books and magazines. That's why you'll need to adjust any dates you are given accordingly.

If you've ever driven north to south through the country in spring, you'll have noticed how the daffodils seem to come out during your journey. That's due to the effect the changing climate has on the growing season. In the far north, the growing season starts three to four weeks later than in middle of the country. Daffodils will hardly be showing through the ground in southern Minnesota, while in northern Kentucky, where the season may be up to two to four weeks earlier, the daffs will be in full bloom. Since the growing season also ends correspondingly later in Kentucky than in Minnesota, it follows that garden plants have a lot longer to complete the season's growth in Louisville than in Minneapolis . That's why your chances of harvesting a good crop of sweetcorn is much better in a southern garden; the shorter, northern growing season may not permit the crop to grow and ripen before frost. A short growing season also condenses your summer bedding displays and limits your chances of a good show of late-flowering perennials. It's not fair, I know, but it's a fact of life.

It's not just when traveling from north to south that you notice the difference in climate. For every additional 1000ft (300m) above sea level, you can knock roughly two weeks off the growing season

Even when the growing season has come to an end, it doesn't mean the garden must be dreary – frost can actually brighten a view.

because the higher you are, the colder it gets; even those few degrees can make all the difference. Close to large bodies of water, like the ocean, or a huge inland lake, the water acts like a giant, night-storage heater. In these areas the temperature is less likely to fall as low in winter, or rise as high in summer, as it does even a few miles inland, where the night-storage-heater effect peters out.

In the middle of a city, the climate is different again, because the heat leaking out of buildings warms the air to create an unusually mild microclimate. This is why you'll often see the tougher indoor plants, such as cyclamen and azaleas, flourishing outdoors in windowboxes, sometimes even in the middle of winter. City dwellers may also also grow tender plants outdoors that you'd otherwise only be able to leave out all year round if you lived in more southerly areas. If this irritates you, tell yourself that you wouldn't want to live in the city – whatever the compensations!

Frost pockets

People in mild, southern gardens might think they've got off lightly when it comes to the climate, but don't bank on it. Frost pockets can occur anywhere. When frost covers a garden at night, the cold air sinks to the lowest point. If your garden is in a dip, or at the foot of a slope with high walls at the bottom, the cold air can't sink any further and gathers there, creating a frost pocket. It might only be a small part of the garden, but plants in that area will be later starting into growth, tender-ish plants will be more prone to frost damage, and half-hardy bedding will need planting slightly later than the rest of the garden. It pays to know.

On a cold, sunny morning, you can spot frost pockets immediately, because you can see the frost lingering there when the rest of the garden has thawed. If you are halfway down a slope, you can often get rid of frost pockets by removing obstructions, such as fences or hedges, or by making gaps in them, so that the cold air can drain away down the slope.

Hardiness zones

We live in a big country with lots of different climate and weather. Our climates range from permafrost in Alaska to baking deserts in Nevada, from sunny and storm-prone plains to snowy mountain ranges and even the odd bit of temperate and subtropical rainforest. Tied to climate is our weather, which can be cold and wet, hot and dry, or somewhere in between, and of course it isn't the same from day to day or from year to year.

Recognizing the differences in the amount of cold temperatures a given area experiences, the United States Department of Agriculture devised a system for determining and indicating the average annual minimum temperatures for throughout North America. From this has developed the system of cold hardiness zones for plants.

Why would you want to know about hardiness zones? Once you know which zone you live in, you can match that to the hardiness rating given for each plant, which is part of the standard cultural information given in gardening books in the USA, including this one (as Z5–9, for example).

Cold and heat and change

USDA hardiness zones are based on the amount of cold temperatures a given area has experienced over a given period of time. Because weather is far from constant and predictable, fluctuations occur over time, and this means that hardiness zone information and their boundaries on the USDA hardiness zone map are periodically adjusted to reflect changes.

It must also be pointed out that cold is not the only thing that determines a plant's suitability for a large part of the country. Heat is a very important environmental factor, and it can be just as important as cold in determining the success or failure of a given plant. Recognizng this, the American Horticultural Society and cooperating institutions have created a similar system for demarcating heat-tolerance zones for North America and have determined heat-zone codes for many plants. This system is becoming widely accepted.

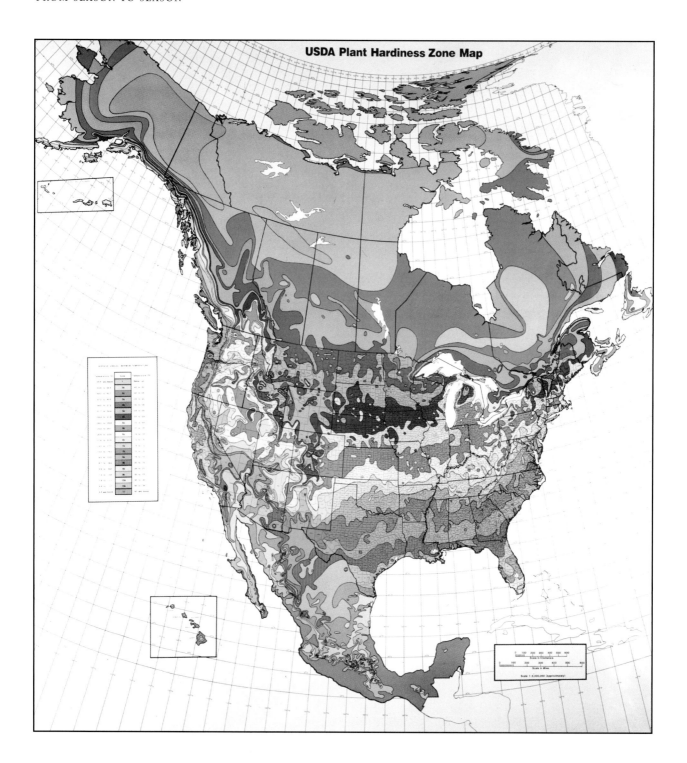

USDA Plant Hardiness Zone Map

It's important to keep in mind that cold hardiness is not the only factor that determines a plant's chances of surviving in your garden. Heat is a major factor (see the box on page 117), as are humidity, exposure to wind and sun, and a wide range of soil factors, including type (sandy vs. clay, for example), fertility, moisture content, and drainage. The microclimates in your garden (see page 116) will further determine the success and failure of a given plant. And of course it's stating the obvious that a plant that is totally hardy in your area and that is adaptable to your microclimate will not survive if you fail to give it the basic care it needs.

It's not just the USA that uses hardiness zones – they've been worked out for most of the world, and it's quite interesting to see which other places have the same climate as you do. But don't get carried away: remember that hardiness zones relate only to *average* minimum winter temperatures. The last I looked, weather was still variable and rather unpredictable.

The weather

You've only to listen to any group of gardeners talking for a few minutes before they get around to the weather, but it's not just because they want to know if the lawn will be dry enough to cut this weekend. The weather doesn't affect only the gardener's plans, it affects the plants in the garden, too. Nasty outbreak of tomato blight? Blame it on the weather. Mildew on the roses, zucchini rotted off, plagues of toadstools in the lawn, hanging baskets fried to a crisp? Yes, the weather is often at the root of the matter. Each season is different, and thank goodness. How boring gardening would be if each year was the same as the last. Where would the challenge be?

Bad weather

In winter, many plants become dormant to avoid wind, rain, and cold. There's a lot you can do to protect plants from bad weather at each end of the growing season – by providing shelter for newly planted evergreens when it's windy, or by covering late or early vegetables with cloches. But when bad weather strikes in summer, it can have a very serious effect on plants. A cold summer means that bedding plants in containers and hanging baskets will be slow to start growing and won't peak until toward the end of summer; vegetables and greens will take longer to mature, and fleshy fruits and vegetables, such as strawberries and zucchini, will be more likely to rot, especially if they touch the soil. If a cold, wet spell coincides with the start of the rose season, many blooms might go moldy before they have the chance to open fully (a condition called balling, which often affects some of the old-fashioned varieties).

Using hardiness zones

First determine your hardiness zone on the map on the opposite page. If you live in Zone 6, for example, any plant that is indicated as being hardy in Zone 6 should survive your winters. Since hardiness is often given as a range, be sure that your Zone falls within that range; a plant with a range of Z5–8 should survive the cold of Zone 6.

Sudden spells of hot dry weather can put plants under stress. With roses, that often leads to an outbreak of powdery mildew.

Small, transparent plastic tunnels are handy for protecting early crops from severe weather conditions.

There are some combinations of bad weather that are predictors of outbreaks of plant disease. Cool, damp weather with dull days provides ideal conditions for fungal diseases, so you can expect blackspot on the roses and gray mold in the greenhouse. Mid-summer rains almost guarantee an outbreak of potato blight, which also affects outdoor tomatoes (the two plants are closely related). Take precautions as soon as you realize the risk.

Although hot, dry weather is generally considered to be good weather by gardeners, that's not always how plants see it. It's bad for most plants if they become too dry, or if the temperature in the greenhouse rises so high that plants scorch in the burning sun. Plants need protection from high temperatures by shading and ventilating greenhouses, and by the vigilant watering of those plants that are susceptible to drying out (see pages 32 and 169–72). The most at-risk are plants in containers, shallow-rooted annuals, and any recently planted youngsters that haven't yet established a far-ranging root system.

Dry, late-summer weather may prevent spring-flowering plants from forming flower buds, which is why you should water rhododendrons in August if the soil is dry. And a prolonged dry spell at any time in summer creates conditions that encourage powdery mildew to develop on roses, honeysuckle, New England asters, or other susceptible plants.

Because the weather can vary so much from year to year, it's easy to be caught off guard. In recent years in some areas, hot, dry summers with watering bans and light winter precipitation in between convinced some people to plant drought-resistant gardens – just in time to receive record rainfall! But then, as H.E. Bates said, "Gardening, like love, is a funny thing, and doesn't always yield to analysis."

Frost

The dates of the first and last frost of the season are turning points in the gardening year. The last frost of spring signals the start of the bedding-plant season, as that's when you can start planting half-hardy annuals outdoors. The first frost of autumn finishes them off, so then you pull them out and put in your pansies, making sure all your tender plants have been carefully stowed in a heated greenhouse or brought indoors.

Frosty weather is fine when it happens on schedule. Cool autumn temperatures that slowly sink to normal winter cold lead plants into a proper dormancy and kill off all sorts of bugs, snails, and slugs. That's what used to happen much of the country had old-fashioned winters with plenty of seasonal cold and snow. The problems occur when the cold snap comes late, after a long, mild autumn, which is what happened afew times in the 1990s. Mild weather ran right into what should be winter and, by early spring, a few sunny days triggered plants out of a sort of shallow sleep, just in time for tender buds and newly opened young leaves to be clobbered by frost. Weeks later, when the real spring arrived, all sorts of odd symptoms appeared; many new leaves had brown edges or peculiar wrinkling. The tight buds had been "nipped" by frost, which killed part of the leaves so that they distorted as they unfolded. In severe cases, a late frost can kill all the buds on a plant, and it may look dead for weeks until it manages to produce a new crop of buds. Don't be in a hurry to dig out "dead" plants after a late frost. They may be resting and recuperating. Give them until early summer and, if there's no sign of life by then, you're probably right to ditch them.

The odd late frost can occur anywhere, once in a while, and it's just bad luck, but if you garden in a frost pocket, or have an east-facing site, avoid growing early-flowering plants, such as camellias, and choose late-flowering fruit varieties. Frosted early flowers are killed if the frozen tissues defrost too quickly, and that's what happens if they are hit by early morning sun. At best, you've lost a season's flowers and, at worst, you've lost an entire crop of fruit. But grow shrubs and trees that flower from early summer onward in that situation, and you won't have a problem.

Frost damage on this leaf has produced typical scorching symptoms.

First and last frosts

These depend on where you live, of course, but frost dates move roughly north and south, with allowances for proximity to bodies of water, altitude, and microclimate. Everything from books and local gardeners to seed packages and the Internet present frost information. Also, take into account the weather of a particular year, which can advance or delay frost dates from two to three weeks in any one year. Local weather forecasters give frost predictions; pay heed.

The year-round garden

Proof (*opposite*) that there can be color and interest in the garden at any time of year:
1 Tulips are spring bloomers.
2 Grapevines color up well before their leaves fall in autumn.
3 Evergreens like this euphorbia look good when rimed with winter frost.
4 In summer, the entire garden seems to erupt into flower.

There's no mysterious secret to creating a stylish, good-looking garden with all-year-round appeal. It just takes a bit of planning to ensure there's a constant stream of plants reaching their peak at different times of year. To make sure it's always interesting, your garden should contain some plants from each of the key seasonal groups (see also pages 16 and 27–29).

Gardening work-planners help to plan the year, but they aren't meant to be followed slavishly. You can't take it for granted that the ground will be in a fit state for seed sowing in March, just because that's what it says on the packet, so read the signs and adjust the dates to suit local conditions and the vagaries of the weather.

The key jobs I've given here for each season are by no means a comprehensive list, but I've included them to make the connection between the things that gardeners need to do and the seasons. Experienced gardeners feel this connection instinctively, but for first-timers, often living or working in urban environments and being somewhat removed from the seasonal changes, the association is not so obvious. There are many more jobs than I've listed, but at least these will give you a clue as to which areas of maintenance need thinking about at what time of the year.

Overview of the gardening year

Season	Plants at their best	Main seasonal jobs
Spring	spring bulbs fruit tree blossoms	cleaning planting and sowing weeding and mulching rose pruning
Summer	roses herbaceous perennials bedding plants	mowing hedge clipping hoeing vegetables fertilizing and watering
Autumn	autumn leaves fruit berries	bulb planting planting trees and shrubs cutting down and neatening lawn maintenance
Winter	colored shrub stems tree bark evergreens	planning and designing construction general maintenance and repairs

Spring

Spring bulbs, tree blossom and flowering shrubs are the highlights of spring, and most people are so relieved to see a bit of color after a long, dull winter that they aren't too worried about creating tasteful color combinations. They want whatever there's most of, and I'm inclined to agree with them.

Bulbs

The great thing about most spring-flowering bulbs is that you can grow them beneath trees knowing that they'll put on a darn good show when you need it. You don't need to worry about the deep shade that envelops them when the trees come into leaf, since that's when they die down anyway. In borders, this useful habit means that you can grow summer-flowering perennials in practically the same spot as your bulbs. Snowdrops and winter aconites are especially worthwhile for a first carpet of color, and they like being naturalized – planted and then just left alone to spread. Once they are in, they don't make any more work.

Daffodils and crocuses are fine for naturalizing in a lawn, as long as you plant in drifts, but if you want a wildflower meadow, then go for species daffodils, such as *Narcissus poeticus*, or the spectacular *Fritillaria meleagris* (snakeshead fritillary) with nodding, checker-patterned mauve or white bell flowers. The starry blue squills (*Scilla*) and chionodoxas are also good for naturalizing in a wild-style garden.

In borders, carpets of dwarf daffodils are much more practical than the larger-flowered ones, because they don't leave tall, messy foliage littering your flower beds as it dies. 'Jetfire' is one I like – neat plants, masses of flowers, and it clumps up well, too.

As soon as buds start to break in spring, and these ostrich ferns (*Matteuccia struthiopteris*) push up their bright green shuttlecocks in ground that will soon be shaded, there is a great feeling of renewal in the garden. Savor every moment!

For containers, the earliest dwarf daffodils, such as 'February Gold', are good, but it's bulbs like tulips and hyacinths that are going to make a real splash when spring arrives in earnest.

Trees

Mid- to late spring is blossom time, and it's an embarrassment of riches. If you have a small garden – especially if it's not very sheltered – don't be seduced by plants such as lilacs and flowering cherries, whose flowers don't last long before turning brown and blowing away. They leave you with nothing very interesting to look at for the rest of the year. In a larger, more sheltered garden, yes; grow them if you love them. Just make sure they have plenty of company to keep the garden colorful when their time of glory is over.

For my money, some of the best flowering trees for a smaller garden are those that give you a second spectacle later in the season – they make better use of the space. *Amelanchier* (shadblow), for example, has white flowers that open at the same time as the bronzed young leaves in spring, followed later by wonderful autumn color. Similarly, crabapples are first wreathed in spring blossoms before bearing a generous crop of bright autumn fruits. Where there's more room, the edible quince (*Cydonia oblonga*) is a superb tree with large, pale pink blossoms in spring and golden pear-shaped fruits that follow.

Spring-flowering evergreens have a good chance of looking handsome all year round, if you choose those with attractive foliage and a strong shape. In mild sites, you might choose unusual early-flowering trees, such as *Azara microphylla*, with fluffy, yellow, vanilla-scented flowers in late winter and early spring. *Ceanothus arboreus* 'Trewithen Blue', which flowers for weeks on end in late spring, also has an interesting shape and dark, glossy, evergreen foliage the rest of the time.

Shrubs

The bulk of the best-known shrubs flower in spring. This is when you can enjoy camellias, rhododendrons, berberis, forsythias, mahonias, many viburnums, the flowering currants (*Ribes*) and ornamental quince (*Chaenomeles*). But it's always good to include a real star like *Magnolia stellata* – that's the shrubby one that doesn't mind a bit of alkalinity in the soil. It makes a good specimen if you don't have room to grow it in a mixed bed. Perhaps plant a few of the less common spring shrubs that you don't see everywhere, especially if you want to make a small garden special. Mezereon (*Daphne mezereum*) doesn't suit everyone's soil, but the scented, pink-purple flowers in early spring are a real joy. It needs very well-drained soil with plenty of organic matter and, though it's known not to be crazy about lime, in practice, it tolerates a slightly alkaline soil as long as everything else is to it's liking.

Putting it all together

Sprinkling seasonal color all around a garden doesn't make much impact, especially if it's a big garden and you only use a few flowers. What works much better is grouping plants together to make seasonal "hot spots." They show up well from a distance and will entice you outside for a better look. A tree, a shrub, and a clump of perennials are a good recipe for a mini-feature, especially if you add a little sculptural something – a big pot or a large, round cobblestone. To brighten up an otherwise out-of-season border, use carpets of spring-flowering bulbs, winter bedding (such as pansies or ornamental cabbage), or low, spreading perennials to create islands of color beneath shrubs and roses.

Key Jobs for Spring

This is the busiest time in the garden. Try to allocate some regular gardening time each weekend, making weeding and planting top priorities; if you fall behind now, you'll struggle to get back under control later. Stay on top now and your efforts will be rewarded.

Early spring
• Spring-clean borders – hand weed or hoe, and mulch with well-rotted organic matter. Fork over vegetable beds.
• Prune roses.
• Plant shallots and onion sets; sow early crops under cloches.

Midspring
• Begin mowing the lawn regularly. Apply lawn fertilizer, and treat weeds or moss. Prepare soil and sow grass seed or lay sod.
• Fertilize beds and borders, specimen trees, roses, shrubs, and hedges with general fertilizer.
• Plant roses, trees, shrubs, and perennials. Move evergreens or conifers. Plant spring bedding in containers and gaps around the garden. Plant dormant dahlia tubers and gladiolus corms.
• In the greenhouse, prick out seedlings, or pot up if they're ready.
• Plant sprouted potato tubers. Most maincrop vegetables, other than frost-tender ones, can be sown now.

Late spring
• Plant tomatoes in an unheated greenhouse and plant late vegetables, e.g. leeks, Brussels sprouts, and cauliflowers outside.
• Prune spring-flowering shrubs after flowering and clip hedges.
• Move or divide spring-flowering bulbs after flowering.
After the last frost:
• Plant half-hardy bedding, dahlias, tender exotics and frost-tender vegetables, such as beans, zucchini, corn, and pumpkins.

Start garden jobs early in spring. Put seed potato tubers in a bright, frost-free place (*left*) to get them to sprout, ready to plant out – sprouted tubers produce larger yields; (*center*) dig up overcrowded snowdrop clumps as the flowers fade, and divide and replant them to make more colonies; (*right*) if you're short of color in spring, you can get it instantly by planting out early-flowering pansies.

Summer

Flowers are the real stars of summer, whether it's bedding plants in pots and hanging baskets on the patio, perennials in the borders, or those old stalwarts, the roses. This is the time for being a bit more co-ordinated with your colors, now there's so much to choose from.

Bedding

Old favorites such as pelargoniums and fuchsias still rate top of the poll, but now that everyone goes so mad on container gardening, demand has given rise to a heck of a lot of new and different patio plants, such as scaevola – the pendent beauty with fan-shaped blue flowers. Modern strains of petunias put on some of the best and most long-lasting shows possible in hanging baskets; choose the 'Million Bells' type, with trillions of small flowers, or the popular 'Surfinia series', which have a wonderful scent if you grow them in a sheltered spot. The equivalent flower-power among the pelargoniums is to be found among the 'Cascade' type; they are a big improvement on the conventional trailing, ivy-leaved pelargoniums. The plants are completely covered in narrow-petaled flowers all summer, like the old favorites seen in those spectacular windowboxes on Swiss chalet balconies, but with a modern twist.

The summer border that you dream about in winter. But it will be like this again – honest!

Perennials

You don't need to have a traditional herbaceous border to be aware of the abundance of perennials in flower during summer, from old favorites like delphiniums, lupines and bearded irises, to loud red-hot pokers (*Kniphofia*), drought-tolerant pinks (*Dianthus*) and penstemons, or trendy euphorbias and alstroemerias – which are both pretty drought tolerant, too.

For damp borders or watersides, you could pick tall rodgersias, with horse-chestnut-like leaves, yellow-spired loosestrifes (*Lysimachia*), and the plant that looks like chains of gold coins, the golden version of creeping Jenny (*Lysimachia nummularia*) 'Aurea'.

But in any situation, don't forget the foliage; plants like heucheras and hostas are handy for separating colors that "fight" or for making individual flowers stand out from the horde.

A summer border awash with color from *Geranium* 'Johnson's Blue' (left foreground), *Lavandula stoechas* (center foreground), aquilegias (the pink columbines), bearded irises (center) and purple sage (right).

Roses

Nine out of ten gardens grow roses, even though very few feature traditional formal rose beds now – the sort with bare soil beneath the plants. Nowadays, you'll more often see shrub roses grown in mixed borders, or prickly species roses, such as *Rosa rugosa*, grown as a hedge. Among the new developments of the past few years have been the compact patio roses, which are brilliant for pots. They have all the long flowering season of bedding but without the need to replant every season, since you can leave them in the same pots outside all year round. Groundcover roses are similar but, instead of being neat and bushy, they are low and spreading – perfect for covering a bank or the front of a border. Standard roses are ideal if you want a bit of height and formality in a border. They look pretty good rising above a carpet of ground-cover roses, or a bed of knee-high perennials, but use them carefully if you want to avoid that retro 1950s look.

Key Jobs for Summer

Fertilizing, watering, deadheading bedding plants, and keeping the grass mowed are major priorities in summer. Perennials and vegetables by now shade the ground, so most annual weeds will be smothered out, but watch out for nasties, such as bindweed.

Early summer
- Apply some sort of shading to the greenhouse.
- Fertilize and deadhead roses after the first flush of flowers.
- Use netting to protect soft fruit from birds.
- Harvest early vegetables and greens, and replant beds.
- Fertilize and water tomatoes, peppers, eggplant, cucumbers, and melon plants regularly.
- Sow seeds of perennial plants and winter bedding outdoors.

Mid-summer
- Pick soft fruit.
- Water containers regularly and fertilize once a week.
- Keep up the fertilizing and deadheading of bedding plants.
- If the weather is dry, raise the lawn mower blades slightly; grass will stay greener if allowed to grow a little longer.

Late summer
- Water rhododendrons in dry weather to help initiate their flower buds for next year.
- Summer-prune soft fruit and trained apple trees.
- Clip slow-growing hedges, such as beech and yew.
- Pick open flowers from patio plants before going on vacation, so you come home to fresh new blooms instead of deadheads.

Close-weave netting (*left*) is a good shading material for a greenhouse. It can be rolled up on dull days. Picking gooseberries (*right*) is a satisfying sort of job – and you can dream of pies and gooseberry fool!

Autumn

Autumn is the fruiting season in the garden, when berries and seed heads are at their best, and the brilliant colors of autumn leaves change the character of the garden within a matter of days.

It isn't just fading leaves that provide autumn color; flowers like these *Anemone x hybrida* 'Honorine Jobert' start coming into their own from late summer onward.

Autumn foliage

In grand gardens noted for their fiery autumn colors, it's the big trees, like oaks and maples in the park, and the giant climbers, like Virginia creeper covering the west wing, that make a splash as autumn comes around, but at home you can still create quite a ripple. Medium-sized trees, such as the paperbark maple (*Acer griseum*), the maidenhair tree (*Ginkgo biloba*), and many hawthorns (*Crataegus*), are just as good. If the soil is acidic, then go for flame-tinted sweet gum and Persian ironwood (*Parrotia persica*) – two of my favorites. For something more unusual, there's the spectacular Katsura tree (*Cercidiphyllum japonicum*), with heart-shaped, smoky pink and yellow autumn leaves that smell of toffee apples when they fall. Pure fairground!

If you have less room to play with, the deciduous azaleas and Japanese maples (cultivars of *Acer palmatum*) are brilliant; those that change from green to red in autumn, such as *Acer palmatum*

'Ôsakazuki', are especially stunning. Some barberries and viburnums color well too, among them *Berberis* 'Pirate King' and 'Buccaneer'. The leaves of the wayfaring tree (*Viburnum lantana*) turn bright cherry red. There are even a few smallish trees that color up well in autumn – the *Amelanchier* mentioned earlier (see page 125); birches (*Betula*) with leaves that turn a buttery yellow, and a few of the ornamental cherries, such as *Prunus* 'Spire', with orange and scarlet tints.

Berries and fruit

Colorful fruit, berries, and hips show up well against green foliage, but combine them with autumn colors and they make the garden look as if someone has walked around turning the lights on – until the birds get stuck in for a meal. Unless the weather is very cold, you should get a couple of months of enjoyment out of them first.

Species roses, such as *Rosa rugosa* and *Rosa moyesii* 'Geranium', are some of the very best for hips, and crabapples (*Malus*) can always be relied on for colorful fruit; cultivars such as 'Harvest Gold', 'Snowdrift', and 'Donald Wyman' are among the heaviest croppers of the lot. Both edible and ornamental quinces have big, knobby fruits, but, while those of the ornamental quince (*Chaenomeles*) are long-persistent, those of the edible quince (*Cydonia oblonga*) fall from the tree long before they're ripe if it's windy.

Cotoneasters and pyracanthas are reliable old favorites for berries, but if you fancy something a bit different, try the spindle bush (*Euonymus europaeus* 'Red Cascade'), with fiery red autumn leaves and vivid pink capsules that split open to show bright orange seeds inside.

Seedheads

Setting seed is what flowers are all about, and, by early autumn, the plumes of ornamental grasses, such as *Miscanthus*, *Pennisetum*, and *Stipa gigantea*, are at their best. You'll also find that some of the species clematis, such as *Clematis tangutica*, are covered with Beatle-like wigs of feathery seeds. Then there are the teasels and honesty heads down in the wild garden.

A great autumn plant you don't see so much of these days is the Chinese lantern (*Physalis alkekengi* var. *franchetii*). It's a perennial with upright stems bearing papery orange lanterns that look good running through a natural-style shrub bed or a wilder mixed border. A good many perennials produce seedheads worth leaving through the winter, including bronze fennel (*Foeniculum vulgare* 'Purpureum'), bear's breeches (*Acanthus*), and sea hollies (*Eryngium*). The seedheads look particularly good when rimed with frost or against snow, so don't be in a hurry to cut them down.

Key Jobs for Autumn

Bringing tender plants under cover before the frost is the first priority. When an autumn is mild, it's the best time for planting new trees, shrubs, and woody climbers; their roots establish well if the soil is still warm and moist.

Early autumn
- Clean the greenhouse; wash the glass, remove shading, and check the heater. Remove plants after harvesting fruits or flowers.
- Bring in frost-tender plants, such as fuchsias and pelargoniums; cut them back, pot them up, and keep them frost-free and in good light.
- Remove summer bedding when it has finished flowering, and replace with winter pansies and ornamental cabbages.
- Plant spring bulbs and spring bedding, such as wallflowers and primroses.
- Prepare soil for new lawns; sow grass seed.
- Harvest pumpkins.

Mid-autumn
- Plant deciduous trees, shrubs, and climbers.
- Lift tender summer bulbs, such as gladiolus, and dahlia tubers (allow frosts to blacken dahlia foliage before lifting); store in a frost-free shed.
- Dig up potatoes and store in paper sacks in a frost-free shed.
- Pick apples before the autumn storms. Store in a shed or the bottom of the refrigerator.
- Protect the crowns of margnally hardy plants with straw tied loosely with string.
- Neaten perennials; cut back dead stems, but leave ornamental seedheads for winter interest and to feed birds.
- Lay new sod any time the ground is not frozen.
- Rake lawn to remove thatch, and apply autumn lawn fertilizer.
- Clear fallen leaves from the lawn and rock garden.
- Put net over fish pond.

Late autumn
- Plant tulips and hyacinths.
- Clear fallen leaves from lawns, paths, flowerbeds, and rock gardens.
- Plant hedging or roses sold with bare roots.
- After leaf fall, move any deciduous trees and shrubs that need it, provided they are not too big.

Store potatoes in the dark in a thick paper sack. They are less likely to sprout than if exposed to daylight.

Winter

You'd be wrong to think of winter as a bit of a washout in the garden, because it's the time when evergreens and colored bark and stems come to the fore. Combine them with what's around in the way of winter flowers, and you have yet another set of new views at your fingertips.

Evergreens

Evergreens are the backbone of the all-year-round garden, and there is an enormous range of golden, variegated, gray, blue, and even russet-colored conifers and evergreens available. I use as many different shapes as possible – bamboos, small trees, and compact shrubs – to bring contrast and variety to the more predictable, wintery outlines of deciduous plants. A varied evergreen framework is a good background for spring and summer flowers, and autumn fruits and leaves, too, but in winter, it helps make the best display of what's around in the way of colored stems, trunks, and flowers.

Bark and stems

Bare bark and colored stems make the best possible contrast to a background of bushy evergreen shapes. Red-stemmed dogwood (*Cornus alba*) is the winter-effect shrub that first springs to mind, but there is also a yellow-green version called *Cornus stolonifera* 'Flaviramea'.

Just when you had given up all hope of another spring, the snowdrops appear (here beneath the red stems of a dogwood), to mark the end of winter and cheer you up.

You can chose from several shades with the shrubby willows; there's the scarlet willow (*Salix alba* subsp. *vitellina* 'Britzensis'), which is bright orange-red, or the pewtery-purple stems of the violet willow (*Salix daphnoides*). All are pruned back hard in early spring to produce more new stems for the following winter's pleasures.

There are birch trunks in shining white, such as those of *Betula utilis* var. *jacquemontii*; the jade green-striped stems of snakebark maple (*Acer capillipes*); the shaggy, rust-red coats of the paper-bark maple (*Acer griseum*), or the polished, mahogany-colored bark of the Tibetan cherry (*Prunus serrula*). Or how about curls? Contorted hazel (*Corylus avellana* 'Contorta') has twigs that are coiled like springs and, in late winter, they jangle with long, sulfur yellow catkins.

Iris 'Katharine Hodgkin' is a staggeringly beautiful winter-flowering iris, most easily admired when grown in a pot.

Winter flowers

Winter heathers and Universal pansies are the obvious choice for bulk color anywhere that the ground is reasonably well drained, but don't overlook bold ornamental cabbages and kales for containers – and toward the end of winter, there are the first colorful primroses coming on.

Witch hazels (*Hamamelis*) are well worth having – their red or gold autumn leaves are followed by the first spidery, winter flowers almost straight away. Several mahonias – *Mahonia japonica* cultivars in particular – bloom from midwinter into spring, with their delicious, lily-of-the-valley scented flowers. But the winter-flowering shrub everyone should know is the winter jasmine (*Jasminum nudiflorum*), which is one of those invaluable plants for a north-facing wall.

Key Jobs for Winter

Now that the routine chores are finished for the year, this is your big chance to get on with any garden planning or redesigning, and to do any building jobs… but don't undertake concreting if it's likely to freeze.

Throughput winter

- In mild areas, continue cutting the grass if it is still growing in spells of warm weather – but don't cut it too short.
- Prune fruit trees, figs, and grape vines when they are fully dormant.
- Protect containers planted with winter bedding, or all-year-round shrubs, from freezing solid. (Even totally hardy plants suffer when all the water in the potting mix freezes.) Stand them in a shed, garage, or sun room, or cover the pots with bubble wrap, or plunge them to their rims in an empty bit of ground for insulation – before they freeze.
- Sprinkle sand or grit on icy paths, not salt, which harms plants.
- Take the opportunity to treat lumber with wood preservative.
- Erect trellises, posts, or arches.
- Order seeds from seed catalogs.
- Float a child's ball or a log on a pond to relieve the pressure exerted by ice. Pour hot water over it to open up some air space for the fish.
- Put your feet up!

People think I'm nuts for washing the trunks of my white birches in winter, but it removes green algae and makes them stand out in dull winter light.

Floating a ball or log on the surface of a garden pond will allow you to make a hole in the ice to let fish breathe in the depths of winter. Just pour hot water over it and then lift it out.

5 WHO'S IN CHARGE?

Weed wars

Weeds want to take over, make no mistake. They can outgrow many native plants, even though the natives are on home territory, as well as fancy man-made hybrids . Weeds live to breed, and they want to overrun your garden. So what's stopping them? You are!

Daisies (the constellation in back) in your meadow - are they weeds? Not if you want them there.

What is a weed?

"A weed is any plant growing in the wrong place." This is an old garden saying that should be tattooed on trowels. Weeds are not just old faithfuls like dandelions in the lawn and greater bindweed in the borders (see pages 143 and 145); there are also some very invasive garden plants that come into the weed category when they come up where they aren't wanted. If you don't believe me, just see how fast the very pretty snow-in-summer (*Cerastium tomentosum*) takes over your rock garden.

The term you'll hear gardeners use for overactive cultivated plants is "thugs," which perfectly describes their unsocial behavior. You can't always spot a thug until you've let it loose in your own garden, because some will display perfect manners on certain soils but go berserk on others.

There are other plants that need watching because of their family connections. In my garden at Barleywood, I grow a stunning variegated form of that well-known nightmare, Japanese knotweed (see page 149), and I can say that – hand on heart – in 15 years, it's never gone as mad as its green-leaved relative, and its chest-high stems have such pretty pink, cream, and green leaves that I don't intend to start worrying about it. Mind you, I still take the precaution of planting it in a large pot that is plunged into the border soil to retard its root spread. The ornamental, variegated form of goutweed (see page 146), on the other hand, definitely has big ambitions, especially when it is grown on moist clay soil.

Contrary to what you might think, wildflowers aren't the same thing as weeds at all. Respectable wildflowers are grown deliberately in wild gardens, or in wildflower meadows, and if they spread or self-seed, they do it in a dignified way that inspires respect and needs encouragement – they don't try to take over. Weeds are plants that do try to gain the upper hand, and they'll succeed if you let them.

Weeds are great travelers, and seeds often arrive on the wind, especially if you live near wasteland, or untended gardens. Maple seedlings will certainly drop in this way if you have a big mature tree close by. Spreading, perennial weeds can creep under the fence from your neighbor's yard, or from fields. But you can also buy in weeds, since they can stow away in manure, topsoil, or the soil mix of your bought container-grown plants.

Weed tactics

The trouble with weeds is that they compete with garden plants for food, water, and, most of all, light. They grow faster than cultivated plants, and, by burying your treasures in foliage, cut out the light from them. This either "starves" them or stresses them so much that they succumb to disease. It also leaves them at the mercy of slugs and snails that find life under a nice weedy canopy most enjoyable, thank you very much. There are two basic types of weed, each with its own means of attack. Both need different treatment.

Annual weeds are the ones that grow each year from seed and live for one growing season. They often germinate at lower or higher temperatures than many garden plants and, since they grow from seed that sprouts wherever it falls, they don't suffer the setback of transplanting, unlike garden plants. This gives them a leg up in the survival stakes. Some annual weeds, such as groundsel (see page 141), produce several generations of seedlings each year and spread even faster.

Perennial weeds have underground reserves in the form of overwintering roots or rhizomes that enable them to spring into action quickly at the start of the season. Their speciality is embedding their roots in those of shrubs or garden perennials, so they aren't easy to get out. Even when they grow where you can get at them, some have a very tenacious grip on life. Some, such as dandelions and docks (see pages 144–45), can be dug out without too much difficulty. The ones to worry about are those that spread by means of a pervasive network of roots or rhizomes. That's what makes bindweed, goutweed, quackgrass, and Japanese knotweed seem so unstoppable (see pages 145–49).

Noxious weeds

These are weeds that are legally considered the worst of the bunch, causing major problems for agriculture, but they can become a problem in your garden, too. Considerable amounts of time and money are spent in an attempt to control them. The official list varies from state to state and can be obtained online.

Well-known weeds

It's not absolutely essential to be able to put a name to each individual kind of weed you meet while you're working your way through the shrubbery on your hands and knees; you just need to be able to distinguish the villains from the tolerables. But knowledge is power, especially in the battle against the bullies.

Everyday weeds

These are the sort of weeds most everyone has – mainly annual ones that appear in any exposed soil in spring and pop up almost at once on freshly dug soil.

Take prompt action

Don't wait until weeds flower to find out what they are. Learn to recognize them as seedlings, so you can remove them as soon as they appear in the garden, without accidentally eliminating flower or vegetable seedlings. Unlike perennial weeds, most annuals pull out easily even if they reach a good size. Put them on the compost pile only *before* they seed – otherwise you'll just be helping to spread them around.

Keeping a hoe going in spring and summer prevents weeds from getting out of hand – but keep it sharp, keep it shallow, and aim well!

Chickweed (*Stellaria media*) (**1**) One of the first to appear in newly turned soil, with masses of tiny seedlings that, at first, resemble a fine green mist. Plants eventually form a low carpet that roots as it spreads. Grows in cool weather and dies in prolonged heat.

Red dead nettle (*Lamium purpureum*) (**2**) The leaves are deceptively similar to tiny stinging nettles, but the plant doesn't sting, it is low and creeping (not tall and upright), and the flowers are mauve. Most reach 4in (10cm) high by 6in (15cm) across by the time flowering begins.

Groundsel (*Senecio vulgaris*) (**3**) A fast colonizer of bare soil, with small clusters of yellow flowers without petals that develop into fluffy seedheads like small dandelion heads. Expect several generations each year. Plants reach about 8in (20cm) tall and 6in (15cm) across.

Annual nettle (*Urtica urens*) (**4**) Short, bushy nettles with small leaves and vicious stings. Unlike the taller, more upright perennial nettle, it's easy to pull out, but don't imagine that its sting is any less painful than that of its big relation!

Everyday weeds:
1 (a) Chickweed (*Stellaria media*) seedling and (b) the full-grown plant.
2 (a) Red dead nettle (*Lamium purpureum*) seedling and (b) the full-grown plant.
3 (a) Groundsel (*Senecio vulgaris*) seedling and (b) the full-grown plant.
4 (a) Annual nettle (*Urtica urens*) seedling and (b) the full-grown plant.

Lamb's quarters (*Chenopodium album*) (**5**) A fast-growing, upright weed reaching up to 6ft (2.2m) tall. It has greenish, plumelike flowerheads that produce and shed masses of seeds and spread like… weeds.

Opium poppy (*Papaver somniferum*) (**6**) Smooth, gray-blue leaves and large, mauve poppy flowers followed by pepperpot seedheads. Plants reach 30in (75cm) tall and 12–18in (30–45cm) across. A weed that's pretty enough to leave in the garden, if it comes up in a suitable spot.

Hairy bitter cress (*Cardamine hirsuta*) (**7**) Although only a short-lived annual, 1–2in (2.5–5cm) high by as much across, it flowers and seeds incredibly quickly and can spread a lot of seeds in its brief life. Pealikeseed pods pop open, flinging their contents far and wide. Can become a major pest.

Goosegrass (*Galium aparine*) (**8**) Also known as cleavers, it is easily recognized by its hooked, scrambling, 2–3-in (5–7.5-cm) long stems that stick to everything they touch. So do the seeds – it's their way of spreading about.

Everyday weeds continued:

5 (a) Lamb's quarters (*Chenopodium album*) seedling and (b) the full-grown plant.

6 (a) Opium poppy (*Papaver somniferum*) seedling and (b) the full-grown plant.

7 (a) Hairy bitter cress (*Cardamine hirsuta*) seedling and (b) the full-grown plant.

8 (a) Goosegrass, or cleavers (*Galium aparine*) seedling and (b) the full-grown plant.

5a 6a 7a 8a

5b 6b 7b 8b

Annual bluegrass (*Poa annua*) (**9**) The tiny blades of grass quickly colonize bare soil and develop into small clumps. It flowers while still tiny, and, if left, plants knit together to form rough, shaggy "sod" that covers large areas, when it takes a fair bit of digging out.

Germander speedwell (*Veronica chamaedrys*) (**10**) These blue-flowered, creeping plants form low, spreading mats that root as they run. A common weed in lawns, but seedlings often appear in borders, too.

Yellow oxalis (*Oxalis corniculata*) (**11**) A frequent hitchhiker on container-grown plants, making low, loose mats of small, shamrock-shaped leaves that often turn purplish red in a dry or sunny spot. The tiny yellow flowers soon form explosive seedpods that shoot seeds everywhere. Another big pest.

English daisy (*Bellis perennis*) (**12**) An occasional weed of lawns because it manages to stay squat – even its flower stalks are shortened so that they can sneak under the mower. The leaf rosettes can be pried out with an asparagus knife.

9 (a) Annual bluegrass *(Poa annua)* seedling and (b) the full-grown plant.
10 (a) Germander speedwell (*Veronica chamaedrys*) seedling and (b) the full-grown plant.
11 (a) Yellow oxalis (*Oxalis corniculata*) seedling and (b) the full-grown plant.
12 (a) English daisy (*Bellis perennis*) seedling and (b) the full-grown plant.

9a 10a 11a 12a
9b 10b 11b 12b

Nuisance weeds

These are the regular perennial weeds that'll often put in an appearance, especially if you leave an area of ground uncultivated for some time, and they are the sort you'll often inherit if you take over a neglected garden.

Clean and clear

Once you have them in the ground, these weeds can take a bit of shifting, especially if they've tangled themselves up with cultivated plants, so it's worth clearing your borders properly before planting if you discover any of these in the ground. Don't put the roots of these weeds on to your compost pile, or you'll just spread them everywhere when you use the compost. But even problem perennial weeds can't survive regular hoeing. Catch them while they are small, and hoe each time new shoots show their heads above ground. Hard work, I know. But, in time, you will wear them out!

Top tips for weed prevention

- Check topsoil, compost, and manure before you buy to ensure it hasn't been infested with weeds, roots, or seeds, because it is too old or has been badly stored.
- Inspect the surface of the soil mix on any plants you buy for signs of weeds, and remove them before planting.
- Learn to recognize weed seedlings (see pages 140–50) and act quickly, removing them early before they can get too established, and especially before they can grow and produce seed.
- Don't put perennial weeds on the compost pile, or you will probably spread them around the garden next year.
- Use any of the following techniques, according to the size and severity of your weed problems: flaming, hand weeding, hoeing, or chemicals (see pages 151–54).
- Consider rootproof barriers to prevent invasive weeds spreading from next door (see page 157).
- Mulch clean ground with organic matter to prevent infestation (see page 154).

Dandelion (*Taraxacum officinale*) (**1**) A perennial weed with a rosette of indented leaves about 8in (20cm) across, yellow double-daisy flowers and characteristic spherical seedheads that distribute masses of seeds that float off on "parachutes." Though seed is the main means of spread, established dandelions have thick taproots, and new plants will grow quickly from any fragments you leave behind in the ground. It's easily done; they snap off instead of coming out cleanly when you pull.

Greater bindweed (*Calystegia silvatica*) (**2**) Public enemy number one for many gardeners. The fast-growing, climbing stems twine tightly around flower and shrub stems. They can uproot perennials entirely when you try to pull the weed up. Left alone, bindweed can soon smother even large shrubs. The thick white roots (known in some areas as "devil's guts") spread quickly, and, being brittle, any attempt to dig them out just turns them into root cuttings, which propagate the beast even faster. Bindweed needs to be caught just as the shoots first show through the ground, when they briefly form rosettes that can be hoed out or spot-treated with weedkiller – one of the few cases where it's justified, if you have a bad invasion. Bindweed is definitely best cleared from ground before planting, because you'll definitely have a hard job keeping it under control if it grows up through cultivated plants.

Dock (*Rumex obtusifolius*) (**3**) The familiar broadleaved weed that you can rub on nettle stings, with rusty red spikes of flowers that grow 2–3ft (60–90cm) high later in the year. They have deep tap-roots that are inclined to snap off if you pull them out, leaving behind little bits that grow back. It's best to dig them out carefully.

Nuisance weeds:
1 (a) Dandelion (*Taraxacum officinale*) seedling and (b) the full-grown plant.
2 (a) Greater bindweed (*Calystegia silvatica*) seedling and (b) the full-grown plant.
3 (a) Dock (*Rumex obtusifolius*) youngster and (b) the full-grown plant.

1a 2a 3a

1b 2b 3b

Stinging nettle (*Urtica dioica*) (**4**) Small clumps are not too much of a problem, because you can dig them out quite easily, but, once established, the roots spread quite a distance to form satellite colonies, and the stems can grow 6ft (2.2m) tall.

Creeping thistle (*Cirsium arvense*) (**5**) The standard prickly job with tough, spiky leaves. The flowers, like tiny pineapples with a tuft of purple threads poking out of the top, produce a mass of thistle-down seeds that blow away on the wind. In gardens, it spreads mainly by thick underground stems, but, if pulled up while small, it isn't too difficult to deal with. Don't let them seed, or you'll have thistles forever. The saying "one year's seed, seven year's weed" is especially pertinent to thistles.

Goutweed (*Aegopodium podagraria*) (**6**) Another real menace if you have it. The leaves and flowers are similar to those of elder bushes (*Sambucus nigra*), but they grow on a short perennial plant about 12in (30cm) high. Goutweed spreads from underground roots to form dense, knee-high carpets that are almost impossible to dig up if allowed to become established. Even small clumps take a lot of shifting, because bits of root left in the ground grow into new plants.

Nuisance weeds continued:
4 (a) Stinging nettle (*Urtica dioica*) young shoot and (b) the full-grown plant.
5 (a) Creeping thistle (*Cirsium arvense*) seedling and (b) the full-grown plant.
6 (a) Goutweed (*Aegopodium podagraria*) young shoot and (b) the flower.

4a

5a

6a

4b

5b

6b

Baby's tears, or helxine (*Soleirolia soleirolii*) (**7**) Helxine forms low, mossy-looking mats that root as they go, and any little piece left behind will regrow. Regular hoeing and raking up the bits eventually gets rid of it from a border. In lawns, treat it with a lawn weedkiller formulated for small-leaved weeds at regular intervals from spring onward until it's all gone, or just keep raking it out.

Quackgrass (*Elytrigia repens* syn. *Agropyron repens*) (**8**) This spreading grass with thin, wiry stems grows from the creeping, white, underground rhizomes that distinguish it from lawn-type grasses. Small clumps can be dug out, but if it invades perennial plants or bushy shrubs, the best answer is to dig up both weed and plant, so you can tease out weed roots from those of the ornamental plant you want to keep.

Creeping buttercup (*Ranunculus repens*) (**9**) These short, squat plants have rosettes of regulation buttercup leaves growing from a crown at, or just above, soil level. This makes them difficult to pull up, and a new plant soon grows from the roots you leave behind. Creeping buttercups spread by runners (rather like strawberry plants) but are more determined, so dig them out with patient perseverance and a small fork.

7 (a) Helxine (*Soleirolia soleirolii*) young growth and (b) the full-grown plant.
8 (a) Quackgrass (*Agropyron repens*) young growth and (b) the full-grown plant.
9 (a) Creeping buttercup (*Ranunculus repens*) young growth and (b) the full-grown plant.

7a 8a 9a

7b 8b 9b

Rogues' gallery

These are some serious problem weeds that either don't respond to "normal" methods or that need handling with care.

Brambles (*Rubus fruticosus*) (**1**) These have deep roots and a habit of rooting wherever their stems touch the ground. Reduce the size of a large bramble by cutting the stems into manageable lengths with pruners. Pile them up around the stump, allow them to dry out for a week or so, and then use a flame gun to burn the lot. Flame any new shoots emerging from the stump as soon as they appear.

Giant hogweed (*Heracleum mantegazzianum*) (**2**) A gigantic and strikingly architectural plant whose sap, on contact with the skin in sunlight, produces a very unpleasant reaction and huge blisters. If it grows on your land, you must prevent it from setting seed. To dispose of live plants, wear protective clothing and a visor over your eyes, leaving no exposed skin, but rather than cut it down while it's growing, which makes it "bleed" sap, I'd wait until it goes woody in late autumn. Use a flame gun to destroy seedlings while they're small.

Tougher, rogue weeds:
1 (a) Brambles (*Rubus fruticosus*) young plant and (b) flowers on a grown plant.
2 (a) Giant hogweed (*Heracleum mantegazzianum*) young plant and (b) in flower.

1a
2a
1b
2b

Japanese knotweed (*Fallopia japonica*) (3) A plant thought to have been introduced by a Victorian botanist who imagined it would look good in his border. It has since escaped and turned into a monster capable of forming huge colonies. There's no easy remedy. If you have it, all you can do is to cut it down or use the flame gun each time new shoots appear, which is just as effective as using weedkiller. With luck and persistence, you will weaken it so much that it can't grow back. If you spot seedlings, or the first signs of a new clump appearing, tackle them at once before they get any bigger.

Horsetail (*Equisetum arvense*) (4) Horsetail has a very deep and far-ranging root system, is strongly resistant to weedkillers, and is especially prolific on damp clay soils, though it can turn up anywhere. In borders, regular hoeing starves it out in time. If it comes up in wasteland or rough grass, mowing frequently will have the same effect but with much less effort. You can also smother it with old carpets, but, because it has large, underground food reserves, it takes an awfully long time to die. Put a rootproof barrier in around your garden if it looks like invading from adjacent fields (see page 157).

Brushwood killer

For those who need a quick fix and don't mind using weedkiller, woody weeds such as brambles and poison ivy, or really persistent weeds such as maple seedlings, are the sort for which brushwood killer was designed. You'll find specific instructions for treating the different problem weeds on the package, but be extremely careful. Follow the instructions to the letter, wear rubber gloves, and don't get the mixture on your skin. Never use brushwood killer close to plants you want to keep.

3 (a) Japanese knotweed (*Fallopia japonica*) young shoot and (b) the business end.
4 (a) Horsetail (*Equisetum arvense*) emerging shoot and (b) fully grown.

Ragwort (*Senecio jacobaea*) (**5**) This is fine in a wild garden, where its leaves can be a food source for caterpillars. In a paddock or grazing land, it should be pulled out and removed completely, because it is very poisonous to livestock. If uprooted and left, the dead plant is even more attractive and dangerous to ponies and other mammals than the living one.

English ivy (*Hedera helix*) (**6**) Ivy makes a great wildlife habitat, so don't get rid of it unless you really need to. Ivy isn't parasitic and doesn't harm trees, although it may damage weak mortar. To remove ivy, saw through the base of the plant close to the ground, then peel it off when it dries out and turns brown. Kill new growth by regular cutting, or treat the stump and new growth with brushwood killer.

Maples (*Acer pseudoplatanus*) (**7**) These are some of the fastest growing seedlings and, if ignored, can turn quickly into a junior sapling plantation. Dig the seedlings out while they are very small. Larger saplings, especially if they are coming up among garden plants where it is difficult to dig them out, are best sawed off close to the ground. Cut off all the new shoots each time they appear.

Tougher, rogue weeds continued:
5 (a) Ragwort (*Senecio jacobaea*) juvenile leaf rosette and (b) in flower.
6 (a) English ivy (Hedera helix) shoot tips and (b) mature leaves.
7 (a) Maple (*Acer*) innocent seedling and (b) full-grown leaf (here, *Acer pseudoplatanus*).

5a 6a 7a

5b 6b 7b

Eliminating weeds

Everyone wants a magic wand. If there were an easy, reliable way to get rid of weeds for good, someone would have made a fortune by now. There are various ways of tackling your weeds, from hand-weeding to more radical techniques such as applying chemicals or flaming them. Clearing weeds takes a bit of work, but, if you know the right way to tackle each kind, even problem weeds don't turn out to be quite as bad as you thought.

Weed clearance on vacant ground

Suppose you want to make a new bed on rough grass or wasteland, or you've just taken over a neglected garden? The first job is to clear the weeds. You can make a good start just by chopping down everything close to ground level with a hand scythe; rake up and discard everything when it's dried. If you have a fair-sized patch to do, I'd rent a bush hog, which is a tough piece of armament designed for cutting down undergrowth. It looks something like a big motor-mower with a hedge-clipper blade along the front instead of normal blades underneath. It won't choke on brambles and the odd sapling, but instead scissors the whole lot off at ground level.

Once you've got rid of the luxuriant top-growth, dig the ground over and take out all the roots. This is where a lot of people go wrong. They rush out to rent a rototiller, which actually makes things much worse. Problem perennial weeds, such as greater bindweed, goutweed, or horsetail (see pages 145–46 and 149), enjoy nothing better than having their roots chopped up small, because each piece reroots. All you've done is to propagate the colony. Even nettles and docks will grow back in thickets where once there were only clumps.

If digging out roots by hand doesn't appeal to you, there are several other options. One is to leave the cut-down weed stumps until they start throwing up new shoots, then blast them with a flame gun while they are still small. This is like "hot hoeing" – you need only touch them with the flame, not wait for them to fry. If you repeat each time a new flush of shoots appears, you eventually kill weeds off completely by starving them out. The leaves don't last long enough to do any useful amount of photosynthesis, so the plants use up all the roots' food reserves; the roots eventually become too weak to send up any more shoots. Then they die.

You can achieve the same result by covering vacant ground with old carpet or sheets of black plastic, so that emerging shoots can't reach the light (see pages 155 and 157). That eventually starves

A flame gun is fine for burning annual weeds off gravel drives, but its effect on perennials is temporary. Only frequent burning will eventually kill off these tough blighters.

them out, too. The trouble is that, though entirely organic, both methods take time to work. Persistent perennial weeds may take two years to die out completely. If you don't fancy looking out over a sea of plastic or old carpet for that long, the other alternative is to rake the area fairly level after clearing it, then sow grass seed to make a rough lawn. By cutting it regularly, you'll automatically keep the weeds chopped back, and a year or two of this treatment will work as well as the old carpet method or regular flame-gunning. It also looks better in the meantime.

Hand weeding

When weeds come up between cultivated plants in established gardens, hand weeding is the very best option. In a bed of trees and shrubs, where there's plenty of room between them, then a border fork is the best tool for getting out fair-sized weeds. It's just like a digging fork (see page 40) but about half the size; perfect for winkling out clumps and tussocks and for breaking the soil down to a reasonable tilth afterward.

Between close-spaced perennials, use a hand fork (see page 43). It's easiest if you get down on your hands and knees rather than bending double; that's a quick recipe for a painful back. Around small plants, such as alpines, an even smaller weeding implement is called for. I find an old dinner fork is as good as anything. And for weeding cracks between paving, an old, short-handled kitchen knife with a pointed tip is just right.

Hand weeding, using a trowel or hand fork for stubborn perennials, is effective and pleasurable – provided you don't need to do too much of it!

Hoeing

There are lots of places around the garden where you can save yourself an enormous amount of time by properly using a hoe. It's perfect for clearing weeds from between rows in the vegetable garden, and, if you are careful, you can use it in shrub beds and flower borders – anywhere that there's at least a hoe's-width of space between plants.

The trick with hoeing is to catch weeds early, while they are still seedlings. At that stage, they have very little root, and all you need to do is disturb them by sliding a push hoe (see page 42) through the ground, barely below the surface. As long as the weed seedlings are small and you choose a hot, sunny day, hoeing is a snap, because the dislodged seedlings shrivel away to nothing; you don't even need to gather them up. Hoeing tiny seedlings is also incredibly quick – professional gardeners run around their borders with a hoe once a week, just disturbing the surface of the soil before there are any weed seedlings to see. It completely ruins a germinating weed's chances of growing.

The trouble is that it's very tempting to put the job off. Once weeds are big, you often need a draw or chop hoe to clear them (see page 42, the sort with a flat blade set at right angles to the handle). Hoeing is then more difficult, since you need to hack your way through the expanding foliage. That's not all: big weeds won't shrivel up on their own, so they need raking up and removing. If the weather is dull and damp they'll just take root again, so pick the right day. The other problem is that you can't see what you are doing for the foliage, so it's easy to find you've cut into cultivated plants with the blade. You'll do this only a few times before you learn to be more careful, but if you remember to hoe sooner rather than later, you'll find it fun and incredibly satisfying – believe me.

The chemical alternative

If you are in a hurry and you don't want any hard work, then weedkiller is the answer, as long as you don't mind using chemicals. Choose a product containing glyphosate (sold as Round-up, for example) for this job, since it leaves the ground fit to plant as soon as the weeds are dead. Don't use stronger agricultural weedkillers; they persist for a long time in the soil.

Water the product on to the weeds – not the soil – using a fine nozzle on a watering can. (Keep a special can for weedkiller only.) The treatment works best when weeds are leafy and growing actively, so late spring is ideal. To tackle large, woody weeds, cut them down first and wait for soft new shoots to appear, then treat them. It takes three to four weeks for weeds to start dying – wait a few weeks and re-treat if new growth occurs, so the weeds don't

Paths and paving

If you're not averse to using weedkiller, then use a special path weedkiller to prevent weeds from coming up between paving slabs, or on gravel paths and drives. Use a suitable product in spring; the effects last for the rest of the growing season. Don't use it on areas where you already have large weeds, since you'll have dead stems and leaves to look at for weeks once the stuff has worked. No, get the big ones out first.

In between paving slabs, the best alternative to weedkiller or weeding by hand is to fill the cracks with cement so that nothing can grow up through them. Old mortar between slabs often crumbles, so keep it in good repair to prevent weeds from growing.

have a chance to recover. A couple of applications are usually enough to kill most perennial weeds, except the real problem ones.

Glyphosate kills everything green that it touches, so protect the nearby plants that you want to keep, and, to avoid spray drift, don't use it on windy days. As soon as the weeds are dead, the ground is quite safe to plant. Although lots of people prefer not to use weedkiller, it does have one major advantage. If you have a mammoth crop of nasty weeds to eradicate, using glyphosate to clear the ground as a one-time treatment does give you a head start, and you can always stay chemical-free from then on.

Preventing weeds

You can save yourself a heck of a lot of work by preventing weeds from coming up in the first place, but, before you get too excited by the idea, it's worth saying that you can't use weed-prevention techniques everywhere.

Mulching

The method of weed prevention most people use as part of their normal gardening routine is to mulch beds and borders in spring. Mulching means spreading a 2–3-in (5–8-cm) deep layer of mulch, for example, compost or well-rotted manure (see pages 50–52 for a full list), on any exposed soil. It actually does three jobs in one: it reduces water loss from the soil, smothers seeds, and improves soil. How does it work?

You'll often hear people say that a mulch helps to seal in soil moisture. What actually happens is that soil behaves rather like a wick and draws water up to the surface, where it evaporates. If the ground is mulched, the loose material stops the wicking action, keeping the soil underneath cool and moist, which is very much better for roots in a hot summer.

They say that a mulch smothers weed seeds. Weed seeds need light to germinate, so what actually happens is that the weed seeds on the soil surface are plunged into darkness by the mulch, so they can't come up. But weed before you mulch, since it won't kill existing weeds.

People also talk about the "no-dig" technique (see page 54), and mulching is basically what they mean. Instead of forking well-rotted organic matter into your beds and borders, you spread it on top and allow the worms to drag it down. It's just as effective, but it leaves you much less work to do.

Mulching is blooming marvelous, but it can't work miracles. It needs the right conditions to work well, which is why mulching is normally carried out at the start of the gardening season, just after you've weeded the borders and while the soil is moist. If you mulch

Cocoa-shell mulch

Cocoa-shell is a waste product of chocolate manufacturing, and it looks like lots of small crispy husks; they often still have a marvelous chocolate scent. It's sold as mulching material to spread on gardens, and it's quite popular because it's lightweight, clean, and pleasant to handle, though expensive compared to home-made garden compost. Spread it 1–2in (2.5–5cm) deep; once it is wet, the shells meld together over the soil. Some people find that neither cats nor snails like to cross this mulch, though whether it's due to the odd, slightly sticky texture or the chocolate scent, I couldn't say. Unlike bark chips, which look similar, cocoa shells breaks down quite fast, so you'll need to renew it annually. Don't let dogs eat the dry mixture from the sack – chocolate can be toxic to dogs.

dry soil, the mulch just makes a semi-waterproof layer so that rain can't soak in; it just stays on top and evaporates instead.

Mulching is not completely infallible. If you have perennial weeds in your soil, they'll grow through a mulch – just as ornamental perennials and bulbs will. If any weeds do grow through, pull them out by hand or spot-treat them.

As soon as you start talking about mulching, someone always points out the obvious drawback, which is that wind-blown weed seeds soon arrive on top of an organic mulch and start to grow. This certainly happens, but not for a while, and, in practice, the mulching material is so loose and fluffy that weeds in mulch are very much easier to hoe or pull out than weeds growing in unimproved soil. But because mulching combines so many attributes that are good for the soil, it's well worth doing, even if it's not the ultimate weed-prevention technique.

Long-lasting mulches

In a shrub border where it's practical to plant and leave well alone, a mulch of gravel or bark chips lasts a lot longer than compost or manure. Even these mulches need renewing every other year in spring, because they slowly sink into the soil as a result of worm action. It's still much less effort, though, than replacing mulch every spring, which is what you need to do with compost and manure. The bigger the bits, the longer the mulch lasts. A surface of gravel or bark shows plants off well, too. Use fine stone chips or very coarse sand to mulch a rock garden, and bark chips for woodland or wildlife areas for a look that is in keeping with its surroundings.

Weedproof membranes

You can take mulching one step further by using a weedproof membrane beneath gravel or bark. Black plastic, woven polypropylene, and similar "landscape fabrics" are specially made for this job. They keep weed seeds permanently in the dark, where they can't germinate, and, because the fabrics are tough, the shoots of perennial weeds can't grow through them. They should, however, let water through. If you're using black plastic, make sure it is the preslitted sort designed for the purpose.

The only drawbacks with weed-proof membranes are that because they are permanent, there's no further opportunity for adding organic matter to the soil once they're in place, and, since they're difficult to fit around existing plants, their use is really only practical before you plant a new bed.

Gravel or very coarse sand makes the perfect mulch for alpines and dwarf bulbs, showing them off well and preventing them from being splashed by mud.

Start by preparing the ground thoroughly. Dig and rake it level, then cover the entire bed completely with the fabric, securing the edges with special pins sold for the job. Work out where you want to put your plants, then cut two crosswise slits in the fabric at each place. Peel back the edges so you can dig the hole and put the plant in, then tuck the corners back around the stem. When the entire bed has been planted, hide the membrane with an even 1-in (2.5-cm) layer of gravel or bark chips.

Synthetic mulches (weedproof membranes) are fine to use where you are growing trees, shrubs, or roses, but perennials and bulbs obviously can't grow through them. It's also no good using an anti-weed membrane where you want to grow annuals. You would need to cut so many planting holes that the weeds would have no trouble getting in to ruin the effect.

Even though it takes time to set up, in large borders of trees, shrubs, or roses, this technique can save hours of work in the years to come. My only reservation is that, where the membrane is allowed to show through the mulch, it looks vile. Personally, I'd rather take time ridding the soil of perennial weeds and then placing my mulch – be it gravel or bark – directly on to the soil. But that's just me.

You can also lay weedproof membrane beneath a bark or gravel path to prevent weeds from growing through, as an alternative to using path weedkiller. You won't eliminate weeds entirely, since some will grow on tiny specks of mud that fall off your boots and vanish between the path material. I avoid using membranes on sloping paths, since both bark and gravel are easily washed downhill in wet weather to end up in a pile by your back door... and I speak from bitter experience. No, it's far better to lay your bark or gravel right bare soil in that situation, since it seems to grip better.

Mulch options

Mulch type	Advantages	Disadvantages
Bark	Long lasting, good looking, and effective, especially in a shady or woodland setting	Nseed an occasional refill because it sinks into the soil; rots down in time
Gravel	Long lasting, effective, and shows plants off well	May need an occasional refill, because it sinks into the soil
Cocoa shell	Lightweight, clean, and easy to handle (and smells wonderful)	Can be expensive and needs renewing annually, because it breaks down quickly
Compost/manure	Very good for soil conditioning and homemade, so very cheap	Needs annual replacement and can be smelly
Membrane	Very effective and permanent	Hard work to install and can look ugly when exposed. Not practical on slopes or for use with flowers

Rootproof barriers

Think of a weedproof membrane standing up on edge – that's a rootproof barrier. A rootproof barrier is the answer if the roots of the huge tree next door come up in your yard and take all the water, or if there is an adjacent privet hedge with the appetite of an elephant. It's also effective as a barrier to next door's pernicious weeds that spread under your fence. Dig a trench 12in (30cm) or more deep along the base of your fence, or wherever you need it, then bury an upright layer of something that roots can't grow through. The very best material is a moistureproof membrane – a tough, chemically treated material that you can buy from builders' supply stores, but I've also known people use heavy duty plastic or even old bits of corrugated iron. In our first garden, which was very small and narrow, we had a privet hedge running down one side, the bottom of which was full of goutweed. I cut alongside the hedge with a spade, severing both the privet and goutweed roots, then inserted old roofing slates to act as a vertical barrier. It worked extremely well, and they are probably still there! Otherwise, use the usual weedproof membrane.

Another good use for rootproof barriers is to contain an outbreak of nasty perennial weeds while you treat it, or to protect the garden from invading nasties when there's wasteland next door, or wandering bootlaces of honey fungus (see page 221), where this is a problem. I'm all for good-neighborliness, but there are limits.

6 GARDEN MAINTENANCE

Garden routines

Gardening can be enormously creative – utilizing every ounce of your artistic talents in terms of landscape design and planting plans. But, as anyone who's ever pulled on a raincoat knows, there's a deal of day-to-day upkeep to consider too.

Now I know that sounds dull, but once you know what you're doing and why, it needn't be dull at all. It can be enormously rewarding. Routine jobs, such as weeding and watering, keep you close to the plants, the soil, and all the other living things, helping you get to know them better. Soon, you develop a bond that makes the garden feel like part of the family. It's a bit like having a dog. After all the early excitement of buying a puppy, it's the everyday grooming, nurturing, and spending time together that makes the relationship grow.

Gardening essentials

When you head out into the garden, it's a good idea to take along a few essentials. That way, when you spot a job that needs doing, you'll have some equipment on hand, and it will save you a trek back to the shed. My essentials are the following:

• Hand trowel (see page 43)
• Hand fork (see page 43)
• Pruners (see page 44)
• Sharp knife
• String, plant ties, or garden wire
• Blank plant labels and a pencil
• Gloves
• Basket or garden cart to put all these in, which can also be used to carry weeds and other refuse away

Learning the language

Just when you thought you understood plain English, along comes gardening with it's specialist vocabulary giving everyday words a totally new meaning.

It isn't done to confuse – quite the reverse. If you know the right technical term, you often save a couple of sentences of explanation, and not just in conversation. In print and on TV, people often use gardening shorthand for speed. There's no need to learn really specialized technical terms, but the well-used ones are worth knowing.

Bolting

A term usually applied to vegetable crops that have run to seed prematurely. It commonly happens to spinach, lettuces, and celery, if they are left too long in the ground once they are ready to eat, or if they experience a check in growth due to dryness at the roots or extreme temperatures.

Check

A sudden slowdown in growth, usually due to cold or hot, dry weather, lack of food or water, or serious attacks of pests or diseases.

Compost

When British people say "compost," there's often a bit of confusion as to exactly what they mean. There's the sort you make in a compost pile (see pages 204–7), and there are composts that are used as growing media – seed or potting composts. It's a little clearer here in the USA, where we call growing media "soil mixes" or "potting mixes" and the like.

Soil-based mixes are formulated with loamy soil as the main ingredient. Soil acts as a buffer that holds nutrients, so you won't need to start fertilizing plants growing in a soil-based mix until about three months after potting. They may be purchased, or they can be made at home if you have the ingredients and the room. A standard recipe for a soil-based mix consists of sterilized soil (7 parts by bulk), peat (3 parts), and sharp sand (2 parts) with a general balanced fertilizer and a little lime added. Variations on the basic theme contain increasing amounts of fertilizer and are used for potting small, medium, or large plants (or short-, medium- or long-term plants). Another is made without lime, the so called "ericaceous mix" for lime-hating plants. A standard sowing and rooting medium is similar (2 parts soil: 1 part peat: 1 part sand), but with less fertilizer, and is used for seeds and cuttings.

Soilless mixes are seed and potting mixes based on peat, coir (coconut waste), or composted bark in place of soil. They include multipurpose mixes (many are available commercially) that can be used for seeds and cuttings and for potting. Soilless mixes weigh less than soil-based ones, but they tend to continue decomposing once in pots, so the texture gets progressively finer and muckier, and thus it does not last as long. Due to their reduced nutrient-holding capacity, you'll need to start fertilizing after four weeks in the case of a seed medium and six weeks in the case of potting. If allowed to dry out, a soilless mix shrinks and is very difficult to rewet, so it's best kept evenly moist at all times.

Lettuce often bolts (runs to seed) if it is left too long before picking, or if it must endure extreme temperature conditions – whether heat or cold.

Compost (sometimes called garden compost) is made in a compost pile. It is the product of the controlled decomposition of vegetable matter (garden rubbish or uncooked kitchen waste) in a compost pile or bin (see pages 51 and 204–7). It's for digging into the soil or mulching the ground, not for potting plants.

Deadheading
Removing dead flowers (see pages 182–83). It's done for several reasons: to prevent fungal diseases, which often grow on dead plant material; to neaten the plant's appearance; or to encourage development of new flower buds by preventing the plant from expending energy on setting seed, thus extending the flowering season (see page 73).

Dieback
The death of a shoot, due to damage or disease that works its way back from the shoot tip and down the stem.

Germination
The process whereby a seed develops into a young seedling given suitable moisture, air, and temperature (see pages 60–63 and 68).

Hardening off
Acclimatizing a plant gradually to cooler, more natural, conditions. It's mostly done with bedding plants to help them adjust from warm conditions in a propagator or greenhouse before being planted out in the garden. They are moved to a cold frame or stood outside on fine days and brought inside at night for one to three weeks before the date of the last expected frost.

Know your poisons

Fungicide: A chemical product for killing, or at least slowing down, the spread of fungal organisms responsible for causing plant diseases.

Herbicide: A chemical product designed to kill weeds; a weedkiller.

Insecticide: A chemical product designed to kill insect pests.

A cold frame (an unheated, glazed structure) is ideal for hardening off greenhouse-raised plants, getting them used to lower temperatures before they are planted outdoors.

Pinching out

Removing the growing tip of sideshoots to encourage secondary branching. Also known as pinch pruning or finger pruning (see pages 180–81).

Potting

Putting a plant into a pot. Potting *up* refers to the first time a seedling or rooted cutting is potted; potting *on*, or repotting, is when a plant is transferred from an existing pot to a larger one.

Pricking out

Transplanting young, newly germinated seedlings to a wider spacing in seed trays of mix using a small, pointed stick called a dibber (see page 65), your finger, a spoon, or similar tool.

Pruning

Cutting off selected parts of a plant in order to encourage more fruit, flowers, or stems; remove dead, damaged, or diseased material in the interests of plant health; or to develop a particular shape or restrict the size (see pages 179–92).

Setting

Seeds or fruit are said to have "set" after the flower has been successfully fertilized, the petals have fallen, and a baby seedpod or fruit can be seen to start swelling.

Standard

A plant trained with a single, straight, branch-free stem or trunk, and a rounded or spreading "head" of branches at the top (see page 184).

Stopping

Removing the growing tip of a plant to encourage the development of sideshoots (see page 181, see also pruning and pinching out above).

Top-dressing

This can mean several things: an alternative to repotting by scraping away the top 1in (2.5cm) or so of old potting mix and replacing it with fresh mixture; the application of organic matter as a mulch or fertilizer (as a top-dressing) to the surface of the soil around a plant or to lawns (see pages 50–53 and 248); the application of a mulch of stones, grit, or very coarse sand to the soil surface, for decoration, or to reduce evaporation of moisture from the surface.

Training

Making a plant grow into a particular shape by pinching out, pruning, and/or tying in its stems to a supporting framework (see page 184).

A standard fuchsia, grown as a tall, single stem, topped by a head of branches, leaves, and flowers.

Organic gardening

To a chemist, organic compounds are those that contain carbon; they are found in, or derived from, living organisms – things like coal and oil, for instance. The term "organic" has a slightly different meaning for gardeners, though the link with living things is still there.

Organic gardening is all about gardening in as environmentally friendly a way as possible, which means using naturally occurring materials rather than manufactured ones. It usually means using alternative (more thoughtful) techniques, or doing a job by hand, instead of using synthetic fertilizers, chemical weedkillers, and strong pesticides.

Some people take organic gardening very seriously, and it's easy to get bogged down in the arguments about precisely what is and isn't acceptable. Real enthusiasts follow the guidelines of the some of the organic gardening gurus and institutions, whose books and magazins you can find in bookstores, and also online.

It's quite possible to have a decent harvest of fruits, vegetables, and flowers without resorting to chemical sprays and potions.

For most of us, it's enough to banish artificial fertilizers, chemical pesticides, and weedkillers from our gardens. At Barleywood, I reckon to be about 99 percent organic – my one weakness is glyphosate-based weedkiller that I use once only to bring rough ground under cultivation. Glyphosate is inactivated on contact with soil and is nonpersistent; as soon as the weeds have died away, I can perform all subsequent cultivations organically without fear of harmful residues. I like to think of my approach as common-sense organic gardening. For me, organic gardening is not the denial of science and a return to muck and magic; it is the utilization of our knowledge of biology and chemistry in a responsible, forward-looking way.

Organic products

Organic gardening hasn't changed much from the way our grandfathers gardened years ago, in some respects. They relied on manure or compost to improve the soil, and on fertilizers, such as dried blood or bonemeal, based on animal remains. Strong plants growing in healthy soil have a natural ability to withstand minor problems, but, if needed, our forbears used natural products, such as soft soap, pyrethrum, or rotenone, to tackle most common pests (see pages 224–25), and sulfur and copper compounds, such as Bordeaux mixture (see page 224), to treat fungal diseases.

These products and their modern alternatives (which are often specific in their action and less persistent in the environment) are now widely available in garden centers, although since the "mad cow" scare began, many people prefer not to use animal-based fertilizers. Poultry-manure pellets are a good alternative, but

Making your own plant food

If you like to do-it-yourself, you can make your own liquid fertilizer by dunking a sack of manure into a water tank for a few weeks. Draw off the manure tea and dilute to about 1:5 with water; use it on your vegetable patch, or for anything around the garden in need of a quick boost. There's an even "greener" alternative. Fill a tub with nettles or comfrey leaves, top it up with water and cover it with a lid, and a few weeks later you have a (rather smelly) brew ready to use. Dilute it in the same way as manure tea. The nettle version makes a high-nitrogen liquid fertilizer that is good for vegetables and salads, while the comfrey extract is a high-potassium fertilizer that's especially good for tomatoes.

"vegetarian" general-purpose fertilizers are available from specialized suppliers. Nowadays, a huge selection of organic supplies is available through mail order catalogs if your local garden center doesn't stock them.

Me? I've settled on a system that allows a steady buildup of natural predators and which makes sure that there is no concentration of any one plant in any one place, so epidemics are less likely. I never spray with pesticides – organic or inorganic – and I have learned to live with the odd nibbled leaf and blemished apple. A garden that teems with all forms of wildlife seems to me preferable to one that is perfect but sterile.

Alternatives to peat

Although peat is a natural material, its extraction damages the natural habitat of a lot of specialized wildlife. Use a substitute wherever you can. Don't dig peat into the ground, use well-rotted manure or make compost instead; both are far more effective at improving soil, and compost doesn't cost a penny. Use soil-based seed and potting mixes wherever you can (see page 161); it's true that they contain a small proportion of peat, but that's a lot less than a peat-based mix.

Soilless mixes based on coir contain no peat at all – but against that you need to balance the environmental cost of transporting coconut waste halfway around the world using fossil fuels. I can't get on with them – too many are dusty, and some produce plants that look distinctly unhappy.

Other types of soilless mixes made from renewable resources are coming on the market all the time and are steadily improving (see page 161), so see what's available and be prepared to adapt your growing technique to suit different materials. Those based on composted bark are among the most promising, but even these don't suit some seeds and seedlings. Carry out your own tests and see what works for you… that's exactly what I'm doing.

Organic techniques

You may think organic gardening is hard work, if you need to pick off pests and weed by hand or hoe and you can't use weedkillers or pesticides (but see pages 224–25). But so great is the gardening public's interest in cutting out chemicals, all sorts of techniques and gadgets have been designed to help.

Natural predators

In the natural scheme of things, nearly all pests have natural predators. Ladybugs and their larvae, for example, feed on aphids.

Mealybugs, spider mites, and scale insects all have natural predators, and several wasps are parasitic on the caterpillars of damaging butterflies. But nearly all pesticides are indiscriminate – they kill predators as well as pests. Give up chemicals and, to attract beneficial insects, grow old-fashioned hardy annuals that are naturally rich in nectar; poached-egg plant (*Limnanthes douglasii*) and *Phacelia campanularia* are especially good for encouraging hoverflies (the adults and larvae consume aphids) and they look lovely, too. (See also Biological controls, pages 226–27; Beneficial insects, pages 230–31.)

Fly screens

Drape crop-protection mesh over carrots and members of the cabbage family from planting time onward to exclude bugs, such as carrot rust fly or cabbage white butterfly.

Fleece

Cover early vegetables with woven horticultural fleece (also known as row cover) to protect them from wind, cold weather, and flying pests, such as insects. Remember to remove it to allow access for pollinating insects when the first flowers appear on plants such as dwarf beans and zucchini. Don't leave fleece over plants in hot weather, when they need a good air circulation.

Horticultural fleece can provide valuable protection for early vegetables.

Small-flowered *Tagetes* (marigolds) planted among tomatoes will often keep whitefly at bay.

Unwanted compact discs strung on fishing line among lettuces, cabbages, and other vegetables can help deter birds – it's the reflection, not the music, that does it.

Companion planting

It's claimed that planting small-flowered marigolds (*Tagetes*) between your tomatoes, garlic beneath your roses, and nasturtiums (*Tropaeolum majus*) around fruit trees and in the vegetable garden will ward off pests. It may be that companion plants emit deterrent chemicals, or it may be that they attract lots of predatory insects, but it works for some, so it's worth a try. Complete charts of companion plants are available from organic suppliers.

Barriers and traps

Create an impassable ring around tree trunks, the rims of pots, and the legs of greenhouse staging (the shelves for the plants), by applying a layer of crop-protection "glue" or grease bands to prevent the passage of caterpillars and harmful creeping insects. Use upturned half grapefruit skins or beer traps for slugs and snails, and pheromone (synthetic sex-hormone) traps for fruit moths to avoid maggoty apples and plums. Hang yellow sticky traps in the greenhouse to snare flying pests, such as whitefly and thrips. Protect soft fruit from birds by using a web of cellulose threads that won't entangle them and which biodegrades at the end of the season – it's much kinder than netting.

Scarers

Humming line, strings of old cans, and strips of foil help frighten off birds; old CDs suspended from fishing twine so that they glint in the light also have a deterrent effect. Electronic devices that emit a high-pitched sound are often effective at keeping other people's cats out of the garden, if the sensors are correctly set to patrol the fence. Transparent plastic bottles filled with water and stood in beds and borders are also said to be good at repelling cats. It may be their own distorted reflections that scare them off.

Watering plants

An outdoor tap is essential for serious gardeners, because if there's one job that needs doing regularly, it's watering – especially in summer. Young and shallow-rooted plants are the top priorities, so plants in containers, the vegetable patch, annuals, and any newly planted beds are the ones to watch. Even during quite long dry spells, you can leave well-established trees, shrubs, and lawns to take care of themselves.

Do they need watering?

Novice gardeners can find it confusing trying to establish when their plants are in need of water, and there is no one answer. Use your senses and try any of the following – you'll soon build up experience (see also pages 169–70 and 221–22):

Look at the color of the soil mix. Your plants need watering if the soil mix is quite pale. In containers you can see if the mix has shrunk away from the sides of the pot, or the plants are droopy and wilting those are two major signs that they need water.

Touch the soil. It should feel like a wet cloth, moist but not soggy. If it's not, water the plants.

Listen for a hollow, empty sound when you gently knock on the side of a clay po; if you hear that, then the pot needs water.

Hand watering

Hand watering is best, because when you are going around with the hose or watering can, you can take a good look at everything you pass and nip problems, such as pests or diseases, in the bud.

With containers, don't wait until plants wilt before watering. Check them regularly; you can tell those that need watering by the color of the soil mix – it's paler when it's dry – but, if you want to be certain, poke it gently with your finger and it will *feel* dry. How dry is dry? Well, think of a freshly wrung-out washcloth. If the soil feels like that, it's damp enough and does not need watering. Whether you use a slow-running hose or a watering can, the art of watering containers is to soak the soil mix *thoroughly* and then wait until it *just* starts to dry out before doing it again.

For those who aren't sure, or who just like gadgets, you can get a water meter with a probe that you stick in the soil to give

Using a hose to water newly planted border plants and shrubs ensures that the water goes exactly where it is needed. Always apply enough to soak right into the soil.

Where water runs off too easily and you need to get it down to the roots of a plant, cut the bottom off an empty plastic beverage bottle, remove the cap, and sink the bottle into the ground alongside the plant to act as a funnel.

you an accurate reading. But if you want to be a proper gardener, throw it away; watering is a skill you need to learn. If you use clay pots, the old-fashioned way of tapping them with a bit of broom handle works well – a damp pot makes a dull clonk; a dry one a clear ringing tone. When potting, always remember to leave sufficient space between the surface of the soil mix and the pot rim to allow for watering – the larger the container, the deeper the gap. Allow ½in (1cm) of space in 3–5in (7.5–12cm) diameter pots; 1in (2.5cm) for pots 6–10in (15–25cm) in diameter, and 2in (5cm) for larger containers.

In open ground, the surface of the soil may look dry, but this is due to evaporation. Soil acts like a wick, drawing up moisture from deeper down, so you don't need to water until there is a danger of roots drying out. That's why shallow-rooted plants, like rhododendrons and bedding plants, need watering long before you need to bother with mature trees or shrubs. You'll now realize the value of a moisture-retentive mulch to shallow-rooted plants.

Watering little and often is actually counterproductive; a layer of dry soil acts as a "dust mulch" that prevents surface evaporation. If you just dampen the surface, the wick starts working again, and more water is lost from the soil. If you *are* going to water plants growing in the open ground, give them a really good soaking, and don't do it again until they really need it. And if you funnel water precisely to where it's wanted – say, by sinking an upturned, bottomless plastic bottle alongside the rootball of a newly planted shrub – you'll do much more good than if you sprinkle water about indiscriminately.

Irrigation systems

The time may come when you end up with more watering than you can do by hand, and that's when you find yourself irresistibly drawn to the idea of an irrigation system. There are many types, but if your water is metered and you pay for every drop, it's worth choosing an efficient system that delivers water precisely where you want it.

Sprinklers are not very efficient; they shower water over a wide area, and much of it misses the target altogether. Originally designed for lawns – on which fewer people waste water nowadays – those with a circular spray pattern are especially wasteful; the watered circles rarely overlap, resulting in both over- and underwatered areas. If you must use a sprinkler, choose the oscillating type that swings from side to side to give a rectangular spray pattern and the most even distribution.

Perforated pipe is plastic tubing with stitches or tiny holes all the way along, through which water slowly leaks out. This is the sort of irrigation system to use in between rows of vegetables, since it's easily lifted when you want to run a hoe through the soil. The water spreads out to between 1½–2½ft (45–75cm) on either side of the tubing, depending on soil type. Leaky hose can also be snaked between newly planted annuals and is easily cleared away once they are established.

Sprinklers are not the most efficient means of applying water, but the oscillating type, which moves back and forth over an area of ground, is far better than the circulating kind.

Hanging baskets really benefit from a drip irrigation system which can be turned on once or twice a day in summer.

Drip irrigation is the most sophisticated system, since it waters each plant or container individually. You can put the bits together yourself to suit any garden layout. It's also great in the greenhouse. The idea is to have a drip nozzle in every pot, maybe two or more for big containers or grow bags. Both this and perforated pipe can be used permanently out of doors to water beds and borders. Run the tubing between plants, then bury the lot under a blanket of bark or gravel mulch.

When to water

In hot weather, it's best to water in the evening so that plants have longer to drink before the heat of the sun makes surface water evaporate. In cold or dull weather, water in the morning, so that plants can dry out before nighttime. This is especially important in the greenhouse in spring and autumn when damp plants are more at risk of fungal infections.

Should you water at midday? Yes, if you see that a plant is obviously wilting – leave it until evening and it may be too late. The old wives' tale that plants scorch if you water them in sunshine is true only of some hairy-leaved plants that hate being splashed whatever the time of day. Just water them carefully and avoid wetting the foliage, whenever you water them.

Timers are the last word if you want to automate an irrigation system. These gadgets can be fitted to your outdoor tap before connecting it to the hose at the start of your irrigation system. You set the timer to switch on for a defined period of time each day, and you can even specify the time of day; it can be a real life saver when you are on vacation.

Fertilizing plants

We enjoy three square meals a day, but plants prefer to "graze." Little and often is what they like best. They don't take in food in solid form; the fine root hairs take in nutrients that are dissolved in water held in the soil.

Stored nutrition

When plants are growing in the open ground, finding their own "food" is no problem; their roots spread a long way in search of the nutrients they need. On well-prepared soils, you can easily get away with fertilizing beds and borders just once or twice a year to renew supplies. Nutrients that aren't used right away are held by clay particles and humus (the residue of decayed organic matter), so it figures that the more clay and humus there is in the soil, the more nutrients it can hold. That's why clay and loam soils are so fertile (see pages 90–92). On soils with little clay or humus (as on unimproved sandy soils), excess fertilizer washes right through the soil with the rain.

A well-fertilized border soon fills out so that no soil is visible, and plants seem to bristle with health.

Well-manured soil, which contains plenty of organic matter, is far more efficient at holding on to nutrients than poor, thin soil.

Solid fertilizers

On outdoor beds and borders, solid fertilizer – the powdered or granular kind – is usually used (see page 52). It's cheap, easy to spread, and, because it shows up against the soil, you can see where you've put it. The idea is to sprinkle solid fertilizer thinly over the soil and hoe or fork it in lightly, so that it mixes evenly into the soil instead of just sitting on top. But before plants can take it up, the fertilizer needs to dissolve and percolate through the soil to root depth, so clearly the ground must be moist. If it's not, either give it a good watering first or wait until the ground is damp.

The best time to fertilize beds and borders with solid fertilizer is in early spring, just before plants start growing. A second dose in early or midsummer will replenish nutrients for the benefit of greedy plants, like clematis and roses, which need a lot of input to keep up their output.

It's a bad idea to fertilize in late summer; the last thing you want to do is to encourage a lot of lush, late growth that will be well and truly clobbered by frost. And there's no point at all in fertilizing in winter; plants aren't growing then, so they can't use it. Bonemeal was traditionally used when trees and shrubs were planted in winter because, being coarse and organic, it took so long to break down that nutrients became available only when plants were ready for them in spring. Nowadays, we know that most of the phosphates bonemeal contains are locked up by the soil anyway. There is more benefit to be obtained by working in well-rotted manure or compost at planting time; it improves soil structure and so coaxes out roots more effectively (see pages 49–55).

Liquid and soluble fertilizers

Containers call for a completely different technique in fertilizing. You wouldn't feed a baby a steak, so it's no good expecting a plant in a pot to take kindly to great lumps of solid fertilizer. It needs liquid fertilizer. That way, the nutrients are already properly dissolved and, by diluting the fertilizer in the right amount of water, you'll be applying a "nutrient soup" at just the right concentration.

If you do use solid fertilizers for plants in containers, remember that the roots are in a restricted volume of soil mix, so there's only so much they can cope with at once. It's difficult to gauge the right dose of a concentrated fertilizer – overdo it, and you end up with a strong salts solution around the roots that actually sucks water out of the plant instead of letting it in (a process called reverse osmosis, if you want to be scientific). An overdose can also damage the root hairs, preventing plants from taking up water. In both cases, plants literally die of thirst. Liquid fertilizers are definitely the answer. That way you know what you are getting and how much to use..

Very little and very often is the right way to use liquid fertilizers. Commercial growers often apply at quarter-strength each time they water; it's done automatically through an irrigation system. At home, that's not practical, so aim to liquid fertilize plants in pots once a week or whatever it says on the back of the pacakge. Give each pot as much of the diluted fertilizer as you'd use if you were watering normally, then you'll automatically be using the right amount. Plants in pots need liquid fertilizing all the time they are growing, from spring to late summer. Plants that are growing all year (such as indoor plants in warm rooms) can use the occasional fertilizing even in winter, though they don't need fertilizer as much, or as often, as in spring and summer. High-nitrogen fertilizers are best for leafy plants, and high-potassium ones – usually sold as tomato fertilizer – are good for anything that flowers or fruits. Just dilute them more for pot plants than for tomatoes.

Slow-release fertilizers

If you tend to forget about liquid fertilizing, then use slow-release fertilizer sticks or granules instead. They work by "leaking" nutrients very gradually; some of the more sophisticated kinds "leak" only when growing conditions are warm and moist, which is when plants need fertilizing most.

Add slow-release fertilizer granules to the soil when you are potting plants in spring, or add it to new mix if you are top-dressing established plants in pots. Otherwise, just poke in fertilizer sticks around the side of your containers in spring, or a few weeks after potting. And read the instructions – the bigger the container, the more fertilizer sticks you need to achieve the right dose.

Running on empty

If you've used slow-release feertilizers in your pots, don't assume they keep working all the while you can see the granules – old ones don't disappear once they are "empty." Make a point of reminding yourself when they'll need replacing. For indoor plants, use the sort that lasts three months or more, and make note of when it's time to add some more.

Fertilizer sticks can be used in hanging baskets and other plant containers, if you have no time for regular fertilizing.

Supporting plants

Most plants can stand up for themselves, but there are some that need a bit of help. They fall into two categories; climbers, which obviously need something to climb up, and floppy plants that just need a crutch in life.

Trellising

A trellis is ideal for supporting plants, such as clematis and honeysuckle, that grow naturally through trees; the close-spaced lattice is the next best thing to twiggy branches. It's good for supporting climbers on walls or fences. You can attach a trellis to horizontal slats screwed to a wall or fence, and fit it with hinges and hooks; then you can lay the trellis and its plant down on the ground if you need to do any painting or maintenance. Slats can act as spacers between the trellis and wall, allowing air circulation and space for plants to grow through.

Structures

Arches, pergolas, pillars, and gazebos are particularly spectacular ways of supporting climbers. If you choose plants that don't cling naturally, you'll need to tie them into the structure. Large structures, such as gazebos, are best built with trellis panels for the sides – you can get arches of the same type of construction – so that climbers can really spread themselves out.

Bamboo stakes

Stakes are ideal for tall, straight-stemmed plants, like delphiniums, or for training plants to *be* straight, as you would for cordon-trained sweet peas – the ones grown for exhibition-quality blooms. Tie stems in at about 8-in (20-cm) intervals with soft garden twine to avoid bruising. Think of a stake as a splint, but one that's used to prevent breaks rather than mend them. Split stakes, which are often about 1½ft (45cm) long and dyed green, are a lightweight alternative to full-sized stakes for supporting smaller plants in pots.

Other stakes

Use sturdier stakes (usually wood or plastic) to hold up heavy-headed plants, such as dahlias. Knock four or five stakes into the ground all around the plant, then tie soft twine between them to make a vertical cradle. It keeps loose-growing or top-heavy clumps upright, instead of allowing them to splay open. Use heavy-duty stakes for trees that need long-term support, or use short stakes at 45 degrees for others needing only temporary help (see page 79).

Against a wall, a trellis provides a practical, yet decorative, support for climbers and wall plants whose stems can be tied in as they extend.

Pea sticks

An informal means of supporting scramblers, like peas, or perennials that are only slightly floppy. Just push a few twiggy shrub stems, or woody prunings, around the clumps before they reach 1ft (30cm) high. Gauge the length of your sticks by the ultimate height of your flowers, and cut the sticks about 6in (15cm) shorter, so that they will be hidden by foliage.

Plant frames

Frames are intended for seriously floppy, bushy perennials. One type looks like a short metal stool with a wire-weave seat; it is placed over a perennial plant while it's still very small so that the stems grow through the wire-weave as they elongate. Another type – looking rather like a partially straightened wire coat hanger – has legs that you push in all around a plant; the right-angled top pieces link the individual units together. Another alternative is the wigwam type (see below). In all cases, you need to choose frames that are a good 6in (15cm) lower than the top of the main dome of foliage when fully grown, so that the support system will be hidden by flowering time.

Woven willow wigwams are great for sweet peas, but renew them annually – they become brittle after a single season.

How to... **put up wires**

Wires fastened to a fence or wall are the traditional way of supporting wall shrubs and climbing roses, both of which have a fairly rigid framework of stems. Wires are also good for really vigorous twiners, such as wisteria, that can wind around them as they grow. By using vine eyes, which have a long "stem," the wires are held a little distance away from the wall, giving twiners room to wind themselves around the vine-eye stems and let a bit of air circulate. Wall shrubs need to have their stems trained out along the wires and secured at intervals with plant ties.

1 Your aim is to attach wires in horizontal rows about 18in (45cm) apart to fill the area to be covered with plants, with the lowest wire 1ft (30cm) above ground. So, mark the wall with a soft pencil at the points where you want each wire to start and finish. Position these points in the mortar between the bricks, rather than on the bricks themselves, since it is softer to drill into. Now drill your holes.

2 Insert wall anchors into the holes, and screw a vine eye into each. Line up the hoops of the eyes so they all face left to right and not up and down. Then secure a length of fairly heavy-gauge wire to the first vine eye and stretch it across to the second, pulling the wire as tight as you can and winding the end around the vine eye to keep it taut. Secure a length of wire between each pair of vine eyes to give you several horizonal wires covering your growing area.

3 Once all your wires are in place, gently tie in the stems of your plant. Use lengths of garden string or plant ties taking the string around the wire and crossing it over before securing it firmly with a knot around the plant. This figure-eight knot needs to be tight enough to support the plant and prevent it from moving and rubbing, while at the same time not strangling it by being tied too tightly.

Pruning

If there's one thing gardeners really get their knickers in a twist about, it's pruning, but when you start breaking it down, it's not half as complicated as people make it out to be. There are lots of plants that never need pruning at all, or only rarely, so it's always a good idea to stop and ask yourself why you think you need to prune.

Woody plants with a branching structure, like shrubs, roses, and fruit trees, are the ones that are most likely to need pruning. You might want to encourage a wall-trained plant to keep its shape, or prevent shrubs from becoming too big and unruly, or maybe you want roses and apple trees to produce more flowers and fruit. You will need to prune, too, to remove dead, damaged, or diseased tissue.

On some shrubs pruning can be dramatic, as with this dogwood (*Cornus*), which is being hard pruned so that it produces plenty of new stems.

Fine topiary pruning, as with this spiral of boxwood, is best done with a pair of sheep shears sold especially for the job.

Trees shouldn't take much keeping in shape. When you buy them from a nursery, the initial shaping should have already have been done, so little pruning will be needed subsequently. If you have older trees that cast too much shade, you can cut off the bottom branches to lift the crown, or thin out the top, but big jobs are best left to an arborist.

A lot of minor pruning jobs are things you probably do every day in the summer without even realizing it. When you are forming the shape of young plants that you've raised from seed or cuttings, or when you are deadheading flowers, or even clipping your hedge, you're still pruning.

Finger pruning

Finger pruning, as the name suggests, is the sort that you do with your fingers, so you can really do it only on soft young growth. It's mostly carried out on young plants to make them branch and form a good, bushy shape. You'll sometimes meet avid gardeners who let the nails on their thumb and forefinger grow longer specially to use as "nippers," but most people seem to manage without such refinements. Fingernails generally do a much better job than the tips of scissors, which can't get in as close to remove small sideshoots – the alternative is to rub them out with the side of a finger.

Stopping

Some plants have stems that want to grow straight up, and, if you want them to be bushy, you'll need to "stop" them. Think of the old-fashioned store-window sort of pelargonium: one long, bare stem with a handful of leaves and a flower at the top. Now, if only that had been stopped when it was 2–3in (5–7.5cm) high, it would have branched from the base, giving it a better shape that would have been packed with leaves and flowers.

Under normal circumstances, plants whose stems display what botanists call "apical dominance," have natural hormones that encourage the bud at the stem tip to keep growing, so that the stem elongates. At the same time, the hormones flow back down the stem to inhibit the development of dormant buds (at leaf joints lower down) into shoots.

When you stop a plant, by nipping out the very tip at the end of the stem, you automatically deflect the growth hormones to the next buds down, which are then triggered into growth and they develop into sideshoots. It's all part of the natural system for making sure that a damaged plant survives and goes on to flower. All we are doing is harnessing it to our own ends.

People often ask when's the best time to stop plants. I always stop rooted cuttings when I pot them up; that way, I can catch them at just the right size to encourage branching right from the base. Some plants, such as fuchsias, need a second stopping. This encourages the first set of sideshoots to "break" again and form a second set of sideshoots; so you can see how this helps to form a nice, bushy, well-branched plant.

Pinching out

Pinching out is exactly the same idea – you nip out the growing tip of the shoot – but here, the aim is more to maintain the shape of an older plant. If you had a lovely symmetrical fuchsia, with one long shoot heading out sideways beyond the rest, you'd pinch the tip out to make it branch at that point, so the plant would just thicken out instead of growing lopsided.

Or you might also want to pinch out the tip of a shoot that has been damaged by pests or disease, or perhaps killed by a late frost. It's dead easy to get rid of aphids clustering around the tip of a stem by pinching out the affected part, pests and all. By removing the damaged part, you help the plant's own hormones ensure that a new shoot replaces the old one as soon as possible.

You'll often see avid gardeners pinching out shoots here and there as they walk around their garden. It's not to be confused with pinching cuttings: that's usually called stealing, which is something quite different.

Allow a young penstemon cutting to grow and it forms a long, single shoot, but cut out that shoot fairly low down (*top*), and the plant will become bushy (*bottom*).

Deadheading

The idea of deadheading is to prevent plants from setting seed. But they will keep trying and, to this end, will produce another crop of flowers in the process. Call it cheating if you like, but I prefer to think of it as improving on nature or, at least, persuading her to be even more generous.

Some people deadhead sooner than others. The very neat like to get rid of deadheads when the flowers are barely faded, but others wait until they actually go brown. Regular deadheading is a good habit to get into. In summer, go over your containers once a week and take off any bloom that is fading. If you are disciplined about it, and keep deadheading from the time the first flush of flowers goes over in early summer until the time the plants stop producing new growth in early autumn, you can keep bedding and patio plants, and modern roses, flowering pretty well flat out for five or six months. It may seem fussy, but it pays dividends.

The question often asked by beginners is, "How exactly do you deadhead?" Avid gardeners take it so much for granted that it's just one of those things that is seldom explained properly. The answer is, it all depends on the kind of dead flower you are dealing with.

Flowers like lupines will produce a second flush of bloom if their flower spikes are snipped off as soon as they fade.

Deadheading techniques:

1 Faded pelargonium flowers should be removed by snapping off the entire stalk.

2 With fuchsias it is sufficient to remove individual faded flowers.

3 When an entire clustered head of roses has faded, the stem can be cut back 6–9in (15–23cm), but before then the faded blooms can be snipped off individually.

4 With bulbs, like daffodils, simply pinch off faded flowers to allow the food produced by the stalk to be transported back into the bulb.

One head of flowers (1) on the end of a longish stalk, as in pelargoniums. Remove the dead flower plus stalk. Snap it off cleanly at the point it grows out from the main stem of the plant.

Lots of short-stalked flowers (2), as in fuchsias and petunias. Nip the deadheads off with your fingers just behind the flower.

Roses (3): when it comes to roses, deadheading is like light pruning; use pruners to remove 6–9in (15–23cm) of stem along with the dead flower or cluster of flowers. Cut just above an outward-facing leaf joint. If you see a new shoot emerging lower down the stem, make your cut just above that; the next flower will appear a lot faster. If only one flower in a cluster has faded, it can be removed individually.

Bulbs (4): pull the deadhead off leaving the stalk behind; nutrients in the dying stem will be drawn back into the bulb and will help build it back up to flowering size ready for next year.

Masses of tiny flowers, like those of alyssum, are impossible to deadhead; don't bother unless you are really fussy. Fine scissors are a help, but please… there are more exciting things to do with your time!

Early deadheading

People growing plants for exhibition will remove unopened flower buds until so many weeks before a show so that a big crop of new blooms (or one single, large bloom) develops all in one go ready for the big day. You need to know what you are doing, and most exhibitors experiment for years to get the timing right.

But if you are going on vacation, try removing all the open flowers from pots and hanging baskets before you go. That way, instead of coming home to a sea of deadheads, everything will be coming back into full flower.

How to... **train a standard**

Training plants is a fascinating art. It's the process of taking a young plant and bending it to your will. Using a combination of stopping, pinching out, and tying in, you can create shapes that plants wouldn't normally grow into – maybe flat, for growing against a wall, or as a standard (the classic lollipop shape), with a long bare stem topped by a rounded, bushy head of leaves and flowers. Fast-growing plants, such as fuchsias, are the most fun to train because you see results quickly.

When you get around to more advanced training, you can create your own topiary, or fan-shaped fruit trees, starting from scratch, by combining pruning or clipping and tying in to the right sort of support, but that takes time and dedication.

1 Remove all sideshoots from the rooted cutting, allowing only the central leading shoot to grow and extend. Move the cutting into a 4-in (10-cm) pot, and push a split stake in alongside it. As the stem grows longer, tie it in to the stake at 4-in (10-cm) intervals to keep it straight.

2 When the plant reaches the top of the stake and fills the pot with roots, repot it into a 6-in (15-cm) pot and retie the stem to a bamboo stake 3ft (1m) long. When the shoot reaches just beyond the top of the stake, stop it by pinching out the growing tip. Allow the resulting sideshoots to grow to about 2in (5cm), and give them a second stopping. Remove any sideshoots that grow from farther down the main stem.

3 Continue pinching out the very tips of the shoots at the top of the plant each time the new crop of sideshoots reaches about 2in (5cm) long, so that the head of branches will slowly grow larger and denser. When the head reaches the desired size, don't do any more stopping. After a few weeks, the plant will start flowering. The leaves on the standard's stem will naturally wither and die as the plant ages, or you can pick them off once the plant is in flower.

Clipping and trimming

Hedges, dwarf edgings, and topiary are the garden's answers to poodles – good-natured, but they need regular clipping and trimming, which again are forms of pruning.

Whether you use trendy, single-handed sheep shears to shape up your lavender edging, a pair of shears to clip your topiary dome, or electric hedge-clippers to trim miles of Leyland cypress hedging (X *Cupressocyparis leylandii*), the operation has exactly the same effect as pinching out the tips of the shoots on your potted fuchsia – the stems below the cut will branch out. So, besides redefining the shape, clipping also builds up a thicker hedge.

The great art of clipping is to know when to do it, so that you don't need to undertake the job more often than is necessary.

Hand shears allow you to clip hedges at a steady rate, and they are a darned sight quieter than electric trimmers!

Leafy formal hedges

Leafy, formal hedges, such as beech and conifers, need clipping twice a year if you like them to look perfect. Clip them in early summer and again at the end of summer, and they'll never look scruffy. If you want to cut down on clipping, you can get away with a single annual cut in late summer, though your hedges may look a bit fuzzy during the summer. Use the same timing for topiary. Formal edgings of dwarf boxwood – used to outline borders or make knot gardens – are best clipped in late spring, but do the job in dull weather to prevent the cut leaf edges being badly scorched. I clip my yew hedges once a year in late summer, or just at the very beginning of autumn. That way they stay crisp and clean-looking right through the winter.

Fast-growing formal hedges of hawthorn or privet are much more work, since they need cutting about every six weeks between late spring and early autumn. Don't make the last cut too late in the season, because clipping encourages a lot of soft young growth, which can suffer if it is hit by a late frost; the hedge won't really recover its good looks until next spring.

It can take ten years or more to encourage a beech hedge to form an archway like this, but then not every job in the garden needs to be done at breakneck speed.

Lavender makes a wonderful informal hedge or curb at knee height and associates well with other herbs and salad vegetables.

Dwarf herb edgings

These are an excellent way of edging flower beds. Clip rosemary after it has finished flowering, in spring. Santolina is good for edging, and, if you don't want it to flower, clip it as soon as you see the buds starting to form in late spring – especially if the chrome-yellow flowers are going to clash with your color scheme.

Dwarf hedges of lavender are clipped after they've flowered. All you are doing is snipping off the faded flower heads and lightly shaping the plants, so it's barely more than deadheading. With lavender, you mustn't cut back into thick, woody, old stems; they are reluctant to resprout. It's much better to give them a light hair-cut each year to keep them bushy.

Clipping technique

Clip a hedge so that its sides are sloping slightly inward to the top. This "batter" looks better and prevents a hedge from being top-heavy, so it's less likely to splay apart. Also, because the base receives more light, the hedge is less inclined to become bald at the bottom.

When clipping, start at the bottom of the hedge and slope your shears or hedge-clippers lightly inward to get the angle of the slope right, and just follow the line upward. If your hedge is taller than you can reach in comfort, use a stepladder, or buy or rent a special platform. Make sure you are standing on something stable. And do plug power tools into an ground fault circuit interrupter or circuit breaker, designed to cut the power if you chop through a cord.

Informal hedges

Most flowering shrubs aren't particularly well suited to being formally clipped, and things like shrub roses and flowering currant (Ribes sanguineum) *are usually much better planted in a row and allowed to grow into their natural shape. But they still need keeping under control, and the way to do that is by pruning them just enough to keep them in shape. Do this in the same way as you'd prune free-standing shrubs, if you want to be correct about it.*

Key pruning

You could go for years without really needing to do any serious pruning, but there are some things you simply must give a good going-over each year. So if you grow roses, some kinds of clematis, spring-flowering shrubs, and shrubs, such as dogwoods, that are grown for colorful winter stems... be prepared.

Where to cut

Always cut just above a leaf joint, a lateral stem (far left) or bud – about ¼in (5mm) away from it – even if you can't actually see a bud, since that is where the new shoot will grow out from.

Don't cut so close that you risk damaging the dormant bud on the stem, but, on the other hand, don't make your cut too high above it, or you'll be left with a short stub or "snag" (left) that will die back. Dieback may spread to the shoot that you're trying to encourage to grow.

Prune just above a bud that faces the direction you want the new shoot to grow in. In the case of a tightly packed bush, cut just above an outward-facing bud so that the new shoot grows away from the center.

For single buds, make the cut at an angle that slopes gently away from the bud; it reduces the risk of rainwater carrying fungal spores into the wound. This isn't possible with paired buds; just cut them straight across, about ¼in (5mm) above the buds.

Tools of the trade

There are several different cutting tools for use in the garden. Each is specialized for the particular job it's designed to do. The main thing about cutting tools is to keep them well sharpened, since this will make the job much easier. These are the main types of tool that you will need for pruning:

Pruners are essential. Use them for cutting through stems up to about ½–¾in (1.5–2cm) in diameter. Avid gardeners prefer the parrot-beak, bypass type that works with a scissors action (see page 44). Bypass pruners give a cleaner cut; at least they do if you keep them sharp and wipe the sap off the blades each time you use them. If you don't want to spend so much, the anvil type (see page 44) is less costly and just as fine. Until you move into the rarefied world of specialized pruning, there isn't really all that much to choose between them, so buy whichever you feel most comfortable with.

Long-handled loppers are more powerful than pruners; the long handles give you greater leverage for cutting through thicker stems. They are also good for reaching into the middle of dense shrubs.

Pruning saws are for branches. Always cut a branch off close to a trunk or main stem. Don't leave a stump that will die back, and don't cut flush with the stem. Leave the raised "collar" at the base of the branch; it encourages bark to grow over the wound, and it heals better.

Long-reach pruners are invaluable if you have tall trees to work on, since they save going up ladders. Keep them well oiled for a smooth action.

Loppers are useful for cutting branches between 1 and 1½in (2.5 and 4cm) thick, that pruners would find too much heavy going.

How to... prune spring-flowering shrubs

What you need

- *long-handled loppers*
- *sharp pruners*
- *container to carry discarded branches away (to be shredded and composted, or bundled up and discarded)*

Some spring- and early summer-flowering shrubs – *Philadelphus* (mock orange) and *Forsythia* in particular – can get very messy unless they are pruned every year. A neglected plant fills up with old stems that don't carry many flowers. You can easily identify these stems, even outside the flowering season, because they have darker bark and look a tad gnarled. The way to prune these shrubs is to give them a glorified deadheading. As soon as the flowers are over, cut back all the stems carrying dead flowers. Follow the stem down until you reach a good strong bud or young sideshoot with no dead flowers on it, and cut just above the point where it grows out of the main branch. Do that regularly each year, and your spring shrubs will stay neater and carry a lot more flowers.

The technique for most later-flowering shrubs is pretty similar, but do it in winter. The rule of thumb is: if it flowers before mid-summer (say, mid-June), prune it immediately after flowering and, if it flowers later, prune it in late winter or early spring. You can apply that rule to almost any plant with woody stems.

1 Shrubs like *Philadelphus* (mock orange) and this *Ribes* (flowering currant) benefit from having a few older stems cut out each year. You can identify the older ones by their gnarled stems and by the faded flowers carried on their sideshoots.

2 Use a pair of loppers to cut out the thickest of the stems, taking them as close to ground level as possible. Make your cuts just above a bud or a young sideshoot. Then use pruners to remove any feeble or diseased stems you find.

3 As a result of this annual renewal pruning, you will end up with a shapely and healthy bush that produces masses of flowers on vigorous young wood each spring, rather than a tired old warhorse that looks ancient and worn out.

Pruning roses (1)

Large-flowered and cluster-flowered bush roses, the sort we used to call hybrid teas and floribundas, are the ones that are cut down hard every year between midwinter and early spring. The latest theory is that they can be pruned with hedge trimmers, but unless you run a parks department with acres of the things, I wouldn't bother. Just prune all the stems back to about 6–9in (15–23cm) above ground level. Cut out all dead wood completely, and cut thin, weak stems back shorter than the strong, thick ones, because the harder you prune, the stronger the new shoots grow. Try to cut just above outward-facing buds. Shrub roses don't need hard pruning in spring; just deadhead them in summer instead, removing 4–6in (10–15cm) of stem along with each old flower.

Pruning clematis (2)

Some clematis need pruning, and some don't. The best way to tell is to keep the label when you buy a new plant, because it comes with instructions. As a good rule of thumb, clematis species, such as *Clematis tangutica* and *Clematis orientalis*, as opposed to cultivated varieties, such as *Clematis* 'Barbara Jackman', don't normally need pruning. If you grow the large-flowered hybrids, wait to see when they flower. There are the late-flowering lot that start flowering in midsummer (e.g. *Clematis* 'Jackmanii Superba') and keep going until early autumn, and it's these that need pruning hard. Cut them down to 12in (30cm) above ground level before new shoots appear.

The other sort start flowering earlier, in early summer, then take a midsummer break before a second flowering nearer the end of the summer (e.g. *Clematis* 'Nelly Moser'). Don't prune these quite so hard, or you'll be cutting off the later flowers and the stems that ought to flower early next year. Cut them back to silvery buds at around waist height in late winter. Varieties of *Clematis viticella* and *Clematis texensis* such as 'Princess of Wales' and 'Etoile Rose' can be cut back to nearly ground level each spring.

Key pruning:
1 Always make pruning cuts on roses just above a bud or a young shoot.
2 In spring, clematis are pruned back to healthy emerging shoots – the height above ground depends on their season of flowering.

Key pruning continued:
3 It is only the young stems of plants, such as this *Salix alba* subsp. *vitellina* 'Britzensis', that give wonderful color right through winter, so prune them back hard each spring to encourage new growth.

Of course, if you reach the stage where any clematis gets too big, then you can prune it back hard in late winter and let it start all over again, or just neaten the excess growth after flowering has finished. Either way, you'll probably miss out on a certain amount of flower next time around, but the plant will look neater.

Pruning for winter stems (3)

Some shrubs benefit from a very hard and regular form of pruning known as stooling or coppicing, which basically means cutting the whole plant down almost to ground level every year or two. It is commonly used on shrubs that are grown for their colorful winter stems, such as the red-barked dogwood (*Cornus alba*) and its cultivars, and shrubby willows, such as the scarlet willow (*Salix alba* subsp. *vitellina* 'Britzensis').

The time to do the job is in late winter or early spring, just before the buds "break" and the plants start growing. The idea is that, by removing all the old stems, which become less colorful as they grow woodier, you encourage a great flush of bright-barked new shoots. If you adopt this kind of pruning, you should mulch the plants well with manure (see pages 154–55) immediately afterward to give them the wherewithal to produce new growth.

Alternatively, remove half the number of stems completely each year – taking the older ones – and allow half to remain. It's kinder and, provided it's the youngsters that are retained, you'll still have plenty of colorful bark.

Rejuvenating old shrubs

Most garden shrubs don't need regular pruning, but, once they are approaching middle age, they may need a little cosmetic surgery to keep them looking good, and if you have really elderly or overgrown shrubs, then a drastic facelift may be called for.

Midlife renewal

The easiest way to maintain the shape of mature shrubs is to prune them lightly as soon as you first notice them starting to look a bit ragged. Winter or early spring is the best time to neaten shrubs that flower after midsummer; prune earlier flowering kinds soon after flowering.

Whatever you do, don't clip flowering shrubs like barberries into the neat domes you sometimes see in overly neat gardens, because all you do is rob them of all character – and you'll probably prevent them from flowering as well.

Don't snip bits off here and there, either. It's much better to take off an entire branch close to the base of the plant or to cut it back close to the junction with a better-placed branch. That way you leave the shrub with a reasonably natural shape. Lopsided shrubs just need the offending branches cut back to restore their equilibrium, so prune just above the next well-placed branch emerging from lower down on the same main stem.

Very strong-growing shoots that push up through the middle of an otherwise bushy shrub can be cut back by half their length or more, in an effort to encourage them to branch out lower down – but if it's a grafted plant (see page 78–79), do check to see whether it's a sucker growing up from the rootstock underground; if it is, dig it out.

You can avoid pruning by growing plants that need very little attention, such as Japanese maple (left center) and fatsia, or Japanes aralia (right), growing here in a well-sculpted border with hostas and Japanese anemones.

How to... restore old shrubs

If you have geriatric shrubs that don't flower well, ask yourself whether it wouldn't be better to replace them rather than try to restore them. Restoration takes time, whereas a new shrub will look better right away. But if you have something special, and it's not too far gone, or you feel too cash-strapped to lay cash down on a new one, then give it a go.

I know it's tempting to try to do the whole job at once, but be patient. If you cut an old shrub back too hard, it'll just fight back by growing lots of strong, leafy shoots that don't flower. If it's a grafted plant, you may end up with a thicket of suckers. It's much better to cut out one or two of the very oldest branches every year – they are the thicker ones with darker, more gnarled bark, the baldest branches, and the ones with the fewest flowers. Winter or early spring is the best time to do the job on mid- to late-summer bloomers. Early-flowering shrubs can be given the chop after flowering. Don't remove more than one fifth of the plant's branches at a time.

1 Some shrubs, such as *Salix alba* cultivars, ornamental elders, and dogwoods, grown mainly for their foliage and/or colored stems, benefit from hard pruning every 2–3 years. Cut all the thick, dark-stemmed old branches down close to ground level with a pruning saw, in spring – just before the plant starts growing but when the risk of severe frosts has passed.

2 Neaten the small, twiggy stems with pruners. Strong young shoots will soon grow out from these stumps to form a bushy new plant.

3 Later the same summer, you'll have exactly what looks like a brand new shrub, with large leaves and strong stems. This is *Cornus alba* 'Elegantissima', grown for its handsome variegated foliage and red stems, seen at their best in winter.

Restoring perennials

While shrubs are rejuvenated by cutting them back hard, the way to breathe new life into really old perennials is to dig them up and divide them.

Now if you look in a lot of the old gardening books, they'll tell you to divide one type in autumn and another in spring, and you'll end up feeling what you really need is a year-planner. Don't panic! The easiest way to go about rejuvenating perennials is just to divide everything in spring. By dividing them up just before they start growing – or even when there are some short new shoots showing – they will recover rapidly.

How do you tell when a plant needs dividing?

Unless you just want to propagate some more plants, there's no point in dividing perennials before they need it, because large clumps flower better than small ones, and they make the garden look more mature. Whether a plant needs dividing or not depends on how it is growing. Perennials certainly need dividing if they are:

Dead in the middle. iIf the middle of the clump has died out or stopped flowering well – leaving a circle of young growth all around the edges – the plant is a prime candidate for rejuvenation.

Overgrown. If the clump has outgrown its spot and started invading and/or shading out neighboring plants, you'll need to divide it to keep the neighbors happy.

Taking leave of the soil. If the clump has grown itself out of the ground, as heucheras sometimes do, then that's another good sign that your plant needs dividing.

How often do plants need dividing?

Some perennials take a long time to reestablish after being divided, so don't disturb things like the ice plant (*Sedum spectabile*), hostas, Siberian iris, and peony until you really need to. You can leave them for five years or more before they need splitting up, and even then they may go on happily for several years more.

Some of the very self-sufficient, cottage-garden perennials, such as hardy geraniums, can be left untouched almost indefinitely. But very vigorous perennials, such bee balm, many daisy-type perennials (including asters and *Rudbeckia*), and phlox, tend to run out of steam unless they are divided every two to three years.

What's wrong with autumn?

Autumn is okay for dividing up the tougher, fibrous-rooted plants, such as New York Asters (Aster novi-belgii), but try carving up the fleshy roots of sedum and hosta, and you leave big, open wounds that just rot when they're exposed to cold, wet soil all winter. If you garden on warm, light, fast-draining, sandy soil, you can probably get away with dividing in autumn in most years, but on wet clay soils, stick to springtime.

How to... divide perennials

You'll often be told that the way to divide perennials is to use two garden forks back to back. The idea is to dig the clump out of the ground, impale it on the two sets of prongs, and lever the bits apart. All I can say is whoever came up with this knuckle-bruising wheeze has never tried to do it. It doesn't work! It's much better to chop the clump into pieces with a sharp spade. You can be quite rough about it.

1 Some plants need dividing more regularly than others. Things like New York asters can be divided every three years. Other plants, such as this geranium, can wait rather longer. Use pruners to cut off all the old, faded plant growth and reveal the healthy young shoots. Cut down the stems as low as possible, so that when you come to handle the plant the cut stems are less likely to get in the way or stab you. With a spade or fork, dig around the clump, then pry it out of the soil.

2 Divide up the decent, healthy young stuff into 5-in (12-cm) diameter clumps by chopping into the main clump with a spade. Be generous in the size of the pieces, because tiny clumps can take ages to start flowering. You can pot smaller bits up and grow them on to give to friends, if you like. Discard the tired old central portion.

3 Improve the soil by forking in some good compost or manure and a handful of general balanced fertilizer. Do this whether you're going to plant the perennials in the same spot, or take the opportunity to move them elsewhere. Replant the best bits at 12-in (30-cm) spacings.

Container gardening

Pots, windowboxes, and hanging baskets are the easy way to personalize all sorts of special places around the garden, from the patio and porch to your rustic gazebo or designer treehouse. They are also a very practical way of growing plants in places without soil, such as a paved courtyard or roof garden. Being portable, containers are ideal for anyone planning to move their household, and, if you are a compulsive rearranger, containers allow you to reinvent your surroundings without the bother of digging everything up. All things considered, it's not surprising they've become so indispensable, but remember, containers do need regular maintenance.

Seasonal color

Think of hanging baskets and pots, and you are immediately transported to a summery scene. But there are three distinct bedding seasons, and as long as you keep tipping out and replanting at the end of each one, you can keep your containers colorful for much of the year.

Summer is simple; in fact, the choice is very wide. You can't beat bedding plants like petunias and pelargoniums for a long, continuous flowering season, but anything with a compact, bushy, or trailing habit is ideal. "Patio plants" is just a marketing term for

Almost any plant can be grown in a container. Here, lavender planted in square pots adds to the formality of a flight of decking steps.

Experiment with containers for bedding – orange tulips look great in a galvanized miniature tin tub.

container-worthy, half-hardy perennials sold in little pots in spring. New kinds come into the fold all the time. These are planted after the last frost and, if properly cared for, should keep flowering until the first seriously cold weather in autumn.

After the first nip of frost, autumn and winter bedding takes over. You can use ornamental cabbages and kales or Universal pansies, or make temporary arrangements of autumn-flowering heaths, winter heathers, and berrying evergreens, such as skimmia and *Gaultheria procumbens*. Yes, I know they aren't annuals, but anything grown temporarily counts as bedding – and with these, you can always plant them in the garden when they are past their best in pots, so it's not nearly as extravagant as it sounds.

Once the worst of the weather is over, in spring, you can replace winter plants with primroses and new pansies; the later you leave it, the bigger the selection of spring bedding you'll find in the nurseries and garden centers. There'll be pots of ranunculus – those giant, turban-topped buttercups with jewel-colored flowers – violas, forget-me-nots, and pots of dwarf spring bulbs just coming into flower. By the time they are past their peak, it's time to start on the summer stuff again.

Summer containers in my garden sport lilies, begonias, and the white bells of galtonia. I love a bright and vibrant mixture – subtlety can be so dull!

All-year-round planting

Year-round container gardens are stylish and practical for people who like the potted look but can't manage the regular makeovers of seasonal designs. They want plants that can stay put for years on end without needing a lot of fuss. The sort of plants to go for must be hardy, of course, but they also really need to look their best all the time.

There are loads of suitable plants. Evergreens and naturally compact shrubs are excellent, and dramatic architectural shapes can look superb. Yes, I know virtually everything you buy comes in pots, but that doesn't mean to say they'll be happy to stay restricted in the long term. If you want year-round container plants, don't bother pot-gardening with monsters like climbing roses, hybrid teas, and blackberries.

Some of the very best year-round container plants are natural showoffs, things like bamboo, dwarf rhododendrons, and Japanese maples, or Chusan palm (*Trachycarpus fortunei*), yucca, and phormium. Most of the smaller clematis are superb in pots – grow them up posh obelisks or rustic tripods.

If you prefer a traditional look, then patio and miniature roses are the answer. I'd go so far as to say they are a better alternative than summer bedding for busy people, because they are just as colorful and flower for as long, but you don't need to throw them away at the end of the season. Just keep them in their pots for next year.

Vegetables and herbs

When you don't have much of a garden, it's smashing to have a few vegetables in pots to bring the supermarket right up to your back door. Salad greens, herbs, zucchini, and climbing beans all grow perfectly well in containers, and, provided you keep up to date with the fertilizing and watering, there's no reason why you shouldn't have crops just as good as you'd expect from a small, intensive garden bed. On a warm, sunny patio, you can add tomatoes and sweet peppers to the list.

Growing edibles in containers is only a little more labor-intensive (in terms of fertilizing and watering) than growing in open ground, but they can look infinitely more glamorous when growing in beautiful containers. Anyway, you'll enjoy looking at them almost as much as eating them, so they'll be good for you on both counts.

If you go for grow bags, you can hide the bright plastic covers under a piece of burlap, pile pebbles over the top, or stand them inside long wooden boxes. Besides looking better, this also helps insulate the soil mix, which keeps the roots a bit cooler in hot, sunny weather.

You can grow even herbs and salad greens in a hanging basket, provided you don't forget the watering.

Container-growing techniques

Gardening in containers is just like growing potted plants on your windowsill indoors; it's only the scale that is different.

But what is it about container gardening that brings out the Scrooge in some folk? I wish I had a fiver for every time someone has asked me why they need to buy potting mix instead of using garden soil to fill their pots.

Frankly it's not worth the saving. Potting mix is like giving plants a dinner party instead of asking them to survive on a bag of chips. Potting mix is specially formulated to meet their requirements; with garden soil you just don't know what you are getting: it may contain soil pests or diseases or it might be short of basic nutrients, badly drained, or just poor quality. Since containers are showpieces, the plants in them need every opportunity to do their best. Sorry, lecture over, but you need to get these things off your chest!

Summer containers: jobs checklist

Planning	Watering	Fertilizing	Deadheading	Dismantling
Decide on shape and size of container, and position (sun or shade, etc). Choose plants accordingly (consider color, shape – upright or trailing – etc). Get your soil mix and water-retaining gel. Now plant up (see page 201).	Check regularly. Do not drown them in their early and late seasons, but they will need watering almost every day at the height of a hot summer. If you are unsure whether to water or not, check the "Do they need watering?" chart on page 169.	Start fertilizing about four to six weeks after planting the container, and follow the manufacturer's instructions on how frequently you should apply. Alternatively, use slow-release fertilizer sticks or granules.	Do this regularly, at least once a week. The more you do it, the more flowers your plants will produce and the longer the flowering season will last.	When the last of the flowers has faded, clear the decks ready for next summer's planting by putting the dead plants on the compost pile and washing and storing your containers, or plant up for winter color.

How to... **plant a container**

If plants are going to stay in the same container for several years, soil-based potting mix is the answer, because it lasts longest (see page 161). Look out for the ericaceous (lime-free) version for long-term lime haters, such as rhododendrons and camellias (see pages 93–95).

Soilless mixes are fine for bedding plants that won't stay put for more than about five or six months (see page 161). They often hold more water, so they're especially good for small containers, hanging baskets, and windowboxes that are notorious for drying out quickly in summer.

You can get water-retaining gel to use in containers. It absorbs moisture every time you water and retains it for the plants to use. It's a real help to container gardeners, but a word of warning, though: follow the instructions, and don't overuse it – the gel expands and can push your plants and potting mix over the edge of the pot.

1 Mix water-retaining gel into the potting mix and wet it until the granules swell up, then mix in a little slow-release fertilizer (follow the instructions given about quantities on the package).

If the pot is tall and might be top-heavy, put a handful of broken pots or stones in the bottom, then partly fill it with potting mix.

2 Tip the plant out of its pot, and tease out a few roots if it is pot-bound. Fill around the plant with more potting mix so that the surface of the rootball sits flush with the surface level of the new mix. Don't fill the container right up to the top – leave a 1-in (2.5-cm) gap below the rim to allow for watering.

3 Firm the potting mix gently – don't mash it down as though you were making bread – and water it well.

Fertilizing and watering

The first thing you notice when you take up container gardening is the way the chores change – you exchange weeding beds for feerilizing and watering pots. In beds, plants scavenge for what they need; in pots, they need a delivery service… you.

The smaller the pot and the hotter the weather, the faster it will dry out. Be handy with the watering can – especially in summer, when you might need to water twice a day.

Water with care early and late in the season when the weather is wet; it's easy to overdo it. But in high summer, the problem is usually keeping containers moist enough, particularly in hot, dry spells or in breezy weather. Once containers fill up with roots, they dry out almost in front of your eyes. Hanging baskets often need watering morning and evening in summer, and large containers probably need watering every day. As a precaution, always use the finger test (see page 169) to see if watering really is needed.

By the time plants have been growing for four to six weeks in soilless mix, you'll need to start fertilizing; use liquid or soluble fertilizer, diluting it exactly as advised by the makers (see page 175). If you know you aren't going to have time to fertilize every week, don't let the job slide; mix slow-release fertilizer into the potting mix before you plant. If you give occasional liquid fertilizer as well when the plants are in full bloom, they'll be as happy as clams.

Care of all-year-round containers
Caring for all-year-round containers in summer is much the same as looking after pots of petunias and fuchsias, but, as the season comes to a close, you'll need to vary your container- gardening techniques to accommodate the changing weather.

Autumn is often lashed by storms, so it's worth moving containers of tall plants closer to the house for shelter and tying them up to a trellis or wedging them between bricks for stability. Not very pretty perhaps, but it takes a long time to regrow a broken plant – and decent containers cost more than enough. As an added precaution, raise containers up on pot feet or bricks so that they don't stand in water. The last thing dormant plants need is wet feet, which encourages rot, so you need to ensure that surplus water drains away quickly.

Winter brings weeks or months of freezing weather, so year-round containers need some protection. Even though the plants may be perfectly hardy, their roots are less protected than they'd be in a border, and if the soil mix in containers freezes solid, the plants may die. Well before they freeze, move containers into a greenhouse, carport, or porch, and they won't come to harm in the shed or garage if it doesn't freeze. Otherwise, sink them up to their rims in a border, or push all your containers together in a sheltered spot and fill the gaps between them with bark chips. Pile some more bark up over the top of the pots to act as a blanket.

Winterproof containers

You can use any kind of container you like for summer designs, provided it has drainage holes in the bottom, but if you want to keep it planted in winter, make sure it's up to the weather. Many ceramic or terracotta containers will crack if the soil mix inside them freezes, because water expands as it turns to ice. Wood, stone, and plastic are naturally resistant. Don't be misled by "frostproof" terracotta – some people think it means that it protects tender plants from frost and cold; it doesn't. It's just a better grade that is less likely to crack. But even so-called "frostproof" pots are not indestructible. "Frost-resistant" would be a more accurate term.

Spring is typically unpredictable, and, if you have early-flowering shrubs such as camellias in pots, don't stand them in an east-facing site; early morning sun shining on frozen flowers spoils them. Avoid a windy spot, too, or flowers will go brown – especially white ones. If the weather is bad, move your pots into a porch or cold greenhouse for protection, which will have the side effect of bringing the flowers on early. If a late frost is forecast after the plants have produced new growth or big fat flower buds, wrap them in horticultural fleece. It gives only a few degrees of insulation, but that's often all that's needed. Don't wrap plants in plastic, because condensation builds up underneath, which might cause plants to rot; by contrast, fleece "breathes."

Making compost

People throw away a lot of stuff to clog landfill sites, when it could be providing vital "roughage" in their garden soil. There's no secret to perfect compost, just a few good tips on technique. Don't believe the old countrymen who'll kid you that the only way to get garden rubbish to rot down properly is to recycle ten pints of beer over it on the way back from the bar. There are other ways, even if they aren't quite so creative.

Compost piles

Compost must heat up to work properly, and one of the most common reasons that compost fails to rot is that it's never been given the chance. Don't economize on the size of your pile; compost needs a certain critical mass to heat up properly, and a cubic yard (cubic meter) is just about right. To go bigger, extend the pile into an oblong shape, but a yard high (about 1m) is probably about the most you can manage, because the ingredients must be stacked in layers.

If you have the sort of garden that generates lots of waste, the way to deal with it is by having two compost piles. It's the same principle as having two gardening shirts, one on and one in the wash.

Start with pile number one: stack it up, cover it, and allow it to rot down (see page 206). Sometime later, begin pile number two. By the time the second pile is made, the first is ready for use. By alternating between the two you can have a constant supply of compost.

You *can* make a free-standing compost pile, but you still need to build it rather than just piling rubbish up, and using a container makes it so much easier.

Every garden should have a proper compost pile. It need not be smelly, and it recycles valuable organic material that builds the soil.

How to... **make compost**

There are several ways to contain compost while it rots down; you can either buy a plastic compost bin, which suits a small garden (see page 206), buy a self-assembly wooden bin of the type shown here, or you can make your own container. You will need a level area of ground measuring 3ft (1 meter) square, with space enough to park a wheelbarrow alongside. Consolidate the ground and hammer in four posts, one at each corner, about 3ft (a meter) apart. Tack wire netting all around the sides, or nail boards across to create solid or semi-slatted sides. Make the front section easily detachable by using galvanized hooks and eyes, so that you can remove the finished compost later. Now you can fill it up...

> ### What you need
>
> - *4 4ft (1.2m) high fence posts*
> - *wire netting or boards for sides*
> - *galvanized hooks and eyes*
> - *coarse drainage material, garden waste, fresh manure, and soil*
> - *piece of carpet or tarpaulin*

1 If you decide to make your own compost bin, follow the instructions above; otherwise, assemble your bought container. Then put a layer of coarse material, such as not-too-woody herbaceous plant stems, at the bottom, for drainage. Spread 6in (15cm) of garden waste evenly over the base. Firm it down by treading, and dampen it if it's dry. Firmness and dampness (not sogginess!) will help the rotting process. Avoid concentrations of any one ingredient. (See page 207 for a list of what you can and can't use to make compost.)

2 Top each new 6-in (15-cm) layer with a couple of spadefuls of fresh manure or soil, which provide beneficial bacteria and act as a compost starter. Make sure that all your waste ingredients to be composted are mixed together before you add them, and remember to water the pile if it looks dry.

3 To keep heat and moisture in, cover with an old piece of carpet or tarpaulin after each time you add more material. Keep building the pile up, sandwich-style, until it's 3ft (a meter) high, and finish with a 1-in (2.5-cm) layer of soil on the top. Cover and leave for 6 months. Compost rots down far faster in summer than in winter. A pile made in spring should have made good, brown, friable compost by autumn, but a heap made in autumn may not be ready until the following summer.

To rot down, compost materials need moisture, air, and a supply of beneficial bacteria. You can add bacteria by adding dry or liquid compost starter bought from the garden center. Fresh, unrotted manure has a good bacteria count, too, and there are plenty in garden soil, so don't bother knocking too much of it off the roots when you are doing the weeding.

If you don't have space to build a compost pile, a smaller compost bin, like this one, is the solution.

Smaller bins

In a tiny garden, you might not have enough waste to make a large compost pile that works, and the answer is to go for a custom-made compost bin instead. Think of a plastic trashcan with the bottom missing.

Stand it somewhere convenient, and just pile all your rubbish in – no need to worry about layers; just mix everything together. Moisten it if it's dry, and firm it with the back of a rake to avoid large air pockets. As long as there's some soil on the roots of weeds to provide the beneficial bacteria needed, you can even forget about adding the odd spadeful of manure or soil. Fill the bin to the top, and put the lid on. The compost should be ready to use in as little as two or three months, or maybe five in cooler weather, when compost doesn't "work" as quickly.

Troubleshooting

Most compost-pile problems boil down to one or two simple things that are usually quite easily made right.

Slimy, smelly compost is often the result of an overdose of lawn clippings. Don't make clippings more than half the total bulk in your compost pile, and mix them well with other material. Alternatively, sandwich the clippings in 6-in (15-cm) layers between weeds and other waste, or use a compost rotter that is specifically designed to prevent grass clippings from turning into dark green slime.

Mummified orange peel and other shriveled but still-recognizable matter are signs that a pile is too dry – make sure that you dampen new materials each time you add them.

Slow rotting may be due to too-coarse, woody materials or thick stalks being used; cutting them up small, or passing them through a garden shredder first, makes them rot faster. Remember, too, to keep your pile firm (by gently trampling it) and damp (by watering it in dry weather).

Rodents can be a nuisance sometimes, even if you don't put cooked foodstuffs in your pile. If you can, arrange to empty your compost bins in the autumn and put them away until spring, or look out for a metal compost bin with a small-mesh base that's rodentproof.

Wormeries

If you generate only a fairly small amount of waste, especially if it's mostly from the kitchen, then you could consider using a wormery instead of a conventional compost bin to convert it. Worms are the modern answer to the traditional cottager's pig. You feed your scraps in one end and what comes out the other, incredibly quickly, is valuable plant food. Worm compost is good as it is and ready to use straight from the worm, whereas fresh manure gives off enough ammonia to "burn" any plants it comes in contact with, so it needs stacking for six months until it is well rotted.

You can buy a kit containing the wormery, worms, and everything you need to get started – the three-stage sort that looks like a pile of sieves is good if you are a bit squeamish about handling the little workers themselves. You can remove the bottom chamber, where the oldest material is ready to use, dump it out, and return it to the top of the stack for refilling. It's the closest thing you'll get to perpetual motion in the garden.

Use your rich, home-grown supply of worm compost – which is pure worm casts – to top-dress plants in outdoor containers or to enrich your vegetable patch. It's great for organic gardeners, because it's 100 percent natural.

A wormery can make efficient compost out of kitchen waste and will also provide liquid "manure" from a tap at the base.

The ingredients for good compost

What goes in...

- Annual weeds
- Tops of perennial weeds
- Spent bedding plants
- Uncooked vegetable trimmings and peelings, crushed eggshells, and tea bags from the kitchen
- Lawn clipping (well mixed with other materials)
- Soft hedge clippings, soft prunings, and spent flowers
- Dead leaves
- Shredded woody stems
- Shredded paper and cotton and wool fabrics

And what doesn't...

- Cooked food scraps, meat, bones, and bread should be avoided at all cost; they may attract vermin
- Diseased plant material and soil pests
- Dog or cat waste
- Weeds with seedheads
- Perennial roots, especially weed roots
- Woody material, such as prunings and Brussels sprout stems
- Synthetic fabrics and any other nonbiodegradable matter

7 KNOW YOUR ENEMY

Prevent and detect

As you've probably realized by now, there are a lot of things that can go wrong with plants. Apart from being attacked by all sorts of insect pests, they also fall prey to diseases caused by microscopic fungi, bacteria, and viruses. But not all problems can be blamed on pests or diseases.

Cultural problems come about when plants aren't given the right care or conditions (see wilting, page 221). They can suffer from physical damage, such as breakage or bruising, and the elements can cause trouble (see frost and wind damage, page 220), hence the well known gardening maxim "blame it on the weather."

But it's not all doom and gloom, because you can garden for years with only minor problems, if you're lucky, or if you take a few simple steps to keep plants healthy. I'm a firm believer in the idea that the best way to tackle plant problems is to prevent them from happening in the first place.

Avoidance tactics

Don't buy trouble. When you're choosing plants at the nursery or garden center, check them for pests and diseases in all the obvious places: on or beneath tender young leaves and the tips of shoots. Spotty or pale leaves, holes, and wilting shoots can all be symptoms of problems you don't want to take home with you (see pages 144 and 212–19).

Once in the garden, there's a lot you can do to keep plants healthy by growing them well. It's a heck of a lot easier – even for the professionals – to keep a good plant healthy than to rescue it after it has gone badly downhill. Healthy plants, well cared for in healthy soil, have a tremendous ability to fend off all sorts of pest and disease problems, whereas frail specimens simply hang up their boots.

Do look plants over regularly. You can often nip a potential problem in the bud just by spotting it in time and doing something simple, such as picking off a mildewed leaf or wiping off an insect, before you have a major outbreak on your hands. In containers or under cover, regular deadheading and dead leaf-picking are easy ways to short-circuit many common problems. It's not difficult to tell there's something wrong with a plant once you start observing.

In the same way that you can tell that a person is out of sorts by their pasty complexion, so you can identify a troubled plant by it's lackluster appearance. What's not so easy is working out why it's not well. That's where the gentle art of gardening turns into something like a Sherlock Holmes plot – and some detective work is called for.

Scrubbing pots in winter might be a dreary chore, but it does make sure that pests are not transferred to plant roots right from the start.

Blow it up

You can get by without the deerstalker hat, but a magnifying glass is incredibly useful. Given a decent view, early symptoms are often all the clues you need to get on to the case. The best type of magnifying glass to use to detect plant problems is the sort that has it's own built-in light. Choose one with a large magnifying head, since those with small lenses are easy to slip into your pocket but don't give you a wide enough angle on the problem. You don't need huge magnification; about four times actual size is usually enough.

Odd spots on leaves may show themselves up to be clusters of baby bugs, or fluffy molds, which are fungal diseases. Holes in fruit or vegetables, magnified to several times life size, often reveal themselves to be made by tiny rodent teeth or boring insects. Holes in leaves may be revealed as damage caused by the rasping mouthparts of snails as opposed to the munchings of beetles.

Gather the facts

As the owner of the plant, you are in a much better position to know what might be wrong than an outside expert, to whom you describe the symptoms or even send a sample. The reason is elementary, my dear Watson. Being on the spot, you know the plant's cultivation history, the garden situation, and the local weather – especially transient occurrences, such as hailstones and late frosts; any of these may have had a bearing.

Keep your ears open. If other gardeners report early aphids or plagues of tomato blight, expect them to reach you, too. And if you've had trouble with blackspot, rust, clubroot, or vine weevil in the past, the odds are you'll have them again. So be prepared for the worst, and, who knows, you may be pleasantly surprised.

Know what to expect

Identifying plant problems is a bit like bird watching. You can safely assume that 99 percent of what you see is quite common, so eliminate the obvious before thinking you have something unusual. It also helps to know which plants are prone to particular problems.

Roses, for instance, are martyrs to blackspot, mildew, and rust (see page 218). All members of the cabbage family are affected by clubroot, and vine weevil larvae (see pages 216–17) are specially fond of cyclamen, tuberous begonias, and rhododenron roots. If you grow peaches and nectarines, you are sure to see peach leaf curl and, if you grow apples, you are bound to find the odd one with a codling moth maggot inside. There are some pests that attack almost anything, notably aphids, spider mites, and slugs, from which little is safe. Greenhouses are notorious as pest and disease hot-spots – the shelter offers them ideal conditions to multiply.

Don't over-react

Don't automatically rush for a spray every time you find a few pests in your garden. A small population can actually be quite a good thing, if it attracts beneficial insects or birds in to feed. When there is a healthy balance between friend and foe, natural predators build up each time pest numbers increase, so damage is kept within acceptable levels. Chemicals may solve the immediate problem, but they wipe out the good bugs as well as the bad, leaving the way clear for pests to reinfest without any competition. Try simple solutions, like picking pests off by hand, before you blast them with some noxious fluid.

Common foes

Sometimes you'll be able to see clearly what it is that's causing a problem with plants – a lot of snails and beetles can be caught red-handed by going out with a flashlight at night. But in some cases, the best way to identify the culprit, be it a pest, disease, or cultural condition, is by recognizing the damage it does.

Pests

As far as a gardener is concerned, a pest is any member of the animal kingdom – from tiny nematodes to rabbits and deer – that likes to eat his plants. They can chomp, they can suck sap, they can nibble roots. And they are a real pain in the nether regions.

Snails (1)
Snails will also go for almost any soft, lush plant, though hairy or furry plants are usually fairly safe. Hostas are a particular favorite. Snails are surprisingly good at climbing, so if you see holey leaves on climbers or wall shrubs, or in containers such as hanging baskets, it's probably snails; slime trails are a dead giveaway. You can also tell snail damage by the way the soft green tissue of leaves is rasped away between the ribs, leaving a "skeleton" behind – slugs eat the lot. Snails also work fast – a lot of people can't believe their eyes as new bedding plants disappear overnight.

Apart from gathering them by hand, you can put out saucers of beer to trap them, or spray at-risk plants with yucca extract (sold in garden centers). Prickly leaves or diatomaceous earth can be piled around susceptible plants, but few methods are really effective. In autumn, set out empty clay flower pots under hedges for snails to hibernate in, then you can easily gather up large numbers in spring. Snails need calcium to build their shells, so they are less of a problem on acidic soil – but on chalky soil, watch out. If you remove snails from the garden, remember that they have a homing instinct. They'll travel a couple of miles in search of Chez Nous.

Slugs (2)
Slugs attack almost anything soft and lush, and symptoms are similar to those of snail damage but lower down on the plant. They are found mostly under leaves that touch the ground, or inside lettuces. Slugs are easily found by natural predators, such as frogs and toads, and they are very successfully dealt with using biological control (scc pages 226–27). You can also lay down half grapefruit skins, which slugs will crawl into, and then you can throw them away.

1

Common garden pests:
1 Snails can wreak havoc in a garden, and they are adept at crossing all kinds of barriers, as my experiments have shown. Gravel, crushed eggshells, oatmeal, and holly-leaf barriers will all be crossed by a snail intent on eating a tasty hosta!

Caterpillars (3)

Caterpillars munch similar holes in leaves to those caused by slugs and snails, but caterpillars don't leave a slime trail and don't hide away so much during the day. They also leave black excrement – the polite term is frass – behind them that makes identification easier. You'll spot them quite easily, especially the tent-forming types that make dense webs around the tips of shoots, or those that live in colonies, such as cabbage white caterpillars. Lots of birds eat small green caterpillars, but few birds eat large or vividly colored caterpillars. Picking caterpillars off by hand is one of the best remedies for nuisance species like cabbage whites. But for solitary ones that don't do much harm, such as the mullein moth caterpillar, which lives on verbascum and buddleja, leave them alone and enjoy them… Oh, come on; there's more to life than worrying about a hole or two in a leaf. Moths and butterflies have just as much right to be here as we do, and there aren't nearly as many of them around as there used to be. Take an interest in them!

Spider mites (4)

Mainly a problem in greenhouses, or on pot plants indoors, spider mites (often referred to simply as "mites") are so tiny that you'll need a magnifying glass to see them properly. They look like animated specks of buff-colored dust . At first you'll see pale speckled patterns on the leaves that show where spider mites have been feeding; in a really bad infestation, you'll later see fine, silky webs at the tips of the shoots and on young leaves. In a very bad case, plants drop their leaves, which dry out and turn brown; "just like autumn." Spider mites can be very difficult to deal with, even when using chemicals. They're best avoided by keeping the air humid (spider mites thrive in a dry atmosphere). Pick off affected leaves, or nip out shoots showing signs of webbing. Standing conservatory plants out in the garden for the summer often helps avoid spider mite attacks (see pages 227).

2 A gray field slug chomping his way through a pea leaf.
3 The caterpillar of the mullein moth is best tolerated; it attacks only the plants in their second year – very considerate.
4 Bleached leaves and fine webbing indicate the presence of spider mite, which is not to be tolerated.

5

6

7

Common pests continued:

5 Spitbugs are more of an irritation than a pest; don't worry about them.

6 Mice, like this wood mouse, can eat everything from pea and bean seeds to this tasty crocus.

7 Ants, here in their red variety, farm aphids and burrow under plants, sometimes causing roots to dry out.

8 The cutworm is the larva of a moth and eats plant roots, especially in the vegetable patch.

9 Scale insects are sap-suckers and cling beneath leaves, usually favoring the thicker-leaved plants that aphids don't like.

8

9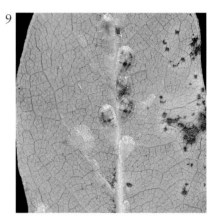

Spitbugs (5)

The frothy white spittle you sometimes find on plants in early summer is a lot less sinister than it looks. It conceals the nymphs of the spitbug, or froghopper, which do very little harm to plants. Wash the "spit" away with a hose if you must, but there's really no need. The adult is a positively friendly creature that'll happily walk onto your hand – it looks something like a cross between a giant aphid and a small grasshopper.

Mice (6)

The worst thing mice do in the garden is to steal big seeds, such as peas and beans – especially the early-sown ones. You'll often find a cache of stolen seeds hidden in the compost pile. They might also nibble tubers or vegetables that you've stored in your shed over winter, or newly planted bulbs, which makes them rot. It helps sprinkle holly leaves in a row just over your pea and bean seeds, or on top of bulbs before burying them, but, if you live in country areas with a big rodent population, it's a good idea to clear your compost pile away each autumn, so there's no cozy winter nesting site for them – or their larger cousins, the rats. And hang your fruit and vegetables (such as potato tubers) up in nets in the shed roof.

Ants (7)

Most of the time, ants do no harm at all apart from aphid "farming"; they like the sticky secretions (honeydew) that aphids leave behind, so they run a sort of protection racket. But in summer, ants make themselves unpopular with gardeners by nesting in dry soil in the lawn, in cracks between paving slabs, in rockeries, or in pots. They create conical mounds of what looks like sifted soil that's been excavated from around the roots. Though ants don't directly harm plants, their underground tunnels can leave roots dangling in thin air, so they dry out. That's what kills plants in ant-infested pots and rockeries if you don't react in time. If ants nest where there is nothing to harm, you can safely ignore them – they'll go away after a couple of months. Otherwise, flood ants out with lots of water in early summer when they begin nesting, so they move elsewhere. Tip out ant-infested containers and wash all the larvae off the roots, then repot the plant in fresh potting mix. Better still, protect pots from ants before they start building by smearing crop-protection jelly around the sides (see page 225) – it will deter snails, slugs, and vine weevil, too.

Soil pests (8)

Cutworms, leatherjackets, and wireworms are the larvae of various moths, crane flies, and click beetle respectively, and all feed on underground roots and tubers. Even if you don't see the grubs, you'll know you have them from the dead patches in the lawn, disappearing bulbs, newly planted bedding plants and vegetables suddenly separated from their roots, or holes in potatoes. Soil pests are most often found where grass has been dug up to make new beds, so if you don't want to use soil insecticide, turn the ground over several times in autummn to bring pests up to the surface, where birds can eat them. Or run your chickens over the patch for a few weeks first; they're a great natural way of eradicating pests, and weed seeds too. A flock of starlings pecking at the lawn is usually a sure sign of soil pests; let them finish what they are doing, then repair any damage.

Scale insects (9)

Yet another greenhouse and conservatory pest, scale insects look like tiny shields clinging to stems or beneath leaves. They are sap-suckers but usually target the kind of plants aphids don't like – the tougher ones with thick, waxy, or evergreen leaves. Citrus plants are a special favorite. You can wipe scale insects away, then wash the leaves in tepid water to remove the sooty mold that often follows in the wake of an attack. Some species attack outdoor plants, such as camellia and euonymus.

More common pests:

10 Black aphids suck sap, secrete sticky honeydew, and transmit virus diseases.

11 Whitefly do the same but are more difficult to control than aphids because their young are tough little scales.

12 Vine weevil is the scourge of modern gardens. The adult weevils, with their 'elephant's trunk' mouthparts, chew the leaf edges of plants such as rhododendrons, and their larvae eat the roots of begonias, cyclamen and many other plants.

Black aphids (10)

These look like big, fat, black, greasy aphids (see page 217), and are mostly found in summer as large, sap-sucking colonies clustered at the tips of shoots, often on elder (*Sambucus*) and bean plants – especially broad beans. As with all sap-suckers, extensive colonies weaken the plant; they'll also prevent bean pods from setting. Birds aren't very big on them (who can blame them?), so the traditional way to shift them is to nip out the tips of broad beans once a good crop of pods has set, and as soon as you see the first balck aphid. You can prune out colonies on elder without harming the plant.

Whitefly (11)

Whitefly are sap-sucking, mostly greenhouse pests that look like minute, arrow-shaped white moths. They fly up from plants in clouds if they are disturbed and are particularly fond of fuchsias and tomato plants. When at rest, they congregate beneath the leaves, out of the light, and it's here that you may also see the tiny, pinhead-like eggs, from which the next generation hatch. One of the best ways to control whitefly is to hang yellow sticky traps from the greenhouse roof (see biological control, pages 226–27), then shake the plants gently to get the pests flying. Or grow a flowering tobacco (*Nicotiana*) in a hanging pot; the whitefly will home in on that and you can then pop it in a plastic bag to get rid of large numbers all at once. In a very hot summer, you may find greenhouse whitefly on plants out in the garden, but whitefly on members of the cabbage family are a different species that attacks only brassicas (cabbage relatives).

Vine weevil (12)

Two pests for the price of one. The adult is a small, buff-brown beetle about ⅜in (9mm) long with Y-shaped antennae. It carves small notches around the edges of rhododendron leaves and other evergreens, but doesn't really do much harm; its larvae are the real problem. They are fat, white, legless grubs about ½in (10mm)long that lie curled up in a C-shape in the soil, close to the roots of their favorite food plants. They are especially fond of primroses and cyclamen, but they'll attack other things and are very common in containers, especially on plants in soilless mixes. The grubs stay safely underground, so the first thing you'll notice is a plant that quickly turns yellow and wilts, showing that it has suffered major root damage.

Once plants have been attacked, it's usually too late to do anything. To deter egg-laying adults, sprinkle a thick layer of grit around at-risk plants, and destroy adult vine weevils if you see them. Repot or top dress all-year-round plants in outdoor containers each spring, and protect them with biological control (see page 227) if you've had problems with vine weevil before. A soil pesticide can be watered on to susceptible pot plants to prevent attack, and crop-protection soil mix containing that pesticide has the same effect. Both offer control for several months. Organic gardener that I am, I do occasionally use these chemicals, because they are contained within pots in the greenhouse and so don't contaminate the wider environment of the garden. And vine weevils are such devils!

Green aphids (13)

Green aphids go for the softest parts of plants: the tips of shoots and the undersides of young leaves. Nearly all are female and, as they give birth to live young without being fertilized by a male (the ultimate in women's lib), one little aphid is all it takes to start a population explosion. Indoors and in heated greenhouses, green aphids are active all year round. Because they feed by sucking sap, they can spread viruses between plants by injecting them with their mouthparts as they move from one plant to the next. Controlling greenfly does a lot to cut down on virus infections.

As green aphids feed, what comes out of their other end is sticky honeydew, upon which black, powdery-looking sooty mold often grows. This is a type of fungus that is not in itself harmful, but it is unsightly and prevents light from reaching the leaves. You can wipe green aphids off plants with your fingers (brace yourself) and wash sooty mold off with a damp cloth (and see biological control, page 227). Alternatively, let birds and ladybugs help themselves to aphids, and allow the rain to clean the plants up. But if you see sooty mold, suspect greenfly.

Aphids aren't always green, though – different species can be pink, red, cream, yellow, orange, or brown. There are other sorts as well, including black aphids (page 216), root aphids, and the waxy-covered cabbage aphids.

13 Green aphids invariably attack the soft and succulent shoot tips of plants, sucking sap and spreading virus diseases.

Diseases

Diseases are plant problems caused by fungi, bacteria, and viruses. The first two are especially encouraged by weather conditions – fungi love damp weather – and viruses can be transmitted by insect pests. Viruses seldom kill plants; fungi and bacteria do.

Blackspot (1)

One of the most regularly occurring fungal disease of roses, blackspot causes irregular, rounded black patches on leaves from midsummer onward. Other than spraying regularly with a specific fungicide all season, the best remedy is to replace badly affected roses with varieties that have some natural disease resistance. Even they will get a little blackspot in a summer that's warm, humid, and overcast – ideal fungus weather – but pick up and discard dead leaves at the end of the season to reduce the risk.

Powdery mildew (2)

This is a very common fungal disease that looks like a light dusting of talcum powder over the upper sides of younger leaves. It affects all sorts of outdoor and greenhouse plants, particularly roses, and plants that are regularly short of water. You can help avoid an outbreak of powdery mildew by mulching and fertilizing plants in spring and by watering thoroughly in long, dry spells. In severe cases, pick off badly affected leaves and discard them.

Rust (3)

Plant ust looks like iron rust – powdery, reddish brown spots. Most rusts are specific to a particular species of plant, so if you have rust on your roses, it won't affect your onions. Rose fungicides are fairly effective, especially if you opt for the latest kinds, but grow disease-resistant varieties if you want to avoid spraying. On plants like pelargonium, prune out affected stems, or discard and replace the plants; some rose fungicides are also suitable for use on other ornamental plants, so check the instructions. It's not worth spraying leeks – simply peel away the rusty outer leaves and eat the rest, but don't put rusted material on the compost pile. Hollyhocks are martyrs to rust, so they're best raised anew from seed each year.

Gray mold (botrytis) (4)

This is the fungal disease responsible for fluffy gray patches on dead or dying leaves and flowers in dull, damp weather, but also causes "ghost-spotting" (small, round, translucent spots) on tomatoes. It's very common in humid greenhouses in winter, when light levels are low and there is little air circulation. Prevent gray

---

Expert diagnosis

If you have a pest or disease problem you can't identify, even with the help of a well-illustrated book, there are several places to find help. Members of your local horticultural club may know the answer; there may be an adviser at a large local garden center, or, if you are going to a major gardening event, such as a big-city flower show, it's worth taking a specimen with you to show to one of the experts at the gardening clinics sometimes held there. Also, don't forget to look into your local county Extension Service.

mold by picking over plants regularly to remove dead leaves and flowers. Space plants out, so there's room for air to circulate, and ventilate the greenhouse whenever you can.

Brown rot (5)

A spectacular rot affecting fruit including plums, apples, pears, and crabapples. It rapidly turns the whole fruit brown with concentric rings of raised white spots. Pick off infected fruits and discard them – never put them on the compost pile – and don't leave infected fruits lying around, because they'll be a source of more fungal spores for next year.

Coral spot (6)

Virulent-looking, raised, coral-red spots on dead or dying wood. Avoid coral spot by pruning properly, just above a healthy bud or leaf joint, so you don't leave short stumps that die back and let fungal infections like this in. It can be a rampant spreader, so prune it out promptly – back to clean healthy wood – to avoid any spread back into living material. Discard infected prunings; don't put them on the compost pile.

Common plant diseases:
1 Blackspot is a common disease of roses – especially those with thin leaves.
2 Mildew can attack all sorts of plants, especially those already under stress.
3 Rose rust is best avoided by growing disease-resistant varieties.
4 Gray mold loves a damp environment and will often attack damaged tissue.
5 Brown rot attacks fruits, displaying its tell-tale concentric rings of fungal pustules.
6 Coral spot is a fungus that attacks dead or dying wood.

Cultural conditions

If there's an advantage to pests and diseases, it's that you have something tangible to blame. But not all plant problems are a result of predatory organisms. Some of the cultural conditions that beset plants are what you might call "acts of God" – late frosts, hurricanes, and hailstorms – which are beyond your control. But most of the things that go wrong with plants that aren't pests or diseases normally boil down to a simple failure to provide the correct set of growing conditions, so if you can't find any other reason for plant problems, double check its soil and situation, as well as basic lapses in your tender loving care.

Frost damage

Young shoots that suddenly look like they've been hit by a flame thrower – shriveled and turning black – are usually a symptom of a late frost. The damage is quite commonly seen in spring, if there's a sudden cold snap after the buds have burst and new leaves have started to open. If a late frost is forecast, drape plants in several layers of horticultural fleece to avoid damage. Otherwise, wait until you can see which bits of affected plants are dead and which are alive, then prune affected stems back to healthy growth. You'll know shoots are dead if they snap cleanly instead of bending, and, when cut, they will be brown or buff-colored beneath the bark. Living, healthy shoots are flexible and are green beneath the bark.

Classic frost damage (*left*) on a rose. The unfurling leaf looks as though it has been burned, when, actually, the opposite is true – it has been frozen. Wind damage here on garrya (*right*), is similar in its effect – it causes drying out and browning of tissue.

Wind

Wind can also cause a scorched appearance, and young growth is most vulnerable, because it's soft. Wind-burn grows out in time, but if a delicate plant is grown in a windy location, it'll never be very happy. Make sure that wind-hating plants, such as Japanese maples, are grown in a sheltered spot.

Wilting

Most people rush to water a wilting plant, but dry soil is not always the problem. A waterlogged plant that has lost its tiny root hairs will also wilt, since it can't take up water, as will one that has lost its roots because of soil pests. Always investigate further before jumping to conclusions.

Toadstools

Mostly harmless, toadstools usually appear in mild, misty autumns and feed on rotting organic matter, often in lawns, or on soil that's recently been enriched with mushroom compost or manure. They disappear naturally after the first frost. Fairy rings in lawns are something you learn to live with, unless you're prepared to dig out the soil to a depth of 1½ft (45cm) to remove all the threadlike underground mycelium (the fungal equivalent of roots), then fill the hole with new topsoil before laying new sod or reseeding.

Bracket fungi on trunks of old trees are often an early sign of a specimen that's on its way out. But the ones to watch out for are clumps of small, ocher-yellow toadstools on the ground close to dying trees or shrubs, especially if there are black "shoelaces" present in nearby soil, or beneath the bark. Then it's worth suspecting honey fungus (*Armillaria*), which can be a real killer. It needs expert diagnosis to confirm it for sure; but if it's in the area, your neighbors will probably know all about it. Dig up and discard infected plant roots, and prevent attack by keeping plants growing well – fertilizing and regular manuring help build up health and resistance.

Toadstools grow on rotting plant material – often old tree roots. I find that the best thing to do is (a) admire them or (b) sweep them off. They don't last long, anyway.

Nursing sick plants

Faced with plants that are a bit under the weather, a lot of people find it easier to cut their losses and replace them. It's certainly the quick solution to the problem, but it can be expensive, and, let's face it, if you love plants, there's a great sense of satisfaction in nursing casualties back to health.

Dealing with a dehydrated plant

One of the most common plant disasters is the dried-out hanging basket or the forgotten potted plant. You spot it only when the leaves are hanging down accusingly over the sides of the container. Often, normal watering doesn't hit the spot, because dried-out potting mix shrinks (especially the soilless types), leaving gaps at the sides of the container, so that water applied subsequently runs right through without soaking in. The answer is to stand the container in 2in (5cm) or so of water for a couple of hours – no longer, or the plant can "drown." By then, the potting mix should have soaked up as much water as it can hold, and you can let the excess drain away. Never leave a plant standing in water, or you'll create a continuous cycle of waterlogging that gives the root hairs no chance of making a full recovery, and the plant will eventually succumb.

A light diet

The first thing most people want to do with a sickly plant is fertilize it, because the leaves look pale, but it's usually the worst thing you can do. The best remedy is a few weeks on an invalid diet. When a plant is under the weather, it isn't working properly; don't add to its stress by making it cope with fertilizer. No, not even liquid fertilizer. Go easy on the watering, unless it's obvious that the only thing wrong with the plant is that it has dried out.

If your sick plant is in a pot and it has suffered root damage due to soil pests or waterlogging, then water it only sparingly for about four weeks. This gives new root hairs time to grow. If the plant normally likes moist air around it, increase the humidity by standing it in a loose plastic bag with a few holes punched in it, or put it in a propagating case; it's a good "intensive care unit" that will help it survive until new roots grow.

Otherwise, deal with the cause of the problem and give the plant time to recover naturally before resuming normal fertilizing and watering. If you really want to give a recovering plant a real shot in the arm, then spray it once a week with foliar fertilizer.

This is the quickest way of getting nutrients into it – especially if the roots are a bit suspect – and it usually regains a healthy color quite rapidly. Don't be tempted to spray on any old fertilizer – foliar fertilizers contain only nutrients that can be taken in through the leaves, and they are very dilute, so there's no risk of scorching.

You'll be able to tell when your nursing has done the trick, because the patient will start to look plumper and glossier and begin making new growth. In the case of a potted plant, you really know that you've won if you see healthy, white, young roots around the edge of the rootball when you gently tip the plant out of its pot.

The kindest cut

In some cases, a spot of surgery can be just what the doctor ordered. Reducing the size of a large plant can help its chances of survival when it's lost a lot of roots for any reason, because removing the leafy top means it's no longer losing water faster that it can take it up. It stands a better chance of recovering – and it'll soon make up the missing growth. As a rule of thumb, aim to cut back the top by a third or a half, if this can be done without wrecking the plant.

Pruning often makes a damaged plant look better in a hurry. If a bushy plant has been broken, or the young shoots have been distorted by a bad attack of aphids, then cutting it back has the same effect as "stopping" it (see pages 179–80 and 181), and encourages a rapid flush of sideshoots.

Plants that are well fertlized and watered are usually much more likely to stay healthy in the face of pest and disease attack.

Nonchemical controls

In the past, spraying was seen as a magic wand for waving away any kind of plant problem, but, today, there are all sorts of other controls that are often just as effective as chemicals and more environmentally responsible. The advantage of these techniques is that you don't eliminate the beneficial critters along with the bad guys.

Organic alternatives

Organic gardeners prefer to avoid problems in the first place, so they'll screen vegetables from pests using barriers; they might trap pests, or pick them off by hand, or encourage natural predators by companion planting (see organic gardening, pages 164–68).

But use even "organic" insecticides with care. Although many are nonpersistent and environmentally friendly, some are simply "organic hammers" that are nonselective in their action.

Insecticidal soap, or soft soap, isn't the kind you use in your bathtub, but a special soap based on fatty acids. It's sold as a liquid that you spray onto pests. Use it against aphids, spider mites, and whitefly; it's one of the few really effective remedies for cabbage aphids, as it can penetrate their natural waxy coating.

Beneficial bacteria, in concentrated form, are available in various products for different purposes. There are those that clear your pond, make your compost pile rot down faster, or treat stored rain or gray water in a barrel so that it can be recycled on to the garden. Some products are used to increase the natural level of beneficial micro-organisms in the soil, and they help make a healthier root environment; they are particularly useful when converting to organic gardening.

Bordeaux mixture contains slaked lime and copper sulfate made into a sprayable liquid. Use it for peach leaf curl, tomato and potato blight, and various fungal diseases of soft fruit.

Sulfur dust is good for powdering on stored bulbs to prevent rot and can also be dusted on to the wound, if you have to cut out a rotten bit of bulb. It is also good for controlling powdery mildew on plants, but use a light puff – don't drench them in dust. Sprayable sulfur products are sometimes available, which are easier to use accurately on plants, and you can also buy sulfur candles to burn if you want to fumigate your greenhouse.

If you really must spray, then choose an environmentally friendly product and follow the manufacturer's directions precisely. Never add "one for the pot."

Crop-protection jelly, or barrier glue, is sticky gunge you apply round the rims of containers, the legs of greenhouse staging, or the bark of trees to protect against crawling pests, like snails, gypsy moth caterpillars, vine weevil adults, ants, and sowbugs, which don't like to cross it.

Rotenone is a natural product, in itcomes from tropical plants. But although it's pretty effective against aphids, caterpillars, and thrips, it is nonspecific in its action (killing the goodies as well as the baddies) and has recently been found to be far more toxic to humans than was originally thought. I avoid it.

Aluminum sulfate, while not acceptable to real organic purists, is a more environmentally acceptable alternative than using slug pellets to tackle slugs and snails – but look out for other, even greener, products such as aerosol sprays based on yucca extract, and copper barrier strips that give mollusks a minute electric shock.

Liquid seaweed extract, used as an addition to liquid fertilizers or sprayed on the foliage, is thought by many organic enthusiasts to act as a natural tonic by supplying trace elements. They often use it to treat sick plants as well as to boost the natural defenses of healthy ones.

Natural disinfectants are available that are made from citrus extracts, which are handy for cleaning up soil and pots or seed trays.

Pyrethrum is also derived from plants (in this case, the flowers of a type of chrysanthemum), and it's used against aphids.

Canola oil is the active ingredient of a natural insecticide that works by blocking up the breathing holes in the skin of small insects, such as aphids, leaving bigger beneficial kinds, such as ladybugs, hoverflies, and lacewings, unharmed.

Crop protection jelly smeared around the rim of a pot will act as a barrier to slugs and snails and other crawling pests.

One plant will often distract pests from another. Aphids will home in on nasturtiums in preference to gooseberries – well it's worth a try!

Biological control

Biological control means really waging war on pests, because what you do is unleash a very powerful living enemy against them. Each biological control agent tackles one particular pest and, although they aren't cheap, results are at least as good as using chemicals, and they last longer.

The idea was originally developed for commercial greenhouses, where specially introduced insects can't fly away, but there are now several biological control agents, including beneficial nematodes (sometimes called eelworms) that can be used very successfully in garden soil or in containers outside.

At home, biological control is particularly worthwhile if you have a conservatory or greenhouse where you want to tackle all the common pests without using chemicals, or if you have a lettuce bed to protect from slugs or containers that you want to protect from vine weevil.

Using biological control agents

Introduce biological controls under cover early in the season, as soon as the temperature is warm enough for them, because they can't overtake a major plague of pests. You'll need to send off for the relevant "agent" by mail. Various suppliers advertise in gardening magazines, and some products can be ordered through garden centers. Use them within a few days of delivery because, being living organisms, they don't keep.

Glasshouse insects are usually delivered as eggs in vials of vermiculite, or as eggs on cards to hang up among your plants – always place them near a group of pests, so that there's a fast food supply for the emerging biological control agents.

Beneficial nematodes are delivered freeze-dried, so you need to reconstitute them in water and apply them to the soil through a watering can at the correct rate. But they all come with full instructions, and it's essential to read these first to get it right.

Caterpillars can be killed by introducing a caterpillar disease called *Bacillus thuringiensis* onto the foliage on which they are feeding. Treated caterpillars take a few days to die but stop feeding very quickly. This bacterium is normally used outdoors, but only exactly where it's needed. It can kill caterpillars of desirable butterfly species, too, so it's not a favorite of mine.

Scale insects, mealybugs, and thrips under cover can also be wiped out with specific biological controls; they are available from a few specialized suppliers, so you'll need to seek them out.

Aphids can be controlled under cover by introducing a parasitic insect called *Aphidius*. It lays its eggs in young aphids, which turn into brown mummies, from each of which a new aphidius hatches out. You can also buy lacewing and ladybug larvae to use in the greenhouse, or to let loose in the garden, to boost your naturally existing populations.

Spider mite can be kept under control with the help of an aggressive predatory mite called *Phytosieulus persimilis*. A warmth-loving creature, it's no use introducing it unless the greenhouse temperature stays above 61°F (16°C) at night. Unless you're prepared to put on the heating, delay introduction until late spring.

Slugs are a real biological control success story. The slug parasite *Phasmarhabditis hermaphrodita* is a nematode that commonly occurs in the wild, so, by increasing the numbers in your garden, you are simply fortifying natural defenses. Use the parasite from midspring onward, when the soil is warm (above 40°F/5°C) and moist. By wiping out your existing slugs, you also ensure there are no eggs in the soil to start up the next generation. Although the vendors claim that the product lasts six weeks or so, many people have found that it takes about a year before the slug population recovers fully in treated areas. It doesn't work on snails, because snails don't spend enough time on the ground, and it's not as effective on cold clay soil. Though not cheap, its often the answer when nothing else works. And if birds eat an affected slug, they aren't harmed by toxins that they pick up from slugs that have eaten slug pellets.

Vine weevil larvae are tracked down by a species of beneficial nematode, *Heterorhabditis*. Apply by watering the diluted nematode "soup" onto soil or pottimg mix outdoors in late spring, early summer, and early autumn, when larvae are most likely to be present. Use it under cover at any time; the pests have a longer breeding season in warmth. If no larvae are present at the time of application, the nematode will die out.

Whitefly are commonly controlled under glass by a tiny parasitic wasp called *Encarsia formosa*. It lays its eggs in the whitefly eggs, so that instead of a young whitefly hatching, out pops another encarsia to keep up the good work. For best results, introduce three batches of encarsia at two-week intervals. There's also another whitefly predator called *Delphastus* that is a relative of the ladybug. This is claimed to be more efficient at tackling larger outbreaks; it's worth a try.

Physical controls, like this sticky, yellow fly-catching paper, though not strictly biological, are an effective way of checking for whitefly in a greenhouse and contain no chemical residues.

Gardeners' friends

There are plenty of creatures out there that'll be only too happy to make a meal of your garden pests for free. What's more, you don't need to do much to attract them. Stop using chemicals, and create a reasonably undisturbed environment where there's food, water, and somewhere to take shelter – especially for winter – and they'll find you all on their own.

Birds

Starlings, I reckon, hatch out knowing that a gardener plus a spade equals lunch – they and other blackbirds are the natural answer to soil grubs, but they'll also take caterpillars and all sorts of nuisances. The thrush's specialty is snails – thrushes use a handy stone as an anvil to smash the shells against, so they can get at the filling inside. Many small birds are like security patrols against aphids; they'll do the rounds of your roses and fruit trees regularly in spring when they have chicks to feed. Wrens take lots of insects from hedges and are also very interested in the springtails and other tiny creatures that often live in and around compost piles.

The way to attract birds to your garden is to feed them in winter with seeds, peanuts, and fat, but make sure there are plenty of trees and shrubs to offer cover so that they can escape from predators. It's also a good idea to grow plants that provide seed heads and berries that birds can feed on in autumn. Provide a supply of clean water all the time, and some birdhouses, and you'll have the makings of a thriving resident bird population.

Mammals

Larger creatures play their part in the life of the garden, too, eating unwanted pests. Encourage wildlife by providing undisturbed areas for small mammals to take refuge in. Leave a few rotting logs in a patch of long grass among shrubs, and they might be persuaded to move in. Even if they don't, they are likely to at least pass through or wander around a quiet garden... if they are in the area.

Skunks are admittedly not the first thing you want to run into when you're walking around your garden, especially at night, but they do a great job on grubs (sometimes too good a job, tearing the grass up badly in their search for them) and they will eat other pests.

Foxes are something suburban and rural gardeners don't always welcome, either, but when they are well fed, they rarely dig holes in the garden or knock over the trashcan, and they usually just pass through. Again they are fun to watch, and they'll eat snails and grubs as well as any scraps of pet food that you put out.

The wise gardener has more than a romantic attachment to insect-eating garden birds, because they play an important part in pest control.

Friend or foe?

Some insects that gardeners traditionally treat as enemies turn out to have some beneficial tendencies as well.

- **Earwigs** are best-known for nibbling flower petals, but they also do a lot of good by feeding on aphids and other small insects. Only among flowers like dahlias and daylilies do they wreak real havoc. Encourage them to linger in places where they can do some good by stuffing flowerpots with straw and perching them on top of short sticks.
- **Wasps** go only for sweet things at the peak of the fruit season; the rest of the time they take aphids and small caterpillars for their larvae to feed on. As long as their nest isn't somewhere it's going to be a nuisance, then leave them alone.
- **Sowbugs** have a bad reputation as eaters of seedlings, but it's debatable whether they damage strong, healthy ones, and, when you find them inside holes in fruit, it's unlikely that they did the initial damage – they are more likely to be sheltering in a hole originally made by a slug.

Pond life

If you do nothing else to encourage wildlife, put in a pond – even if it's only a small one – as long as it has at least one shallow, sloping edge. Birds will visit to take a bath, and a wide range of wildlife will drop in for a drink. But you'll also attract frogs and toads, which are among the very best natural controls for slugs. The adults don't spend all their time in the water; they wander around between plants hunting for snacks.

A garden pond will encourage all manner of beneficial wildlife that will do its best to help with general pest control.

Beneficial insects and their relatives

For many years, gardeners were brought up with the idea that the only good bug is a dead one, but attitudes have changed, which is good for the garden, because lots of insects help by hunting down plant pests. Attract the adults by growing nectar-rich hardy annuals, lavenders, and flowering herbs. Poached-egg plant (*Limnanthes douglasii*), *Phacelia campanularia*, and *Convolvulus tricolor* are particularly good. And do learn to recognize the larvae as well; for years people went around bumping off ladybug larvae without realizing what they were.

Encourage beneficial insects to stay in the garden in winter. Don't clear your perennial beds properly until spring, so they have lots of safe hiding places. If you must clean up, leave a fringe of long grass and plant stems around the edge of the garden, so that beneficial bugs are on the spot, ready to go to work when they emerge in spring.

How do you tell a good bug from a bad one? If it moves slowly, it eats plants; if it moves fast, it eats other insects. Obvious, really!

Ground beetles (1), rove beetles, black beetles, call them what you will (there are several different types): are all well worth making friends with. They live in soil, under stones or logs, and in debris under hedges and feed on slugs, cabbage root fly, flea beetles, weevils, and other soil pests. Their larvae have a similar diet, so the entire family does a lot of good. They're easily distinguished from vine weevils. Good beetles are generally black, shiny, and move fast; they have two separate antennae on the front of their heads – bad vine weevils are smaller, buff-brown, and have Y-shaped antennae. A black beetle with a purplish tinge is probably a violet ground beetle – another goody.

Ichneumon flies (2) lay their eggs in the caterpillars of the large white butterfly caterpillars (alias cabbage whites) – the ones that reduce members of the cabbage family and nasturtiums to lace – and parasitize them, which prevents them turning into new butterflies.

Lacewings (3) look like transparent-winged greenish moths. Both the adults and larvae eat aphids and other small pests. If you find them, allow them to hibernate in the shed in winter. To encourage them to stay in your garden all year, you can buy lacewing "hotels" made of bundles of hollow stems mounted in a frame.

Hoverflies (4) are those stripy jobs that look like slimline wasps, except that they don't sting and they have a remarkable ability to hover on the spot. Both the adults and the larvae take huge numbers of aphids from early summer onward, once the sunny weather sets in.

Spiders (5) are great hunters and trappers; the wolf spider is the one you sometimes see sunbathing on a leaf with its two pairs of front legs stretched out together – they run down insect prey. Web-forming spiders catch flying insects, and even tiny spiders feed on aphids. Daddy longlegs, which look like small-bodied, long-legged spiders, take newly hatched caterpillars and sowbugs. If you catch them indoors, put them out in the garden.

Ladybugs (6) come in red or orange and with varying numbers of spots; both the adults and larvae take huge numbers of aphids. Ladybug numbers are slow to build up in summer; in winter, they hibernate in large "roosts."

Velvet mites (7) look like minute, bright red spiders; you sometimes see them scurrying around in hot, dry corners – they are a natural predator of many small insects, including spider mite.

Centipedes (8) are the flattish, red-brown, fast-moving creatures that snake their way through moist leaf litter and debris, hunting for springtails, mites, slugs, and other food. The slow-moving, tubular black jobs with waves of rippling legs are millipedes, which eat plants.

Beneficial insects:
1 Ground beetles polish off all manner of soil pests.
2 Ichneumon flies lay their eggs inside caterpillars – gruesome, but very welcome.
3 Lacewings are aphid eaters.
4 Hoverflies eat large quantities of aphids.
5 Spiders feed on all kinds of insects, from aphids to house flies.
6 Ladybugs eat aphids – very helpful.
7 Velvet mites feed on pests such as spider mite.
8 Centipedes are fast movers that will demolish everything from slugs to mites.

Using chemicals

Chemicals are, to my mind, very much a last resort. I am very rarely persuaded to reach for a bottle if the only alternative is losing a good plant. If you feel the same, the one thing I'd say is don't use anything more powerful than you really need. If there's a product that tackles the specific problem, then use it. It will have less impact on the rest of the garden community than a broad-spectrum product that kills lots of things. Treat only the affected plant – don't blitz the entire garden. In extreme circumstances, I think it's far more responsible to use a specific inorganic pesticide than a nonselective organic one.

Types of product

A glance at the chemicals department of a big garden center can be daunting, since there are so many bottles, packets, pots, and potions on sale. They fall into several categories, so look out for key words:

Systemic products are taken up into the sap stream of the plant and move around inside it. Systemic weedkillers are taken in through the leaves and kill the roots as well as the leaves and stems. Systemic insecticides kill sap-sucking insects for some time after treatment, so one spray can protect plants from attack for two weeks or so.

Contact products work only on what they touch. They kill leaves but not roots. Contact insecticides kill only those pests that get sprayed. With these, it's vital to cover the entire plant thoroughly.

Stomach-acting insecticides work by being sprayed on to plants and then eaten by pests along with the leaves, so they are good for killing munching bugs like caterpillars.

Combined products contain a cocktail of ingredients. Path weedkillers, for example, usually contain one chemical to kill off existing weeds and another to kill emerging seedlings. Some rose fungicides contain several ingredients to treat different diseases, plus an insect killer or foliar fertilizer. Combined weedkillers and fertilizers are available, usually as lawn "feed and weed."

Total weedkillers kill everything green that they touch.

Selective weedkillers "choose" what they work on; the only example of this type of product is selective lawn weedkiller that kills broadleaved weeds and leaves grasses unharmed.

Stay safe

The important thing when using any kind of chemical is to read, understand, and follow the instructions. Safety must always come first, so I make no apologies for nagging.

Check the days-to-harvest period before using a pesticide on edible crops. It tells you how many days must elapse between spraying the product and eating treated fruit or vegetables. You can't put treated produce in the freezer to bring out after the harvest interval is up – that doesn't count.

To avoid damage, read the small print to see if the plants you want to spray are unsuitable for treatment with that product. If you make a mistake, wash the plant off well and flush the potting mix or soil through with plenty of water.

Concentrated liquid products *must* be diluted for application, whether by sprayer or watering can. The directions often assume you need large amounts of the diluted product, so calculating the right dose for small areas can be tricky. If you know you're not a whiz at mental arithmetic, work it out on paper, or use a calculator. Once diluted, chemicals don't keep, so make up only as much as you need, then dispose of any surplus safely (see below).

Stick to the dilution rates given in the instructions. Avoid using products at a stronger dilution than suggested – far from working better, they are usually less effective.

Avoid the use of weedkillers just before it rains; most need at least 12 hours in contact with the leaves to be absorbed properly.

Safety with chemicals

- **Do** wear rubber gloves and cover any exposed skin when applying garden chemicals.
- **Do** wear safety goggles or a visor when mixing liquids to avoid chemicals splashing into your eyes.
- **Don't** breathe in the spray.
- **Don't** spray in windy conditions, because droplets can reach plants you didn't mean to treat. Protect nearby plants if you're using weedkiller, even in still conditions.
- **Don't** decant products out of their original container or use anything that's lost its label; you won't know what it is or how to use it.
- **Don't** pour unwanted chemicals down the drain. Even if there's only a bit left, dilute it as per instructions and water it thinly over a patch of gravel or vacant ground. For advice on disposing of larger quantities, contact your local authority; they have arrangements for dealing with what they call hazardous household waste.

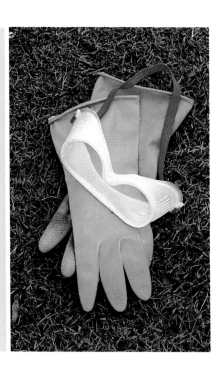

8 THE GREEN CARPET

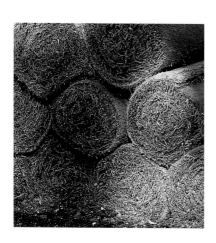  

Grass in gardens

To most people, grass is "outdoor carpet," as indispensable in the garden as wall-to-wall wool or nylon in the living room. Yes, fashions change, and hard surfaces – paving, gravel, and decking – are on the increase outdoors, in much the same way as seagrass matting, or polished wood floors, are indoors. But there are very few gardens that don't have at least a small patch of lawn.

There's something about a striped lawn that brings out the neatnik in a homeowner - nothing says "perfectionist" like this!

Grass is still the cheapest and most traditional outdoor floor covering, particularly for large areas, so it's easy to take it for granted. But don't think of it as a self-renewing carpet; see it instead as thousands of tiny individual plants growing tightly packed together in each square yard of soil. It is not maintenance-free. Although grass doesn't take quite so much time and effort as a border, it still needs looking after.

Which grass?

When I was a lad, you had two sorts of grass. In the back garden, you had your everyday bluegrass dotted with springy heads of rye-grass that popped up from under the mower instead of being chopped off – just like that lump of hair on the back of your head that wouldn't lie down. Out front was the posh lawn that you kept off; it was there to impress the neighbors. Both were nearly weed-free and were stripe-mowed at the correct length for the entire season, and leaves and other debris were removed soon after they appeared.

Things have come a long way since then. Today's lawn is a much more natural style of grass that the family can use fully for all outdoor activities. Weeds are no longer a dirty word and, to some gardeners, are even classed as desirable wildflowers to be welcomed. Stripes have almost vanished now that so many of us have rotary mowers instead of cylinder mowers, and you'll sometimes find "feature" lawns that don't contain any grass at all but are covered with herbs or flowers instead (see pages 255–57).

Yet despite all the emphasis on contemporary design and trendy hard surfaces, people are still making new lawns. Modern strains of ornamental blue- and ryegrasses are bred for looks, compactness, and hard-wearing qualities, so you have the best of both worlds, without the stiff seed heads that made 1950s lawns so uncomfortable to sit on. You'll find various grass seed mixtures: some suitable for damp, shady areas; others for dry, sunny spots; some slow-growing "low-maintenance" blends; and other mixtures with wildflower seed added. On the sod front, you can choose from several grades of cultivated turf, which are extensively farmed as a crop, and you can find places that sell it by the piece or by the truckload (see page 238).

Nowadays, many people have several types of lawn; they'll have distinct areas – perhaps a patch of "best" with grassy paths, rough turf for the kids and dogs to play on, and maybe a feature lawn or a wildflower meadow. At Barleywood, I have a bit of everything, but the greensward binds everything together in a kind of verdant unity.

Sports turf

Not many people would really want a lawn like a bowling green if they knew what was involved. Proper sports turf needs colossal amounts of maintenance, because it's trying to do two things: provide a hard, flat playing surface that stands lots of wear, while growing grass that is cut routinely to keep it at the correct height. That's why clubs and teams employ groundsmen to do all the maintenance – the rolling, serious slashing of the lawn's surface, and regular reseeding – none of which you'd want to do at home (and, frankly, you shouldn't need to).

What a lawn does better than any other surface is to bring together all the elements of the garden.

Lay sod as soon as possible after arrival, and within a month or two you'll have a usable lawn.

Sod

Sod is pregrown grass that is cut from the ground ready for you to unroll as an instant lawn. Cultivated sod gives a good-quality lawn, but meadow turf, possibly with weeds or bare patches, is cheaper, if you can find it. Once sod has rooted into your soil, you can treat it as a normal lawn. But, be prepared to water it if the weather is dry. If you lay sod in early autumn, there should be plenty of rainfall to do the job for you.

You usually order sod by the square foot. It is delivered in strips measuring about 3 x 1ft (100 x 30cm), folded or rolled up so that it's easier to handle. Arrange to have it delivered just before you want to lay it; if you can't get on with the job for two to three days, don't leave it rolled up. Unroll the pieces and lay them flat, with the grass exposed to the light, and water them, if necessary. If you leave your sod rolled up, it will turn yellow in a matter of days. It will look vile, be weakened as a result, and may die out in places.

How to... **make a lawn from sod**

The great advantage of laying sod is that one day you have what looks like a building site, and the next you have a lawn. You're not limited as to timing, either. You can lay sod as long as the ground is not frozen and is not too dry or boggy. It's a bit of a risk putting it down in summer, although you might get away with it if the weather is unusually cool and wet and you keep it heavily watered. Busy folk tend to forget and, before they know it, their green carpet tiles have shrunk and turned brown at the edges.

Fast results come at a price. Sod is ten times more expensive than grass seed, and, if you go for high quality, it costs about the same as good carpeting. Sod is fast, but, although it looks the part right away, don't walk on it until it has rooted down into the soil and started to grow.

What you need

- *sharp spade and garden fork*
- *garden rake*
- *special lawn fertilizer or autumn lawn fertilizer (without weedkiller)*
- *pieces of sod, enough to cover the area*
- *wooden board*
- *sharp kitchen knife*

1 Dig or fork the ground over in the same way as if you were preparing a new flower bed (see page 66). Rake it roughly level, removing stones and roots as you go. Sprinkle on fertilizer at the recommended rate, then rake it in. Walk over the entire area, sinking your weight well down into your heels to consolidate the soft patches. Rake again to cover the footprints, leaving a fine seed-sowing "tilth."

2 Without walking on the prepared ground, lay a line of pieces in a straight row along one end of the area, butting their short sides up together. Pat down with the rake head so that each piece makes contact with the soil beneath.

To avoid making footprints and dents, place your board on the row you've just laid and walk along it as you lay the next row, staggering the joints between the pieces like joints in brickwork. Repeat, patting each new row down with the rake.

3 When you've covered the entire area, trim the outer edge of the sodded area with a sharp kitchen knife, so the lawn edge follows the shape of your beds.

If it doesn't rain for several days after laying, turn the sprinkler on. Repeat every few days until the sod has knitted into the ground. To test, try to peel back the corner of a few random pieces – if you can't lift them, then the grass has rooted down.

How to... **make a lawn from seed**

What you need

- *digging spade and fork*
- *garden rake*
- *special preseeding lawn fertilizer or autumn lawn fertilizer (without weedkiller)*
- *grass seed: allow 1–2oz per sq.yd (25–50g per 1sq.m)*
- *twiggy pea-sticks, if birds are a problem*

Growing grass from seed costs a lot less than using sod (see pages 238–39), but there are only a couple of windows of opportunity for successful sowing; midspring (April–May in most of the country) and midautumn (September–early October). It takes 4–6 months before you have a usable lawn, so most people sow in autumn. It gives new grass plenty of time to turn into a proper lawn before heavy demands are made upon it. It also means natural rainfall keeps your grass seed watered – sowing just before the start of summer makes it much more likely that you'll need to use a sprinkler while the new lawn establishes. Weed seedlings are also less of a problem in autumn than in spring. On the whole, although you need to wait longer for a lawn from seed, it's less arduous than laying sod.

1 Prepare the ground in the same way as if you were laying sod (see page 239): dig or fork over, rake, spread fertilizer, rake, tread, and rake some more. You are aiming to produce a level, evenly firmed seedbed, which will lead to a level lawn.

2 Divide the total amount of grass seed in half. Sprinkle one lot north-south, then repeat, this time spreading east-west. You don't need to take a compass to it, but the general idea is to make sure the seed is spread very thinly and evenly all over, with no bare patches.

3 Rake over the area again very lightly, starting at the far end of the "lawn," scuffling the seed into the ground. You won't cover all of the seed – expect to see about half of it still showing when you've finished. If you anticipate a bird problem, lay twiggy pea-sticks over the ground to prevent birds from eating the seed and from taking dust baths.

And after?

It's quite exciting watching grass seed come up – in a rather Zen-like way. For days there's nothing but bare soil but, after a couple of weeks of mild weather, crouch down and look across the surface of the soil and you'll see a green haze over the ground that will rapidly turn into green stubble. Water if you need to, and keep off the new grass while it's looking a bit thin and wispy. Don't worry about lots of weeds coming up – that's quite normal, and they won't stand a chance once you start cutting the grass.

As the lawn starts to thicken up and once the longest tufts are 2–3in (5–8cm) long, cut the grass very gently with a mower set high enough to take only the tips off the grass blades. Remember: all you are trying to do is take the tips off the grass, which helps it root in more firmly and makes the grass seedlings bush out and develop into tiny clumps. Make sure your mower is sharp, or it will rip the young plants from the soil rather than scissoring off the ends of the leaves.

For the first proper cut, choose a day when the grass has dried out completely: if it's wet, the blades will, again, just tear and pull bits up instead of cutting cleanly. Adjust the mower so that the blades are at their highest setting, and leave the grass bag on to catch the clippings.

Apart from essential cultivation, keep off the grass until it has been cut several times and starts to look like a proper lawn. Keep the blades set high for the first few cuts, then lower them gradually, but don't cut any shorter than 1¼in (3cm) to start with. The good news is that within the first few cuts, virtually all the weeds will disappear as if by magic. If you find typical lawn weeds, such as dandelions and plantains, pull them up by hand or wait for six months or more, then you can start to use normal lawn weedkillers, or combined fertilizer and weedkiller treatments – not before.

If you have a small lawn, make it an even shape that is easily mowed, then maintenance will not become a problem.

Under the surface

Lawns are a bit like swans – the top may look serene but, below the surface, there's a lot of frantic activity going on. Here's a worm's-eye view of the sort of situations your grass must put up with as it grows older.

Thatch
Thatch is a buildup of dead bits of grass and tough horizontal stalks that knit together on the surface of the soil beneath the lawn like a fibrous underlay. You can check for it very easily by cutting a small square of grass out of your lawn and looking at it edgeways on – thatch is the strawlike layer between the roots and the green leaf blades. Thatch is quite natural in lawns that are getting on a bit, and a lot of people – mistakenly – think that the springy surface of a badly affected lawn is a sign of quality. It isn't. The trodden-down thatch acts like a spongy umbrella, preventing rain from soaking down to the grass roots, where it's needed, and keeping moisture at the soil surface, where it encourages disease.

You probably won't have any trouble with thatch until your lawn has been down for five years or more, but it builds up faster if you don't use a grass bag on your mower. Once it's there, it needs raking out regularly. Autumn is the best time to do this, as part of a regular lawn-care program (see page 251).

Surface compaction
This is another regular problem to expect once lawns have been in place for a few years. It's the frequent trampling that does the damage. When the ground is wet it's softer than usual, so your feet sink in, and standing garden furniture on it, or running heavy whelbarrows over it, squashes the lawn down badly. Then, as with any well-trodden patch of soil, plant roots have more of a struggle to push through the hard ground, and puddles form in wet weather.

Compacted soil has a lot of the air spaces squashed out of it, which is why it's a good idea to spike the lawn with a fork. Spiking alleviates compaction and, by making some airways, helps the grass grow. Again it's a job that's best done in autumn. On small-particled soils, like clay, follow up by brushing gritty sand into the vertical drainage channels (about a bucketful per square yard), so that the "pores" aren't squashed shut again next time you walk over the area. You won't brush it all in, but the surplus works into the surface over time, making it firmer to walk on yet better drained in wet conditions.

A plastic or wire-toothed lawn rake is an efficient way of getting rid of thatch. Power dethatchers make the job easier but will do nothing for your stomach muscles.

Lawn pests

Even the best-kept lawns can suffer from the occasional attentions of unwanted visitors, but, if you're vigilant and know what to look out for, you can nip problems in the bud before they reach epidemic proportions. It also pays to know the difference between problem pests and the creatures that you can happily live with.

Sweep off excessive numbers of worm casts – with a spring-tined rake or special broom known as a besom – on a dry day, and they will add to the lawn's fertility.

Earthworms

Worms are actually beneficial in the garden – they make hundreds of tiny drainage channels in the soil. They also drag organic matter, such as dead leaves, into the ground, helping with soil enrichment. Of the many species of earthworm, only a few leave worm casts on the lawn's surface, and then mainly in spring and autumn, so don't over-react; earthworms are a sign of a healthy soil. Wait for a dry day and sweep worm casts off with a rake or broom – the sort made out of a bundle of twigs – and they will quickly disintegrate before you start to mow.

Ants

Ants like nesting in dry soil in lawns in summer, when they push up little volcano-like cones of fine soil. They will defend their nests, often giving you nasty nips if you sit down near them – red ants are the worst. Ants usually target patches where the grass is thin and bare soil is exposed, so a lush, well-maintained lawn is less likely to be bothered. Keep an eye open for nests in early summer. If you soak new nesting sites thoroughly with water, you can often drive ants away. If they are well entrenched, take heart; in late summer, much of the colony will disappear. Soak the area well when the ants vacate, and you will wash a lot of the loosened soil back into place.

Moles

Moles burrow beneath lawns in search of their favorite food – earthworms. Years ago, pesticides were used to kill the worms in the hope that the moles would leave, too, but those toxic products are no longer available, even if you wanted to use them. You can often deter moles by flooding new runs with water, by placing prickly holly leaves inside, or filling the runs with something smelly, such as the contents of the cat's litter tray. Don't connect the exhaust pipe of your car up to gas them out – it does more harm to the car. Some people swear by burying something noisy inside the run – a musical birthday card or a transistor radio, wrapped in a plastic bag, and tuned to one of the noisier pop channels. You can buy electronic mole repellents (which work better on clay soils than on sandy ones), or sink empty wine bottles into the runs, so that

Moles are a pain to get rid of, but their molehills are an excellent basic ingredient for homemade potting soil.

the wind makes an eerie howling noise when it blows across the bottlenecks. They usually work for a while if you "plant" a row and keep moving them, so you sweep your mole out of the lawn, but it pays to change your strategy regularly, because moles get used to anything in time.

Moles are quite territorial, so even if you persuade the current incumbent to leave, the vacant patch soon attracts a new tenant. If your garden is surrounded by farmland, you've little chance of winning, so it's probably best to learn to live with them. Just be sure to clear molehills away before mowing the lawn, or you just end up with big bare patches where the grass has been smothered. If possible, wash the soil back into the hole, so that you don't end up with a sunken lawn. Not very satisfactory, I know, but it's about the best we can do these days. Unless you want to call in the molecatcher...

Solitary bees

These creatures sometimes turn up in garden lawns, but they are quite shy and don't do any harm. You are most likely to see them if you have a wildlife garden where the lawn isn't cut very often, or – how shall I put this delicately – on a rather neglected lawn with a lot of bald patches. Each bee, which looks like a small bumble bee, excavates a round hole about as wide as a pencil, with a few honeycomb-like cells below ground in which she rears her family. All you'll see is the queen bee flying in and out of the hole. You may find several holes in the same area, but solitary bees don't make colonies. Frankly I'd leave well alone – they nest only in spring, and by autumn they've moved on. You're unlikely to find them in a smart, well-maintained lawn, because they don't like being disturbed.

If you do find them, consider it an honor and a privilege; you can also feel pleased with doing your bit to conserve a self-sufficient little beauty.

Leatherjackets

If you see hordes of long-legged crane flies dancing over your lawn in autumn (especially in the Northwest), be prepared for an invasion of their larvae – leather-jackets – the following year (see page 47). Leatherjackets eat grass roots, and the first thing you know about it is lots of little yellow patches, or flocks of starlings probing for grubs. Since the chemicals that were once recommended for use against lawn soil pests have now been withdrawn, your best bet is to let nature take its course. You can repair a pecked-up surface after the birds have done their bit. Alternatively, nip the problem in the bud by gathering the craneflies when they congregate for an orgy.

Regard the arrival of a solitary bee as a compliment, and congratulate yourself on doing your bit for conservation.

Lawn maintenance

Rough grass can be left to look after itself for much of the time, but a proper lawn needs a little regular attention if you want to keep it looking its best. The amount of trouble you are prepared to go to depends on how much of a lawn perfectionist you are.

My rotary mower, with its heavy rear roller, has resulted in quite a decent lawn that even has stripes.

Mowing

Although it's more convenient to cut the grass on weekends, it really needs cutting every time it grows about ½in (1cm) longer than you want it. The time it takes to do that varies during the year, according to the growing conditions. I know that regular care isn't always possible, but it is the ideal to aim for. If you leave a lawn to grow long and shaggy and then cut it short, the odds are that it will look unhappy for a while, because you will have cut into the thick brown or yellow stems at the base of the plants, instead of through lush green leaf blades. Regular mowing produces a greener, denser, harder-wearing lawn.

To keep a lawn looking really good, it helps to vary the height at which you cut it during the year. Start mowing in spring, as soon as the grass is dry enough, with the blades set high – maybe 1½in (4cm) – just to slice the top off. Lower the blades as the lawn gets used to being cut. Aim for a height of ¾in (2cm) for a very fine lawn; 1in (2.5cm) for a family lawn, and 1½in (4cm) for rough grass beneath trees or in a wild garden. If the weather turns dry in summer, raise the blades again to reduce stress to the grass. Grass will remain greener if it's allowed to grow a little longer until the conditions for encouraging growth are better. As the weather turns cooler in autumn, raise the mower blades back up to their spring level, but don't give up cutting the grass. It keeps growing until it's really cold, so, if it is still growing, top it lightly whenever it dries out enough.

It's entirely up to you whether you prefer to use a grass bag or not; high-quality lawns look the better for it, and, if you use a cylinder mower with a roller on the back, you'll be able to make those snappy-looking stripes for which the British are justly famous. Rotary mowers with a heavy roller can produce stripes, too.

A rotary mower without a grass bag is much quicker to use because you don't need to keep emptying out clippings, but mow frequently, so that the short clippings disappear quickly into the lawn. Otherwise, go for a mulching mower that shreds the clippings into fine bits and then blasts them back down into the lawn.

Using a mower without a grass bag once every two weeks is a recipe for disaster. Long grass, if left in clods on the surface, will kill the lawn and make it patchy. Added to which, the freshly cut lawn looks a real mess. Nothing at all to laugh at.

Edging

After cutting the grass, trim around the edges with edging shears – the long-handled sort – to neaten the tufts of grass that stick out sideways over the margins. But before you can use edging shears, you need a properly made lawn edge – a shallow, neat-edged gully all around your beds and borders with a vertical drop of 2–3in (5–7.5cm). Hold the blade of the shears against this flat surface as you cut.

Lawn edges need redefining each spring, because rain tends to wash the soil from the adjacent beds down to fill in the edges; this prevents you from using your shears properly. That's why, before your first lawn-mowing session each spring, you should go around all your lawn edges with the back of a spade to reshape them.

Edging shears will provide the finishing touch – a neat, clean rim to the lawn.

It doesn't take long, but it does make edging so much easier for the rest of the year, not to mention making the whole garden look neater. If the edges are badly broken, more heavy-duty maintenance may be needed (see pages 252–54). Some folk can't be doing with this sort of perfectionism. I find it worryingly therapeutic.

Fertilizing

A heck of a lot is asked of lawns – they are "pruned" more regularly than any other plant in the garden, and then they are walked all over. So they need fertilizing if they are to look good, especially if they must stand up to heavy wear. The most important time to fertilize is in early spring, since that's the start of the growing season, but real lawn enthusiasts often keep fertilizing every six weeks until autumn to keep grass looking lush. When the soil is dry, the grass is already stressed and can "scorch" if it's fertilized, so don't fertilize unless growing conditions have been favorable for a few weeks and the grass has recovered.

What to apply? Spring and summer grass fertilizers are high in nitrogen and so produce a rich green lawn, but, as summer comes to an end, lawns need a different nutrient blend. Use an autumn formula that is low in nitrogen but high in phosphorus and potassium to toughen up the roots for winter. If that sounds too much like hard work, then try an organic lawn fertilizer once a month. It will not scorch the grass, and it releases nutrients over a longer period of time than other lawn fertilizers. It's always best to use a proper lawn fertilizer – either granular or liquid – for fertilizing grass. Some people economize and use a general-purpose fertilizer instead, but if you do, you won't get the same flush of lush green grass, and the large granules need a lot of watering in. If your aim is to improve the lawn without making it grow any faster (so it doesn't need so much mowing), simply use an autumn lawn fertilizer during summer instead. Organic gardeners can now find organic lawn fertilizer with little difficulty.

Weeds

The sort of weeds that are a real pest in lawns are the ones that lie flat and pass safely under the mower instead of being chopped off. These are the rosette-forming weeds, such as plantains and dandelions, and the low-spreading sort, such as trefoils and speedwell. These weeds are known as broadleaved weeds in chemical-company speak, and they are easy to eradicate with selective lawn weedkillers.

Organic lawn fertilizer is easily applied by hand from a bucket, though for ease – and accuracy with inorganic kinds – a wheeled spreader is a safer bet.

You can either spot-treat individual weeds with a ready-to-use product that comes in a "water-pistol" pack, or as a waxy, deodorant-style stick, or you can sprinkle a combined "weed-and-feed" treatment over the entire lawn.

For small-leaved weeds like trefoil, you'll need a liquid weedkiller that is specially designed for this type of weed. Dilute it and water it on with a can. It's always a good idea to feed the lawn around the time you kill the weeds. Dead weeds leave bald patches in the lawn that are quickly colonized by weed seeds and moss, unless you encourage the grass to thicken up and fill the gaps.

If you don't fancy lawn weedkiller, then use an aspargus knife to lift individual weeds out by hand. With trefoils, which grow out from a central root in the shape of a lace doily, find the middle, gather the doily in one hand, and twist until the whole plant lifts out.

Organic gardeners cannot use lawn weedkillers, but there are several products on the market that will encourage grass at the same time as discouraging weeds from colonizing. The basic premise is that if the grass is growing vigorously, there will be little room for invaders.

For best results

Use lawn weedkillers in spring when weeds are growing fast but before they start flowering; by the time they flower, weeds will have become too tough to respond well to treatment. Apply liquid lawn weedkiller on a dry day, so that it has at least 12 to 24 hours to be taken in through the leaves. If it's washed away too soon, it won't have a chance to work.

If you opt for a granular "weed-and-feed" treatment, you need to time the application carefully, because although the weedkiller needs the same 12 to 24 hours' absorption period, the fertilizer needs to be washed in as soon as possible afterward. Turn on the sprinkler, if it hasn't rained after 48 hours, to make sure that the treatment is effective.

Moss

I wish I had a fiver for every time someone has told me that their lawn weedkiller didn't touch their moss. Well, it won't. You need a completely different product. Some moss killers also work on green lawn slime and on liverwort (that crusty green growth that looks like an alien invader), but not weeds.

The best time to treat moss is in spring, and you can buy liquid lawn mosskiller, or products that combine mosskiller with lawn

Regular spiking with a fork to improve surface drainage will help discourage moss on lawns.

fertilizer. You need to fertilize the lawn, so that it thickens up and fills gaps where moss has been, to prevent weeds from coming in.

Lawn sand is an old-fashioned, but effective, preparation that acts as a fertilizer, weed-, and mosskiller, but it can scorch the lawn if applied too heavily. That said, some gardeners swear by it. Buy it or make it up yourself from 4 parts (by weight) ammonium sulfate, 1 part iron sulfate, and 20 parts fine silver sand. It must be applied in dry weather, but when the soil is moist, at the rate of 4oz per sq.yd (115g per 1sq.m). It is used in spring and early summer, rather than in autumn.

Most mosskillers take a couple of weeks to work and you know when they have, because dead moss turns black. A light infestation may well vanish on its own after that, but it's usually recommended that you rake the dead stuff out. Frankly, I'd sooner rake the stuff out in the first place and save on the chemicals. It's hard work, so I use a power lawn raker. On damp, shady lawns, moss will keep coming back whatever you do, so you'll probably need to treat it in spring and autumn to keep on top of it. Anything you can do to let in more light and improve the surface drainage – spiking and sanding – will also help.

Lawn-care calendar

Just as your car needs servicing, your lawn needs maintenance, too.

Spring
• Fertilize and apply weedkiller or mosskiller, if needed.
• Start mowing regularly.

Summer
• Raise your mower blades and mow regularly, even if the grass isn't growing rapidly, to control upright weeds.
• Don't use fertilizer or other treatments in hot, dry conditions.

Autumn
• Mow the lawn from top to bottom, then from side to side.
• Rake to remove thatch and moss, then spike with a fork to aerate.
• Apply autumn lawn fertilizer to prepare grass for winter.
• Top dress with gritty sand or turf dressing, if needed.
• Clear fallen leaves regularly.

Winter
• Keep off the grass as much as possible; lay a board or "portable path" if you need to use a wheelbarrow.
• In mild areas, mow when conditions allow.

It will all have been worth it in the end when the final result is a good-looking, hard-wearing lawn.

Renovating lawns

If you've taken over a badly neglected lawn, or the grass takes a battering because the family uses it as an outdoor leisure center, it needs more than just routine care. One dose of intensive restoration work should be enough to put a neglected lawn back on its feet, but grass that receives regular hard wear will need a session once a year, in spring or autumn, whichever is the most convenient. The recipe sounds simple, but it means a lot of hard work, I'm afraid. The good news is that you'll notice a difference within a few weeks – and the improvement will continue as time goes by – if you keep up with normal, routine maintenance during the rest of the year.

Where to start

Begin by giving the lawn the annual autumn lawn treatment as described on the previous page in the lawn-care calendar. If you are doing this as part of a program of lawn restoration, it can be undertaken in spring or autumn. If a neglected lawn is in a really bad state, there's no reason why you shouldn't renovate it in summer, as long as the weather is cool and the soil is moist; but don't attempt it in a drought or a heatwave. Since summer is the barbecue season, be aware that the treatment will make the lawn look worse before it gets better, and it won't impress your guests!

After you've mowed, and mowed again at right angles to the first cut (to catch the bits that usually just get flattened by the mower), rake and spike the lawn, then use autumn lawn fertilizer – even if it's spring or summer. It's the best for thickening up the grass and stimulating the roots, which is what you want. Then, while the lawn is moving into top gear, see what other problems there are that need tackling.

Bald patches

Some bald patches are bald because that particular piece of lawn is in constant use by regular heavy foot traffic. If that's the case, you would be better off putting in a proper path, or at least sinking a series of paving slabs into the surface to use as stepping-stones.

Some patches may look a bit thin because the grass isn't growing very well, and spiking and fertilizing may be all it needs. Other patches may simply be "scalped" bumps; that happens when the mower "grounds." Leveling will put them right (see Peaks and hollows, page 254). But if there are bald patches where large rosette weeds have been removed, or because the lawn is in very poor condition, the quickest way to deal with them is to reseed.

You can buy "patch" kits that contain grass seed mixed with a soil mix. Alternatively, you can buy the two separately, mix them in a bucket, and sprinkle the mix thinly over bald areas, after spiking them well to loosen the soil surface. Rake the seed-and-compost mix in lightly, then stick in some stakes to prevent people from walking on the area until the grass has come through. Autumn or spring are usually the best times to "patch" lawns. but, as long as it's only a few spots, you can do the job in summer, provided that the weather isn't too hot and you keep the areas watered.

Broken edges

Broken lawn edges don't just look messy, they make mowing difficult and proper edging almost impossible, but they are very easily fixed. All you need to do is take a sharp spade and cut out a square of turf that has the broken edge along one side. Turn it around and fit it back into the gap, so that now there's a complete straight edge around the outside of the lawn and the broken piece is on the inside. This leaves a hole in the lawn. Fill the hole with topsoil and firm it down, so that it doesn't sink below the level of the rest of the lawn. Then reseed it as if it were a bald patch (see page 252). If you do this in autumn, by late spring you'll have a complete lawn and you won't even see the joints.

Doing repairs to lawn edges are easily carried out. Remove a square of turf (*top*), which includes the broken edge. Reverse it and pat it back into place (*bottom*), then re-seed the bald patch, which is now within the lawn area.

Peaks and hollows

Long after a lawn has been laid, it's not uncommon to find that parts of it sink, so that you end up with a slightly uneven surface. In a wild garden, this looks very natural. It's not so good in a fine lawn that you keep closely cut, because the mower tends to scalp the peaks, leaving them permanently bald. That's bad enough if you want a good-looking lawn, but it's hopeless if you want to play croquet; the ball shoots off in all directions.

Shallow dips on a lawn can gradually be filled in by raking topsoil or potting mix into them.

To flatten peaks, don't bash them down with the back of a spade or take a garden roller to them. That just compacts the soil even more and the grass still won't grow. Instead, strip the turf off the peak, remove some of the soil beneath, and level the spot before putting the turf back. Easier said than done, I know, but you'll be glad that you did it.

Hollows are treated in the same way, but in reverse. Remove the turf, add topsoil until the hollow is level, and put the grass back. If the dip is very shallow, just fill the hollow in easy stages by top-dressing. Use sieved topsoil or turf dressing, which you might find in bags at the garden center. Sprinkle it thinly and evenly over the area, and brush it into the grass. Don't put on more than about ½in (1cm) of dressing at a time, or you'll smother the grass and kill it. But if you top-dress the dips two or three times a year, it's amazing how quickly they will even out.

Alternative lawns

If the traditional close-cropped lawn doesn't fit your style of garden, there are plenty of other kinds to choose from. Some contain grass along with other ingredients – wildflower lawns, for instance – but there are others that don't have any grass in them at all, such as herb or flower lawns.

Don't make the mistake of thinking that nongrass lawns are direct substitutes for grass. Grass is the *only* type of lawn that you can use for running around on – the rest don't stand up to very much wear at all. They are fine for small areas, where you don't need to walk all the time, and great for areas around a garden seat. My advice is, if you need somewhere for the family to play, stick to the traditional lawn at the back of the house, and save the other sort for quieter places, well out of harm's way. Treat the special lawn as an occasional walk-through flower bed.

Wildflower lawns

A wildflower lawn is just a patch of grass that isn't cut quite so short as usual – say 2in (5cm) instead of 1in (2.5cm) – where you encourage low-growing flowering plants such as primroses, violets, and cowslips. Some people also like to encourage Germander speedwell, trefoils, and other plants, which, to traditional gardeners, are lawn weeds.

A wildflower meadow is wonderful in summer and a great butterfly attractant, but remember that you will still need to cut it a couple of times a year in early spring and autumn.

You can either let the wildlings come up naturally and weed out the ones you don't want, or you can plant the flowers of your choice into the turf in spring; they'll self-seed once established. A wildflower lawn doesn't need fertilizing, but it does need mowing regularly, even though it's allowed to grow taller than usual. Don't confuse a wildflower lawn with a wildflower meadow; the latter is where tall wildflowers grow in long grass. Meadows are cut only twice a year and look completely different.

Clover lawns

Clover is the sort of "weed" that traditional lawn fans spend years trying to eliminate from fine turf, but, on it's own, white clover (*Trifolium repens*) makes a very good "lawn." Sow it in the same way as a normal grass lawn, using clover seeds that you can buy at garden centers. It's much less trouble than grass – clover stays green in dry weather when grass looks like hay, and its full height is only about 2–3in (5–8cm), so it doesn't need regular mowing.

If you sow clover and grass seed together, you'll have a more conventional-looking lawn that needs mowing but fertilizes itself; clover roots "fix" nitrogen out of the air and enrich the soil. Clover is a mass of flower in summer and very attractive to bees, so if you want a "play" lawn for children, simply mow down the flowerheads to prevent your kids from being stung by foraging bees.

Flower lawns

The classic flower lawn is chamomile, which, ironically, is usually made of the nonflowering form, *Chamaemelum nobile* 'Treneague'. You can also grow a lawn of creeping thymes, a mixture of mat-forming alpines, or one of the flowering chamomiles, such as the double-flowered Roman version, *Chamaemelum nobile* 'Flore Pleno'.

Good flowering lawns look superb, and the idea is that they don't need mowing, just a clip over after flowering – a bit more often in the case of nonflowering chamomile. You probably won't want an extensive area, because flower lawns need to be weeded by hand, but it's not quite as bad as weeding a flower bed. Once the plants cover the ground densely, the foliage smothers out a lot of weeds. Think of these lawns more as low-growing groundcover.

A lawn of chamomile, other herbs, or alpines is very fussy about its growing conditions. A sunny spot with first-class drainage is essential, so on "normal" ground, dig plenty of very coarse sand or gravel into the area. Improve the drainage even more by spreading a 2-in (5-cm) layer of gravel over the area, with some sort of edging in place to prevent the lawn from creeping into your flower beds.

Put the plants in through the gravel so they have a deep collar to protect them from moisture, which can easily make them rot off at the crowns. You don't need to plant a continuous carpet of the same type of flower – you can mix different creeping herbs or alpines together to create more of a Persian-carpet effect. You could add pieces of paving so you have somewhere to put a seat, or some containers with sun-loving plants. If drainage is a bit iffy, be prepared for such a lawn to need quite a bit of restoration work in spring. Yes, an herb-rich sward is lovely, but it's more fun if it's small.

Creeping thymes make a fragrant "lawn," even though they don't take a lot of wear and tear.

Mossy glades

If you want a mossy green carpet for a damp, shady area, then you can't do better than real moss. It's sometimes sold in pots for creating Oriental-style gardens. In the right spot, moss will appear all on its own, so instead of fighting it, why not go with the flow? The odds are you won't get all that many weeds in a damp, shady corner, but if you don't want to weed by hand, then use a weedkiller that does not harm moss. They can be rather nasty chemicals, though, so take all the recommended precautions and follow the intructions to the letter when you use them.

Alternatively, in milder areas, you can achieve a good mossy effect with helxine or baby's tears (*Soleirolia soleirolii,* see page 147). Several forms, including gold, silver-edged, and green, are sold as houseplants, but the plain green is the hardiest one and the best to use as a "lawn." But be warned: once you have it, you'll never be rid of it, and it can be a terrible weed if it comes up where it's not wanted.

Epilogue to Part One

If you've just finished Part One, you're probably feeling a little punch drunk. There's so much to learn and so much to remember. Relax. If gardening becomes a worry, it is not worth the effort. It should be looked upon as a challenging pursuit, not as a chore. I know there are some dreary jobs to do, and that it always seems to be raining just when you need dry weather to mow, fertilize, or whatever. But once you get in touch with your basic earthy self – and that, as much as anything, is what this book is about – then you'll start to become an instinctive gardener who realizes that common sense is the most important attribute of any son or daughter of the soil.

Part Two of *How to be a Gardener* concentrates more on plants. Now that you've come to grips with the basics of cultivation, you can open your eyes to the real magic of it all and the reason for learning all this stuff in the first place – to grow flowers, fruits, and vegetables better, whatever your situation, and to realize just how much variety there is to be had, wherever you garden, and whichever style appeals to you.

Whatever the weather... well, you know the rest.

Introduction to Part Two

It has always struck me that gardening is a basic skill that is not so much learned as uncovered. Why else would academics and intellectuals suddenly go off into raptures about the simple task of growing their own zucchini, or raising impatiens from seed? It is, purely and simply, because gardening is deeply instinctive. It satisfies our basic urges in a way that few other pursuits can.

It seems to me perfectly obvious that we were always meant to grow things. Other people are convinced that we are meant to understand how a mobile phone works. I am happy not to be of their number; new mobile phones appear that are ever more complex and that offer functions I am never likely to demand. Nature, bless her, has no need for such frequent "improvements."

In Part One of *How to Be a Gardener* I explained simple growing techniques and showed how plants work. If you understand how something works, you can better equip yourself to deal with it – which is probably the root of my mobile phone problem. Once you know how plants grow, and how to make them grow, you have become a gardener. But that does not mean that you will have a beautiful garden. To do that, you need to know how to put different plants together: you need to know which plants will grow best in which situation, and then how to group them with other plants of a similar disposition that will make them look even better.

The architect Sir Frederick Gibberd said that gardening was the most complicated of all art forms because as well as using shape, form, color, and texture, it also used time. Time changes the picture – over the seasons and over the years. What was once a perfectly formed planting design can become overblown and over the hill.

By now you have probably convinced yourself that you will never become a proper gardener. But take heart – none of us has ever cracked it completely. Provided you know the pitfalls, you can anticipate them. You won't always avoid them, but you might learn to enjoy the challenge.

Part Two of *How to Be a Gardener* lets you in on the ways to make your garden look good and feel right. There is no accounting for taste, or for fashion, but even allowing for these influences, there are still ways of having a garden that reflects your own personality. And that is the key – your garden is for you – not for the neighbors, who will have their own likes and dislikes, or who may be slaves to fashion.

Oh, you will be influenced by current trends – if you are a receptive sort, you will have no option. But basic rules of thumb are as valid in the garden as they are on the catwalk, and you can come to grips with them more easily than you would think. A bit of planning and a few basic design guidelines will avoid most pitfalls, and you will have great fun trying different designs and different planting designs over the years.

It is a mistake to think that a garden is ever finished. It is not a room filled with inanimate objects. It is a living, breathing, passionate, fiery creation. Or it should be. Anyway, you'll see what I mean – I hope. And you will get more out of your garden as a result.

9 YOUR DESIGN

Garden design in history

In the beginning, nobody set out to design gardens at all. They just happened. But then, in the beginning, the garden as we know it today did not exist. Early gardens were either strictly practical or for limited recreational use. Gardeners simply endeavored to make the best use of the space and the small range of plants and materials available. Down-to-earth common sense was there in spades, but for anything fancier, you'd need to wait several centuries.

Medieval practicality

For medieval peasants in the Old Country, the space around the family hovel was little more than a farmyard, and, if they wanted a few herbs for the pot within easy walking distance of the back door, they needed to fence them off to prevent livestock from eating the lot. People didn't much go in for vegetables at that time; meat, bread, or a "potage" made from dried peas, beans, or grains made most meals, and the staples came from a personal strip in a communal field. Flowers didn't get included, because hard-working folk didn't waste their time on anything they couldn't eat.

At grand establishments, such as castles, gardens were enclosed within fortifications, where the ladies could walk safely and sit and talk, but there wasn't much to grow except wildflowers that came up naturally, so you had flowery meads and turf seats to take away the smell of dawning civilization. The serious horticulturists were in monasteries. Monks – the doctors of the day – grew medicinal herbs in well-ordered beds with paths in between, so they knew where everything was. Later, the same layout of beds and paths was used in apothecaries' or "physic" gardens, placed close to "hospitals," since plants were still used for medicines. There's still a good example in London, at the Chelsea Physic Garden, and an American version of one in Philadelphia .

Better times

As living standards improved, Elizabethan English peasants evolved into self-sufficient cottagers. At the back of the dwelling, they'd have a well-stocked vegetable garden and a pig in the sty, and out front would be a cottage garden where they kept bees, a jumble of wildflowers, and a few cultivated plants grown from bits passed on between neighbors. These treasures were shoved in anywhere there was room. Smallholders became yeomen farmers, with bigger houses, more livestock, and several employees.

In the apothecary's garden, plants were cultivated for their medicinal properties rather than their beauty.

As the big landowners grew richer, their houses were enlarged, and their gardens became places to show off. They would surround themselves with formal grounds, creating wonderful views of fountains, parterres, and clipped hedges from the terraces. Rare flowers, such as tulips, would be displayed in flower beds that were like a stage set, with bare soil and contrived backgrounds that were intended to drive visiting toffs wild with envy.

In the meantime, America was developing, and Americans tended their plots and gardened according to their means, much as had been done in the Old Country, and following European styles.

Just as everyone who was anybody had finished creating their formal gardens, fashions changed. In the early 18th century, the European craze for Arcadian landscapes came in, and wealthy Americans followed suit. William Kent, Lancelot "Capability" Brown, and their American followers turned uppercrust grounds into vistas of trees and lakes decorated with grottoes, follies, and ruined temples. The idea was to improve on nature. The parkland beyond the house would be full of deer and prize herds of cattle, which were kept at a suitable distance by a ha-ha – a steep-sided ditch that didn't obstruct your view. It gave the distinct impression that you owned everything as far as the eye could see – an early example of what garden designers today call "borrowed landscape."

Ostentation was the name of the game in the 18th century, when the Arcadian landscape was all the rage.

In other parts of the world

Long before we carved out the wilderness and created American gardens, they were being made by other civilizations around the world.

The Mogul gardens of ancient India and Persia were based around elaborate water gardens with formal canals, waterfowl, and trees – like the Taj Mahal.

Oriental gardens were places for meditation and to be close to nature. Zen gardens contain sand raked into patterns like waves on a beach, or they echoed the natural landscape with moss, trees, and water. Very symbolic, but few flowers.

Islamic gardens were high-walled courtyards with fountains, statues, beds, and intricate detail as elaborate as any woven carpet. They were designed to keep women entertained within the grounds and to prevent people from seeing in.

Victorian and Edwardian gardens

By Victorian times, for anyone concerned with keeping their place in society on both sides of the Atlantic, a conservatory and walled kitchen garden – complete with a range of greenhouses – were essential for entertaining guests at country-house parties. Elaborate, formal carpet-bedding designs came into fashion, showing the world that you could afford both the tender plants and the greenhouse to produce them, and that you had a properly trained staff capable of tackling the latest fashions, however outlandish. Mathematical geometry was a vital part of a gardener's training in those days.

As the 19th century progressed, the style became more romantic, so at country houses you'd see formal lily ponds, pergolas, and rose gardens for a quiet tryst. William Robinson published his *English Flower Garden* in 1883, in which he made a plea for naturalness and lack of formality in gardening. By Edwardian times, Gertrude Jekyll, often designing in collaboration with the architect, Sir Edwin Lutyens, was being creative with her book *Colour Schemes for the Flower Garden* (1908), and the sort of themed "garden rooms" you see at Sissinghurst and Hidcote Manor were beginning to evolve. It was to be a century of gardening contradictions and extreme variety.

Modern times

Since the early part of the 20th century, gardens have gone through several short, sharp phases. During the Second World War, gardening was all about Victory Gardens, so you dug up your back lawn to grow vegetables and planted potatoes and fruit trees to provide food and show solidarity.

Then came "fifties formal," when you'd have cut a geometrically shaped flower bed out of the middle of your front lawn and filled it with straight rows of salvias. During the "low-maintenance" sixties, you crammed the garden with shrubs and groundcovers, or dwarf conifers, to save work.

In the "sun-loving seventies," you pulled it all out again to make a patio, which gradually grew until the garden became, for a lot of people, a complete outdoor living room. Organic gardening took off in the "earthy eighties," as did a passion for herbaceous perennials, and both have been growing ever since.

Instead of just being a genteel hobby for the retired generation who'd become real enthusiasts, by the nineties gardening had become the height of fashion for younger people and families with children. Everybody was at it, and the thing you needed was style. Prairie gardens, minimalist gardens, water gardens – you name it, you could have it. If you had a big enough space, you could enjoy the lot all at once by dividing your space up into separate "rooms" and "decorating" each one differently. In the new millennium, gardening and yardwork has become very popular on account of its "close to the nest" appeal. You can go out into the yard, and you and your family can have a good time without leaving home. Gardens became fun instead of hard work, and hard-bitten traditionalists may be sniffing in despair.

The future

We've been pinching design tips from gardens of the past ever since I can remember, but with the dawn of the new millennium, we have – at last – started to look ahead and develop totally new ways of thinking about what goes into a garden. That's why you see so many contemporary gardens in magazines and on the TV these days. Yes, I know some of them are experimental and not necessarily the sort of thing you'd want to live with every day, but there are lots of bright ideas you can adapt to suit yourself. And what today seems difficult to live with may well be commonplace tomorrow.

Now that we tend to stay put instead of moving every few years as we once did, we are more inclined to make changes to our present situation instead of just trading it in for a new model somewhere else – so the trend is to make the most of the space and really develop it fully. There's never been more scope.

Today, gardens are individually created to suit the needs and artistic preferences of their owners, but they are still influenced by changing fads and fashions.

What's right for you?

The way most people make a garden is very hit and miss. You know the sort of thing – first-time buyers move into a starter home, put up a laudry spinner and park trashcans where they won't be bumped into, plonk some paving down outside the patio doors, put in a patch of grass for the kids to play on, and a path down to the shed. The rest slowly fills up with whatever takes their fancy at the garden center. They'll probably move on before the lot gets overgrown, leaving the result for somebody else to sort out. Well, it doesn't need to be like that.

A garden should suit both house and owners. This dull yard (*below*) has been transformed into a cottage garden (*above*) that complements both dwelling and family.

Evolution versus revolution

In my experience, people are either evolutionists or revolutionists when it comes to making a garden.

Evolutionists like to start with something that's already there and alter it gradually. There's a lot to be said for this method. You never need to put up with a plot that looks like a building site, you complete one project at a time, and you can stagger the work – and the cost. When the children grow older, you can turn their play area into something more adult, and, if you spot something on television that catches your fancy, you can replace an old feature with something new. If you take over a big garden, as I did at Barleywood, you don't ned to try to finish it all at once.
You can tackle a different bit every year or so, as I did, then start redeveloping the original bits when you think up better ideas.

An evolutionist's garden is never finished, but then, no garden ever is. The big problem with this type of development is that it's very easy to wander off track and end up with a mess, so you do need to make long-term as well as short-term plans.

Revolutionists are the exact opposite. They prefer to scrap everything, start with a completely clean slate, and get the whole job over with at once so they can spend the next few years just enjoying it. They are the type of people who are most likely to sit down and plan the garden fastidiously, or call in a designer and a team of landscapers to do everything. This is very much the way we work on *Ground Force* – we must, if we are to get the job done in the time – and, at home, it suits a lot of people with small yards who want to see the full effect right away. But you can take things too far and end up with plans so detailed that you hardly dare impulse-buy so much as a single flower in case it throws your entire design out of synch. Don't get me wrong; having a plan is a good idea. Just don't get bogged down in the fine details at the start, and definitely be flexible.

You don't need to be a professional designer to transform a tiny rectangular patch of ground (*above*) into a well-crafted garden (*below*). Once you know a few secrets, you can achieve wonders by doodling and playing around with lines on a sheet of paper…

Thinking it through

Whichever approach best suits your natural instincts, begin by asking what you are trying to achieve. Otherwise, you can spend a lot of time and money and end up with just a collection of ingredients that don't make a garden. It's like trying to pick two socks that match without turning on the light; you stand no chance. Look at your lifestyle and what you want from your garden.

Do you want a stylish space for outdoor entertaining in summer? In which case, a courtyard garden in a Mediterranean-style or contemporary look is worth considering. Or, if you lead a busy life with no time for chores, then a low-maintenance garden that looks good all year round might be the best choice. Think about gravel and paving instead of grass, a fountain or pebble pool instead of a pond, and a few outstanding, all-year-round specimen plants instead of lots of time-consuming flowers and containers. Maybe you want to grow your own produce, encourage wildlife, or cultivate special plants you've enjoyed collecting or have propagated yourself? These gardens need more time, but you'll spend it doing those things you enjoy, so it won't feel like a chore.

If your home has period character, with masses of architectural detail, then a garden with lots of curving beds, winding paths, and small features will look very much at home, but if you have a very

This garden has been designed to suit a family with little time to spare. The plants are easy to maintain, there is little lawn to mow, and somewhere to sit in the sun during precious leisure time. Perhaps an hour or two's work a week is needed – that's all.

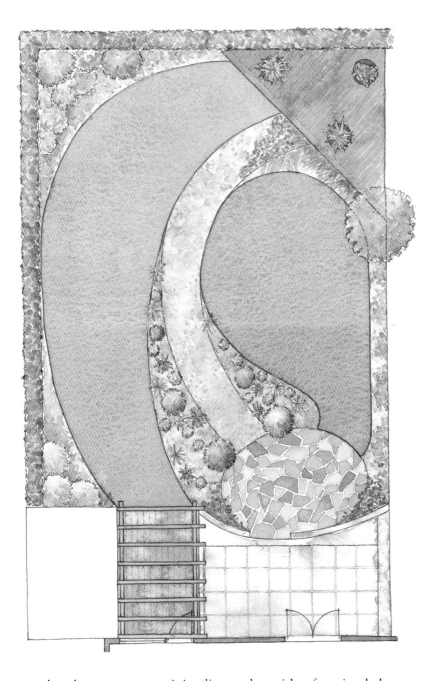

This plan of the low-maintenance garden opposite shows the following time-saving features:

1 Low-maintenance planting design of shrubs and grasses.
2 Small lawn area that is quick to mow.
2 Decking made of railroad ties, positioned to catch the evening sun.
4 Slate mulch in planting beds to minimize watering and weeding.
5 Pergola to provide shady and scented seating area.

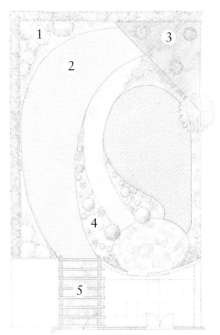

modern house, a more minimalist garden with a few simple but stylish shapes will be the best match. The style that suits you will be different in each case. It sounds obvious, I know, but if you don't ask yourself the right questions, you'll be amazed at how easy it is to end up with the "wrong" kind of garden.

So the first rule of garden designing is: always start with the big picture, and leave the details until last. From pages 276–298 there are some of the garden "looks" that are available to you, but, before you go straight to choosing a style, there is another important factor you should consider that might influence your decision.

Working with nature

Some gardens start out with natural characteristics that are very difficult and expensive to alter, so if you have seriously boggy ground, a patch of shady woodland, or a steep rocky site, my advice is: don't fight it. Instead, see the "problem" as nature's way of telling you that this is the perfect place to develop a particular style of garden. That will be a heck of a lot cheaper than trying to change the soil type, clear trees, or level rock, and because you've built on the garden's natural characteristics, you'll end up with a garden that's the envy of your friends and that people with "normal" sites would have spent a fortune to achieve.

Which brings me to rule number two of garden design: the easy way is often the best.

This seaside garden makes good use of plants that can endure a maritime location. The nautical atmosphere continues with a gravel path, a painted shed, and a striped deck chair.

Problem solving with style

Even in places where you might think a "proper" garden is out of the question, there's a lot you can do just by following the lead that the landscape gives you. The result is a garden that looks totally at home in its surroundings and that is very easy to look after, because you are doing only what comes naturally.

Gardens near the ocean

Strong winds, often laden with sand or salt, are a feature of coastal gardens. The soil is usually pretty grim – all pebbles and sand and with hardly any fertility to speak of. In these conditions, normal garden plants don't stand a chance of flourishing.

Design solution There are two real choices; a normal-ish garden or a seaside-style one. The late Derek Jarman's garden at Dungeness is a great inspiration. Team plants with beach paraphernalia, such as a bit of breakwater, driftwood, chunks of chain or fishing nets, a mulch of shells – which you can now buy in bags for the purpose – and lots of pebbles.

Suitable plants If you want a normal-ish garden, then plant a defensive barrier of tough plants around the edge for some protection. Inside your shelter belt of plants, such as Japanese black pine (*Pinus thunbergiana*), maritime pine, (*P. pinaster*), Monterey cypress (*Cupressus macrocarpa*), or *Euonymus japonicus*, you could go for a summer garden of hardy fuchsias, escallonias, and annuals. If you want to leave your sea views open, stick to really tough seaside plants that'll stand the conditions, such as sea holly, (*Eryngium*), thrift (*Armeria*), and pinks (*Dianthus*). If, however, you want to make a seaside-style garden inland, you can use plants that look nautical but don't actually enjoy coastal conditions, such as euphorbias and ornamental grasses.

Wet ground that never dries out, even in summer

Most normal garden plants need reasonably good drainage because their roots rot if they are left standing in "soil soup," particularly in winter.

Design solution Make a bog garden, adapting features found in real swampy places, such as knotty branches and chunks of tree trunk, willow panels, a rustic gazebo on stilts, and banks and ditches.

Suitable plants Stick to plants that are naturally adapted to living with their feet in water. Most marginal plants will grow in anything from very wet ground to a couple of inches of water. Use this type of plant in the lowest-lying places, where puddles collect in winter. For the not-quite-so-soggy parts around the edges, choose moisture-loving perennials, such as hosta and candelabra primroses, and plants like *Darmera peltata*, which is found on stream banks in the wild. Where you have a large space and you need what designers call a "bold statement," then the giant prickly rhubarb *Gunnera manicata* is perfect. But in a small garden it will eat you out of house and home.

Hunt for inspiration

It takes imagination to find a stylish solution for seemingly impossible spots, so don't be afraid to borrow ideas from people who have already done it. Visit other gardens in your locality, and take a camera and notebook and pencil with you. You'll discover a lot of good private gardens on your doorstep by visiting those that open in aid of good causes for a few days each year,. such as the Garden Conservancy and many local organizations.

On boggy land, use plants whose roots are naturally adapted to growing in soggy soil – they'll happily thrive.

A bare, sun-baked terrace (*above*) can be turned into a flower-filled garden (*below*) using plants that are naturally equipped to cope with hot, dry situations.

Sunny, sloping sites

The ground dries out quickly, plants suffer from drought, and, in heavy rain, the soil is washed down the slope.

Design solution Unless you fancy a vineyard – and this is a good spot for one – then the best plan might be to turn the steepest part of the slope into a series of shallow terraces. Create winding paths between the stone retaining walls of the terraces, and make beds on the terraces for naturally drought-tolerant plants. If there's good rock just under the surface, expose it and make the most of it.

Suitable plants Go for sun-loving shrubs, perennials, and rock plants that don't mind drying out a bit in summer. Use plenty of evergreens so the view doesn't just evaporate in winter; if the ground is well covered, there's less risk of soil erosion. Don't worry about using lots of small plants, because on a sloping garden they are brought closer to eye level.

Shady gardens under woodland trees

Summer shade makes it difficult to create a colorful garden using conventional border plants.

Design solution Make a woodland garden. Big trees would be a problem if the soil is dry underneath, but proper woodland is different. It has a light canopy of branches overhead with deep, rich leaf mold or a thick layer of organic matter on the ground, making perfect growing conditions for all sorts of choice shade lovers and woodland treasures. If you need to let more light in, call an arborist in to thin out or lift the crowns of big trees.

Suitable plants Choose spring bulbs, which complete their growing cycle before the tree leaves emerge, as well as perennials, such as hellebores and violets, that love damp shade. Where shade is light, grow Japanese maples (*Acer palmatum* cultivars), shade-tolerant grasses and woodlanders, such as bugle (*Ajuga reptans*) and primroses (*Primula*) and cut "rides" through for access. If the soil is acidic, which it often is in this situation, then lime-hating woodland plants, such as rhododendrons and camellias, will thrive.

There are plants to suit every situation, however difficult, so the third rule of garden design is: if you don't have a problem, then don't look for one. Think about the style of garden you'd like, and don't feel pressurized by current trends – remember that the garden is there to please you and yours. Do show off a bit, but not at the expense of the garden's original purpose to provide pleasure and relaxation.

There is a world of difference between a patch of dreary and unkempt wilderness (*below*) and a wild garden (*above*). With a little crafty planning and planting, the one can be transformed into the other.

Contemporary gardens

Contemporary gardens are all about breaking away from tradition. They are not plant-lovers' gardens; they generally appeal to younger or more design-conscious people, who may or may not know much about gardening – but they know what they like. This sort of garden looks quite out of place around a traditional house, but if you have an unusual space to fill, such as a rooftop terrace, or modern-style home or office surroundings to landscape, then a contemporary exterior is often a very good choice.

By using a small selection of hard landscaping materials and utilizing bold and dramatic curves, a garden instantly takes on a contemporary look.

What's it all about?

Contemporary style is all about shapes, textures, and patterns. Plants are only part of the picture. If you go contemporary, you'll use fewer plants than in a more conventional garden, but they will need to be the architectural kinds that look almost like living sculpture. Alternatively, you could go for carpets of plants contrasted with blocky shapes of clipped hedging to create a more formal contemporary style. Color is often provided by the walls, furniture, or floor, with the plants providing the plain green. The secret of this rather abstract look is that the empty spaces become as much a part of the design as the plants.

Hard surfaces, containers, and abstract artefacts are major ingredients, and the more way out they are, the better. Glass nuggets, stainless steel catering vats, and lengths of copper water pipe are *de rigueur* in contemporary gardens, but what you are really trying to do is to use materials in unexpected ways. You can dream up all sorts of creative uses for things most people would never think of putting in a garden. Don't bother trying to achieve a natural look; that's not what this style of gardening is all about, and that really gets up the nose of some traditionalists. If you like it, don't worry about them!

Contemporary gardens aren't easy to make unless you have a naturally artistic eye or some design training, but a good one is certainly eye-catching. If you feel like dabbling with this style, I'd strongly suggest taking a look at some examples that really work and using one of these for inspiration. Adapt it to suit your own taste, of course, but don't be frightened of using it as a starting point. You'll see superb examples in the display gardens at the bigger flower shows, and they sometimes turn up on television in more off-the-wall make-over programs and in the trendier type of home and gardening magazines.

There's one thing you can say about a contemporary garden, and that is: because there are very few plants and probably no lawn, it will be a lot less work to look after than a more traditional garden. Routine chores? It's more like housework. Which may be a good or a bad thing, depending on how you look at it.

A restrained use of color creates a clean, cool, and highly sophisticated atmosphere in this modern water garden (*below left*). Take care not to create a multicolored nightmare when using colored gravels. This garden (*below right*) just about gets away with it.

Choosing paintwork to complement the shades of the planting design has a unifying effect.

Good contemporary plants

The way many designers go about choosing plants for contemporary gardens is to think first of the shape they want and then put a plant name to it. For spiky shapes, go for plants like the New Zealand flax, (*Phormium tenax*) and hardy yuccas, if you must leave them outside all winter. If you have a sunroom to overwinter containers, you can use less hardy plants, such as *Agave americana* and Chusan palm (*Trachycarpus fortunei*). If you want to make a carpet of identical plants, then low ornamental grasses are good – and, no, you don't need to mow them – but don't forget that if you choose a species that dies down in winter, you will lose the effect. Evergreen grasses, such as blue fescue (*Festuca glauca*), or the red sedge (*Uncinia rubra*), are a better bet for year-round looks, and the leaves make a repetitive pattern that reeks of the trendy. Block-shaped, evergreen knee-high hedges, low pillars, or other architectural shapes can be clipped in boxwood (*Buxus sempervirens*), arborvitae, or plain evergreen euonymus – choose a cultivar with small leaves; large leaves, which you can't help cutting in half when you use shears or hedge-trimmers, end up looking ratty.

Hard surfaces

Contemporary gardens at shows contain lots of novel combinations of paving and other hardware, including some outlandish materials. I've even seen paths made from rusty washers and broken windshield glass. This strikes me as a touch uncomfortable, but there's big business in recycling glass from bottle banks as colored nuggets about the size of cough lozenges to use in the garden, and they also make glass gravel. The edges are supposed to have been rounded for safety, but I'd still wear gloves for handling them, just to be firmly on the safe side. These sorts of materials are too expensive to use for paths, but you can use them for top-dressing containers, for mulching, or for making imitation pools.

Garden artifacts

Don't think you can't have water features just because you've gone contemporary. You can, but a traditional lily pond won't look good in an ultra-modern setting. This is the place to take off on a flight of fancy with a floodlit fountain, or go the other way entirely with something very stark like a plain, shiny bowl of water.

Reflective surfaces are very fashionable, so besides stainless steel for covering vertical surfaces, look at mirror acrylics from DIY stores, which are a lot cheaper. You don't need to spend a fortune to be stylish; some of the trendiest containers are just large tin cans that have been washed out and stood in a row with plants in them.

Which brings me to rule number four of garden design: it's not how much you spend, it's the forethought that counts.

Five ways to make your garden contemporary

Materials	Color	Lighting	Plants	Keep it simple
Be adventurous – think manufactured materials rather than traditional ones, such as glass, stainless steel, copper piping, or rendered concrete.	Look beyond planting to introduce color. Paint walls, fences, floors, and outbuildings in bright colors as an effect in their own right, or as a background to dramatic planting.	Whether for practical or fun use, lighting can create instant contemporary impact. Use lights to highlight dramatic plants, focal points, water features, or reflective surfaces, or simply to illuminate paths or dining areas.	Choose dramatic, architectural plants with well-defined shapes, such as phormiums, tree ferns, Chusan palms, agaves, ornamental grasses, or clipped evergreen plants such as boxwood or euonymus.	Contemporary gardens are about order, incorporating strong shapes, clean lines, a few simple textures, and bold, minimalist planting designs – this is not the place for packed, busy borders and the natural look!

Natural gardens

Conventional gardening involves rearranging the landscape and planting non-native species and plants that have been mucked about by plant breeders, but these days a lot of us are feeling the call of the wild. Natural gardens are firmly back in fashion. They'll suit anyone who likes the idea of a slice of countryside on the doorstep, even if they live in a city. It doesn't matter if your garden is measured in square feet instead of acres; a corner at the far end of a "normal" garden is enough. It helps if you have the leave-it-alone philosophy, because this isn't the type of garden for a control freak or a serial neatnik.

What's it all about?

Natural-style gardens use flowers, trees, and shrubs that grow wild in this country (or a specific part of it), planted very informally to mimic the way they grow in nature. They aren't evenly spaced out in the way you find plants in a "proper" border, and you won't find the tallest at the back and the shortest at the front. You might not find any borders at all; wildflowers are often just grown in grass, and paths may only be roughly marked out with fallen logs and surfaced with bark chips.

It takes a degree of planning and careful planting to create an apparently artless wildflower bank.

Natural-style gardens are quite cheap to create, since many wildflowers are easily raised from seed, and, once your favorite kinds are growing, they'll usually spread by self-seeding. Bulbs like camassias need only to be planted once and then left to spread naturally, and native species of trees and shrubs can be the cheapest kinds to buy from nurseries and garden centers. You don't always need to *buy* wildflowers and native trees and shrubs – very often, if you give up conventional gardening, they'll find you.

There's no reason why you shouldn't stop using weedkiller on your lawn if you are happy to call it a wildflower meadow!

Good plants

It is plants that give a natural, wild-looking garden its character. Go for native trees like mountain ash (*Sorbus americana*), birch (*Betula papyrifera*), or black cherry (*Prunus serotina*), but plant them in close groups of three if there's room. That's the way they often grow out in the countryside.

If you want a hedge, forget about cultivated conifers, and go for the sort of mixed hedge you see out on a country walk, made from a mixture of viburnum, hawthorn, wild rose, and dogwood – the red-stemmed kinds with clusters of white flowers that ripen into excellent bird food. You don't need to clip a mixed hedge tightly – a relaxed row of plants allowed to grow into small trees makes a good, bird-friendly windbreak – but if you do clip it more neatly, let the occasional hawthorn or dogwood, or maybe a holly seedling, grow up through the hedge and turn into a small standard tree.

Wildflowers like spring beauties and violets are good for growing in short grass, while gaillardia and ratibida give long grass more character. Choose woodlanders, such as lobelias and black cohosh, for shady areas under trees.

Inspiration taken from the wild can be used to give any garden a more natural feel, even where quite hard curves and lines are employed.

Try to include as many different habitats as you can. A patch of flowering hay meadow looks truly rural and needs cutting only in spring and autumn. Otherwise, encourage a grassy lawn to grow short wildflowers, such as spring beauties and violets, by not using fertilizers and weedkillers, and topping it at about 3–4in 8–10cm) instead of cutting it short.

If there's room, have a small wooded area – birches are good here since they don't cast too much shade, so woodland plants and bulbs will thrive underneath. If your site is suitable, have a shallow pond or a patch of boggy ground, since they both lend opportunities for increasing the range of wild plants and flowers you can grow. They're also great for encouraging birds and amphibians, such as frogs, toads, and newts, into the wild garden.

Don't feel you need to stick only to genuine wild plants; if you want to add "tame" ones feel free, but plant them in random drifts, so they look as if they grew wild, and go for those that look the part so they don't stick out like sore thumbs. You'll find that anything too big, blowsy, and brilliantly colored might look really out of place.

Five ways to make a natural garden

Plants	Water	Materials	Wildlife	Natural boundaries
Use native plants – flowers, trees and shrubs that grow wild in this country rather than cultivated species. Don't plant them as you would for a conventional border: go for a more informal feel. Include some wild-looking exotics.	Dig a shallow pond or set aside a patch of boggy ground to encourage wildlife to visit and set up home. Damp areas also increase the range of wildflowers and plants you can grow.	Go back to nature – incorporate logs, woven-twig fences, wood, willow, and stones in your design. Reclaiming natural materials can be environmentally friendly – as long as you are getting them from reputable sources!	Attract wildlife into your garden by planting trees and hedges with berries, wildflowers, and grasses to supply food and hiding places for small animals and birds. Leave the garden undisturbed, and they will seek you out.	Natural gardens look best with boundaries made of natural materials. Woven-twig fences blend into the planting, as do wild hedges. Other fences can be smothered with climbers to give a more natural-looking effect.

Other ingredients

The simpler and more back-to-nature your design is, the better it will look. Tree stumps and old logs are vital – rotting wood supports 40 percent of forest life, so don't be too neat. You don't need to leave them littered about, if you can't bear it; they will be just as attractive to wildlife in a stack.

Even a wild garden deserves a few decorative touches. Natural dips and hollows in the ground can be enlarged or emphasized. Woven-twig fences make good natural arbors, path markers, and dividers. Or you can even add "wild" ornaments, such as wooden mushrooms, a willow sculpture, or a tree house. But don't try to be too clever – let the plants have the limelight.

Wildlife accommodation is very in-theme. You can make or buy bat hibernation boxes, woven coir roosting pockets to wedge in hedges for birds, and insect "hotels" made of hollow bamboo stakes or dried grass stems crammed into wooden frames to hang in trees. One thing I wouldn't be without is a seat. A fat fallen log is all you need for a quiet afternoon's nature study.

Family gardens

This is a good example of what I said earlier about choosing the type of garden that will suit everyone who uses it. Most people need a garden like this at some stage in their lives. If you have a huge place in the country, it's not hard to have a great family garden, but it's not so easy to create something attractive around a typical suburban house on a quarter acre.

You can have lots of different gardens in one, so that every member of the family has a spot they feel happy in. At this end of the garden the patio provides a place to sit and soak up the sun...

What's it all about?

A growing family needs room to run around, so it's no good planning a garden full of fragile flowers and breakable features. But it still needs to look attractive. After all, you'll be looking at it for several years. Play safe with a garden filled with child-friendly features, but don't forget to include things the whole family can enjoy: a sunny patio, a barbecue for Dad to play with (yes, I know there are only so many days a year when he can fiddle with it, but it's the thought that counts), and some flowers, herbs, and a vegetable patch somewhere out of harm's way. You can easily alter the playground feeling to something more sophisticated later.

Family-friendly plants

The perfect plant for a family garden is one that you can fall into but that bounces back without either of you coming to any harm. Into that category I'd put most of the reliable old favorites – dogwood, forsythia, flowering currant, mockorange, and winter jasmine. An ancient apple tree is good for a natural climbing-frame-cum-summer-sunshade; two are even better for hanging a hammock, and it's not a bad idea to have some tough groundcovers, such as *Cotoneaster horizontalis*, that withstands most things.

Whatever else you grow, a patch of lawn is essential for running around, but I wouldn't worry about laying a top-quality lawn: something rough and ready is the answer. As long as it's well fertilized and not cut too closely, it'll stand up to lots of hard wear.

It's worth thinking about what to leave out of a family garden if there are small children around. Steer clear of poisonous plants – laburnum and aconitum are among the worst offenders. Even so, it's best to teach small kids not to put anything they find in the garden into their mouths, unless it is presented to them on a plate.

...and at the far end of the garden, a curved path surrounds a lawn where toddlers can do whatever strikes their fancy..

Avoid prickly plants, such as barberries, roses, and pyracantha, and anything sharp, which includes many ornamental grasses and bamboos. Irritants, such as euphorbias, which have very unpleasant sap, and rue, whose leaves contain an irritating oil, can both cause severe skin reactions.

While children are small, I'd pass on a pond, even if it is quite shallow, or you'll always worry. Water features are something to save until they are a bit older and wiser. If you want one while they're small, I'd stick to a fountain or pebble pool, in which most of the water is kept safely in a reservoir underground.

Other ingredients

It's worth putting things into a family garden that children will enjoy – a wildlife corner, or a place to keep pets such as rabbits safely fenced from predators. Start them on the right tracks by showing them how to grow their own sunflower seeds to feed the

Five ways to make a family garden

Plants	Water	Play area	Grow your own	Lawns
Think robust – the plants might be victim to a stray ball, and trees might become climbing frames for children. Also know your poisonous plants and try to remove them from the garden, or at least out of reach of small, tempted hands.	If you have children, avoid open water features, such as ponds, and choose water features that keep water in secure, underground reservoirs, where it doesn't present a danger.	Devote a section of the garden to the children for swings, slides, sandboxes and climbing frames. Cover the floor area with bark chips – they make a good, soft landing pad.	Encourage children to take an interest in plants, while indulging an adult passion for growing your own fruit and vegetables. Even a few pots of tomatoes on the patio can be very satisfying on a summer's day.	If your family garden is not complete without a lawn, make sure the grass you choose is a durable variety. A more expensive, delicate kind won't stay immaculate for long when your lawn becomes a playground.

birds, or salad green for the rabbit. Specialize in things that grow quickly, such as lettuce and nasturtiums. Children can be impatient, but fast-growing plants will harness and retain their interest.

If the garden is big enough, you can create a special play area covered with bark chips – they are a lot kinder to tiny knees than gravel and won't get muddy in wet weather, as grass does. Use it to park a playhouse, swing, and slide. If you are talked into building a sandbox, make a cover for it – a trellis will do – to prevent cats from using it for their personal convenience.

Fruit, vegetables, and herbs have a great place in family gardens, and kids usually enjoy helping to grow things they can eat or cook on the barbecue. But because time is bound to be short, think about growing just a few things that everyone likes, say cherry tomatoes in tubs on the patio. If you are serious about growing edibles, then make a couple of deep beds where you can grow a lot in a small space without too much work. Family gardens, in particular, are the kind it does pay to cultivate organically; there's no risk of kids coming in contact with pesticides or weedkillers. If you really must use garden chemicals, lock them safely away when they aren't in use, and keep kids and pets off treated areas until the stuff has dried, even when it's been diluted and properly applied.

You don't need vast amounts of space to create a family garden – it can be achieved almost effortlessly in the tiniest of spaces.

Paved gardens

A paved garden is probably one of the easiest kinds for a novice garden planner to make a big hit with, because half your plants are in containers, so the "garden" is portable. This makes it easy to shift things around every time you come up with a better design idea, and you can also update the area each season just by buying a few new plants or containers. A paved garden is ideal for first-time gardeners, small gardens, and for fashion victims who like to update their "look" regularly: for anyone, in fact, who appreciates stylish outdoor living without making a lot of work for themselves.

What's it all about?

The hot, sleepy siesta style goes down well in sunny patio and courtyard gardens, where there's no grass to cut, just gravel and paving with terracotta pots and a few sun-loving plants. It's a garden with a natural vacation feeling that you can build on by adding a state-of-the-art barbecue, sophisticated outdoor furniture, an awning, or parasols, outdoor lighting, and all the trimmings. Go as high-tech as you like.

Families with small children need a decent-sized patio to double as a play area, especially when the lawn is soggy. But if the surrounding planting is used to soften the effect, it need not look like an airport runway.

In summer, sheltered corners of a patio make a good home for house-plants and potted tender perennials.

Typical paved garden plants

Plants in pots are essential in a paved garden. Annual bedding plants are the traditional choice, but don't feel tied to them – use something that will create the particular effect you have in mind.

On very hot, sunny paving you can create a Mediterranean look by using terracotta pots planted with pelargoniums and aromatic, evergreen herbs. A lean-to pergola can support a grape vine. In summer, you can stand pots of bougainvillea up against a trellis on a sunny wall, or dot potted lemon trees and pots of oleander all around the place.

Without changing the structure of the patio, you can give it the tropical treatment by using containers of canna, pittosporum, and gazanias, with *Trachelospermum asiaticum* growing up the wall – that's the evergreen climber with white jasmine-scented flowers all summer long. You could almost think you are in Hawaii.

Alternatively, you can create a desert-island paradise decorated with palm trees – the tougher ones, anyway, such as cabbage palm, (*Cordyline australis*), and the dwarf fan palm (*Chamaerops humilis*), with some potted bamboos and banana plants (*Musa basjoo*). All it takes is a little imagination and somewhere warm to keep tender plants in winter, since they won't stand frost.

Other ingredients

Don't overdecorate a paved garden, or it'll end up looking like an architectural salvage yard, but there's no doubt that pots are very good scene setters. Don't just settle for cheap plastic kinds. Terracotta is a classic material for pots, but brightly colored ceramic looks more tropical, and the understated earth shades with brush-stroke markings are inscrutably Oriental. A lot of people pick the pots first and then find plants that go with them; it doesn't matter which way you do it, just so long as you know what you are aiming at. Unity of theme is important, whichever your garden style.

A variety of textures underfoot add enormously to the interest in a paved garden, especially in winter, when you only have your evergreens for company. Don't design your paving so it's dead square, and do leave out the odd slab, either for planting or to allow you to vary the texture by covering the soil with gravel, or with cobblestones set into a bed of cement. You don't want to become bored with your flooring, because it's the one thing that's difficult to change once it's down.

A variety of textures and colors work well in a garden space and add interest to your design, but keep them to a minimum for maximum effect.

Furniture is likely to be your biggest outlay, so pick something you'll be happy to live with for a few years. It needs to be comfortable and suit your chosen style. Unless you have lots of room in your garage, go for hardwood (taking care to look for the tag that shows it is from sustainable forests), or cast aluminum because it looks classy and, most important, you can leave it outside all year round. Just be sure to bring the cushions in when you aren't using them to keep them dry.

The smallest sitting area can be made spectacular with the bold use of paving, containers, and plants. This one isn't subtle, but it's individual and exhilarating.

Five ways to make a paved garden

Flooring

Paving slabs are the most conventional material, but add a bit of interest to it by removing (or leaving out) some slabs and replacing them with gravel, cobblestones, lawn, or ground-cover planting.

Pots

There is a wide range of containers available, from terracotta to glazed pots and more contemporary steel ones, which come in all different shapes and sizes to suit any style of garden.

Plants

There are many plants that will happily grow in pots – from summer bedding plants to herbs, and even palms or small trees. Your only restrictions are the size and exposure of your property.

Hi-tech

A paved garden is perfect for technology extras such as lighting, outdoor heaters, and barbecues – and anything else to lure you outdoors on a sunny day!

Furniture

This might be the most visible part of your garden and will probably be the biggest outlay, so choose carefully to make sure you select the most comfortable and the most aesthetically pleasing pieces.

Cottage gardens

The romantically cluttered look of a cottage garden makes it an ideal style for plant lovers. You can cram a lot of different plants into a small space without losing the overall character. A quaint country cottage isn't essential. There are people who make cottage gardens on suburban subdivisions or in cities. If you can't stop buying plants, or if you are a compulsive plant propagator, this could be just the kind of garden for you – a patchwork quilt of your own particular floral pleasures.

Here, boxwood balls provide a touch of formality alongside the paved and gravel path and are a nod to the old cottagers' love of topiary. Horizontal lines – the path and the pergola – are perforated by the verticals of the pots and the verbascums and delphiniums.

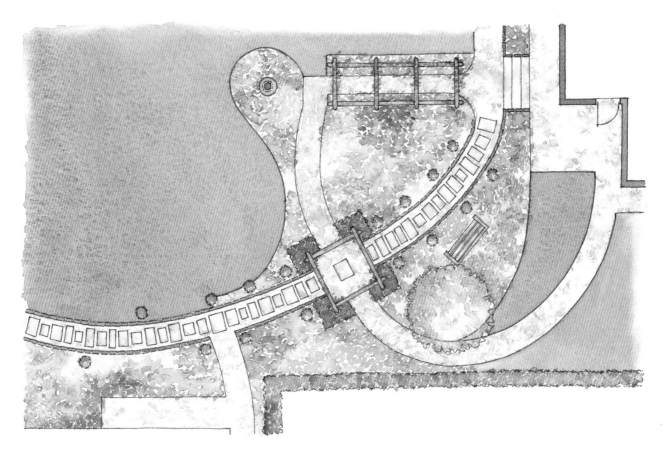

What's it all about?

Cottage gardens are about plants and very little else. The original cottage gardeners didn't bother with grass, because it took up valuable growing space. Cinder paths, which nowadays have been replaced by gravel, did for getting around, and everything else was wall-to-wall plants, all jumbled together with recycled bric-a-brac. Cottage gardeners simply stuck things in wherever there was room. Design didn't come into it – the garden just "happened."

Even today, cottage gardeners are the sort who'll keep nipping a bit out of the lawn to enlarge the flower beds any time they need more room. Guidelines? Forget 'em. This type of garden breaks all the rules. If there's a tree, it will have a couple of climbers growing up it and a shrub underneath. Every shrub will be underplanted with perennials *and* bulbs. The porch will be weighted down with climbers and the steps congested with plants in geriatric clay pots.

Although it goes against the grain for anyone with an instinct for cottage gardening to do any garden planning, it's still well worthwhile. It's the only way you'll see all the various plant characters properly and to make sure that they don't end up swamping each other. You also need a little bit of architecture or hard landscaping to set them off, or you end up not seeing the garden for the flowers.

The paths in this cottage garden are supremely practical in that they lead from the door of the house to the garage and garden gate, but the planting and design softens the hardness of the practicality, and the chosen plants give a truly cottagey feel.

Cottage garden plants

Old cottage gardens were stuffed solid with easy-going plants, such as hardy annuals and the sort of spreading perennials that would probably be called "thugs" in most modern gardens. They'd also have old roses, useful plants including herbs and vegetables, and wildflowers and plants providing nectar for bees, because every garden had a couple of hives.

The only trees and shrubs would have been the sort that provided fruit for the house. Flowers like gladioli, sweet peas, and dahlias were often grown in rows to sell as cut flowers at the garden gate – few evergreens would have found a place at all. The emphasis was on self-sufficiency, with the chance to earn a little pocket money on the side.

Nowadays, you can make a low-maintenance cottage garden border by teaming self-seeding hardy annuals with rampant, spreading perennials, or you can make a nostalgic border by mixing together flowers for cutting and the prettier vegetables and herbs.

Five ways to make a cottage garden

Plants	Hard landscape	Climbers	Recycling materials	Containers
In a cottage garden, the more plants, the merrier. Plant whatever you fancy – from flowers to trees, shrubs, bulbs.	Most cottage gardens avoid this except for the occasional small path to allow access to the garden or beds – plants are the key ingredient.	If you don't happen to have a porch, try to introduce some verticals in the garden over which climbers can grow. Pergolas, gazebos, a trellis, or trees can provide support.	Old sinks, chimney pots, and other antique or second-hand paraphernalia add a cozy, relaxed feel to a cottage garden.	Cottage gardeners soon run out of space in their beds and borders, but containers provide room for yet more plants and can be placed on paths and patios and into gaps throughout the garden.

But your average cottage garden houses a huge mixture of choicer plants, too. It might contain flowering shrubs, a clematis collection, a formal herb garden, unusual perennials, topiary, natural-looking ponds and streams, or containers of alpines shoe-horned into every inch of available space. The 21st-century cottage garden is definitely an enthusiast's garden.

Restraint is not a familiar word in the cottage gardener's vocabulary. The planting wraps right around the house (*opposite*) and billows out over snaking paths (*above*) as you amble down the garden.

Other ingredients

Cottage gardeners are born recyclers; the Victorians did so out of genuine poverty, but today it's usually because they would rather spend their money on more plants. If a wall came down, if the kitchen sink was replaced or a bucket sprang a leak, or a tile floor was relaid, the plunder would be reused somewhere in the garden.

Nowadays, to achieve the look, people will buy (or better still, acquire) second-hand items, such as old chimney pots or stone butler's sinks from salvage yards. Twist-topped tiles are good for edging paths, and old bricks make good raised beds for special treasures. Rickety rustic structures made from pruned tree branches, and plant supports made out of rural materials such as hazel and willow wands, look very much at home in this sort of garden. And so do distressed, reproduction antique garden knick-knacks. But go easy on the paraphernalia – the final effect should give more of a nod toward that greeting-card picture than the junk-yard of Sanford and Son.

Formal gardens

Formal gardens are a carryover from the grand gardens of the past, and what makes them stand out is their geometry. They don't even try to look natural. Lines are straight, angles are right, and corners are squared. You might think you need a junior stately home to carry it off, but not so. A lot of tiny urban gardens look good with a formal layout, but, if you have a big enough space to divide into several "rooms," there's something peculiarly refreshing about wandering straight from a wildly casual patch into an area with a strong sense of order and calm.

What's it all about?

The character of a traditional formal garden is created by rectangular blocks of grass, clipped evergreen hedges, and elaborate topiary with bags of architecture, whether it's walls and paving

Squares and circles, rectangles ,and avenues are the backbone of the formal garden (*below*). You don't need acres of space to create a similar feel: this style can work well even in the smallest area and with a limited range of plants (*opposite*).

or classical sculptures – there is none of your abstract stuff here. Only Corinthian columns, stone cherubs, and Grecian urns need apply. Water features might be the square, lily-pond variety or the circular sort complete with a skinny-dipping nymph clutching the fountain.

Yes, there are flowers, but they'll be very well behaved, or else strictly staked, growing in a proper, rectangular herbaceous border with a brick wall or a yew hedge running along the back. Or there could be a double border, which is simply two borders face to face with a path running through the middle, the whole inside a "room" enclosed by walls or hedges.

Look to stately homes for inspiration. Many of them have features such as formal parterres, with flower beds edged with clipped dwarf hedging, or geometrical herb gardens, divided into segments like an orange, with a sundial in the center. They may seem to demand a large amount of space, but they can be successfully duplicated on a smaller scale to suit your own plot.

Five ways to make a formal garden

Design	Features	Plants	Materials	Order
Straight lines, square corners, right angles, and geometry are the crucial factors in designing a formal garden – it is a style that demands a strong sense of order.	Formal gardens demand a strong architectural feel that can be provided by hard landscaping, such as walls and paths, or features such as statues and follies: the most important word to remember is elegant.	Traditionally, formal gardens are characterized by hedging and topiary. Yew and boxwood are best. Other plants should be suitable for disciplined beds or borders.	From paving to statues to furniture, the materials in a formal garden should be classy and expensive-looking. Synthetic or cheap materials will stand out and ruin the effect.	Good order is key in a formal design – hedges will need to be kept clipped, and borders and pathways must be kept neat and clearly defined. Seating at the end of paths and along borders allows you to survey the order you have created.

Blocks of dahlias and mushrooms of yew make a classic combination at Hinton Ampner, one of my favorite Hampshire gardens.

Formal plants

Whatever else you decide on, you'll need a hedging plant that will stand being closely clipped, and normally the choice is between yew and boxwood, both of which can also be trained as topiary. Go for yew if the site is sunny and the soil well drained; in a shady garden, boxwood is best, though it's also happy in sun if the soil doesn't dry out too badly. If you want dwarf edgings, go for dwarf boxwood (*Buxus sempervirens* 'Suffruticosa'), since the other boxes won't stand being clipped this short. Otherwise, use evergreen herbs, like an upright form of rosemary, santolina, or one of the dwarf lavenders, such as *Lavandula angustifolia* 'Munstead'.

Other ingredients

Whatever you have, it must be classy. Paving needs to be good-quality bluestone or sandstone or even better. Statues should be of lead or stone, or you might stretch a point and order a little something in wrought metal. Forget gaudy garden chairs: the sort to go for are classic wooden Lutyens-style benches or cast aluminum copies of Edwardian ironwork garden seats.

In case you're worrying that it all sounds a bit expensive, that's certainly the impression you want to make, but, since quality lasts, a garden like this keeps going for years without needing expensive refurbishment. But you can always cheat. Any competent do-it-yourself fan can make their own wooden seats and tables, and reconstituted stonework looks just like the real thing these days.

Finding formal ingredients

Some larger garden centers have big display areas where you can see a good selection of different types of repro garden furniture, outbuildings, and accessories, and most large gardening shows will have a good range of products available at the maker's booths. Other places to look are architectural salvage yards and businesses, especially those out in the country. They often have amazing pieces that will instantly make your garden.

Making a plan

Once you have some idea of the style of garden you fancy, start to put something down on paper. It's too soon for a shopping list at this stage; the way I always start is by drawing an outline of the garden. This will become the template upon which you try out various ideas as you build up your dream garden in several stages. There's something hugely intimidating about a blank piece of paper, but once you've drawn in the house and the boundaries, you can fiddle about and see what starts to fall into place.

Drawing the outline

It's worth drawing your garden outline to scale; otherwise, when you start filling in some details later, you'll have no idea if the features you want are going to fit.

If you like working with paper and pencil, you'll find graph paper makes life much easier. Choose a scale to fit. One square to the foot or yard usually works for a small garden, but if you own rolling acres, you'll soon be off the edge of the page.

Use your computer if you prefer; that's the way I planned my television gardens. You don't need to buy a proper design program unless you particularly want to; I just use the drawing tools to make straight lines, formal shapes, or freehand beds and borders, then I can play about with various ideas and print them .

From simple sketch to colorful design, what was once a blank and lackluster patio now becomes an exciting viewpoint for the tiers of bright planting on the slope.

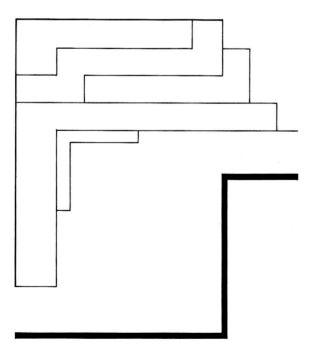

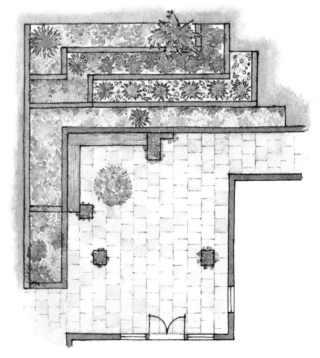

Proper measurements will make your plan realistic – you'll then know exactly what you can fit into a given space.

Measuring

If your plan is to work, the information needs to be accurate in the first place, so measure up very carefully. Landscapers normally use a 100ft (30m) tape that retracts into its own carrying case, but there's no need to buy one specially. You can make do with an ordinary retractable handyman's tape measure. That's a lot easier than struggling with a school ruler, and it has the big advantage of being flexible. Have an assistant to help; measure your boundaries, then convert them to the right scale and mark them on your plan. If all else fails, you can always just pace the length and width of the garden, then multiply the length of your stride (it's usually about a yard/meter) by the number of paces. That'll probably be good enough for a small garden.

Next comes a bit more measuring, because you need to mark the exact position of the house on your plan, and show where the windows and doors are, so you know where you'll be looking out or going in. Then measure the position of all those things that have to stay put, such as immovable paths, utility meters, air conditioners, huge trees, and tall fences that you can't or don't want to remove, and mark them on your master plan, too.

Draw in a small compass rose so you can see which way faces north and south. If there is anything outside your garden that you need to take into consideration, such as superb country views you don't want to lose, a messy neighbor that you want to hide, or overhanging trees that create heavy shade – make a note on the plan so you remember to take them into account as you work.

Now take a copy of your plan, or lay a big sheet of tracing paper over the top so you don't make a mess of the original, and experiment with some basic shapes. Take your time and have fun – it's nothing to worry about.

Pick of the best

Stick to basic shapes for now, and don't be tempted to start filling in minute detail. That will come later. For now, concentrate on making perhaps half a dozen different designs. Pick out the bits you liked best from each, then see if they can't be combined in a different way to make something you like even better.

The "experimenting with ideas" stage is an important one, so take your time. That's why most people choose winter to design the garden, when there isn't much doing outside and it's very pleasant to sit inside, just thinking and planning. Once you have a basic layout you are reasonably happy with, that's the time to start thinking about specific features, plants, and hardscaping.

Playing with shapes

Just because your garden is square or rectangular, it doesn't mean that you need to keep it looking that way. It's amazing how something as simple as changing the shape of the lawn can alter your whole perspective on the rest of the garden. So whether you have an existing garden to adapt, or a whole new garden to start from scratch, just play around for a while. It won't commit you to anything, and it might be the start of some good ideas.

There are lots of possibilities to explore, and when one jumps out that makes you feel right, move on to the next stage. So take your basic outline and gradually keep adding the next degree of detail. The picture slowly builds up until you have a finished plan showing everything. You'll find the Master Plan is a great help, whether you are making the garden a bit at a time, or just deciding what to buy at the garden center. That way you will know where to put it when you get home, because you can fit it into the plan.

Design tips – conjuring up ideas

Don't just sit there staring at a blank sheet of paper waiting for inspiration to strike. Look at photos of good gardens in books and magazines, preferably ones that are roughly the same size, shape, and style as the one you are trying to create for yourself. If you've taken pictures of gardens you've visited during summer, now is the time to dig them out. There's no need to copy someone else's ideas exactly, but if you see something you really like, there's no harm in borrowing it as the basis for your own garden. By the time you've added your own personal touches, it'll look quite different. Confidence is hard to come by when you're starting from scratch, so never be afraid to rely on other people's experience.

And if you simply cannot design on paper? You are not a failure. Go out onto the soil and do it there; use lines of sand to mark your shapes, and scuff them out if they don't work. Use stakes to indicate prominent trees and shrubs. You will not be alone in your preference for designing on the ground – William Robinson (the "father of English gardening") insisted on it. You're in good company. Sometimes I do it myself.

Over the next few pages, I've looked at some simple ideas for laying out the garden shapes you are most likely to encounter. You don't need to copy them, but if you've never done this sort of thing before, it's helpful to have a starting point. Just adapt them as much as you want. And remember to be practical. Choose lawn shapes that are easy to mow, and beds and borders that are large enough to accommodate a decent number of plants. Even in tiny gardens, it is worth remembering the KISS rule – Keep It Simple, Stupid!

Diagonal lawn

If you want a rectangular lawn, there's nothing to say that it has to run parallel with the garden fences. Try laying it diagonally across the garden, but instead of putting it right through the middle, offset it slightly to leave differently sized shapes in the corners.

Two diagonal lawns

You could try for similar effects by using two diagonally placed rectangles that overlap each other – they can be the same size or different, if that fits the space better. It gives a dynamic sense of movement and leaves several planting spaces of interesting shape.

Round lawn

Superimpose a circular lawn on to your garden plan. See what it looks like in the middle – the basis for a formal garden, perhaps? Or offset it to one end of the garden, or over to one side. See how the shapes between the edge of the lawn and the boundary round the garden change? Imagine what they'd look like filled with plants, but don't get drawn into fine detail – at this stage it's just a question of opening your mind to ideas.

Two round lawns

Why settle for one round lawn when you can have two? Some of the most stylish modern gardens are based on two overlapping circles. They don't both need to be the same size, and they don't need to overlap equally. Try placing them up and down the garden, then see how it looks if you place them diagonally from corner to corner. Again, notice how the shapes alter between the circles and the edge of the garden, where you'll be putting your planting. See what happens if you draw a quarter circle in one corner and overlap it with a section of a second circle. If you are on a sloping site, one circle could be higher than the other, so you need to step down where they overlap.

Nobody can tell you what you like or don't like – it's instinctive – but you can at least make sure you know all your options. Will it be a diagonal lawn or two diagonal lawns? A single grass circle or a double one? Only you can decide.

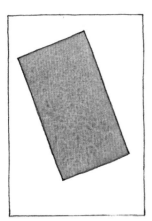
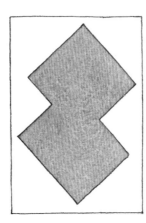
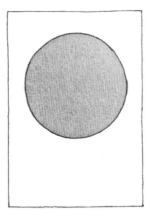
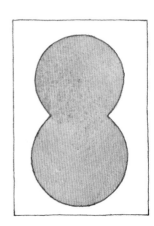

How to... transfer paper plan to site

Once you are happy with the shape, size and positioning of your beds, paths, and other features on your Master Plan, it's time to see what it looks like for real, out in the garden. You haven't committed yourself yet – there's still time for fine adjustment. Convert the lines on your plan into life-size measurements. You'll find it easier if you write them on the plan as a ready reference. Stick to either imperial or metric measurements – don't mix them up, or you'll get in a muddle. (But bear in mind that some building materials might be sold in metric.) It's also a good idea to cut yourself a straight piece of lumber exactly one yard long as an instant measuring stick.

What you need

- *some 1ft (30cm) wooden pegs sharpened at one end*
- *plenty of string*
- *cans of landscaper's spray paint or an old plastic beverage bottle filled with dry sand*
- *tall bamboo stakes*

1 Starting at one end of the garden, hammer a peg in to mark the position of the corners of all your main features, then link them together with string. Use taller stakes to represent trees and important focal points. Take a look out of all your windows, particularly the upstairs ones, to get a feel for the way it's looking, then make any necessary alterations.

2 Use a measuring stick or a tape to add up the dimensions of important features. This way you can work out if they will be large enough to put chairs and tables on, and you will be able to calculate accurately the amount of materials that will be needed to build them.

3 Once you are happy with the layout, go around spraying landscaper's paint or trickling sand directly underneath the strings. With the markings in place, you can take out the pegs and string, leaving the shape of the garden outlined perfectly. Tackle the hard landscaping first – paths and patios – then move on to plant features, such as hedges, beds, and lawns.

Regulation rectangles

Ultra-modern designs can look good in small gardens and also be practical. The curving lavender wall masks the ugly shed and is outfitted with a seat for soaking up the sun.

A few pages back I showed you how something as simple as changing the shape of the lawn can make a plain rectangular garden look completely different. Well, now I'd like to show you some other ways you can make the same shape more interesting by dividing it up into several smaller areas or "rooms."

"That's all very well if you have a huge garden," I can hear you say. Well, yes if you *do* have a big garden, dividing it up into "garden rooms" is the best way to pack it full of interest, but you can do the same thing on a small scale in quite a tiny garden. Only here, instead of having tall features to divide it up, you just use shorter ones that you can see over. It's not as radical as it sounds; most of the good small gardens you know will probably have a patch of paving, some borders and a feature of some sort, such as a pond, or a specimen tree with a seat under it. So there are three quite distinct areas for a start, even if they aren't kept apart by real physical barriers.

Because you are only playing about with ideas on paper at the moment, it doesn't matter how your thoughts turn out; nobody is going to see them except you. So experiment with some different basic shapes inside your space – diagonals and circles; the odd lazy "S," teardrop shapes such as you find in Paisley patterns, and long sweeping curves. Then start to adapt them into beds, borders, and lawn, or paving and paths. Don't start thinking about specific plants yet, because we are still working on the big picture.

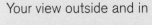

Your view outside and in

Imagine you are looking out from the windows you marked on your plan, and make sure they overlook a good view of the garden. If you have big borders right in front of them, they'll make the room dark and spoil the view. You don't want to be able to see the entire garden from indoors, either. Screen part of it off to give some inducement to explore.

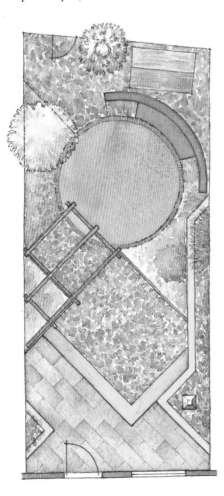

The modern design (*far left*) is one solution in this "no space" garden, but if you prefer something more formal and traditional, then a simple arrangement of paths at right angles to one another, along with dwarf boxwood hedging, seats, and focal points, may suit your taste.

Long and lean

There are more long, lean gardens around than you might think. Mostly they are older, urban gardens where, in order to make sure everyone had at least a little bit of road frontage, the original planners carved the building plot up into a lot of thin slices.

By its very nature, the long, thin garden draws your eye straight to the far end, where it loses interest. There are several tricks that will remedy this; the idea is to find a way of slowing the eye down by creating some interesting diversions on the way.

One way to do that is to divide the garden up into several smaller and squarer shapes, which each make a "room" that could have quite a different character. You might have a lawn and flower

This is the plan that was decided upon (*left*) but there is an alternative (*right*) which is every bit as workable. It's all a matter of taste.

Avoid long, straight lines

The thing to avoid at all costs is having a path that runs the full length of the garden. It acts like a visual wind tunnel, carrying your eye straight past everything else to the end of the plot. Stagger your paths so you need to cross the garden from side to side, or cross a diagonal, or walk around a segment of a circle to move from one "room" to the next. It looks better when you see the garden from the house or the upstairs windows, but when you are out there walking around, it helps you lose your sense of direction and makes you feel that you are wandering around aimlessly instead of being confined inside a regular shape.

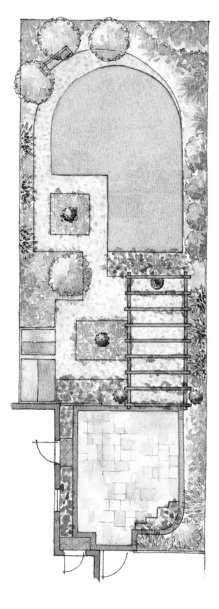

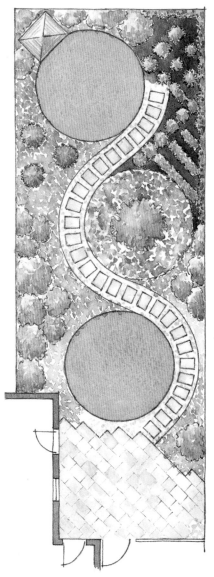

garden in one, a paved seating area with containers in another, and perhaps a formal ornamental vegetable and herb garden in another.

You could base the overall design for the space on a giant "S" shape, but to make it foreshorten the length of garden slightly, don't sit it square in your space; it will be more effective if it is angled so that it runs diagonally from one corner of the garden to the other.

Alternatively, you can go for a more geometrical look based on a series of dynamic diagonals to create a zigzag pattern running down the garden.

The difficulty usually lies in knowing when to stop and when a design is becoming over elaborate. As a general rule, use strong, hard lines – even if they are curving – and avoid fussy, itty-bitty spots. These will probably irritate you after a while and can be very difficult to maintain – especially if they make the lawn hard to mow.

This garden (*below*) was completely empty – a blank canvas. In a way this situation is the most daunting – there is nothing to inspire. But once a list of requirements was drawn up – somewhere to sit in the sun, a lawn for toddlers to play on, a few vegetables and herbs, and the accommodation of two small sheds, it started to take shape.

Tricky triangular

Not all gardens are symmetrical; in fact, few are. But the owners of those odd-shaped spaces around the edges of building plots often despair of finding a way of organizing their lopsided patch into something that looks like a garden.

    If that's your problem, then you are a lot luckier than you think. Irregular shapes can be a lot easier to divide up into separate areas, precisely because you don't have the straitjacket of a formal square or rectangle outline dominating your thoughts and trying to duplicate itself every time you drop your guard.

Just because a garden is asymmetrical and oddly shaped, it does not mean that it cannot be visually satisfying. Think of it as uniquely challenging!

Once you set it down on paper, an odd shape often dictates how best to divide itself up; circles and diagonals that touch odd-angled boundary walls make all sorts of interesting shapes.

A point at the end of a triangular garden can be squared slightly by lopping off the tip, leaving you with a handy bit of land in which to screen off your shed or compost piles. Alternatively, you could use the space for a big specimen tree against a background of evergreens, or to plant a bamboo grotto with a bit of garden stonework. They'll all help disguise the odd shape of the garden and, at the same time, leave you wondering if there isn't something else leading off around the corner. Keep 'em guessing, and the garden will look all the more interesting.

One thing that often looks attractive in a slightly triangular-shaped garden is to have a straight path that runs parallel to one of the sides and going part of the way across the garden. Instead of a plain path, you can substitute a walk-through pergola to cover with climbers or a fruit tunnel.

Once you have taken a bold decision and plotted it in, you start to see a new set of shapes within the garden that suggest all sorts of ideas. So don't worry about dirtying paper; have a go at it, and find out for yourself what works and what doesn't.

The plan (*above left*) is the layout of the garden opposite – it is a languorous feast of sweeping curves. The alternative could have been the layout above right. This design centers around a formal pool and interlocking paths that bisect the garden and its packed formal beds.

10 VERTICAL GARDENING

What's it about?

Vertical gardening is just a handy umbrella term for things that go up, like fences, walls, pergolas, and arches, in contrast to things that go along horizontally, like lawns and flower beds. It's a good way of making a flat garden look more three-dimensional, besides giving you extra space to grow plants you might not otherwise have room for. So make more of your verticals – they can practically double your growing space!

How verticals fit into the grand design

Boundaries go around the edge of the garden like the margins around a piece of paper; they are your fences, walls, and hedges. They mark the outer extent of your property, giving you an enclosed place to escape from the outside world. They shelter the garden from wind and weather, they provide a background for the garden, and they can also act as your fortifications, keeping intruders out and pets and children in.

Garden structures are also verticals, but they appear more like punctuation marks. Think of sheds, summerhouses and arbors as the periods at the end of a path, or pergolas as parentheses that enclose or frame a chunk of space. Pillars and obelisks are the exclamation points in your borders, while arches are the page breaks, allowing you to step from one chapter of the garden into the next.

As well as being used to lift a garden above the flat, a climber-covered screen will also act as a divider, which tempts the visitor to explore further or which masks an ugly shed or garage.

When you begin adding details to your basic plan, start from the outside and work in. Think about all of these taller, more solid features – boundaries and structures – first. They are the things that give your garden its permanent framework, and they help you organize the view into bite-sized bits, so that it's not just a solid mass of unbroken greenery from which nothing stands out.

Verticals in small gardens

Tall boundaries are usually a mistake in a small garden. They can make it dark and dingy, and, because you feel hemmed in, they make the space seem even smaller than it really is. It's much better to keep the boundaries lower and lighter, or even partially see-through, by using a trellis, open lattice, or rustic fences. Add height within the garden by using structures and tall plant supports.

Rustic poles and pillars are a great way of growing climbing roses when you don't have a wall, decorative plant supports are perfect for growing a clematis in the middle of a border, and annual climbers trained up an obelisk are ideal for growing in pots on the patio. Anywhere there is a natural opening – such as over a gate at the side of the house – you can add an arch, which immediately makes room for another two climbers, besides adding extra interest without taking up any space.

Verticals in bigger gardens

Where there is more space to play with, tall features can give the garden more of a sense of mystery. Hedges can be used to divide the space up into a series of outdoor rooms. Instead of being able to look straight to the end of the garden, you need to go outside and walk around to investigate the hidden areas. Don't be ashamed of having a low boredom threshold – pander to it instead.

A pergola or tunnel can turn a straight path into an interesting feature. An arch positioned over the top of a bench turns it into an arbor, and a curved hedge behind a large garden ornament acts like a living frame, creating an instant focal point.

In a bigger garden, you'll also have more room for outbuildings, which not only provide useful storage space but also add all sorts of new possibilities to your views around the garden.

Problems solved

Vertical gardening can also be a solution to all sorts of problem situations. You can use the principle to turn an ugly chain-link fence into a flowering hedge by covering it with evergreen climbers, disguise a derelict outbuilding by growing ivy over it, or screen off next door's junkyard behind a clematis fence. When it comes to a coverup, climbers and wall plants are the best things for the job.

Not all forms of vertical gardening need to rely on visible structures – this clematis has overtaken its support system to make a cascading dome of flowers.

Hedges

The only thing you needed to think about when choosing hedging years ago was cost. In urban areas, it was invariably privet, while big suburban gardens went mostly for hemlock, holly, and others that could be bought cheaply as bare-rooted saplings. Out in the country, they'd have hawthorn or osage orange to keep the cows out.

The craze for conifer hedges meant buying more expensive plants growing in pots, since that was the only way they'd transplant well. Nowadays, people who need only a small length of hedge are just as likely to choose container-grown shrubs from a garden center to plant as an ornamental screen.

Today's hedges don't only go around the outside of the garden. You are just as likely to meet smaller, more decorative hedges acting as garden dividers or dwarf edgings around beds or paths. And hedging plants may be clipped into frivolous features, such as topiary, "living architecture," or "cloud" formations.

Hedging plants come in many forms, which makes them capable of being put to many different uses – from clipped orbs of lavender cotton (*Santolina*), to dwarf curbs of boxwood (*Buxus*) or towering yew.

How to... **plant a hedge**

By far the cheapest way of making a hedge is to buy bundles of bare-rooted, deciduous hedging plants. These are normally available only in late autumn and early spring, but small ones cost very little. Stand the plants in a bucket containing a few inches of water for 2–3 hours to rehydrate them when you get them home. If you can't plant them right away, heel them in by planting them temporarily in a hole or trench somewhere in the garden to keep them fresh.

Alternatively, pot-grown hedging plants can be planted at any time of year when the ground is in a suitable state, but spring or autumn is best. However, they will be considerably more expensive than bare-rooted plants.

> **What you need**
>
> • *enough plants*
>   *(see spacings below)*
> • *well-rotted organic matter*
> • *general organic fertilizer*
>   *(in spring)*
> • *garden line*
> • *spade*
> • *fork*
> • *hose for watering*

1 Prepare the ground thoroughly. Run out a line to mark the position of the hedge, then dig a trench 12in (30cm) deep and 18in (45cm) wide. Spread plenty of well-rotted organic matter along the bottom of it, and, if planting in spring, sprinkle a general-purpose fertilizer along its length. Fork this into the bottom of the trench.

2 Space the plants out evenly. For a dwarf or medium-sized hedge, plant a single row spaced 1–2ft (30–60cm) apart. If you want a hedge more than 4ft (1.2m) tall, plant a staggered double row, with the plants 30in (75cm) apart. They will make a thicker, stronger hedge. Adjust the spacing slightly before you plant so that the plants fill the space completely and you don't run out of plants before reaching the end of the row.

3 Plant pot-grown plants as you would normal shrubs, but for bare-rooted plants, dig a hole that is plenty big enough, then spread the roots out well in the bottom before covering them with soil. In both cases, water the plants in well and mulch them with an 3in (8cm) thick layer of well-rotted manure or compost. They will establish all the better for this. After planting, you need to do some trimming (see p.62).

Immediate aftercare

With container-grown conifers, shrubs, and evergreens, just trim the sides slightly and prune the top out of the leader (the main, central shoot). One or more shoots will soon grow to replace it, so it won't prevent the hedge from growing taller, but it helps encourage bushy growth lower down in the meantime. If you want a tall hedge, it's a good idea to stake the plants for extra stability.

Thinking of having a hedge?

Hedges are "green," wildlife-friendly, and resilient, and they last for many years, but there is a down side. A new hedge takes several years to reach its full height; it takes up more room around the garden than a fence of similar height, and there is also clipping to think about. Most hedges need trimming once or twice every year. If you choose a fast-growing hedge, it'll reach the required height quickly, but you'll need to clip it much more often to keep the shape. If you live in a city or have a small garden, how are you going to get rid of all the clippings? And don't forget that your hedge is going to grow on your neighbor's side, too.

It is tempting to leave hedging plants at their full height after planting, but you'll encourage more vigorous growth if you cut them back by up to half their height. Then, like this rose hedge (*below*), they will become thicker and more impenetrable.

Bare-rooted deciduous plants need cutting down to about 6in (15cm) from the ground, or, if they are already branching from the base, then you need only to shorten them back by one-third. It's tempting not to bother, but it ensures that the hedge fills out from the ground up – otherwise, you can be left with a gappy bottom, which you will curse later. As the hedge grows, clip it lightly, little and often during the summer, until it reaches the required size, so that you are continually forming the shape as it grows up.

How to... **clip a hedge**

A hedge up to about 5ft (1.5m) high can be clipped by a person standing on the ground. For taller hedges, use a stepladder or a special hedge-cutting platform, which you can rent. Make sure the ground is firm and level before you start; a wobble could be serious if you're holding a moving hedge trimmer. With electric trimmers, *always* use a circuit breaker to cut off the power instantly should you cut through the cord. When using power tools, *always* wear goggles, long sleeves, long trousers, and strong boots. I know it's a bother, but it helps keep you out of the emergency room.

Soft clippings from a hedge that you cut little and often, such as privet, can be put on the compost pile, so long as you mix them with plenty of other ingredients. Bag up or bundle woody clippings as appropriate to dispose of them. If you want to compost them, put them through a shredder first, and allow a little longer than usual for the material to break down. Interesting tidbit: yew clippings are being investigated for their possible use in the manufacture of anti-cancer drugs.

What you need

- *shears or power hedge clippers*
- *stepladder or platform (for tall hedges)*
- *posts or sturdy stakes taller than the hedge*
- *ball of string*

1 If the hedge has been left a bit too long since the last cut, and the shape has been badly blurred by a fuzz of new shoots, knock a post or a sturdy stake in at each end, then stretch a taut piece of string along it at the required height. This will act as a visual guide when cutting the top.

2 Trim the sides first, angling them in slightly from bottom to top to give the hedge a "batter." This makes the top less likely to splay open, and it prevents the top of the hedge from shading the bottom, so there's less risk of it going bald at the base. Use a power trimmer in broad sweeps, making sure the blades are kept parallel to the hedge.

3 Cut the top last. You can cut it perfectly flat for a very formal finish, or round it slightly for a more informal look. In areas that have a lot of snow in winter, clipping to a formal point or a high dome allows snow to slide off more easily. This reduces the risk of a weight of snow building up on top and bending the hedge over or splitting it apart.

Which hedging plants?

When you are deciding what sort of hedge to plant, think about how tall you want the hedge to be – not all hedging plants grow tall. Don't choose a tall-growing kind and expect to be able to keep it small and healthy. It (and you) won't like it one bit.

Think about how much work it's going to make, too. A slow-growing hedge needs clipping twice a year, but you can get away with just doing it once. A fast-growing hedge needs may need clipping every six weeks between late spring and early autumn.

Formal clipped hedges

These are the sort of smart, tailored hedges that you see at stately homes and around traditional urban or country gardens. They look like a wall of leaves.

Yew (*Taxus*) (**1**) makes a good slow-growing, evergreen hedge in the 5–8ft (1.5–2.4m) range. It looks good all year round, and it's very versatile. You can train it for topiary, clip a hedge with a fancy turret-top, or grow an archway in it. A single row of yew can be clipped into a much narrower hedge than any other, as little as 12in (30cm) wide. A yew hedge doesn't take as long to reach its full height as everyone tells you (mine puts on a good 6in (15cm) a year), and it needs cutting only once a year. It's also less fussy than people think – it does need well-drained soil, but it can be alkaline or acidic. Z5–8.

Boxwood (*Buxus*) (**2**) is ideal if you want a shorter evergreen hedge, say 2–5ft (75cm–1.5m) high. It takes to clipping and training just as well as yew, and it's slow growing, so it doesn't need a lot of cutting. It also stands quite a bit of shade. It doesn't want total gloom, though, but in a site that gets about an hour of sun during the day, boxwood will do. The disadvantage is that it has recently begun to fall prey to a disease called boxwood decline, which can kill out great lumps of it. Take a chance if you're desperate for boxwood, but buy from a reputable nursery. Otherwise, go for yew. Z6–9.

Beech (*Fagus*, Z3–9) (**3**) and **hornbeam** (*Carpinus*, Z4–9) are the traditional, slow-growing, country garden hedges, suitable for growing from 5–8ft (1.5–2.4m) high. They aren't evergreen but do hang on to their russet-brown dead leaves in winter, so you're not left with a wall of bare twigs. You can alternate green beech with purple (or copper) beech when planting a new hedge, for a mottled look that some people like. Hornbeam is fashionable but duller than beech; its matte leaves do not reflect the light nearly as well.

1 Yew (*Taxus*).

2

3

4

5

Privet (*Ligustrum*) (**4**) is the hedge everyone loves to hate and it does need a lot of clipping, but it withstands everything from traffic fumes and dense clay, to summer storms and the odd collision with the riding mower without turning a hair. Privet is great if you want a hedge about 5–6ft (1.5–2m) high. There are evergreen, semi-evergreen, and deciduous types to choose from. Z3–9. *Lonicera nitida* (box honeysuckle, Z 6–9) is a good substitute.

Arborvitae (*Thuja*) (**5**) is the nearest thing to the hedge we would all love: an evergreen hedge that can be kept to about 4–5ft (1.2–1.5cm), but it can be much taller. It needs a couple of light clips a year, but, unlike Leyland cypress, it won't go berserk. If you have a reasonably sunny spot with soil that isn't too wet and want a good-looking, reliable conifer hedge, this is a good choice. Z2–9.

2 Boxwood (*Buxus*).
3 Beech (*Fagus*).
4 Privet (*Ligustrum*).
5 Arborvitae (*Thuja*).

When to clip

Clip slow-growing hedges of beech, hornbeam, and arborvitae twice a year – first in mid-to late spring, and again in mid- to late summer.

Clip boxwood in late spring on a dull day, so that the cut leaves will not scorch. Shears produce a better finish than power trimmers.

Clip yew once in late summer when it has stopped growing, and it will stay crisp in outline right through the winter.

Clip fast-growing privet and *Lonicera nitida* as often as every six weeks between midspring and late summer.

Remember, don't make the last cut too late, or you'll encourage a late flush of soft young growth just in time for it to get clobbered by an early frost, which doesn't look good.

× Cupressocyparis leylandii

There are plenty of horror stories about Leyland cypress behaving badly, and, yes, it can grow very fast and very tall, if you let it. While I certainly wouldn't encourage anyone to plant it around a small garden, a hedge that is topped at 6–8ft (2–2.4m) and clipped to shape twice a year can easily be kept under control. In a big country garden or close to the ocean, it makes a good windbreak. A Leyland cypress hedge that has grown too tall can be cut back to about 2ft (60cm) below the height you want it in midspring, and the new growth will soon hide the stump. To keep it that height, you'll need to keep pruning out the new leader that grows back each time, and be prepared to cut the sides back harder, as leylandii *will try to grow out if it can't grow up. You can't renovate a ratty or overgrown Leyland hedge by cutting the sides back hard, as you can for yew and laurel. Brown stems will not turn green again – they will remain bare and twiggy – so you must take steps before things get that bad. But if you don't have* Leylandii *already, think twice before you plant it.*

Informal leafy hedges

The big difference between this sort of hedge and a formal one is that they have big leaves, so you can't clip them with shears without cutting a lot of leaves in half, which then turn brown at the cut edges – it looks awful. This type of hedge is much better pruned with pruners in late spring so that it looks more natural, rather like a continuous row of shrubs. But even though you don't need to do it every year, don't underestimate how long the job takes to do.

Prunus 'Otto Luyken' (**1**) is a low, dense evergreen, sometimes grown as a high groundcover, with flowers like white candles in spring, but if you want a good low hedge about 2ft (60cm) high, this is it. Prune it to shape after flowering. Z6–9.

Cherry laurel (*Prunus laurocerasus*) (**2**) is not to be confused with the culinary bay, *Laurus nobilis*. It's good for a hedge of 5–10ft (1.5–3m) high or more. It will grow as tall as you're ever likely to want to cut it and, if it becomes neglected and overgrown, you can usually get away with cutting it right down to stumps, about 3ft (1m) high, in late spring and training it as a new hedge from scratch. Give it some fertilizer to help it along. Z6–9.

1 *Prunus* 'Otto Luyken.'
2 Cherry laurel (*Prunus laurocerasus*).
3 Spotted laurel (*Aucuba japonica* 'Crotonifolia').
4 *Elaeagnus* × *ebbingei*.

Restoring an old hedge

If you inherit an old hedge that is in bad condition, don't despair – with a bit of care and attention, you can restore it to its original glory. Don't be too hasty to write it off: restoration may take some time, but it will be less time than growing a new hedge from scratch.

Deciduous hedges, such as hawthorn, beech, and hornbeam, can be restored in late winter or early spring before any new growth appears. However, evergreen hedges, such as *Lonicera nitida*, yew, holly, escallonia, privet, and boxwood, can be restored in midspring.

1 Restore one side of the hedge one year, and leave the other for the following year, to avoid giving it too great a check. Cut back the side you are restoring much harder than usual, so that you are cutting into quite thick stems. You can go to within 1ft (30cm) of the center line of the hedge, but it's not essential to go quite that far if you don't want to.
2 Trim the top and the other side of the hedge as usual.
3 Fertilize and mulch the hedge well to stimulate new growth. Later in the summer, clip the new shoots lightly to encourage them to branch and thicken out, but make sure you shape the hedge so that it slopes slightly inward toward the top. Let the hedge grow progressively thicker – the new growth will soon hide the ugly stumps of the severed branches.

Aucuba japonica (3) is the spotted laurel, which comes in plain green, but is usually grown in the gold-spotted or speckled versions. It puts up with appalling conditions, including traffic fumes, pollution, and poor soil in dry shade under trees, which makes it a good choice for an urban hedge from 4–6ft (1.2–2m) high. Z6–10.

Elaeagnus × *ebbingei* (4) has large, gray-green leaves and tiny, greenish bell flowers hanging down from old twigs well inside the shrub in late autumn, so all you really notice is the scent that seems to come from nowhere. A row of plants makes a good hedge, 6–8ft (2–2.4m) high, especially in seaside areas, since it will put up with salt- and sand-laden winds. Z7–10.

Flowering hedges

Most folk never think of hedges as having flowers, but they all do, even if the flowers are relatively insignificant. Constant clipping often removes flowering shoots from some hedging plants, but others will produce their blooms even when trimmed.

Flowering hedges make colorful garden dividers, but because few keep their leaves in winter, they aren't the best choice for the outer boundary of a garden. Some are suitable for fairly formal, clipped hedges, but most are best grown as a continuous, single or double row of flowering shrubs that needs only light pruning.

1 Hips on *Rosa eglanteria* (Sweetbriar rose).

Roses (**1**) can make good informal flowering hedges, if you stick to shrub roses; they don't need hard pruning like modern bush roses. *R.* 'Fru Dagmar Hastrup' (Z2–9), with single pink flowers in summer and red hips in late summer and autumn, is good for a hedge about 4ft (1.2m) high and is good for a windy garden; *R.* 'Buff Beauty' (Z6–9)is the same height, with scented cream-buff flowers. No clipping is needed for a shrub rose hedge; just prune out a few old stems in winter. They look a bit bare and twiggy out of season, but the thorns ensure their role as a living security fence.

Forsythia (**2**) tends to be rather messy when it's grown as a shrub, but if planted as a hedge and allowed to grow about 5ft (1.5m) high it makes a sheet of sheer yellow in spring, and, by clipping it just hard enough to take off the dead flowerheads and roughly reshape it immediately after flowering, it stays a lot neater. Z4–9.

Escallonias (**3**) have a long flowering season – early summer to early autumn. They make good evergreen hedges, 5–6ft (1.5–2m) tall, and are best clipped formally, as soon as the flowers have faded. *Escallonia macrantha* is the one for seaside gardens. Z7–9.

Fuchsia magellanica (**4**), the so-called hardy fuchsia, makes wonderful hedges in mild climates; it'll make a deciduous or semi-evergreen hedge 4–5ft (1.2–1.5m) high. In colder climates, the plants die down to ground level in winter. Leave the dead stems until midspring before cutting them off; they provide a bit of protection for the crowns. Spread a 2in (5cm) layer of bark chips over the roots for insulation. Either way, you have dangling flowers all through summer and autumn, right up to the first frost. Z6–9.

2 Forsythia.
3 *Escallonia bifida.*
4 *Fuschia magellanica* 'Versicolor'.

Dwarf hedges

Dwarf hedges are a long-lasting way of edging a path, flower bed, or formal herb garden. Most hedge plants grow too big; you need something that can be clipped to 1ft (30cm) high or less. If they are too short to trim with hedging shears or power clippers, use single-handed sheep shears.

Dwarf boxwood (*Buxus sempervirens* 'Suffruticosa') (5) is the classic, elegant evergreen edging; plant 4–6in (10–15cm) apart and clip to 6in (15cm) twice a year in the first few years in late spring and late summer. They are slow growing and easy to root from cuttings if you want to grow your own. Z6–8.

Lavender (6) looks less formal, but the bigger cultivars get very floppy, so go for one of the dwarf varieties such as 'Hidcote' or 'Munstead' (Z5–8). They make a lovely, scented, evergreen dwarf hedge about 12–18in (30–45cm) tall. Clip them immediately after flowering to trim and deadhead the hedge simultaneously.

Rosemary (7) makes a neat herbal hedgelet that almost looks like conifer with its needlelike leaves, but in spring it's smothered in blue flowers. And, on a hot day, you have a heady Mediterranean fragrance. Prune to shape after flowering. Z8–10.

5 Dwarf boxwood (*Buxus sempervirens* 'Suffruticosa').
6 *Lavendula angustifolia*.
7 *Rosmarinus officinalis* 'Miss Jessopp's Upright'.

Unconventional hedges

If you prefer a less solid boundary, plant a row of bamboos. *Fargesia murielae* (Z8–10) and *F. nitida* (Z7–10) are good for this. Let them grow up as a living bamboo screen that looks light and airy, even though it grows to 6–10ft (2–3m). Or plant long, bare willow cuttings in autumn or early spring so that they criss-cross to look like a lattice fence. When they take root and start to grow, clip the new shoots back twice a year for a feature that is a hedge in summer and a rustic fence in winter when it loses its leaves.

The simplest of wooden structures can make a pleasing fence, provided the carpentry is sound.

How high?

Fence panels are very popular with first-time gardeners because they are relatively cheap, easy to put up, and, let's be honest, a nice tall fence prevents the neighbors from seeing in. If I could say one thing to first-time gardeners, it would be this: don't do it. You might just make your own garden dark and closed in; a tall, solid fence has a lot of wind resistance, which makes it prone to being blown down in a storm, flattening everything in its path; and the odds are that neighbors can still see in through the gaps, anyway. No, a lower fence looks much better, costs less, and lasts longer. If you want a taller fence, go for one with an open trellis at the top, which lets more light in but still helps deflect prying eyes.

Fences

Although hedges have a lot going for them as bird-nesting sites and wildlife havens, when it comes to saving labor, there's a lot to be said for fences. Compared to hedges, they make an instant boundary – there's no waiting for anything to grow – and they take up a lot less space. Whereas a hedge needs about 2–3ft (60–90cm) of space all around the edge of your garden and takes a lot of water and nutrients out of the borders in front of them, a fence occupies next to no space and takes nothing out of the ground.

It's not all plain sailing; there is a bit of maintenance to do when a fence has been up for a few years, and some have quite a limited life. Because fences have a big influence on the garden's character, it's important to choose one that creates the right atmosphere.

Post-and-rail fences (1) are the type they put around paddocks out in the country – the rails slot into the posts, leaving a lot of open gaps, so though they are good for showing where your boundary is, they don't do much for garden shelter, privacy, or security. If you have a country garden, a fence like this makes a grand support for a big climbing rose, and it'll flower along its entire length when it's trained horizontally. You can also use a post-and-rail fence as the foundation for willow or similar panels, or for bamboo screening. Just unroll some bamboo screening along the fence and attach it to the posts and rails with builder's staples or wire.

Picket fences (2) are the type that you often see around cute little cottagelike houses, usually painted white. They look neat and make more effective boundaries than post-and-rail fences because the gaps filter the wind, yet they don't make a solid obstruction that is easily blown down. The gaps are too small for animals to get through, but picket fences aren't so good for growing climbers on, because they need regular repainting.

Trellis screens (3) are not strong enough to use as garden boundaries, but for dividing space inside the garden they are superb, since you can choose a style to match the effect you want to create. There are diamond- or square-lattice panels, curved panels, panels with arched or dished tops, or you can put wooden finials on top of the supporting posts for a more classical look. Trellis panels are also good for making simple garden structures, such as an arch, arbor, or open-fronted gazebo. A trellis is great for growing climbers, especially for the lighter, airier kinds, such as annuals, or clematis that can be cut down when you need to treat the wood.

Hazel or willow hurdles (4) look very rustic, so use rustic poles to support them instead of sawed lumber. They were originally homemade fences, and, since the rods used to make them are thin, the panels dry out and become brittle. They last only about five to ten years. Their life will be prolonged to its maximum if you spray them with preservative using a knapsack sprayer – a brush is impractical. In a cottage garden or wild garden, grow ivy over aging hurdles, and, as the ivy stems "set" they help hold everything together, so your fence grows old gracefully and lasts a bit longer.

Willow and bamboo panels (5) are not hugely long-lived, either. Plan for maybe ten years, but if you don't need a lot of them and you want bags of style, it's well worth it – and, anyway, you might fancy something completely different by the time you need to think about replacing them.

Panel fencing (6) lasts about 10–15 years, depending on how well it's treated. It is a good, cheap choice and widely available. Panel fences may not be as attractive as other options, but they can be "improved" by painting or by growing climbers over them.

1 Post-and-rail fence.
2 Picket fence.
3 Trellis screen.
4 Hazel hurdle.
5 Bamboo panel.
6 Panel fencing.

How to... **put up a panel fence**

Panel fences are one of the quickest ways to fence the garden: you should be able to fence a smallish garden easily in a weekend. You can use wooden or concrete posts; wooden ones often look better, but they will need more maintenance. Concrete posts come already equipped with grooves for slotting the panels into and will last forever.

There are many alternatives to interwoven panels, and they can provide quite a different effect in the garden. Woven willow screens and interwoven hazel hurdles both have a very rustic feel. You can prolong their life by treating them with a suitable wood preservative or with linseed oil, but neither material will be as durable as most lumber. You are looking at a probable life of 8–10 years for alternative panels, whereas lumber will last up to twice that long.

1 Measure carefully, so that you order the right number of fence panels and posts. You need one more post than panels. Dig a hole that is as deep as one-third the height of the final fence, and position the first post in it. Use a level to check that it is perpendicular, then ram moist concrete (6 parts ballast to 1 part cement) around it.

2 Brace the post and leave overnight for the concrete to harden. Dig the other post holes now, using a gravel board as a measuring guide or to mark their positions. The next day, run a level string line from the first post along the line of the fence and secure it at the far end. If the ground slopes, this line needn't be at fence height, but all panels can be leveled to it.

3 Fasten the first gravel board to the bottom of the first post with the hardware provided, and check that it is level. Use wedges underneath it if the ground is sloping. Any gaps below it can be filled later with soil or gravel. Misaligned gravel boards look dreadful, even if the fence above them is level.

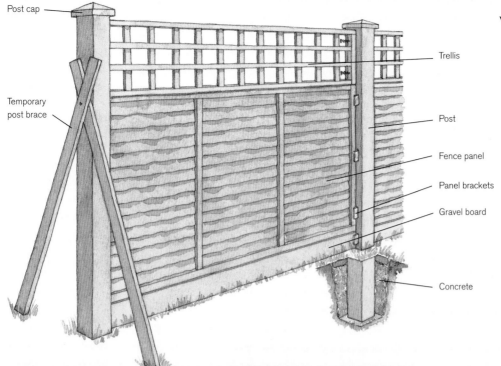

Post cap

Temporary post brace

Trellis

Post

Fence panel

Panel brackets

Gravel board

Concrete

4 Sit the first panel on top of the gravel board, then screw it to the first post with the hardware provided. (These are usually U-shaped brackets.) A second pair of hands is very useful and saves on the bad language when the panel topples off the board.

5 Lower the next post into its hole and fasten it to the end of the fence panel. With the level, check it is perpendicular, then tamp concrete around the base to secure it. Continue to the end of the run, cutting the last panel to fit if necessary. Fasten trellis panels in place (if you have chosen to use them) before cutting off the tops of the posts 1in (2.5cm) above the panel or trellis and securing post cappings to them.

Wood treatment

Wooden fences need treating with preservative every year or two to prolong their life and prevent the color from fading. There's no need to stick to traditional wood-colored preservatives – lurid orange or dreary brown. One of the quickest ways to give a small garden a brand new look is just by changing the color of exposed woodwork. Pale green, dusky lavender blue, terracotta... you can use it on fences, the shed, a trellis or even decking. The most convenient time to treat lumber is in winter when plants have died down, but make sure the wood is dry at the time of painting and rain is not forecast.

If you want to grow climbers on fences, grow them on trellis panels suspended from the fence by hooks, so the plant can be lifted down and laid flat on the ground when you need to treat the wood.

Walls

Walls are solid and permanent. They cost a lot more than fences and take skill to build – anything over about 3ft (1m) high is really a job for a professional. It shouldn't be higher than that if it's next to a public road, and, if you want one more than 6ft (2m) high, you may need your local government's consent.

Walls say a lot about the style of your garden. Old red-brick walls suggest antiquity, while pale bricks are more modern. Glass bricks look very contemporary but are mainly used for designer features inside a garden, rather than as external boundary walls.

Concrete-block walls can be rendered and painted, and sixties-style screen-block walls can be disguised with climbers. You can also build drystone walls nowadays from reconstituted stone blocks that you glue together – they are good for building the low walls that surround raised beds.

Color can be scary in a garden, but exhilarating. And the effects achieved by different colors are startling. The purple wall (*below left*) gives depth to the garden and provides a strong background for the planting. If it were painted yellow (*below right*), it would make the garden appear smaller and overpower the plants.

The shelter effect

Walls are good places to grow slightly tender plants, because they soak up warmth on sunny days and release the heat slowly at night, rather like giant storage radiators, at the same time as providing shelter for plants grown against them.

But, odd though it sounds, less solid boundaries are actually better at sheltering the garden. That's because when wind hits a solid vertical surface, it rushes up over the top, which creates tumbling air the other side. These eddies can mean that the wind is actually stronger than if there were no wall there at all. In a very exposed garden, it's better to use windbreaks made up of about 50 percent holes, since they let some air pass through. They are less likely to be blown down than a fence, and they don't cause turbulence like a wall does. As a general rule, you can reckon that a permeable barrier will shelter a distance of roughly ten times its height.

Wall shrubs

Wall shrubs are ornamental trees or shrubs that are trained to grow flat against a wall, as an alternative to climbers. They grow a lot slower than climbers, and, being naturally twiggy, it's simple to train them out over the area you want to cover and easy to keep them under control.

The sort of plants that are used as wall shrubs are mostly those that are a touch tender and that benefit from the natural protection of a wall. But wall-training is also a good way to grow shrubs that are naturally messy or that normally grow too big to fit into a small garden.

Wall shrubs aren't only for walls – you can grow them against fences or a trellis, but if you opt for the more tender kinds, it's only against a wall, with its hot-water-bottle effect in winter, where you'll really see them at their best.

General training and pruning of wall shrubs

Some garden centers sell shrubs that have already been trained flat, ready for planting against a wall – they are usually tied up to a small piece of trellis. With these, it's just a case of untying them from their support and planting them so they stand flat against the wall. As they grow, tie the main stems to a trellis or horizontal wires attached to the wall so that they spread out and cover the required area. In time, sideshoots will grow to fill in the gaps between the main framework of branches. The only real pruning you need to do is to cut off any shoots that stick out from the wall and to remove those that aren't needed to extend the main framework.

Adding height to a low wall

If you have a 4ft (1.2m) wall where you'd rather have one at about eye level, don't try to build it up higher. It won't have adequate foundations and it may not be very stable; top it with a trellis instead. Put in some strong posts on your side of the wall, and screw the trellis to them. Not only will you now have more room to grow climbers, you've also made the garden more secure – intruders can climb over a low wall very easily, but they are less inclined to tackle a trellis, since it will break under their weight, leaving signs of forced entry.

Pre-trained wall shrubs can be expensive, and only a limited range is available, but it's not difficult to train your own. The best way is to start with a rooted cutting, then pinch out the sideshoots that grow where they aren't wanted, leaving only those that make a flat shape. To train your shrub into a fan or espalier shape, tie some ordinary garden stakes together to form the outline and attach that to the trellis or wires on your wall. Then plant your young plant at the base and train one stem along each stake.

Training a pot-grown wall shrub

A quicker option, if you're not a perfectionist, is to find an ordinary pot-grown shrub in a garden center that isn't as bushy as it should be, and simply prune out a few stems to make it a flatter shape so that it's suitable for growing against a wall. The stems will probably still be supple enough to tie in to a framework. You don't need to bother training it into a formal shape at all – if you prefer, you can just leave your wall shrub as a two-dimensional bush tied informally to stiff netting or a trellis on the wall.

Trained wall shrubs like this pyracantha often have some wayward stems. These stems should be tied in regularly, and any protruding shoots must be cut back to keep the plant close to the wall.

How to... attach a trellis to a wall

A trellis is the best form of support for climbers that climb by means of tendrils of one sort or another. This includes clematis, which need something to wrap its leaf stalks around, and for plants such as sweet peas that hang on using twining tendrils. It's less useful for self-clinging climbers, which use adhesive pads or aerial roots; they prefer sound, flat surfaces to cling to. On stuccoed walls, where self-clinging climbers can pull off the rendering in one large sheet, it is worth equipping the wall with a trellis, which is much more likely to take their weight.

What you need

- *wall anchors*
- *power drill and masonry bit*
- *screwdriver and screws*
- *two wooden slats 2 × 1in (50 × 25mm)*
- *trellis panel*

1 Mark the required position of the trellis on the wall, and cut slats to fit its width. Drill holes in the slats, then corresponding holes in the wall to take wall anchors. The slats need to be about 1ft (30cm) from the top and bottom of the trellis.

2 Push the wall anchors into the holes, and then screw the two slats to the wall. Paint them with a suitable color of wood preservative once the slats are in position.

3 The soil at the base of a wall is often pretty grim, since there will be footings in the way, so dig your planting hole at least 1ft (30cm) away from it, and do a really good job of soil improvement before planting your climber. Spread the stems out along the bottom of the trellis so the plant starts spreading out right from the very base; otherwise, you'll end up with a distinct fan shape.

Wall shrubs for sunny, south-facing walls

This is too good a spot to waste on anything that you could possibly grow anywhere else, so stick to the real warmth-loving exotics that will make your mouth water.

Cytisus battandieri (**1**), the pineapple broom, is one of the most striking wall shrubs, if you have room for it. It has large, silky leaves and yellow cockades of flowers that both look and smell like pineapples. It's big, at least 15 × 15ft (4.5 × 4.5m), and really needs to be trained out over horizontal wires on the south side of a house. I know that's a lot of room for one plant, but it's worth it; it flowers from mid- to late summer, and the foliage looks good, too. Z7–9.

Sophora microphylla **'Sun King'** (**2**) is a relatively new plant and one that I've really enjoyed growing in my garden. It has dark evergreen leaves with tiny leaflets that give it a frothy appearance, and its bright yellow clusters of flowers appear in late winter and early spring. It's tougher than many sophoras: mine is 5ft (1.5m) high and growing in the open. Great for out-of-season brilliance, and it makes a good background to other plants when not in flower. Z8–10.

1 *Cytisus battandieri.*
2 *Sophora microphylla* 'Sun King'.
3 *Abutilon vitifolium.*
4 *Ceanothus* 'Puget Blue'.
5 *Fremontodendron californicum.*
6 *Grevillea rosmarinifolia.*

Abutilon vitifolium (3) is a good choice if you have a tall, narrow, sunny wall, say 10 × 5ft (3 × 1.5m); it's an upright shrub with gray, grapelike leaves and big, nodding white or lilac-purple flowers hanging in clusters from early summer to autumn. Z8–9.

Ceanothus (4), such as the evergreen *Ceanothus* 'Puget Blue' and *C. thyrsiflorus* var. *repens*, are excellent wall shrubs for a hot, sunny spot; most ceanothus flower for several weeks in early summer, when they turn into a fluffy sheet of blue. Once the flowers are over, you can clip the plants quite closely with hedging shears to neaten them up, which also prunes them correctly. Cut off anything that grows beyond its rightful area at the same time. Allow at least 6 × 3ft (2 × 1m), and more for the most vigorous varieties. Z8–10.

Fremontodendron californicum (5) is a slow-growing evergreen and a very good choice if you have a small space about 6 × 6ft (2 × 2m), though it will get bigger if it's really happy. The big, waxy yellow flowers completely cover the stems from midspring until early autumn. It's a well-behaved plant that won't take over. Z8–10.

Grevillea rosmarinifolia (6) is a plant worth the risk if you fancy something really exotic-looking, and I reckon it's tougher than most of the books crack it up to be. Mine has survived some pretty cold spells without turning a hair. It is bushy, with evergreen needles like a delicate rosemary, and reaches 6 × 3ft (2 × 1m). From late autumn through winter and into early summer, the stem tips are crowded with clusters of tubular pink flowers with spiky stamens sticking out all around – not the time of year that you expect flowers like these at all. Z9–10.

Even in winter on a chilly wall, tough plants like *Cotoneaster horizontalis* can look good when rimed with frost.

1 *Camellia japonica* 'Mercury'.
2 *Crinodendron hookerianum*.
3 *Garrya elliptica*.
4 *Jasminum nudiflorum*.

Wall shrubs for north-facing walls

A north-facing wall is the one most people dread, but there's more you can grow there than you might think.

Camellias (**1**) do very well when they are trained out flat; in a smallish garden, that's a good way to grow them, since they don't take up much room. Ideally, I'd aim to keep a wall-trained camellia pruned so that it fits on a trellis panel measuring 6 × 3ft (2 × 1m), but if there's more room, you can just train it to fit anything up to 8 × 6ft (2.4 × 2m), or more if it's a big cultivar. Being evergreen, it gives you something to look at even when it's not in flower. Camellias need acidic soil. Z7–8.

Crinodendron hookerianum (**2**) is also ideal for acidic soil and a sheltered spot; it makes an unusual evergreen with red lantern flowers that hang down from the branches for a couple of months in early and midsummer. It's quite slow growing but it will eventually need a space about 6 × 8ft (2 × 2.4m). It's usually wider than it is tall when grown on a wall. Z9–10.

Garrya elliptica (**3**) is something that's mostly seen as a tree or bushy shrub, but it's a very good wall shrub for a north-facing spot. It's evergreen and has long, gray-green catkins that last all winter. On a wall, it teams very well with variegated ivy, and it looks great when illuminated at night. Z8–10.

Jasminum nudiflorum (**4**), winter jasmine, is a star in this situation; a naturally floppy shrub, it needs a trellis to prop it up. The yellow, star-shaped flowers are very welcome in winter and early spring. It doesn't have much in the way of leaves, and the green stems can look a bit scruffy, so it's a good idea to team it with some gold-variegated ivy to liven it up. Allow about 6 × 3ft (2 × 1m). Z6–9.

Wall shrubs for east-facing walls

East walls are a potential problem. It's tempting to plant early flowers to take advantage of the morning sun, but late frosts can really wreck flowers that are defrosted too fast on a sunny morning – it's safer to stick to shrubs that flower later in the year.

Cotoneaster horizontalis (5) has masses of tiny white flowers in early summer, berries from late summer and well into winter if the birds don't spot them, and those herringbone-shaped stems pile up well against a wall. It's semi-evergreen, but even if it sheds its leaves in winter, it has a great-looking skeleton. About 3 × 6ft(1 × 2m). Z5–7.

Chaenomeles speciosa (6), the flowering quince, looks best trained on a wall; it makes such a scruffy shrub. You can espalier it, and it looks very cottagey with its main branches tied to horizontal wires or a trellis. The spring flowers may be white, pink, or red, and there are many fine cultivars available; allow 6 × 4ft (2 × 1.2m). Z5–8.

Euonymus fortunei (7) can be grown as a small, evergreen, free-standing shrub, but if you plant it against a wall, it flattens out and scrambles up; it doesn't need much training at all. The gold-variegated 'Emerald 'n' Gold' and 'Blondy' bring splashes of color to uninspiring spots. It'll grow to 15 × 3ft (5 × 1m) against a wall, but you can cut it back to whatever size you want. Z5–9.

Pyracantha (8) is a beautiful wall shrub as an espalier and festooned around doors and windows. Even without fancy training, it's good just tied to horizontal wires or a trellis. Clip the plants just after the flowers fade, removing most of the current year's new growth, but not the faded flowers, which produce berries. In autumn and winter, you'll have a wall of orange, red or yellow bunches against a backdrop of evergreen leaves. Allow 6 × 5ft (2 × 1.5m) or more. Z5–9.

5 *Cotoneaster horizontalis.*
6 *Chaenomeles speciosa.*
7 *Euonymus fortunei* 'Emerald 'n' Gold'.
8 *Pyracantha.*

Wall shrubs for west-facing walls

A west wall is the second best place for wall plants in any garden. Because it's not as hot and dry as a south wall, it's a good place for sun-lovers that like more moisture at root level, but there are some seriously splendid contenders for the space. Any of these can also be grown on a south wall, as long as the soil is rich and moist.

Abeliophyllum distichum (**1**) isn't well known, but it's a wonderful shrub for a sunny wall, with white, almond-scented flowers on bare stems in late winter and early spring. It's slow growing and quite small, so you need to allow only about 5 × 3ft (1.5 × 1m). Z5–9.

Magnolia grandiflora (**2**) is the evergreen tree that puts on a big summer show on a huge wall. Think of rhododendron leaves and a giant magnolia flower, but in summer. This will eventually cover the complete side of a four-story house, so it's not one to take on lightly, but if you have acidic soil and a good set of ladders so you can keep the stems tied in, you're in business. You can keep it to two stories by pruning – and it does take time to grow. The variety 'Exmouth' flowers at an early age. Z6 (some cultivars)–9.

1 *Abeliophyllum distichum.*
2 *Magnolia grandiflora.*
3 *Azara serrata.*
4 *Carpenteria californica.*
5 *Itea ilicifolia.*
6 *Phygelius capensis* 'Sensation'.

Azara serrata (3) is pleasingly out-of-the-ordinary and produces large clusters of fluffy yellow flowers in late sring and early summer that are followed by small white berries. It has oval, serrated, evergreen leaves, and it grows to around 12 × 10ft (4 × 3m). Grow *Clematis texensis* through it for late summer color. Z9–10.

Carpenteria californica (4) looks like a giant potentilla with huge, fragile, single white flowers in midsummer and is perfect for creating an exotic look. As wall shrubs go, this one isn't too big – it'll cover a wall up to 6 × 6ft (2 × 2m). In a sheltered, sunny spot with well-drained soil, it should be fine. Z8–9.

Itea ilicifolia (5), sweetspire, is another shrub you don't often see. This is what you'd call sophisticated rather than startling, with evergreen, holly-shaped leaves and, in late summer, 1ft (30cm) long strands of greenish flowers that look like giant catkins from a distance. Very classy. It's slow to get going but eventually makes about 8 × 6ft (2.4 × 2m) against a wall. Z7–9.

Phygelius capensis (6), the Cape figwort, grows as a shrub in sunny borders, but it does even better up against a wall, where it will grow 5–6 × 3ft (1.5–2m × 1m) across. It has rich red flowers with a dash of yellow at the throat and will flower itself silly from midsummer until midautumn. Where marginally hardy, this is often about the only way to grow it reliably, but I'd recommend trying it in the open ground, too. It's often tougher than you'd think. Z6–9.

Itea ilicifolia provides a double whammy – evergreen foliage and long, pale green tassels of flowers.

Garden structures

Arches, pergolas, and outbuildings aren't essential by any means, but they are superb for giving the garden character – and fast. Stylistically, you can choose from rustic twigs or a trellis, and smart-formal or even classical. Victorian and Edwardian designs are always popular, and I suppose it won't be long before we start to see contemporary interpretations.

Any structure of this sort is good for adding height to a flat garden and for giving you somewhere to grow climbers that you might not otherwise have room for. Think carefully about where to place these structures. An arch looks natural where two boundaries meet, making it obvious that you are coming to the end of one part of the garden and are about to enter another. A summerhouse or gazebo stands out like a sore thumb parked in the middle of the lawn, but tucked into a corner, half hidden by planting, it acts as a natural focal point for its own "garden within a garden." And for lifting the back of a border, pillars and obelisks are unequaled.

A well-furnished pergola extends an irresistible invitation to explore.

Simple obelisks made of wood or steel can be used to add instant height to a border and to support climbing plants, such as clematis and sweet peas.

Pillars and obelisks

These are the most basic kind of garden structures. Pillars are straightforward poles, usually pushed in to the back of a border, allowing you to grow a few climbers there instead of the traditional evergreen hedge. Rows of pillars that are linked by thick swags of rope, with climbing or rambler roses trained out along them, are known as colonnades or catenaries.

Obelisks are shorter, more decorative uprights, maybe made of wrought iron or willow or hazel twigs, and they can be pushed into a border – probably nearer the front – or used in containers.

Both are meant for growing climbers, but due to the size restriction, you need to stick to smaller climbers that won't just rush up to the top and then dangle over. Smaller clematis and annual climbers are your best bet here.

Arches and their offspring

If you knock four pillars in to make a square and join the tops together with lumber, you have turned them into an arch. You can make your own out of rustic poles or sawed lumber, or buy arches ready made from various materials, including metal. Either way, if you cover the sides and top with netting or a trellis, you'll make them even more climber-friendly.

A row of arches makes a tunnel, which is a trendy feature to put over a long, straight path. Cover it with a mixture of different climbers, or one or two really huge kinds, such as Virginia

Mixing climbers together

You don't need to limit yourself to one climber per upright; you can grow two or even three in the same space. This extends the flowering season of your structure, if you choose plants that peak one after the other. Or use evergreen foliage plants, such as ivy, to add winter interest to summer-flowering climbers when they've lost their leaves. If you plant them all in the same spot, you should improve the soil over a larger area than you would just for one. Pruning can be a problem when you have several climbers intertwined, so take care to team only those kinds that can all be left to grow without any pruning, or which all need hard pruning, so you don't need to bother working out which stem belongs to which.

An arch (*above*) is an effective way of marking a change in mood between sections of the garden; an arbor (*above right*) is a calming place to sit; and a summerhouse (*opposite*) is a welcome retreat.

Persuading climbers to climb

Self-clingers need help to start with, because you can't persuade the existing growth to hang on. Only new growth will produce the aerial roots it needs in order to climb. When planting a self-clinger, such as ivy or climbing hydrangea (see p.344), cut the new plant back hard so that the new growth starts to grip to the upright surface right from the base of the plant. Otherwise, lay the stems down horizontally along the base of the structure, and new sideshoots will grow up from there and cling on.

creeper (*Parthenocissus quinquefolia*). Some people train cordon fruit trees over the "ribs" to make a fruit tunnel, and others choose laburnum, so that its flowers hang down into the space beneath.

A pergola is really just a traditional, formal tunnel with a square top instead of an arched one. A pergola is meant to go over a path or paving, so you might have one running down or across the garden. They are also often found in their lean-to form against the back of a house. You can make a Mediterranean version by using rustic branches for the roof struts and growing grape vines over the top. Alternatively, keep it traditional and grow something like a wisteria, or a collection of different clematis, one up each "leg." These are the sorts of structure that are meant to be almost hidden under climbers, so go as heavy on them as you like – scramblers and twiners welcome.

Arbors and gazebos

Think of these as big arches with seats underneath. The difference, if you want to be quite correct about it, is that an arbor is supposed to have an evergreen hedge planted around three sides for shelter, with a climber growing over the top as a "living roof." A gazebo, on the other hand, is more open-plan, made of a trellis, and with climbers growing all over. It has an open door and maybe "windows" through which to gaze out at the view. Climbers are a big part of the equation, and all your twiners and scramblers will do just fine here, too.

Summerhouses

A summerhouse is simply a solid gazebo – a good-looking garden building with a proper roof, walls, doors, and glass windows. It will form part of the view when you are looking at it from a distance, and it gives you somewhere to sit and enjoy the garden when the weather is a touch iffy for enjoying drinks on the lawn. It's also a safe, dry place to store your garden seats and croquet set.

When it comes to growing climbers over it, the effect needs to be slightly restrained, so you need to choose nonrampant types, or your glamorous building will be swamped in foliage. And if you grow the self-clinging climbers, the woodwork may be wrecked, so I'd go for a discreet clematis or some annual morning glories growing on some netting or a trellis on one side. If you want an economy summerhouse, you can always decorate the shed with windowboxes and trellises, and glamorize the inside. If you do prefer a more natural look and want to grow plants over it, choose small, slow climbers so that your summerhouse won't be swamped. Magnolia vines (*Schisandra* species) are mostly deciduous climbers with fairly showy flowers in red, pink, yellow, or white, followed (on female plants) by red or pink fruit. They can reach 30 ft (10m) but are far from dangerously vigorous. Team one of them with *Ampelopsis glandulosa* var. *brevipedunculata* 'Elegans', which has mini grape leaves in pink, cream, and white with pink tendrils. Neither needs any proper pruning; just cut out any bits that die back at the end of winter.

Matching plant to place

Small, slow-growing climbers will never muster enough oomph to cover a complete pergola, though they'll be good for pillars or in containers, or shimmying up an obelisk.

Big climbers, such as Clematis armandii, *can't be kept small enough to grow on a single trellis panel in a tiny garden – if you prune them too hard, you'll never see any flowers. Grow them in less disciplined situations, such as over a pergola, on a long fence, or over a large outbuilding.*

Real whoppers, such as Virginia creeper, can also be grown up through trees, but don't risk that with sun-loving species like passionflower, or they won't get enough light to trigger flowering.

How to... **build a pergola**

The very simplest way to build a pergola is to buy a kit from the garden center, which comes complete with all the lumber cut to length and pre-notched or with metal brackets included so you just slot everything into place. Otherwise, be prepared for a spot of DIY. The big advantage here is that you can design and build your pergola to any shape and size, even adding overhangs, which are a great decorative feature of pergolas and give you somewhere to put hanging baskets. But, most importantly, remember to allow enough headroom – aim for around 7½ft (2.5m).

Pergolas are great for framing views and for encouraging the visitor to explore. They make a sort of 3-D invitation. For this reason they are often best positioned near the house rather than at the far end of the garden, where much of the invitation effect is lost. Traditional pergolas may be directly attached to the house and may have sloping rafters, in which case make sure that at the lowest height they still offer ample headroom.

What you need

For the frame

- *4 × 4in (10 × 10cm) lumber for the uprights – spaced about 6ft (2m) apart. Lengths of 9½ft (3m) will allow them to be buried for 2ft (60cm) while allowing 7½ft (2.5m) headroom.*
- *6 × 2in (15 × 5cm) lumber the length of the pergola for the two main rails.*

   (If the pergola is to be built against a house wall, you will need posts only on one side. The other end of the rafters will be supported by a wall plate, made from 6 × 2in (15 × 5cm) lumber bolted to the wall.)

For the rafters

- *6 × 2in (15 × 5cm) lumber, one piece at each end and the others at roughly 3ft (90cm) intervals along the length of the pergola. Each rafter needs to be the full width of the pergola, plus an extra 1ft (30cm) at each end to allow for a well-proportioned overhang.*

- *wood screws and bolts*
- *power drill, saw, and hardware tools, level, and set square*
- *digging tools and concrete*
- *wood preservative*
- *stakes and string*
- *you'll also need several helpers for holding things in place*

1 Mark out the position of the pergola, and calculate how much lumber you will need. When you are confident you have all your materials, mark out the position of the holes using stakes and string and check that they are square with a set square. Dig holes 2ft (60cm) deep and 1ft (30cm) across for each post.

2 Position the vertical posts in the holes and check that they are a) in exactly the right spot, b) perpendicular and c) at the correct height. If the pergola is being built against a wall, fasten the lumber wall plate to the masonry with anchor bolts once you have checked that it is level.

Side members

Rafters

Post

Concrete

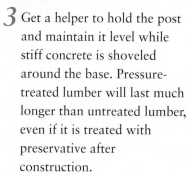

3 Get a helper to hold the post and maintain it level while stiff concrete is shoveled around the base. Pressure-treated lumber will last much longer than untreated lumber, even if it is treated with preservative after construction.

4 Tamp the concrete into place with a wooden rammer. Make the finished level a few inches below the soil surface so that it can be dressed with soil or gravel once construction is complete. Allow a day or two before the rafters are fixed in position, so that the concrete has time to harden.

5 Bolt the two long members down the sides of the pergola at the top of the posts, and then position the rafters. Exclude these on a small pergola, as here; the rafters can be placed directly on the posts in a criss-cross fashion. Cut a square notch into the top and bottom membes so that the two marry together as a simple joint. Secure with screws and apply wood preservative.

A mixture of *Clematis* 'Prince Charles' and *Rosa* 'Kiftsgate' growing over a colonnade, where swags of rope are used to link wooden poles.

Climbers

Unlike wall shrubs, which are relatively easy to keep to the shape and size you want by annual pruning, large, fast-growing climbers tend to head off on their own and can quickly get out of control. When you're choosing a climber, you do need to take into account practical considerations, such as sun or shade and soil type, but the thing you really must look at is how big it can grow. With climbers, big usually equals fast, and while hard pruning can keep them in check, it may also reduce their flowering capabilities.

Climbers for a north- or east-facing wall

Climbers that will grow happily on a north- or east-facing wall will also grow on other exposures as well, but on a north wall they will often "lean" forward to try to find more light, so be prepared for a bit more tying up than usual.

Berberidopsis corallina (1) is a distinctly choice and unusual climber that you don't often see. If you have acidic soil that doesn't dry out badly and a fairly mild, sheltered garden, give it a go. It's evergreen and reasonably slow growing, to 25 × 6ft (7.5 × 2m) eventually, with attractive long, heart-shaped leaves and bunches of red flowers dangling like rows of red beads in late summer. Give it something to twine through, like netting or a trellis. It's not easily pleased, but if you have the right place for it, I can promise you: it's sensational. Z8–9.

Hydrangea petiolaris (2) is a climbing hydrangea that is a good go-anywhere plant with large, white, lacecap flowers in summer and golden leaf tints in autumn. You don't need to bother holding it up, since it clings to the wall with its aerial roots, but, like ivy, it's not for anywhere with shaky mortar. Slow to establish and to start flowering (give it four years before panicking), it needs generous mulching, fertilizing, and watering to get it going. It will eventually reach 40 × 8ft (12 × 2.4m). Z4–9.

Akebia quinata (3) is a semi-evergreen climber with rounded green leaves that are tinged with purple when the weather turns colder in winter. The early spring flowers are a dusky maroon and spicily aromatic, and sausage-shaped purple seedpods follow them. Akebia will scramble its way up a wire-covered wall or through a tree to a height of 30ft (10m) but can be kept smaller by pruning. Give it a try if you fancy something refreshingly different and don't mind visitors asking, "What's that?" Z5–9.

Schizophragma integrifolium (4) is a sort of flashy cousin of the climbing hydrangea, with summer flowers that can be up to 30cm (1ft) across and long, decorative bracts. Like the climbing hydrangea, it is perfectly happy on a north-facing wall, although it usually flowers even better in sunnier spots. It will eventually grow 40ft (12m) or more high but can be restricted by pruning when grown against a wall. It is often slow to start, so be patient. The rewards are great, eventually. It isn't a particularly well-known plant, so don't expect to find it easily. Z5–9.

Parthenocissus henryana (5), the Chinese Virginia creeper, is a cousin of the Virginia creeper; the latter grows far too big, and too fast, for most gardens. It'll reach 70ft (21m) or more, and really looks its best for only six weeks in autumn, when the leaves color up, just before they fall off. No, for most gardens, the Chinese version is much better. It is smaller, at 32 × 6ft (10 × 2m), but it can be pruned hard in winter. It is more colorful generally, since the five-lobed leaves are tinged pink with silvery midribs all summer, and it looks slightly variegated, then the whole lot turns scarlet in autumn. Z6–9.

More climbers for north walls

Clematis – *C. alpina* and *C. macropetala* cultivars (blue or white); C. 'Comtesse de Bouchaud' (pink); C. 'Marie Boisselot' (white); C. 'Nelly Moser' (light and dark pink).

Roses – *Rosa* 'Albéric Barbier' (cream rambler); *R.* 'Bleu Magenta' (grape-purple rambler); *R.* 'Danse du Feu' (red climber); *R.* 'Madame Alfred Carrière' (scented white climber); *R.* 'Souvenir du Docteur Jamain' (claret-red climber, best trained flat against a north wall).

1 *Berberidopsis corallina.*
2 *Hydrangea petiolaris.*
3 *Akebia quinata.*
4 *Schizophragma integrifolium.*
5 *Parthenocissus henryana.*

Climbers for south- or west-facing walls

The soil is not all that great at the foot of a wall, thanks to the builders' rubble and footings down there, but when it's also hot and sunny, then conditions are particularly tough for plants. Prepare the soil very well if you want to grow climbers. Make a bed at least 2–3ft (60–90cm) wide along the base of the wall – remove the old soil entirely, if necessary. Dig out a trench 18in (45cm) deep, and fill it with a mixture of topsoil and well-rotted organic matter. If you grow mildew-prone climbers, such as roses, clematis, or honeysuckle, in a hot dry spot, keep them well watered in dry spells to avoid bringing on an attack.

Actinidia kolomikta (**1**) is grown for its foliage, but you need patience, because the leaves don't develop their spectacular pink and white tips until the plant is several years old. It needs a reasonable space to grow in; it reaches 15 × 10ft (4.5 × 3m) or more. Once established, it has tiny but well-scented cream flowers in summer. Z5–8.

Vitis vinifera (**2**), the common grape vine, makes a very attractive climber with a couple of very useful bonuses up its sleeve. One is that you'll have a harvest of edible grapes. The plants you'll most often see offered for sale are the sour sort for making wine, but, if you buy from a specialized nursery, you'll find some decent other kinds like *V.* 'Concord'. *V.* 'Brant' has bright orange autumn tints and edible grapes, and *V. v.* 'Purpurea' has purple leaves and small, sweet, purple grapes. The other big plus with grape vines is that they stand hard annual pruning – chop last summer's young growth back to a single permanent woody main stem about 5ft (1.5m) high. Do this in midwinter when they are dormant, or the stems will bleed badly, which can kill the plant. Z6–9.

1 *Actinidia kolomikta.*
2 *Vitis* 'Brant'.

Wisteria (**3**) is probably the first climber most people think of, and it causes the most heartache if you buy a shy one. Always choose a grafted plant, which should flower within three years. Train the main stems out over a wall, tying them to horizontal wires supported by vine eyes, and prune regularly to build up flowering spurs. Don't let them run rampant. There are two species that are commonly grown, both twiners capable of growing about 30 × 8ft (9 × 2.4m) or more, with dangling bunches of scented flowers in purplish shades or white. *W. floribunda* (Z5–9), the Japanese wisteria, flowers in mid to late spring; Chinese wisteria (*W. sinensis*, Z5–8) flowers earlier. Both come in a range of named cultivars with flowers in various colors. If you've set your heart on a wisteria and don't have a big enough wall, grow it up a pole in a large container and train it as a standard. It'll flower a lot sooner, and it's an easy way to keep it manageable.

Pruning wisteria

Once you have your basic shape trained out over the wall, go over the plant every year in July and cut back all those long, whippy tendrils of new shoots to within 6in (15cm) of where they originate.

If the climber has grown as far as you want it to go, this is also the time to "stop" the new growth at the end of the main framework of branches so that they don't grow any longer. Just cut the ends off.

In winter, shorten all sideshoots to finger length. This is quite straightforward, but it can be time-consuming when you come to tackle a full-grown specimen.

Solanum crispum 'Glasnevin' (4), the Chilean potato vine, will eventually cover the side of a house, say 20 × 20ft (6 × 6m). Its great claim to fame is the purple and yellow "potato" flowers that it carries during much of summer. It will attract a fair number of insects, including butterflies. Z9–10.

Passiflora caerulea (5), passionflower, looks almost tropical with its 2in (5cm) wide, lavender and white, rosette-shaped flowers that keep coming all summer. It bears yellow, egg-shaped fruits that aren't worth eating, though they won't poison you. In winter, it may keep its leaves if the weather is mild, but usually looks scruffy. In a cold area, it can be killed back to ground level. Either way, it needs neatening up in spring, just enough to cut back stems that have died back. Over a summer, you can expect it to cover about 10 × 6ft (3 × 2m). It needs a trellis or netting to climb on, because it clings with tendrils. The white-flowered form, 'Constance Elliot' is scented, though perhaps a bit more tender – probably best grown in a pot and moved into the conservatory in winter. Z6–9.

3 *Wisteria floribunda* 'Alba'.
4 *Solanum crispum* 'Glasnevin'.
5 *Passiflora caerulea*.

Out instead of up

Just because a climber is capable of growing 30ft (9m) high, it doesn't necassarily mean you need to let it do so. Instead of allowing it to grow up, train it out sideways along a wall or fence. Tying the main stems horizontally has a hidden benefit, because it encourages flowering climbers to bloom all along their length, and you can do this with foliage climbers to turn a fence into a "hedge" that doesn't need clipping. And if you use prickly plants, such as roses, you turn your garden fence into a free-flowering, fortified boundary.

1 *Jasminum officinale.*
2 *Lonicera periclymenum* 'Serotina'.
3 *Trachelospermum jasminoides.*

Climbers for scent

You only need to flip through a nursery catalog to see that there are supposed to be lots of scented climbers – but the trouble is, in the sort of places you grow climbers you can't often get close enough to the flowers to have a decent sniff, so they need to be pretty strong to "carry." Aside from roses (see pages 357 and 359), these are my top three.

Jasminum officinale **'Grandiflora'** (1) is the jasmine of old cottage gardens, but the perfume is big in aromatherapy circles, so it won't seem out of place in a more modern garden, either. It's a big twiner, reaching 20–25 × 6ft (6–7.5 × 2m), with sweet-scented white flowers lasting throughout most of summer. Z9–10.

Lonicera (2), honeysuckle, isn't always as strongly scented as you'd expect from its reputation. One of the best for general garden use is a cultivated form of the woodbine, *Lonicera periclymenum* 'Serotina' (Z5–10), the late Dutch honeysuckle, a twiner with clusters of small, curved-trumpet flowers that are purplish outside and yellow/cream/buff shades inside. Unlike some supposedly smarter cultivars, this one flowers constantly from midsummer to midautumn, and it'll grow to about 20ft (6m) long. You can wind its stems around a pillar, train it onto a trellis panel, or let it run up into a tree. Other honeysuckles are hardy in Z4–10.

Trachelospermum jasminoides (3) could be considered the ultimate scented climber. It has everything – it's an evergreen twiner with masses of strongly jasmine-scented white flowers in summer. It doesn't flower quite as long as real jasmine (*Jasminum*, above), but the flowers are more spectacular, and, because it's evergreen, you aren't left with a lot of bare stems to look at in winter. Perfect for a pergola, arch, or gazebo. It grows to 25ft (8m). Z9–10.

Clematis

By growing a mixture of large-flowered hybrids and species clematis, it's possible to have a clematis in flower for much of the year. Large-flowered hybrids are the familiar ones, with flowers that are often striped like grandad's pajamas; the species often have flowers more like nodding bells or small, open bowls. What they all have in common is that they like to be grown where their roots are in cool shade, but where their stems and flowers can grow out into the light. In a sunny spot, surround clematis roots with low plants, pebbles, or pieces of tile to keep them cool.

Watch out for... clematis wilt

The only serious problem with clematis is clematis wilt, which affects mainly the large-flowered hybrids. Young plants are the most often affected, but older ones aren't immune. Affected plants collapse suddenly, as if they need watering badly, and the leaves start to dry out. If you are sure that the plant isn't simply short of water, cut all the stems off close to the ground and dispose of them (don't put them on the compost pile).

Keep the roots cool and moist, and fertilize occasionally with a dilute liquid fertilizer, and new growth should appear – though this may not occur until the following year. Wilt can sometimes affect the same plant several times, but repeat the treatment, and it'll usually recover and grow normally. It's not really a good idea to plant a new clematis where one has already died of wilt, even though, in theory, the disease isn't spread through the soil.

If you want an alternative to large-flowered hybrids for growing where clematis wilt is a problem, go for any of the *Clematis viticella* or *C. texensis* cultivars, since they are not affected.

Planting clematis

Unlike most plants, clematis need to be planted deeply. Dig a planting hole about twice the usual depth and plant so that the top of the root ball is buried 4–6in (10–15cm) below the surface of the soil. This is so that if the stem of the plant is damaged – by careless hoeing or mowing, or an attack of clematis wilt – there will be plenty of buds below ground from which new shoots can emerge, so the plant regrows instead of being killed.

Clematis are very heavy feeders and need moisture at the roots, so they like lots of organic matter. If you want to grow one up a wall, where the ground is usually poor and dry, dig a very large planting hole and fork in lots of well-rotted organic matter, then plant so the roots are 12in (30cm) from the wall.

Pruning clematis

People worry about how and when to prune clematis. The easy approach is to keep the label when you buy a new plant, because the pruning instructions should be written on the back. If you have an existing clematis and don't know the name, leave it alone and see when it flowers.

As a general rule, the ones that flower from June onward, continuously through the summer, need pruning hard every year. The time to do it is any time during the winter up to the time the plants start growing again. Simply cut the whole plant back to about 1ft (30cm) above the ground and remove all the debris, leaving the trellis clean.

The kinds that flower in May or June, and then again in September, can be pruned more lightly. Just shorten the main stems back to a fat pair of buds, about 3ft (1m) above the ground. Do this in late winter or early spring.

Clematis texensis and its hybrids can be cut back almost to ground level in late winter. Most of the other species don't need any pruning. If they get too big or messy, you can either cut them back just enough to neaten them after flowering (if they finish flowering before the end of June), or in winter if they flower later. *Clematis montana*, on the other hand, will eventually resemble what a friend of mine calls a "disemboweled mattress." The plant is adept at covering sheds and garages, but, like many vigorous climbers, it doesn't know when to stop. Pruning can be a daunting thought, and so is usually avoided. But if you feel you must tackle it, do the job immediately after flowering in late spring. Cut it back as hard as you like, but be prepared to have a lean show of flowers the following year. The plant will subsequently make a full recovery.

Layering clematis

Clematis don't root well from cuttings, so the easiest way to propagate more plants is by layering. You can do it at any time of year, but late spring is usually best.

Look for a strong young shoot that originates close to the base of the plant. Improve the soil at the foot of the plant by forking in lots of well-rotted organic matter, then bend the shoot down and bury 4–5in (10–12cm) of the middle section, between two sets of leaves, in the prepared ground, holding it down with stones or a wire "hairpin." The length isn't critical; just make sure that the tip of the shoot sticks out of the ground.

Expect a layered shoot to take a year or so to root properly; you can tell because the new plant starts to grow strongly. Wait until it's a reasonable size, and then dig it up in spring or autumn, sever it from its parent, and replant it.

The layered stem of a clematis is conveniently held in contact with the ground by a large stone.

How to... grow a clematis in a container

Clematis make excellent climbers for containers, and this is a superb way of growing them when you don't have much wall space, if you expect to move, or you simply like to move your various garden "ingredients" around, rather like rearranging the furniture indoors. Although clematis normally have a very informal feel to them, by growing in containers like square Versailles planters with obelisks to match, you can turn them into a formal feature: stand a pair on either side of a front door, or run a row along the side of a path or up each side of a flight of steps.

Clematis are very greedy feeders and drinkers, and at the first sign of drought they will suffer. For this reason they need to be coddled a bit when grown in pots. Some varieties are more suitable than others for this kind of cultivation. Try early flowerers, such as *C. alpina* and *C. macropetala*, and the spectacular *C. florida* var. *sieboldiana*, plus the large-flowered 'Barbara Dibley', 'Miss Bateman', 'Elsa Späth', 'Nelly Moser', and 'The President'.

What you need

- *container 15–18in (38–45cm) in diameter*
- *one clematis – choose a small cultivar with a long, continuous flowering season*
- *an obelisk, the feet of which fit inside the pot*
- *soil-based potting mix*
- *a bucketful of smooth stones or other suitable mulch*

1 Put in some potting mix, enough to bring the clematis to the correct planting level - the crown should be a few inches below soil level. Take the clematis out of its pot and stand it in the center, after teasing out a few of the biggest roots if they have made a solid ball.

2 Fill the container with potting mix to within 1in (2.5cm) of the rim. Firm lightly, water well, and then cover with a mulch of large pebbles or other suitable mulch, such as bark chips.

3 Stand the obelisk over the plant, then firm the feet down around the inside edge of the container. Untie the clematis and spread its stems out around the base of the obelisk; weave them very gently through the framework, then tie them in place. Keep the plant well watered, and apply diluted liquid tomato fertilzer weekly from May to September.

Clematis species

There are about two hundred species of clematis and at least twice as many cultivars that have been bred from them. In general, the species don't flower for such long periods, but the flowers are often more delicately lovely and, in some, appear at times of the year when not much else is happening. These are some of my favorites.

1 *Clematis montana* seen here growing along a laundry line.

Clematis montana (1) is a large species, and one that most people know. It grows to 20–30 × 5ft (6–9 × 1.5m), with lots of small white flowers in mid to late spring. *C. montana* var. *rubens* has pink flowers and bronzy foliage. There are also larger-flowered white forms, such as *C. m.* 'Alexander'; and several scented forms, such as *C. m.* var. *rubens* 'Elizabeth', with pink flowers. *C. montana* cultivars are no trouble at all to grow, don't need pruning, and are good for any exposure that gets a fair bit of sun. But because they are so big, they aren't the best kinds for growing on a trellis; use them for covering a wall or large fence, or grow one up through a fair-sized tree. Complete butchery immediately after flowering is the way to renovate one that has got totally out of hand. Z6–9.

C. alpina cultivars (2) are small plants and fill a space of about 6 × 3ft (2 × 1m). They have nodding blue or white bell flowers in spring. Alpinas enjoy a cool spot and are good for growing on a north wall, though any exposure is fine. They are easy and don't need any pruning. Z6–9.

***C. cirrhosa* 'Freckles'** (3) is a winter-flowering star. It's an evergreen species that flowers in winter, with nodding, cup-shaped, cream flowers speckled with red. They always reminds me of bird's eggs. It grows slowly at first and won't flower well until it's several years old. It reaches maybe 20ft (6m) but doesn't need pruning, so it's good for growing through a tree or large shrub, in a sheltered spot close to the house. Where not hardy, it's good for an unheated conservatory. Z7–9.

C. florida* var. *sieboldiana (4) (also known as *C. florida* 'Sieboldii') grows only to about 6 × 2ft (2m × 60cm), so it's ideal if you have one small piece of trellis to cover, and it is also excellent for containers. The flowers, produced throughout summer, are a decent size and look like giant passionflowers in purple and creamy white. It needs a warm, sheltered spot and doesn't need pruning. If you like this one, you'll also enjoy its close cousin, *Clematis florida* var. *flore-pleno*, which has enormous white, double, rosettelike flowers. Z6–9.

C. texensis cultivars (**5**) have 2in (5cm) long, elongated, bell-shaped, red or pink flowers from midsummer to midautumn, on stems reaching about 10ft (3m). They like any exposure except a north-facing one. With these, hard pruning is a good idea – you can cut them back to the ground each winter. Z4–9.

C. viticella cultivars (**6**) come in many colors and some look like large-flowered hybrids, but their blooms are only about half the size; they are produced in large numbers from mid- to late summer. Plants grow 10–20ft (3–6m) long and can be pruned or not, as you prefer. They enjoy any exposure except a north-facing one. They are a good choice in a garden where hybrid clematis are affected by clematis wilt, because viticellas don't suffer from it. Z5–9.

C. armandii (**2**) is a monstrous evergreen species that will fill a space to 30 × 6ft (9 × 2m). It has architectural evergreen leaves and scented white flowers in March and April. *C. armandii* needs a sheltered spot facing south or west and, again, doesn't need pruning. The pink form 'Apple Blossom' is harder to find but worth seeking out. The leaves are poisonous to dogs – be careful. Z7–9.

2 *Clematis alpina* 'Pamela Jackman'.
3 *C. cirrhosa* 'Freckles'.
4 *C. florida* var. *sieboldiana*.
5 *C. texensis*.
6 *C. viticella* 'Polish Spirit'.
7 *C. armandii*.

Large-flowered hybrid clematis

Large-flowered clematis hybrids are the most popular kinds, with flowers the size of saucers. They are great for growing up a trellis or through small trees or large shrubs, and, with a few exceptions, they grow mostly to the 8–12ft (2.4–3.6m) size range. If you want a bigger plant, go for *Clematis* 'Jackmanii' or one of the other 'Jackmanii' cultivars; they can reach 15–20ft (4.5–6m). Large-flowered clematis hybrids fall into two groups, depending on when they flower, and it's worth knowing which are which, because then you will know which ones to prune and which to leave alone.

All-summer flowering
These flower continuously from early summer to early autumn. Generally, these are the ones you can prune hard. All Z4–9.

Clematis 'Niobe' (1) has single, rich, deep velvety red flowers.

C. 'Comtesse de Bouchaud' (2) has single mauve-pink flowers.

C. 'Jackmanii' (3) has single purple flowers that have a really rich, velvety texture.

1 *Clematis* 'Niobe'.
2 C. 'Comtesse de Bouchaud'.
3 C. 'Jackmanii Superba'.

4 C. 'Perle d'Azur'.
5 C. 'Duchess of Edinburgh'.
6 C. 'Nelly Moser'.

Early- and late-flowering clematis

These have a couple of bursts of flower. The first is in mid to late spring, then they stop for the summer before putting on another late burst of bloom in late summer or early autumn. They generally don't need hard pruning; otherwise, you'll be cutting off the growth that should carry the second batch of flowers. All Z4–9.

C. 'Perle d'Azur' (4) is incredibly generous with its single lavender-blue flowers, which are produced from early summer to early autumn. It can cope with sunny or shady walls and can be pruned quite hard in late winter or early spring.

C. 'Duchess of Edinburgh' (5) produces very double white flowers in the first summer flush that look like first-prize rosettes, and then, in September, it produces single white flowers. It does best with little or no pruning.

C. 'Nelly Moser' (6) has pale and dark pink-striped flowers and, again, like many of the striped kinds, appreciates a little shade to avoid the bleaching effects of sunlight. It does well in an east-, west-, or north-facing spot. In some years, it will flower until it's stopped by the frosts.

Climbing roses

Roses are *the* traditional climbers for covering walls, pergolas, and arbors, but few cultivars have a truly continuous flowering season, so team them with honeysuckle or clematis to fill the gaps.

Climbing roses need a permanent framework of stems to cover the designated area; the flowers are borne on sideshoots that are pruned back annually. They are good for training on walls, fences, or trellises, up pillars, or over arches. Choose one that fits the space available, so that you won't constantly be chopping it back to size.

Pruning climbing roses

When you first plant a climbing rose, it's essential to space the main stems so that they cover the space evenly. Position them in place by tying them to horizontal wires, a trellis, or wall nails. Tie new shoots in to fill in the framework so that you cover the space with a network of stems 8–12in (20–30cm) apart. Anything you don't need is cut off. The rose will flower on short stems growing from the framework. As the flowers fade, remove them, leaving behind 3–4in (8–10cm) of stem. This does two jobs at once: deadheading and summer pruning, so the plant stays neat. With old climbers, cut an occasional old, unproductive stem back to a junction with a young stem, which can be trained in its place – do that in winter.

Climbing roses are pruned quite lightly immediately after flowering, the flowered shoots being pruned back to leave finger-long stems.

Training a climbing rose on a pergola

If you let a rose run straight to the top of a pergola post, all the flowers appear at the top of the stems, where you can't see them. Roses flower best on stems that are as nearly horizontal as possible, so if the stems spiral around a post, they'll flower all the way up.

At the side of a post, dig a planting hole three times bigger than the pot that the rose came in. Add lots of well-rotted compost and mix in a handful of rose fertilizer. Plant the rose with the bud union (the bulge where the cultivar joins the rootstock) about 1in (2.5cm) below the soil surface. Water and mulch generously.

Cut off any dead, weak, or sticking-out stems, leaving the most strongly upright ones. Gently wind them around the post, then tie firmly in place with garden twine. As the shoots grow, continue winding them in while they're still flexible, keeping them fairly close together, like a coiled spring. When they reach the top of the post, let them run along the pergola top, but keep them tied down. Prune exactly as for a normal climber. If they're on a pillar, cut the top off flush with the top of the post. Do this each year in winter.

When growing roses up a pergola, tie in the flexible stems in spiral fashion as they extend.

Climbing roses

There are many varieties to choose from, but here are four – in a range of colors – that will seldom let you down. Z 5-9 unless noted.

Rosa **'Compassion'** (**1**) is a medium-sized climber for walls and fences and has highly perfumed peach and apricot flowers. It needs very little pruning once it's trained. Allow 8 × 6ft (2.4 × 2m).

R. 'Danse du Feu' (**2**) is a very free-flowering climber with scarlet flowers in two flushes each season; good for a north-facing wall or a spot in light shade. Give it about 10 × 8ft (3 × 2.4m).

R. 'Golden Showers' (**3**) has scented yellow flowers from early summer to autumn. It needs heavy fertilizing. Roughly 8 × 8ft (2.4 × 2.4m).

R. 'Madame Alfred Carrière' (**4**) is an oldie, with scented, pink-flushed white flowers. Good for a north wall; 12 × 10ft (3.6 × 3m). Z6–9.

R. Swan Lake (**5**) is one of the best white-flowered climbers. It makes quite a small plant with unusually weatherproof flowers. It's good for growing on pillars and posts, or on a wall. 8 × 6ft (2.4 × 2m).

Roses for scent

R. 'Albertine' (rambler with pale pink flowers); *R.* 'Gloire de Dijon' (old climbing rose, with large buff-peach flowers); *R.* 'Alchymist' (climber, with egg-yolk yellow flowers); *R.* 'Wedding Day' (huge rambler with single white flowers); *R.* 'Madame Grégoire Staechelin' (climber with large, frilly pink flowers); *R.* 'Zéphirine Drouhin' (climber with almost thornless stems and mauve-pink flowers, good for arches); *R.* 'Crimson Shower' (rambler with red-crimson flowers).

1 *Rosa* 'Compassion'.
2 *R.* 'Danse du Feu'.
3 *R.* 'Golden Showers'.
4 *R.* 'Madame Alfred Carrière'.
5 *R.* Swan Lake.

Rambler roses

Ramblers are vigorous roses that flower on long canes, almost like blackberries, with large clusters of fairly small flowers at the tips. They are less disciplined than climbing roses, and the bigger cultivars are best allowed to scramble up trees, through shrubs, along fences, or over outbuildings. Not all ramblers are huge, uncontrollable monsters, though; there are lots of smaller cultivars that are more suitable for covering modest structures.

Pruning ramblers

Prune ramblers after they finish flowering. Some cultivars have one flush of flower that is over by midsummer, but others have two flushes of flower, so wait until autumn, when the second flush is finished, before pruning. (If you inherit an unnamed rambler, leave it unpruned until autumn in the first year so that you can see whether it flowers once or twice.) To prune, cut back all the stems that carried flowers to just above an unflowered shoot. That removes a lot of the current year's growth and makes the plant look much neater but leaves all the stems that will carry next year's flowers. The new, vigorous, unflowered shoots are the ones to leave.

Rambling roses are pruned after flowering. Remove the older, flowered stems as close to the base as possible and train in young, vigorous, unflowered shoots, which will carry next year's flowers.

Ramblers

These are a fairly well-behaved bunch, but there is one monster that you can let loose if you have room. Z5-9 unless noted.

***Rosa* 'Albéric Barbier'** (**1**) is medium-sized by rambler standards, at about 15 × 12ft (4.5 × 3.6m). Yellow buds open and mature to rich cream. It's good for pillars or on rustic poles at the back of a border.

Watch out for... blackspot, mildew, and rust

Some roses are notoriously affected by fungal diseases, others are more resistant. The traditional remedy is to spray thoroughly every two weeks from late spring to early autumn with a rose fungicide that tackles all the three main rose diseases – some brands include an insecticide as well.

In my garden, I prefer not to spray, and that means making sure that the roses are never under stress (shortage of water is the fastest route to mildew and blackspot). Organically enriched soil and thick surface mulches are a great help. I also plant disease-resistant cultivars when I can and keep all my plants well fertilized.

***R.* 'Albertine'** (**2**) is another medium-sized rose, about 15 × 12ft (4.5 × 3.6m), with copper-pink flowers. Good for walls and trellises.

***R.* 'Bleu Magenta'** (**3**) is a good choice for a north wall or light shade, with grape-purple flowers and few thorns; 10 × 8ft (3 × 2.4m).

***R.* 'Kiftsgate'** (**4**) is huge, easily reaching 30 × 10ft (9 × 3m) or more. The large, fragrant white flower clusters are like those of 'Wedding Day' and 'Rambling Rector', which are both about the same size; they are the best for growing up large trees or on post-and-rail fences and are all extremely vigorous. Z6–9.

1 *Rosa* 'Albéric Barbier'.
2 *R.* 'Albertine'.
3 *R.* 'Bleu Magenta'.
4 *R.* 'Kiftsgate'

11 PATIO GARDENING

Perfect patios

The ideal patio is a cross between a living room and a garden – a sheltered suntrap or shady spot where you have privacy to eat, entertain, or simply sit and enjoy fine weather.

When planning your patio, think about what you will be using it for. Deciding on where to put patio furniture and accessories is a bit like arranging furniture inside a small living room. Start with the biggest items first, such as seats and tables, then add decorations such as pots and plants, where they won't be in the way. If you will be using the patio mainly as a dining area, make sure there's room for seats and tables conveniently near to the barbecue. The barbecue needs to be placed fairly near to the house, and with nothing in your way when you walk from there to the table, patio doors, or the kitchen – you don't want to be tripping over steps or beds of plants when you are carrying food or drinks.

If you are including a table, make sure that there's enough room for walking around it easily without knocking into plants. If you have a garden hose, be sure to site it so that it has a clear run to your outdoor tap without catching on furniture or knocking pots over. Hang a hose reel on the wall so that it's easy to put away.

If you don't have a shed or garage for storing patio paraphernalia when it's not in use, a "garden chest" on the patio makes a handy place to keep folding chairs, cushions, or barbecue gear, besides hoses and spare pots. But however elaborate it becomes, a patio or deck isn't finished without plants.

You can create whatever atmosphere you want on a patio. Here the choice is for a calm and secluded haven, surrounded by plants.

Siting

Most patios are built at the back of the house so that you can walk straight from the living room into the garden and vice versa, without getting mucky feet. Nowadays, the original French windows have largely been replaced by sliding patio doors that can make the patio seem like an extension of the living room when they're wide open in warm weather.

But you don't need to have a "standard" patio layout. If the back of the house doesn't happen to face the right direction to catch the sun, it's perfectly acceptable to build a patio in a sunnier part of your yard. Alternatively, if you prefer to sit in the shade, you can add awnings or a pergola and wall fountain to turn a too-sunny patio into a cooler and shadier haven where you can sit outside without risk of sunburn.

For a more contemporary look, you might forgo the usual paving and go for the wooden equivalent – decking – instead. It's easy to construct, durable, and relatively cheap.

Planning

A patio is one of the most expensive garden features to build and – since everything is stuck down – one of the hardest to change, so it's worth taking a bit of trouble to get it right. Start by planning it out on graph paper or on your computer.

Choose a shape, size, and materials that complement the style of your house and its construction. The shape need not be formal and rectangular or completely flat – you can build a patio on the diagonal, or include steps and a change of level. You might want to build in a water feature or barbecue. And you might like to surround part of it with a low wall to separate it slightly from the rest of the garden, or incorporate screening to give you some privacy from the neighbors.

It's a good idea to avoid having large areas of identical pavers, which can look boring, even if you choose an expensive type. Be adventurous. Leave out occasional slabs to make internal beds in which you can grow plants, or fill them with gravel, pebbles, crushed stone, or smaller slabs to make contrasting textures. Leave some soil beds at the foot of a wall, because that makes it much easier to grow climbers later.

If you don't have much time for watering lots of small, portable containers (and potted plants need a lot of water in hot, dry weather) think about building raised beds. They hold a much bigger quantity of soil, and they don't take as much watering as pots and hanging baskets.

Brick patios

It requires more skill to lay a brick patio than one constructed of slabs, but the overall effect can be very pleasing and suitably intricate in a small area. You can lay the bricks (frostproof engineering bricks are best) on a wet or damp mortar mix laid over crushed stone. Allow the mortar to set before you fill in with dry grouting (wet grouting can stain the bricks). You can lay in the traditional bonds in staggered rows, or in herringbone fashion. Panels of brickwork are very useful for breaking up long runs of paving.

Patio furniture is instrumental in creating atmosphere – here, traditional furniture imparts a homey feeling.

Including lighting in a garden creates a whole new world after dark, especially if the lights are positioned to highlight focal points or works of art, like this bonsai tree.

Patio furnishing

Patios have moved on from being simple paved areas decorated with pots into what are, in some cases, fully furnished outdoor "rooms," complete with sophisticated cooking, eating, and leisure facilities. You can even install an outdoor Jacuzzi, put in outdoor lighting, and bring out the portable patio lights.

Garden lighting

A patio is the first place to think about outdoor lighting. Security lights are fine in their place, but they do nothing for the after-dark ambience. Something more subdued is what's needed. Arrange several small globe lights around the edge of the patio, on the wall, or just above your table – much the same as you'd have wall lights and table lamps indoors. Include a couple of lights around your barbecue so that you can see what you are doing. And use marker lights to illuminate steps or low beds with a weak pool of light – this sort of lighting looks good and helps avoid accidents.

Then there are the more ornamental effects. Use a spotlight to highlight something special, maybe a giant urn or a climber on the wall. Or you could uplight a tree or sidelight an architectural plant to cast dramatic shadows. If you have a built-in water feature, consider underwater lights – they will dramatically help bring water to life after dark.

Building a slab patio

A lot of people prefer to have a contractor do it, but building a patio is a job that avid DIY fans can do for themselves, given time. There are a few golden rules to remember when laying a patio, and positioning it is very important. Always make sure that you leave at least 6in (15cm) between the foundation of the house and the surface of the patio. Also make sure that the patio slopes very slightly away from the house, so that rainwater runs away freely; you need a slope or fall of ½in per yard (1cm per meter).

The patio will need a foundation, and for this you should dig out to twice the depth of the paving slabs to allow for the mortar bed that you'll set them in. The bedding mortar should be made by mixing 4 parts sharp sand to 2 parts soft sand to 1 part cement. Alternatively, you can save yourself the bother and buy bags of ready-made mortar mix that just needs water added. Make the mixture slightly stiff. For filling cracks between slabs, the recipe for jointing mortar is a dry mix of 3 parts soft sand to 1 part cement.

Top paving and path materials

Slabs	Gravel	Setts	Bark	Slate
Settle for gray or buff stone, which shows off plants well, or, if you love colors, there are plenty of other building stones avaialable in a wide range of colors and qualities.	The cheapest hard surface in the garden, and the easiest to lay. This comes in assorted shades. Pea gravel is the multicolored stuff that is very often used loose or bonded.	Setts are available in manmade stone or granite. They can be laid on the square or in concentric circles and are very attractive to look at – especially as feature panels in paving.	An inexpensive and practical material, ideal for nonsloping paths and areas under swings or climbing frames, where it provides soft landings for lively children.	Very fashionable. Slate "paddles" (smooth, flat slate pebbles) make a great mulch and are surprisingly easy to walk on when laid loose on top of crushed stone to make a path.

How to... **lay a patio**

If you have decided to go ahead and lay the patio yourself, follow this method. It is applicable to most types of paving. You can brighten up the paving with some fancy finishes – you could leave out one or more paving slabs to make a "panel" with a contrasting surface. Good surfaces include gravel, loose pebbles, or crushed bluestone or similar stone, and they can be laid over the existing soil. Alternatively, for a cobbled panel, spread bedding mortar (see p.365) to within about ½in (1cm) of the surface, select even-sized cobblestones or largish smooth stones, and gently press them to about half their depth, then lay a straight board over the top and tap gently with a rubber hammer to make sure all the stones are submerged to the same depth.

If you want a soil bed, you may have to remove some soil if it's poor quality, then replace it with good topsoil from elsewhere in the garden. Alternatively, you could use a commercial soil-based mix.

1 When you've marked out the area with pegs and string and checked that it is the right shape (both visually and from a practical point of view) excavate the area to a depth of 6in (15cm) using a spade. Avoid loosening the soil beneath that depth. If you are laying paving stones up to your house, make sure to lay the patio 6in (15cm) away from the house to allow for drainage and expansion.

2 Spread a layer of crushed stone over the area and firm it with a power compactor. Aim for a finished depth of 4in (10cm). Hammering wooden pegs into the ground so that they indicate the finished depth of the stone will make sure you maintain an even covering. Aim for a slight slope away from the house so that water runs off the finished patio and away from the building. Use a level and a long board to achieve this.

3 Lay out the slabs in their final positions. This is important if you are using random sizes of paving. Fitting the puzzle together before you lay the slabs on mortar will avoid mistakes later. Aim for a pleasing pattern, with different-sized slabs next to one another. Start laying near the house wall (or from a fence or wall if the patio is elsewhere in the garden) and work outward. Leave ½in (1cm) gaps between the slabs to allow for grouting.

If you want a bed at the edge of your patio, improve the soil by adding compost or topsoil.

Lay slabs on a 4in (10cm) bed of firmed crushed stone, topped by 2–3in (5–8cm) of bedding mortar. Make sure that they slope away from the house to drain water away .

Occasional slabs can be left out to allow for planting pockets or different-textured materials, such as gravel or stone chips.

4 Lift a few slabs to one side, remembering where they were positioned. Mix a barrow-load of bedding mortar at a time. Make it reasonably sloppy so that it can be easily worked with a builder's trowel. You are aiming for a bed between 2 and 3in (5 and 8cm) deep, which will be fine for domestic traffic. Use the point of the trowel to texture the surface of the mortar into "waves."

5 Lower each paving slab in to place, and tap it firmly with the handle of a mallet. The waves in the mortar allow for the height and level of the slab to be adjusted. Use a level to make sure that the slight fall away from the house is maintained, and that the slabs are positioned evenly within this fall. Keep off the newly laid paving for at least 24 hours to allow the mortar to harden.

6 Once the slabs are set, fill in the gaps between them with the moist grouting mixture. Firm it into place with your fingers (gloves prevent cement from dessicating your hands!) and then rub it smooth with a grouting iron. The mixture will take up water from the soil and crushed stone below by capillary action and eventually set hard. Sweep away any excess with a hand brush and then over the entire area with a soft broom.

Building decking

Decking often looks more stylish than slabs in a contemporary garden, and it lends itself better to angular or geometrical shapes; there's lots of potential. It looks good as a stand-alone feature in the garden – a deck can be built overhanging a pond or can be raised up above ground to create a platform.

Decking is also the easiest way of making a level surface on sloping ground. You can have banisters and built-in bench seats, or make a square wooden platform just above ground level and surround it with plants, grasses, a patch of wild garden, or pebbles and cobblestones. You can easily incorporate all sorts of other wooden features with decking, such as a trellis, pergola poles, or bamboo screens to add even more design opportunities.

Whatever its detractors may say, a well-built deck in the right place can look simply stunning and is wonderfully practical.

Decks are much easier to build than patios, they last a lot longer than some people would have you believe, and they aren't that difficult when it comes to maintenance. They are certainly no more labor-intensive to maintain than wooden fences or a shed. A blast with a pressure hose will quickly remove any slippery algae.

Decks don't need to be huge or elaborate. Sometimes good decks come in small packages – like this recycled cable reel.

Since none of the wood actually touches the ground – it all sits up on wooden legs or brick piers – there's plenty of air circulation underneath. This reduces the risk of wood rotting, as it inevitably does if it touches the soil, and good air circulation helps ensure that it doesn't remain wet for long.

Pressure-treated lumber has already been treated with preservative to prevent rotting, and this method ensures that the preservative penetrates the wood deeply. But it is still a good idea to paint the finished deck with two coats of wood preservative. You can either go for a natural wood color, such as pine or cedar, or use a colored product to paint your deck a stylish shade such as dusky lavender, or perhaps a more subdued and weathered-looking pale gray. If you reapply it every year, the color remains pristine, and you will ensure the maximum life for the wood.

If you are worried about losing things down the gaps, then make sure the gaps are narrow – ¼in (5mm) is ample – or raise the deck sufficiently to make sure that you can rake them out. If you are worried about vermin nesting under the deck – don't. Provided the ground is cleaned and mulched to start with, and there is good air circulation, there is no reason for them to make a home there.

Cheat's decking

Where you already have a firm, level surface like a path or patio, you can cheat by laying ready-made decking squares, using the existing hard surface for foundations. Left loose, decking squares are liable to skate about when you walk on them, so nail them down to rows of horizontal boards to act as underdecking, or fit them inside a retaining wooden frame. Choose heavy-duty, solid decking squares; the thin, lightweight kinds are best used as temporary stepping-stones in gravel paths, grass, or borders.

How to... build decking

First, draw up a detailed plan first on paper to calculate how much lumber and other materials you need. If possible, adjust the dimensions of your planned deck to fit in with floorboard widths (plus gaps between) and standard lengths available from DIY stores. This minimizes cutting of boards to fit. When spacing the concrete foundation pads, note that the boards should overlap the joists by 2in (5cm) all around. If you want a deck longer than one board, stagger the joints in successive rows. And if using the more expensive hardwoods, make sure they're from sustainable forestry.

1 Roughly level the site with a spade. Remove big weeds, but leave the soil firm. Lay out the joists 18in (45cm) apart, and mark the spots for the posts to support them: one at each corner, then at 5ft (1.5m) intervals around the deck. Dig a hole 1ft (30cm) square and deep for each post, and sit half a concrete building block firmly in the base. Sit the post on the block and fill around it with stiff, damp concrete, ramming it thoroughly. Use a level to ensure it's straight. Leave two days to set. Spread an 3in (8cm) layer of gravel over the site on a weed-suppressing mat, if necessary.

2 Attach the joists that will form the rim of the deck. Fasten them to the outside of the posts at the required height with galvanized bolts, and check that they are level. You can leave the posts long and link them with swags of rope later, or cut them off flush with the joists for a plain area of decking. Once the outer framework is in position, further joists are added on the inside at 18in (45cm) intervals. Attach them to the outer members with joist hangers or screws. To maintain stability, spacers ("noggins") of lumber should be secured between the joists at staggered intervals of 4–6ft (1–2m).

3 Lay the decking boards on top of the framework: placing them at 45 degrees to the joists can look more pleasing than at right angles. Cut some spacers (thin slivers of wood) so that the decking boards can be held ¼in (5mm) apart to allow for drainage. The boards should overlap the framework by at least 2in (5cm). Attach them to the joists with counter-sunk screws. Stagger the joints for a better appearance. Draw a line to mark the final edge, then cut all the boards in one go so that the 2in (5cm) over-hang is maintained. Paint the deck (if required) with a preser-vative, but make it muted.

What you need

- *pressure-treated softwood lumber – hardwood is even better but much more expensive*
- *4 × 4in (10 × 10cm) posts for the uprights*
- *6 × 2in (15 × 5cm) joists to support the decking boards*
- *4 × 1in (10 × 2.5cm) grooved boards for the deck floor*
- *galvanized bolts, joist hangers, and countersunk screws*
- *concrete for foundations; 6 parts ballast to 1 part cement*
- *spade, power drill/screwdriver, wrenches, and saw*
- *set square, tape measure, and level*
- *precast concrete blocks to sit in the support post holes*
- *gravel or weed-suppressing mat*

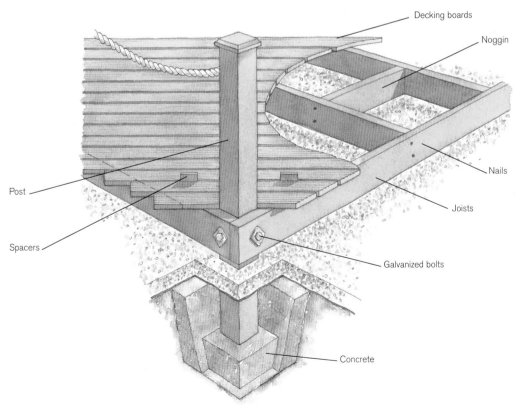

Decking boards

Noggin

Nails

Joists

Galvanized bolts

Post

Spacers

Concrete

Filling in the gaps

A good way to give a large patio character is to grow plants in the gaps between some of the paving slabs. The secret of getting plants to grow between slabs is advance preparation. You can't just chip out a hole in solid mortar, force the unfortunate plant in, and hope it'll survive. When laying the patio, make sure there's some decent topsoil underneath the parts you want to plant, and just bed those slabs onto blobs of mortar instead of laying them on a continuous bed of it. Leave wide gaps between your paving, and put small plants in, then fill what's left of the crack with gravel. If you are thinking of planting into cracks in existing paving, you need to lift the slabs first and improve the soil underneath, then re-lay the slabs on blobs of bedding mortar. If the gaps are too small to put plants in, use "plugs" (tiny plants grown in cells a bit like egg cartons), or sprinkle suitable seeds in soil-filled gaps instead.

However careful you are, though, plants will sometimes be stepped on. That won't bother the tough, wiry kinds as long as you don't make a habit of it. A patio is often in a hot, sunny spot, so choose plants that can stand the conditions; the following are good choices.

1 *Alchemilla mollis.*
2 *Armeria maritima.*
3 *Dianthus gratianopolitanus.*
4 *Parahebe catarractae* 'Miss Wilmott'.
5 *Thymus serpyllum.*
6 *Anthemis punctata* subsp. *cupaniana.*

Alchemilla mollis (**1**), lady's mantle, if grown anywhere in the garden, will most likely self-sow its seedlings into the gaps in your paving, where they will come up and look good with their fan-shaped evergreen leaves and sprays of airy, lime green flowers that form mounds about 12 × 12in (30 × 30cm). You can plant small plants, but they aren't as tough as self-sown ones. Z4–7.

Armeria maritima (**2**), thrift, grows wild at the seaside, making 4–6in (10–15cm) tufts of tough, grassy, evergreen leaves with wiry stems and round pink flowerheads on top, a bit like nautical chives – a good tough one for growing in cracks between paving. Z3–9.

Dianthus species (**3**), grow wild in dry, rocky places, such as on rocky coasts, so the maiden pink (*Dianthus deltoides*, Z3–10*)* and its cultivars, and Cheddar pink (*Dianthus gratianopolitanus*, Z4–9) will be quite at home in paving or gravel. They look like slim-line versions of garden pinks with fine, almost needlelike, gray-green leaves and miniature pink flowers, in single or double versions. They have no scent that you'd notice, which is a pity. If you must have perfume, though, there are a few of the alpine pinks (Z5–9) with a wonderful clove scent that might do the trick – try the red-flowered *D.* 'Hidcote' or the dark-eyed, pale pink *D.* 'Little Jock'.

Parahebe catarractae (**4**) is another plant I'd particularly recommend. Look for it in a garden center or nursery with a good rock garden department. It's a small, mound-shaped, bushy shrub, about 12in (30cm) high and 18in (45cm) across, that's covered with small blue flowers, just like speedwell, for most of the summer. Delicious. Z9–10.

Thymus serpyllum (**5**), wild thyme, and its cultivars make good springy, evergreen mats about 2in (5cm) deep and, when fully grown, may be 2–3ft (60–90cm) across. They release a wonderful fragrance when walked on. In summer, the mats are dotted with pink flowers and bees in roughly equal numbers. Z4–9.

Anthemis punctata subsp. *cupaniana* (**6**) is one of the many rock plants that would do well in this situation, since it is one of the low, mound-forming, evergreen, drought-resistant kinds that are the ones to look for at the garden center. It has silvery green, chrysanthemum-like leaves and big, white, solid-looking daisy flowers with yellow centers, like fried eggs stuck all over the mounds, which grow to perhaps 1ft (30cm) high by 2ft (60cm) across in time. Z6–9.

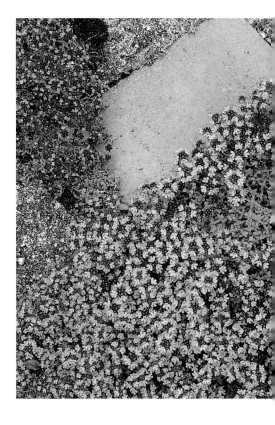

There's something really satisfying about positioning carpeting plants around paving slabs – visually it always works very well.

Plants for patio beds

Where you've made a proper bed in the patio, or left a gap in decking to grow a plant through, you can afford to go for plants that grow taller, look more architectural, or which simply don't stand being stepped on. Treat a bed such as this like a big container – the plants will need fertilizing and watering, even though they are growing in the ground. Drought-tolerant evergreens are the labor-saving option here, too; once established, you can almost forget them.

Drought-tolerant plants (1) include rock plants, such as *Sedum acre* (Z4–9) and *S. spathulifolium* (Z5–9), and both of these do very well in dry conditions. Sempervivums (Z4–10) do, too; they start out as fat rosettes 1–2in (2.5–5cm) across and grow in clusters, but, in summer, they suddenly send up a thick spike studded with pink, red, or greenish yellow flowers about 12in (30cm) high.

For a more traditional flower-border look, drought-loving perennials, such as *Sedum spectabile* (Z4–9), artemisias, and eryngiums (the sea hollies), would cope well, but for solid flowers all summer, consider *Alstroemeria* (Z7–10). Don't go for the old-fashioned ones; new strains come in various heights from 10–36in (25–90cm). Look for cultivars with 'Princess' in their name; they flower the entire summer, as long as you remember to deadhead them. Do it just as though you were pulling sticks of rhubarb; they come out quite cleanly, allowing the show to go on.

Although phormiums (New Zealand flax, Z9–10) are not grasses, their swordlike leaves have a similarly architectural effect, and they are quite tough provided they are not in cold, wet soil over winter.

Grasses (2) are good for a contemporary look. If it's hot, sunny, and dry and you won't remember to water, the one I'd stick with is the blue fescue, *Festuca glauca* (Z4–8). There are several even bluer cultivars, such as 'Elijah Blue' – you can't go wrong with them. Some of the evergreen grasses and sedges prefer some moisture in the soil, so grow these only if you can provide suitable conditions.

Another grasslike plant is the black-leaved lily turf, *Ophiopogon planiscapus* 'Nigrescens' (Z6–10). It is a bit of an oddity and isn't everyone's cup of tea, but, in the right spot, it is very eye-catching. The narrow, strap-shaped evergreen leaves are about 6in (15cm) high, and they spread to make a thinnish patch that looks good interplanted with dwarf bulbs, such as crocus, hardy cyclamen, and colchicums. Plant a carpet of them in a bed in a contemporary patio or deck to make a surrealist "lawn" that Salvador Dali would have envied.

Spiky phormiums (New Zealand flax) in a glazed pot, and pink nerines alongside *Miscanthus sinensis* 'Zebrinus', are set off well by the chunky construction of this solid wood patio.

1 *Eryngium alpinum*.
2 *Ophiopogon planiscapus* 'Nigrescens'.
3 *Juniperus communis* 'Compressa'.
4 *Hebe* 'Watson's Pink'.

Conifers (3) go well with the sorts of grasses that don't like to go short of moisture, but the only ones that put up with hot, dry conditions without being badly browned off are the junipers. Any of them would be happy here, and you can make an attractive cameo from a group of spreading, upright, and bushy ones. If I could only have one it would be *Juniperus communis* 'Compressa' (Z2–6), the dwarf "Noah's Ark juniper," which grows into a perfect flame shape about 30in (75cm) tall.

Hebes (4) are wonderful evergreens with fluffy bottlebrush flowers; they're good for anywhere hot and sunny with good drainage. They flower from early to late summer, and some keep on right into autumn. I'd go for *Hebe* 'Gauntlettii' for its tight-packed tubes of pink-purple flowers that last until October, if the weather is kind, or 'Great Orme', with feathery pink bottlebrushes; both come in at just over 3ft (1m). 'Watson's Pink' is a bright pink summer bloomer well worth having. In windy areas (where the big-leaved hebes may scorch), or in contemporary gardens, the starker, khaki-green mounds of a whipcord type, such as *Hebe ochracea* 'James Stirling', might work better. Z8–10, mostly.

This cobbled path at Barleywood might not be the smoothest surface to walk on, but it looks good in all kinds of weather – especially when rain gives it a high gloss.

In this cottage garden (*opposite*) we used paving slabs set in gravel to make the going easier underfoot but still informal.

Paths and steps

However attractively you lay out your front yard, the mail carrier and other regular callers may sometimes take the quickest way to the front door, even if that means taking a short cut through a flower bed. That's why you need two kinds of path – the direct kind that takes people straight to the places they need to go, and the slowly meandering variety for ambling around and enjoying the garden.

When designing a garden, it pays to anticipate where people will take the shortest possible route. That's the place to put hard-working paths with smooth, level surfaces – make sure they are wide enough for a delivery man bringing a sofa. Leave your romantic, rambling paths – made of gravel, bark chips, or broken tiles – for a walk through the flowers, which is where you want to encourage people to slow down.

If you have a sloping path that needs steps at the steepest parts, they should follow the same rule. Always construct steps with risers (the face of the step) of even heights, and with treads that are wide enough to accommodate your feet. Serious steps that are used for access should be built of solid materials, with nonslip surfaces and maybe handrails to make sure they stay safe in all weather. The sort of steps you use occasionally, or that are more decorative than useful, can afford to be made of less formal materials, such as railroad ties or long logs, which can be sunk into the soil and backfilled with soil or crushed stone and topped with gravel.

Proper paths

If you want a paved path, lay slabs in place on top of the soil so you can see where they need to go, then mark around the edge with the spade and move the slabs offside. Skim off the top 2in (5cm) or so of soil from the marked-out area, leaving the ground beneath undisturbed. This gives a firm base that also acts as a mold. Make up a barrow-load of bedding mortar, using the same recipe as for laying a patio (see page 365), and lay your slabs a few at a time till you reach the other end. Don't make too much mortar at a time, because it'll start to set before you can use it.

You can make a serious gravel path by excavating the shape to a depth of 3–4in (8–10cm). Then bang in wooden pegs and nail wooden shuttering to them, or set twist-topped tiles on edge along each side of the path. Then spread a layer of crushed stone and firm and level it with the head of a sledgehammer. Rake 2in (5cm) of gravel over the top. You need a proper edge to a gravel path to prevent the stuff from walking out into the grass or borders.

Frivolous paths

The sorts of paths that you use for wandering slowly around the garden don't need the same sort of base as serious paths by any means. There's no reason why you shouldn't simply excavate your path to 1–2in (2.5–5cm) deep, put wooden shuttering in the sides (nailed to short, wooden holding pegs), and fill the depression with gravel. That way you can plant scented things, such as wild thyme (*Thymus serpyllum*), into the gravel.

If you like a firmer feeling underfoot, you could sink an irregular line of pavers into the gravel to make stepping-stones. Bed them onto blobs of bedding mortar to keep them firm. Alternatively, you could set bricks on to a firm, level, excavated soil base, so they are packed tightly together in the traditional herringbone fashion. They need to be buried to about half their depth in the soil to seat them firmly, and the edge bricks are best mortared in to keep the whole lot in place.

You could also make a bed of mortar (recipe as before) and press small, rounded pebbles in to make a cobblestone path – like the one I made at Barleywood leading up to my tree fern grove. The construction is serious, but I defy anyone to walk quickly on it – you really need to slow down and enjoy the garden!

Marker lights

A row of small, low-voltage lights is quite bright enough to mark the position of a path for when you come home after dark, and it's an especially good idea on steps. If you don't want the bother of organizing an electricity supply, solar-powered lights are very easy to use. You just push them in wherever they are needed. They charge up during the day and come on automatically after dark, unless you turn them off using the manual override that some models have. Mind you, don't expect a lot of light from them – think of them as candles rather than lamps.

How to... **build a gravel path**

There's something special about a gravel path. Its very crunchiness makes it attractive, and there's the added advantage that you can hear people coming – even uninvited guests. But gravel is also an affable material – it goes with all kinds of plants. It can look smart in an urban setting, or suitably "cottagey" in rural areas. But I suppose the greatest attraction of gravel is its relative cheapness and ease of use. You are required to be a master mason to rake out a load of gravel, but you do need to do your groundwork properly if the path is to be durable, attractive, and well-drained. Gravel and lawnmowers do not mix, or if they do, the outcome is often costly, so always provide a barrier between path and grass.

Once your gravel path is in place, an occasional raking is all that is needed to keep it looking good, and maybe a bit more added every couple of years to replace gravel that has been carried inside the house or simply walked away in the treads of people's shoes.

1 Mark out the path and excavate the soil to a depth of 4in (10cm), removing grass and weeds. Put the edging boards in place as markers and drive the pegs in to hold them, keeping them vertical. When all the pegs are in place, fasten the boards to them with galvanized screws. The finished pegs should sit 1in (2.5cm) below the top edge of the boards.

2 Spread a generous layer of crushed stone over the surface of the soil, then rake roughly level. Make several passes with the compresser to firm and level them, adding more stone to even out any dips. You can run right up to the edge of the boards so that the stone is flattened all the way across the path to a level about 1½in (3cm) below the top edge of the boards.

3 Add gravel to a depth of around 1in (2.5cm) and rake level. If laid any deeper, the gravel will be difficult to walk on. The finished gravel level should be about ½in (1cm) below the top of the boards. You will end up with a path that looks good and is instantly accessible. Weeds seldom spring up through the stone and gravel, and any that do are easily pulled out.

Steps

If you want a flight of steps on a long slope, you need a builder. It's a serious construction project that must have proper foundations to be safe and sound. But if you only want two or three steps leading up to the patio, or to make small changes of level within the garden, then you can quite easily do it yourself.

If you have a naturally sloping garden, it's quite simple to use a spade to chop out two or three wide, shallow steps where you need them, leaving the soil beneath very compact. Make sure that they are level, and that each riser is the same height, then put a good layer of bedding mortar on top and set paving slabs in place.

Alternatively, you could lay a railroad tie to make the riser for your step. Hammer a long metal peg in front of the tie, one close to each end, to make sure there is no chance of it slipping, and fill the tread with 1in (2.5cm) of gravel to make it nonslip. To give your feet something to grip on a very shallow slope, you can do the same thing using long, thin logs with wooden pegs knocked in front of them. Clearly you'd need to check these regularly, because the steps will become unstable if the wood rots – they're fine for a woodland walk, though.

Steeper steps need more support. Cut the steps out as before, and use bricks and masonry mortar to make a low wall for each riser. When they've set, fill any gaps with more masonry mortar. Trowel 1in (2.5cm) or so of bedding mortar over the tread, then lay paving slabs on top. Give them several days to dry before you use them. Check steps regularly, and repair loose slabs immediately.

Coping with a slope

Rather than make a single run of steps straight up a steep slope, which is tiresome to walk up, you could cut a longer, shallow path across the slope, like a hairpin bend on a mountain road. It makes walking much easier, especially when you have a cart or mower to move up the hill. If necessary, you can put in the odd step without needing to do major construction. Don't use loose gravel on a sloping path; you'll slide on it, and it will all end up in a heap at the bottom. Wet bark chips make a slope slippery, too. Add a rustic handrail on the steepest part.

For the garden do-it-yourselfer, wood is often easier to work with than stone, and old railroad ties make particularly good steps.

Container gardening

These days it's not enough to have a few geraniums in pots on your patio; you need style. That means not only picking the right plants to suit the spot, but also choosing containers and other inanimate objects that fit your theme. It's almost like recreating a theatrical stage set in your garden.

Changing the pots in a doorstep display to add seasonal brightness makes sure that the display is never taken for granted.

Traditional style

The traditional patio look is for bedding plants everywhere – in boxes, pots, troughs, windowboxes, and hanging baskets. Old favorites, such as lobelias, petunias, fuchsias, and pelargoniums, are guaranteed good performers, and it's fun to try some of the new patio plants that come out every year. A traditional display is a patchwork of summer color, and you can plan a new color scheme each year if you want, but I warn you: it's a lot of work. If you don't have much time for daily watering, put in a drip-feed watering system, and let the timer take the strain. It'll cost more than a few dollars, but it's worth it for peace of mind. There's still all the fertilizing and deadheading to be done so that the show doesn't grind to a halt halfway through summer.

Contemporary style

The minimalist look is handy, because you use less to say more. Not only do you need fewer plants and pots, there's a lot less watering to do. Forget bedding plants – cut down the chores by using a few architectural all-year-rounders, such as phormium, grasses, bamboo, or *Fatsia japonica* in striking containers. Keep an eye on the glossy magazines; they always reflect the latest trends.

Cottage garden style

The chintzy, cluttered, chocolate-box look of an old-fashioned country garden can be carried through onto a patio using containers of hardy annual flowers, such as nasturtiums, miniature sunflowers, and the short-growing, knee-high sweet peas. Add a piece of potted topiary to give it a modern cutting edge that still looks in character. If you are a plant fanatic, you could use stone troughs filled with a mixture of drought-tolerant plants, such as sedums, sempervivums, and alpine pinks.

Tropical style

Tropical exotics are very fashionable right now, and, if you are going for genuinely tender plants, you'll probably need a heated greenhouse to keep things such as cannas, potted tree ferns, outdoor palms, and bananas safely through the winter. Cacti and succulents also do well outside in summer if you fancy a desert-island-castaway touch – big aloes and agaves look great against a background of giant leaves. If you have a hot, sunny wall or pergola, I think it's worth risking a slightly tender climber, such as *Campsis* × *tagliabuana* 'Madame Galen' or *Trachelospermum jasminoides* (see page 348) whose flowers have a decidedly tropical perfume. In warmer areas, they're both reasonably hardy. A tinkling fountain goes well with this look.

Oriental style

A genuine Oriental garden looks a bit – well, it needs to be said – staid to most western eyes, but you can get into the mood with pots of Japanese maples, bamboos, and a cloud-trimmed conifer. Add a pebble pool and some paving surrounded by gravel and large, smooth, round stones. Plant clumps of *Sisyrinchium striatum* and wandflower (*Dierama pulcherrima*) to grow through the gravel for a splash of color. Oriental gardens look very stylish all year round, and there's comparatively little work involved.

Mediterranean style

At its simplest, you can bring in a hint of the Mediterranean by using the plain old clay pots that you found at the back of the shed, planted with scarlet, single-flowered pelargoniums. Stand them on shelves above plain paving – old bricks and boards will do the trick. Alternatively, you can go upmarket with pricey pots or your citrus, olive, and bougainvillea collection.

Use terracotta flooring tiles underfoot (outdoor ones, or they'll flake from winter weather). Don't forget that if you want to use truly tender plants, you'll need a greenhouse or a conservatory to protect them through the winter except in very mild areas.

Often a single architectural plant, such as this agave, is all that is needed to make a focal point against a stark background.

How to... plant bulbs in containers

What you need

- *John Innes No. 2 potting compost*
- *bulbs*
- *deep tub, 30–45cm (12–18in) in diameter, with pot feet or bricks to stand it on*
- *gravel or broken clay pot 'crocks' for drainage*

The best way to be sure of a really good show of bulbs in containers is to pack as many as possible into the available space. And the best way to do that is to plant them in layers like a club sandwich. This technique is mostly used in autumn to plant spring bulbs, the most popular sort for containers, but you can also use it in spring to plant tubs of lilies, which are great for summer scent and colour on a patio.

For a spring display you can use several layers of the same variety of daffodil or narcissus or you can do as shown below and plant larger bulbs such as daffodils and narcissi in the bottom layers, and smaller bulbs such as muscari and crocuses higher up.

1 Stand the container on pot feet or bricks where you want the bulbs to flower, because it'll be too heavy to move later. Fill the bottom 2.5cm (1in) of the tub with crocks so that surplus water will drain away quickly. Cover the drainage material with 5cm (2in) or so of compost and plant your first layer of bulbs. Space them just far enough apart so they don't quite touch each other or the sides of the container. Press them gently down into the compost so they stand up.

2 Cover the first layer of bulbs carefully with more compost, using just enough to bury the tips, then plant a second layer of bulbs. If there's room, repeat the process with a third layer of bulbs, and again cover them with compost.

3 Finish off with a layer of bedding plants such as dwarf wallflowers, winter-flowering pansies or forget-me-nots to go with spring-flowering bulbs. Use something trailing, such as lobelias, to go with summer bulbs. Just water lightly until you can see the bulb leaves appearing – if you keep the compost too wet, too early on, the bulbs will just sit in water and rot.

Top of the pots

There are so many plants you could grow in pots on patios that it's almost impossible to pick out a few real favorites. I've chosen a mixture of traditional and modern to suit most styles of patio, but nowadays, it's fair to say that almost anything goes in containers – even if only temporarily.

Patio plants

The term patio plants is simply marketing-speak for a wide range of short, bushy plants with a long flowering season that are good for growing in containers. You'll sometimes meet patio plants for autumn, winter, or spring use, but the term usually means summer-flowering, half-hardy annuals and tender perennials that are treated as annuals. These don't withstand frost and can't be put outside until mid- or late May, but if they are kept well dead-headed, fertilized and watered all summer, you can expect all of the best kinds to keep flowering until they are killed by the first proper frost in the autumn. Real troupers, they are. Some can be kept under cover in winter to use again next year.

Some don't like it hot

Don't assume that all house plants will enjoy a baking on your patio. Those that naturally grow in shady tropical rainforests will not appreciate being moved into an environment that is closer to the Arizona desert.

All kinds of plants can be mixed together on a patio, provided that they enjoy the prevailing conditions.

The eryngium (on the left of the picture) is a sun-worshipper, while the caladium (on the right) prefers shade and shows its displeasure by turning crisp on a sun-baked patio.

Argyranthemums (1) are a good choice for summer containers. Also known as the marguerite, they have daisy flowers and foliage like a cut-leaved chrysanthemum. The best known is probably the single yellow 'Jamaica Primrose', but argyranthemums also come in pink and white and with double or single flowers. These go with everything; they're as much at home with fuchsias as lobelias. Z10–11.

Helichrysum petiolare (2) is a great foliage plant for containers. There are several – the gray-leaved species, the brighter 'Limelight' with pale gold leaves, and 'Variegatum' with cream-edged green leaves. The woolly foliage tells you that this is a plant that tolerates sun and drought, so it makes a good partner for pelargoniums and other sun lovers, though it thrives in most container conditions. Easy from cuttings and is no trouble to overwinter. Z10–11.

Brachyscome (3), the Swan River daisy, has small, blue daisy flowers and goes full tilt all summer where it's cool. It looks good with fuchsias that have a blue or purple "skirt," and the ferny foliage doesn't mask the flowers. It's difficult to overwinter but inexpensive to buy or grow from seed. Annual.

1 *Argyranthemum* 'Jamaica Primrose'.
2 *Helichrysum petiolare* 'Variegatum'.
3 *Brachyscome multifida* 'Blue Mist'.
4 Diascia.
5 *Pelargonium* 'Lord Bute'.
6 *Fuchsia* 'Alice Hoffman'.

Diascias (4) are relative newcomers, with spikes of small, mask-shaped pink flowers and, as long as the compost doesn't dry out badly, they keep on flowering all summer. You can treat the ones sold as patio plants as annuals and buy new ones each year, or take softwood cuttings (see page 553) and keep young plants growing in a bright, frost-free place during winter. Z7–9.

Pelargoniums (5) are the best known of the lot, often called geraniums. Zonal pelargoniums are the bushy, upright kind, named for the darker zone that patterns the leaves of some cultivars. Ivy-leaved pelargoniums are the trailing ones with ivy-like leaves. Cascade pelargoniums are a prolific ivy-leaved strain with very narrow petals and so many flowers that the plants are almost entirely hidden by them. All pelargoniums are very free-flowering, sun-loving, and fairly droughtproof – they won't keel over if you forget to water occasionally. They root well from cuttings and are easy to keep through the winter, provided you don't overwater them. Generally hardy to 36°F (2°C).

Fuchsias (6) are reliable and easy to grow. Trailers are naturals for hanging baskets or around the edge of a big container, where they sprawl elegantly down and hide the edges. Bush fuchsias are good for the center of a large pot or for training as standards. You often see them with pelargoniums, but fuchsias actually prefer cooler, moister conditions and light, dappled shade. Easy to grow from cuttings and are no trouble to overwinter – just cut them back hard in autumn and take cuttings from them in spring. Z8–10.

Petunias (7) are great for a slightly shady, wind-sheltered spot. The Surfinias are one of the most reliably long-flowering plants for containers. The scent is entrancing; you'll notice it most in a porch or gazebo, where it's not wafted away on the breeze. Regular dead-heading is vital, but the flowers are huge, so it's quick to do. New strains of petunias with much smaller, more bell-shaped flowers are excellent for containers, especially in windier spots. Don't bother to root cuttings – they're too prone to viruses; buy new plants at the start of each summer, or grow from seed. Usually grown as annuals.

Trailing verbena (8) has been around for a long time, but it's become a container essential only since named cultivars have been promoted as patio plants. It was 'Sissinghurst' and a few other good performers that got the ball rolling, but there are lots of different varieties available in a good range of colors. It's easier to buy new ones each year than to overwinter them – you don't need many. Z7–11.

7 Petunia.
8 Verbena.

7

8

385

Container plants for summer scent

Scented flowers are a definite plus for containers. Choose those with a long flowering season or that have aromatic leaves, so you really feel the benefit all summer.

Position aromatic foliage plants close to a patio or sitting area, and their fragrances will be released whenever the plants are brushed against.

Aloysia triphylla (1), lemon verbena, is the lemoniest scented plant I know, and great for containers. It has intensely scented leaves and insignificant white flowers. It reaches about 30 × 18in (75 × 45cm) in a container on its own over the summer – it'll be smaller in a container with other plants. Easy from cuttings; keep it in a frost-free greenhouse in winter, and enjoy brushing past it. Z8–11.

Salvia rutilans (2), pineapple sage, doesn't look a bit like herb sage. It has large, pointed-oval leaves and spikes of long, red, pipe-cleaner flowers. It enjoys the heat and, when bruised, the leaves have a strong and sweet pineapple scent. It needs a heated greenhouse in winter and is easy to grow from cuttings. Z8–10.

Heliotropium arborescens (3), heliotrope, is a good plant for a sunny container, with large, wrinkled leaves and big heads of tiny lavender- or violet-blue flowers that smell strongly of hot cherry pie. It'll reach 1ft (30cm) high by as much across during summer but is happy crammed into a pot between other plants. Grow from cuttings or seed, or overwinter in a frost-free greenhouse. Z11.

Scented-leaved pelargoniums (4) are old favorites. There are different cultivars that smell of anything from oranges and lemons to roses or spice if you bruise the leaves gently. Don't expect a fragrant version of the zonal pelargonium; they look little like them, though they grow to about the same size. A few have bright flowers, but most are unremarkably small and pale-colored. Overwinter indoors; propagate from cuttings. Generally hardy to 36°F (2°C).

Matthiola bicornis* subsp. *bicornis (5), night-scented stock, is my first choice where there isn't much room, but – as you'd expect – it's scented only at night. The flowers aren't exciting – light mauve, pale pink, and off-white stars dotted on skinny plants 6in (15cm) tall. Shoe-horn a clump in between more spectacular plants, or sow seeds straight into the container – they are annuals.

Mentha x piperita* f. *citrata (6), Eau-de-Cologne mint, has attractive, round leaves that smell like scent out of a bottle, plus lavender flowers. Mix it with herbs or cottage-style flowers – it grows about 18in (45cm) high. *Mentha spicata*, spearmint, is twice as tall but very minty, and a pot will prevent it from spreading. They are quite hardy, so leave them in the garden over the winter. Z3–7.

1 *Aloysia triphylla.*
2 *Salvia rutilans.*
3 *Heliotropium arborescens* 'Marine'.
4 *Pelargonium* 'Lady Plymouth'.
5 *Matthiola bicornis* subsp. *bicornis.*
6 *Mentha × piperata* f. *citrata.*

Container plants for autumn and winter

There's more scope for winter containers than ever. There are a few good winter-flowering bedding plants that would do, but you can also grow evergreens and winter shrubs in containers just for a single winter before planting them out in the garden – twice the value for your money!

Keeping patio plants through the winter

Even though you can't leave tender plants outside in winter because they'll be killed by frost, quite a few patio plants can be used again next year.

Dig the old plants up in autumn before there's a frost, cut the tops down to about 6in (15cm), and put them in pots in a greenhouse or conservatory with just enough heat to keep the frost out. You can replant them outside again in late spring after the last frost, usually around mid- to late May.

Otherwise, root shoot-tip cuttings in late summer, and keep them in a frost-free greenhouse or on a windowsill indoors for the winter. Young plants produced this way usually look better and flower more profusely than old ones. They also take up much less room than the old plants.

Evergreen shrubs (**1**) are invaluable for temporary use in pots; you can plant conifers, boxwood and *Viburnum tinus*, but the ones that I reckon make the best show are skimmias (Z7–9). *Skimmia japonica* 'Rubella' has triangular bunches of rosy pink buds that open in spring to masses of small, star-shaped flowers – it's a male form. *Skimmia japonica* 'Veitchii' is a female plant that carries big red berries in winter. You need both, so plant one of each in the same pot; it will look like one plant and produce buds *and* berries. They are slow growing and can stay in the pot for several years. The secret weapon of the winter containers is a little thing called checker-berry (*Gaultheria procumbens*, Z3–8). It's a short, spreading evergreen with long-lasting red berries. Although it prefers acidic soil, it'll survive in normal potting soil for a few months. Try it in hanging baskets with ivies, or in pots with winter-flowering heathers.

Winter-flowering heathers (*Erica carnea* cultivars) (**2**) are an excellent choice for winter containers; they are compact, flower from November to March, and are very wind resistant, so if you have an exposed patio they won't shrivel up like your average winter bedding. Acidic soil mix isn't essential for this group of heathers, since they are fairly lime-tolerant. The plants go well with ornamental cabbages and kales and with all those evergreen shrubs I've described (and more besides). With these combinations, you can make colorful winter displays. Z5–7.

Universal pansies (3) have been the biggest advance in winter bedding over the last quarter century or so, and they're great for containers. None of the other winter-flowering pansies go on so relentlessly in all but the most atrocious weather. Look after them well and grow them where the soil mix won't freeze solid or become waterlogged, and they'll flower from early autumn until you need to pull them out in May to make way for summer plants. Keep an eye open for the brand new Panola – a cross between a pansy and a viola – which has the universal pansy's ability to recover after bad weather but the greater flower production of the viola. Z4–8.

English ivies (*Hedera helix* cultivars) (4) are very versatile and, if you track down a specialized nursery, you'll find a much wider range than you see in your average garden center – lots of colorful variegated forms and unusual leaf shapes, including maple-shape, curly, ferny, and bird's-foot cultivars. They make classy winter container plants on their own, but they're also good mixers – use them as leafy fringes around pots of evergreens and as trailers for windowboxes and hanging baskets with winter bedding – they're good fillers for gaps anywhere, really. Z5–10.

1 *Skimmia japonica* 'Rubella'.
2 *Erica carnea* 'Springwood Pink'.
3 Pansies.
4 *Hedera helix* cultivar.

Container plants for spring

Once spring comes around, garden centers miraculously fill up with small flowers for planting colorful seasonal containers – it's an embarrassment of riches.

Bulbs and tubers (1) are now sold in spring in pots just as they are coming into flower, for the benefit of people who forgot to plant bulbs in autumn and for those who have not the patience to wait. It's an expensive way of buying them, but the big advantage is it's instant. You can pick several pots at exactly the same stage of development so you don't end up with a lopsided-looking container, as you might if the flowers don't all come out at once. You'll find various kinds of tulips, grape hyacinths (*Muscari*), and perhaps snake's-head fritillaries (*Fritillaria meleagris*) sold in pots in spring, but my favorites are dwarf daffodilss – not too top-heavy for pots, and small enough to plant in windowboxes if you wish. The double forms of *Ranunculus asiaticus* are better known as turban buttercups. They are not available until spring is fairly well under way, but if you are looking for something a bit different and instantly glamorous, this is probably it. They come in a good range of colors, and the flowers do look just like turbans on stalks.

Perennials (2) can be grown in containers first (particularly early spring perennials) and then planted out in the garden, but if you want one good one, go for pulmonarias. Most are compact, with red, blue, or white flowers out at the same time on the same plant, and some, such as *Pulmonaria saccharata* (Z4–8), have spotted leaves that go well with almost any neighbor. They're good for filling the gaps around the edge of a container of spring bulbs.

1 *Fritillaria meleagris*.
2 *Pulmonaria officinalis* 'Sissinghurst White'.
3 *Primula vulgaris*.
4 *Viburnum tinus*.

Primroses (3) – colored primroses, cultivars and hybrids of the wild English primrose (*Primula vulgaris*, Z4–8) – are some of the earliest spring flowers, sometimes appearing soon after Christmas. The weather then is too unreliable to plant them outside safely in many areas, so unless you live somewhere mild, put them in your porch or somewhere equally sheltered. By March or early April, it's fine to plant them out almost anywhere. The Polyanthus Group (Z6–8) are a bit later flowering, usually coinciding with the main rush of spring bulbs. Years ago, we planted them in autumn for formal spring bedding, but, frankly, I prefer buying them in flower in spring and planting them in containers to give an instant burst of color.

Shrubs (4) can look wonderful, even if temporarily, in a pot, and one of the best for this is a viburnum: *Viburnum tinus* (Z8–10) gives you a good return for your money, since the buds look good against the evergreen leaves all winter, and then they open out to small white flowers in spring, so you have two seasons' worth from the same plant. But if you want a real winner, look for *V. carlesii* (Z5–8). It doesn't flower until late spring, when the leaves are already out. The flowers are pretty – a pale, peachy pink – but the scent is one of the best you'll meet in any garden. It'll reach 6 × 6ft (2 × 2m) in time, but a "baby" in a pot can be moved to wherever you want some concentrated perfume.

I love grouping small pots of spring-flowering bulbs like this. Here are *Narcissus* 'Tête à tête', *Crocus chrysanthus* 'Snow Bunting', *Hyacinthus* 'Carnegie', and *Hyacinthus* 'Blue Magic'.

Once they've filled a decent-size container, patio plants need not be potted on each year but can be given a shot in the arm each spring. Remove the old soil mix from the top of the pot, then replace it with a fresh topdressing of new mix that contains slow-release fertilizer.

Container plants for all year round

When you're too busy to bother replanting containers every season and don't have time for the constant attention that bedding plants need, then choose long-lived plants, such as hardy shrubs and perennials, that can stay in the same pots for years.

All-year-round plants can stay put for years without being repotted, as long as you topdress them every spring and mix slow-release fertilizer into the new soil mix that you use to replace the old stuff you trowel off. Even if the plants you choose are capable of reaching a fair size in time, the pot acts like a corset, stopping them from growing too big. Most all-year-round shrubs will need a 15–18in (38–45cm) pot to do well; fill it with soil-based potting mix instead of a soilless peat-based one. In winter, don't let the soil freeze solid, or the plants will dry out (they can't use frozen water): move them into a greenhouse, conservatory, or even the shed if you experience freezing temperatures for more than a few days.

Bamboos (1) are very cool for pots and look great, even though, in theory, a lot of species grow too tall and top-heavy. Any bamboo will do well in a container, but if you want colored canes rather than a thicket of leaves, the ones to go for are the wonderful golden-stemmed bamboo (*Phyllostachys aureosulcata* var. *aureocaulis*, Z6–10) and the black bamboo (*Phyllostachys nigra*, Z7–10)). Don't be fooled by the name; black bamboo has bright green stems to start with that turn black only when they are two or three years old, but the plant is still spectacular. They'll both reach 10ft (3m) or so, eventually, so give them a large enough container.

Topiary (2) is very fashionable, and boxwood (*Buxus sempervirens*, Z6–8) is the best for the job. The garden center will sell you the finished article, at a price, or you can train your own designs. Work free-hand if you are feeling confident, or buy wire frames that you pop into the pot over the top of a small plant then just clip around the outside when it grows through – easy.

Patio roses (3) are the all-year-round answer to bedding plants. These roses are one of the few shrubs that flower for as long as summer bedding, from June to September or October – and they don't grow much bigger than a lot of bedding plants. Most cultivars make about 12–18 × 12in (30–45 × 30cm). Prune them as you would normal bush roses in spring. Z5–9.

Subtropical plants (4) are frequently featuring in gardens now as people find themselves pining for palms. Among the best are the Chusan palm (*Trachycarpus fortunei*, Z9–10) – that's the one with windmill-shaped leaves – and the dwarf fan palm (*Chamaerops humilis*, min. 45°F/7°C) which has, well, fan-shaped leaves. They are both slow growing, evergreen, and will take ages to reach much more than 4–6 ft (1.2–2m), but the fan palm is the bushier of the two. Unless you live in a mild, sheltered area, they need protection in winter – and even in marginal areas the leaves can get very brown and battered in winter– so they are best moved under cover when the weather gets rough.

Herbaceous perennials (5) don't really count as year-round plants, since they die down every winter, but I'd make an exception for hostas (Z3–8), because if ever a perennial was designed for container living, this is it. There are lots of cultivars, with big, round, blue, elephant-ear leaves, or elegant, yellow- or cream-variegated heart shapes, growing in clumps about 1ft (30cm) or more high. A good colony growing in a wide wooden box looks stunningly traditional, but grow them in a big, modern-looking ceramic pot, and they suddenly take on a contemporary flavor. They're good for growing in light shade, though they put up with sun if you can keep them moist enough – the trick is to grow them in something without drainage holes in the bottom and keep an eye on the watering.

1 *Phyllostachys nigra*.
2 *Buxus sempervirens*.
3 *Rosa* 'Flower Power'.
4 *Trachycarpus fortunei*.
5 Hosta.

The year-round patio

The patio isn't a five-month wonder; there is life after summer is over. Even if it's too cold to sit out there, you'll still want to be able to enjoy it from the warmth indoors. And, with luck, you might even get some of those fine early spring days when you can sit out there and bask in anticipation of the summer to come.

With just a single container (see below) you can have it every way and make sure of a bright display in every season. Some plants, such as phormium (New Zealand flax) and ivy might be permanent residents, and temporary occupants can be added and subtracted as they come in and out of flower. Alternatively, in a large pot, you can plant a taller evergreen shrub, such as *Viburnum tinus* (see p. 391), or a small, colored-stemmed dogwood, such as *Cornus alba* 'Sibirica', to form your centerpiece.

Create an evergreen framework to give the patio a basic winter structure, then add a few winter pots to act as focal points. Don't just think in terms of winter bedding, because there are lots of shrubs with evergreen leaves and other kinds of winter interest that you can plant for one season only before planting them out in the garden. Double the value for your money!

The ivy, hebe, and phormium (New Zealand flax) are the permanent residents in this metal planter, but the seasonal display changes with the seasons. In spring (*far left*) daffodils and hyacinths provide the color, followed in summer (*second left*) by petunias, verbena, and gray-leafed senecio. In autumn (*second right*) dwarf perennial asters bring their color to the picture along with an ornamental cabbage, and in winter (*far right*) pansies and heathers change the design yet again.

Plant a formal row of evergreen edging plants, such as dwarf boxwood (*Buxus sempervirens* 'Suffruticosa'), santolina, or rosemary, around the edge of internal beds, plus the perimeter if you fancy a formal look. Stand a matching pair of trimmed bay trees (*Laurus nobilis*) on either side of the patio doors to make a glamorous entrance and exit.

In milder areas, line a wire-framed hanging basket with a green-fiber mat (or a similar very open-textured liner that won't hold much water), fill it with potting mix, and plant it with ivies or other evergreen foliage plants. Add winter-flowering pansies if you like, but remember that woody evergreens will stand up to winter conditions far better than flowers. Hang the baskets up in your most sheltered places, such as under the eaves or in a corner, to provide protection from stormy weather.

In late winter, give the patio a good going-over. Clean the paving off with a stiff broom and hot, soapy water, or a pressure washer, to get rid of decomposing leaves and moss. Weed the gaps between slabs, and wash down any furniture that is left outside in winter. Repaint it or treat it to a lick of wood preservative if it needs perking up. While it's quiet in the garden, take the opportunity to clean any unused pots so that they're all ready for planting in the growing season to come.

12 BEDS AND BORDERS

Placing plants

Beds and borders are your plant features. For plant enthusiasts, these are the most important part of the garden around which everything else revolves, but in contemporary and low-maintenance gardens, they often take second place to hard landscaping (also called "hardscaping") and bold, architectural features. That may be why some dyed-in-the-wool gardeners have a problem with decking, gravel, and blue paint.

As a general rule, the more beds and borders you have, the more work it will take to maintain the garden, but a lot depends on the type of plants you grow – bedding plants and perennials need more attention than an area of shrubs, naturalized bulbs, and groundcover plants. Somewhere along the line there is a compromise – a happy balance. And you do want to be a gardener, don't you?

Borders go around things – maybe the edge of the garden, along the edge of a path, or around a gazebo or shed. Beds are entirely surrounded by something else, such as lawn, paving, or gravel.

These dahlias at Hinton Ampner in Hampshire, England, are grown in traditional formal flower beds surrounded by clipped yew hedges.

Formal beds and borders use a lot of straight lines; they have geometric shapes, maybe round, square, or octagonal for a formal bed. Formal borders are normally rectangular. They may contain one particular type of plant, such as herbs, annual bedding, dahlias, or herbaceous flowers, though you can have mixed planting in formal borders. Double borders are a great feature of formal gardens: they are simply two rectangular borders facing each other with a paved or gravel path or swath of fine lawn running between the two.

Informal borders are curved to create a more natural, casual style, while island beds are often teardrop-shaped, or landscaped to fit into natural contours in the ground, like an island in a sea of lawn. The casual style suits mixed planting designs especially well, so you can mix small trees, shrubs, evergreens, perennials, bulbs, and flowers to give year-round interest, which makes good use of a small space.

This exuberant garden has a relaxed arrangement of informal flower beds stuffed with a glorious mixture of plants.

Design rules

Many people end up reshaping their beds and borders for years without ever being happy with the result. It'll save a lot of work later if you can manage to avoid most of the common mistakes from the start and if you can first plan your beds on paper (see page 45).

Define your edges

If you are going for a formal look, make sure straight edges are really straight and circles really round. In an informal garden, curves should be gentle and generous; violent bends and sharp angles look overly fussy, besides being a pain to mow around.

Stick to a sensible size

Beds and borders should be in proportion to the size of the garden. Don't make borders too narrow or put in lots of fussy little beds. A few big ones usually look much better, and they are less effort to look after because there are fewer lawn edges to trim. But don't make them too big, either – you are much more likely to keep beds and borders hoed regularly if you can reach all the soil without standing on it. That's one reason why island beds are so popular.

Deep borders are not only spectacular because of their generous proportions; they also allow more room for plants to grow. Gentle, sweeping curves along the front of the border are easy on the eye, and the path makes cultivation easy, while preventing plants from flopping onto the lawn.

Give hedges a wide berth

If you want to save work, avoid making narrow traditional borders with a hedge along the back, because they *are* hard work. A hedge makes a perfect depot for weeds, such as bindweed, and slugs and snails. It takes all the water and nutrients out of the soil, and, when the hedge needs cutting, you find it's a struggle to avoid stepping on your plants. If you must make a border in front of a hedge, leave a path along the back especially for the purpose – which means giving up a lot of space. Borders are best running alongside paths or in front of fences or walls; otherwise, go for a free-standing island bed instead.

Soil preparation checklist

• Get rid of weeds – it's fine to turn in annual weeds without any seed-heads, but dig out perennial weeds. If there are persistent perennial weeds, such as quackgrass or bindweed, take time to eradicate them properly first. Use a glyphosate-based weedkiller, which kills the roots as well as the tops; alternatively, hoe or use a flame gun regularly until the weeds stop growing back.

• Improve the soil structure – dig in as much well-rotted organic matter as you can. On heavy clay soil, use gritty horticultural sand as well – up to a barrowful per sq. yard/meter. I know it sounds like a lot: it is a lot. It works.

• Final preparation: sprinkle a general-purpose organic fertilizer over the soil shortly before planting then rake it in, breaking down clods to produce a crumblike tilth. Gather up any big stones (ignore smaller ones), roots, or rubbish as you go. If planting in autumn, just break down the clods for now and wait until spring to apply nitrogenous fertilizer.

Plan your beds and borders

When deciding on a plan, work from the back to the front for the borders and from the center out to the edges for island beds. That way you'll be sure you have your framework plants where you want them, making a long-term background for the smaller plants at the front and those with more temporary effects.

Before you start to plant

First, prepare your soil – you can do it at any time of year as long as the ground is neither boggy, nor frozen, nor bone dry – then draw up your planting plan (see p. 402). When you've chosen and bought the plants, stand them roughly in position – in their pots – so that you can make last-minute changes before planting. If you change your mind later, you can always dig them up and move them.

Tips for the plantaholic

Avid plantspeople, whose main interest lies in finding room for the particular plants they want to grow, will find the same technique works for them – they just need to go about things the other way around.

Start by considering the shapes, sizes, and general requirements of the plants you want to grow, mark them in on your plan, and design everything else around them. Your "key" plants will look a lot better if you use this approach than if you just cram them in anywhere there is room. This is what all too often happens, and that's why so many plantspeople's gardens contain great plants that you can't really appreciate, because they don't do each other any favors. Planning is vital, whatever your style.

Sketch out a rough planting plan, showing not only how the plants are positioned to make an attractive picture, but also how many will be needed in each group.

Preparing a planting plan

This is the bit plant buffs can't wait to get to, when you actually start thinking about precisely what you are going to grow.

The way to go about it is to decide on the framework planting first – those plants that create the year-round "bones" of the garden (trees and evergreens), followed by deciduous flowering shrubs. Leave the flowers for last, since they tend to be smaller plants that have a more temporary effect on the look of the garden.

Don't worry if you aren't a plant expert or you don't have any design experience. It's much easier to work with abstract shapes for now and put names to them later. Work out roughly the shapes and sizes of plants that you need – some grow tall and upright, some are wide and weeping, and others are low and spreading and form carpets.

I always like to arrange plants as a series of triangles, putting contrasting shapes, textures and sizes together. Your triangles should be different sizes, and they should overlap each other by varying amounts. They won't look completely triangular once they are filled out in plants, but it's a good way to start, and it avoids creating a spotty look.

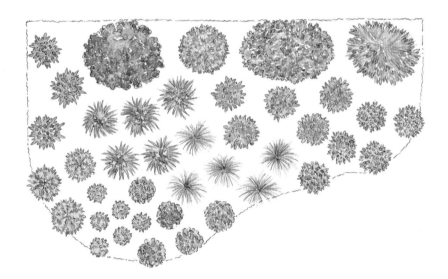

Converting your plan into real, live plants

When you are deciding which plants will suit your plan, you need to know which shape they are, the size you can expect them to reach in five years, which growing conditions they need, and what they do – do they have big foliage or masses of flowers – if so, which color, and when? You also need to know which category of plant you are looking for.

It all sounds so daunting, doesn't it? But take your time and do your research, and it will become a fascinating pleasure. Think of it as a puzzle for which only you can find the answer. If you start working it out in winter, you're bound to have it sorted by planting time in spring! Who's rushing?

From a design point of view, there are three kinds of plants. The stars are the architectural specimens that need to be focal points or centerpieces. Then there are the domed, upright, or bushy shapes that make up the main contents of the triangular shapes in your beds and borders. This group also includes more distinctive upright spikes and spires. Finally, there are the everyday fillers – plants that may not be individually exciting but which are essential for showing off the stars. They make your various triangles hang together, or they fill out the shapes in contemporary gardens. These are the dumplings of the border.

Horticulturally speaking, plants are grouped into trees, shrubs, evergreens, perennials, alpines, bulbs, and so forth. Knowing the type of plant usually gives you a rough idea of shapes and sizes and whether they keep their leaves in winter or disappear underground entirely at certain times of year.

The labels on the plants at the garden center will give you most of the basic information about size and growing conditions, but you can do a lot of research at home using reference books.

Still in their pots, arrange your plants in triangles or groups of odd numbers so that the look of the bed is just right before you start digging.

Trees

Use trees in your framework planting, around the edge of the garden, at the back of mixed borders, or toward the center of larger island beds. Especially striking or architectural selections also make good specimen plants or focal points to grow in the lawn. Trees are there to add height, interesting shapes, and seasonal features, such as striking foliage, flowers, or fruit. There's lots of choice. Unless otherwise stated, the ones I've included here are happy in most reasonable garden conditions.

The best time to plant new trees, whether they are bare-rooted or container-grown, is in mid- to late autumn, late winter, or very early spring, when they're still dormant. If you do it then, they're most likely to get plenty of rainfall to help them establish. They will still need watering in dry spells; I think lack of water is the biggest single reason for failure of new trees, so go to it! A mulch of about 3ft (1m) across at the root zone will help keep in the soil moisture and keep down competing weeds, but keep it clear of the immediate trunk. In theory, you can plant container-grown trees any time the soil is workable, that is when not too dry, too wet, or frozen – but the later in spring you plant, the more watering you'll need to do if your plants are to establish properly.

The Judas tree (*Cercis siliquastrum*) smothers its branches with rose-pink, pea-shaped flowers that open in spring before the leaves appear. The leaves are kidney-shaped and take on stunning autumn tints before they fall. It grows slowly to 20 × 20ft (3 × 3m).

Trees for small gardens

Yes, size does matter in a small garden. But just as important is that, in a small space you want good value from your plants, and that means several features of interest. The trees on the following pages fit the bill.

Crabapples (1) are real three-in-one trees. They have white or pink blossoms in spring, small yellow, orange, red, or purplish fruit in late summer and autumn, and, in winter, the bare trees reveal their attractive shape. *Malus × schiedeckeri* 'Red Jade' is an architectural, weeping form, about 12 × 18ft (3.6 × 5.4m). It's very free with its pink and white flowers in late spring, and the red, cherry-sized fruits can hang on the tree until late winter. *M. × zumi* 'Golden Hornet' is a more upright shape, around 15 × 10ft (4.5 × 3m). It's good for the back of a border, and its wonderful golden fruits hang on the tree until after Christmas. Mostly Z4–8.

***Gleditsia triacanthos* 'Rubylace'** (2) is a standout, if foliage is your main priority. It's a purple-leaved form of the honeylocust, with ferny foliage on prickly stems and a loose, domed shape. The leaves change to bronzy green from midsummer onward. Don't be alarmed by the ultimate height of 30 × 10ft (9 × 3m); it takes ages to get there. Use it as a specimen tree, or plant it in a border. Z3–7.

***Cornus controversa* 'Variegata'** (3) is sometimes called the pagoda dogwood, because its branches are arranged in flattened tiers. It's a beautiful small tree, to 25ft (8m) in time, but if you find the right space for it in a small garden, it will not outgrow its welcome. The biggish heads of creamy white flowers open in midspring, but it is the foliage that takes your breath away – the leaves are slightly twisted and a wonderful mixture of creamy white and green. In autumn they fall to reveal deep plum-purple stems. I love this tree; it always reminds me of a wedding cake! Z6–9.

1 *Malus × zumi* 'Golden Hornet'.
2 *Gleditsia triacanthos* 'Ruby Lace'.
3 *Cornus controversa* 'Variegata'.

Rule of thumb

Don't be put off planting trees because of bad publicity surrounding a few that have caused problems close to buildings. If you stick to decorative garden trees, you can plant them as close to the house as the height they can be expected to grow. Remember that, as a general rule, the spread of the tree is even more important than its height. The sky's the limit when it comes to height, but wide-spreading trees cast a lot of shade, and it's the big, fast-growing, thirsty woodland or forest species that cause problems close to houses, especially if they are growing on the sort of clay that shrinks badly when it dries out. Avoid at all costs willows and poplars – the prime causes of shifting foundations. If you are worried about existing large trees, a local arborist or tree expert should be able to advise you.

Fruiting and berrying trees

These are good for attracting birds to the garden, but some have an edible bonus that we can enjoy ourselves.

Mespilus germanica (**1**), the medlar, is a most attractive medium-sized, dome-shaped tree, roughly 18 × 20ft (5.5 × 6m), with largish white flowers in spring and big, long, oval leaves that turn gold in autumn. The 2in (5cm) diameter, green-brown fruits hang on the tree after the leaves have fallen, looking just like round, carved wooden ornaments. You can eat them, but you're supposed to let medlars "blet," or almost rot, before they are fit to eat or make into jelly. It may have been a medieval favorite, but thanks, I think I'll pass on that one and just enjoy it as a garden tree. Z6–9.

Sorbus hupehensis (**2**) is a mountain ash good for the back of a border. The bunches of white, pink-tinged berries stand out well against a blue sky. Z6–8. In a wildlife garden go for the plain *Sorbus aucuparia* (Z4–7), whose red berries are among the first fruits to ripen in late summer. Also look out for *S. aucuparia* 'Aspleniifolia', which has finely divided, ferny-looking leaves and an upright-conical habit. Allow about 20 × 8ft (6 × 2.4m). All mountain ashes have good autumn colors and are happy on acidic soils. On thin, alkaline ones, they tend to be short-lived.

Morus nigra (**3**), the black mulberry, grows into a craggy, domed tree, with large, heart-shaped leaves and edible fruits that look like big, dark red loganberries. They ripen in late summer and taste wonderful eaten raw, straight from the tree. You know they are ripe when they feel soft and come off at a touch, but they make a filthy mess of your clothes – the juice stains horribly. If the fruit is your main reason for growing it, look for a named cultivar, which will start cropping within a few years; unnamed plants can keep you waiting ten years or more. Allow 15 × 15ft (4.5 × 4.5m). Z5–9.

1 *Mespilus germanica.*
2 *Sorbus hupehensis.*
3 *Morus nigra.*

4 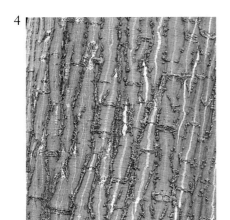   5    6

Trees with attractive bark

In winter, when the leaves have fallen, trees with exceptional bark are the ones that stand out most in the garden. Even if you don't have acres to play with, it's worth trying to find room for a small one.

Acer capillipes (4) is one of the snakebark maples, so called because of the wavy, gray-green stripes running up and down the trunk. The leaves are three-pointed maple leaves that turn bright red in autumn and, in spring, the young shoots are bright red, too, so there are plenty of seasonal attractions. It makes a dome-shaped tree that eventually gets to the larger side of medium, but it's slow-growing, so anticipate 15 × 15ft (4.5 × 4.5m). Z5–7.

Eucalyptus **species** (5), mostly Z9–10, include many with striking, flaking bark that leaves peculiar stripy, python-skin patterns, and the best of these is probably *Eucalyptus pauciflora* subsp. *niphophila* (Z8–10), the snow gum. The older, thicker trees are the ones that have the most characteristic bark patterns. This means you'll have quite a large tree, because it grows fast and reaches maybe 20 × 15ft (6 × 4.5m) or more, but it doesn't cast much shade. Older trees often lean over and grow into angular architectural shapes, which makes them good as "character" specimen trees.

Betula **species** (6) make good, small to medium-sized garden trees, but if I were only allowed one, it would need to be *Betula utilis* var. *jacquemontii*, Jacquemont's birch, Z5–7. It has the typical open, spreading birch form and, like other birches, doesn't cast a lot of shade. What's special about it is the peeling, dazzling white bark: I wash mine twice a year! In theory it can grow quite tall, but in gardens it'll take a long time to grow to more than 30 × 15ft (10 × 4.5m).

4 *Acer capillipes.*
5 *Eucalyptus pauciflora*
  subsp. *niphophila.*
6 *Betula utilis* var. *jacquemontii.*

Tree sizes

It's hard to give the ultimate size of trees accurately, because size varies according to growing conditions. The sizes given are roughly what to expect of a tree within 10–15 years. If trees outgrow their place, you can cut them down and use the space for something else, or call in an arborist to reduce and thin the crown. Preventing a potentially big tree from getting bigger needs professional pruning before it becomes a problem. If it's tackled regularly, this also stops the roots from spreading further – a good thing if it's close to a house. Trees are to be loved, but they do have a finite life. Try to recognize when that life is at an end. Thank the tree, cut it down, and plant another. Gardening is about renewal, not mindless preservation.

Flowering trees

Everyone goes mad over magnolia and cherry blossoms in spring, but these are not always the best flowering trees to go for – in a windy situation, the flowers last no time at all, and if the weather is wet at flowering time the petals turn brown, so you might only see them at their best one year in three. Don't let me put you off if you like them, but don't say I didn't warn you.

Buddleja alternifolia (**1**) is a relative of the butterfly bush (*Buddleja davidii*). Left to itself it makes a big, ungainly shrub; it's much better trained on a single stem to make a tree. It then grows into a rounded mushroom sort of shape and has clusters of scented lavender flowers arranged along semi-trailing stems in early summer. It'll reach about 12 × 8ft (3.6 × 2.4m), which makes it suitable for most small gardens. Best at the back of a border. Z6–9.

***Prunus* × *subhirtella* 'Autumnalis'** (**2**) is an altogether better bet. Okay, the flowers are smaller than most cherries, but there are lots of them, and they are more weather resistant – white, and produced in batches from autumn until spring whenever the weather is mild. The tree is graceful, dome-shaped, and eventually reaches 25 × 20ft (7.5 × 6m). Its cousins, of similar size, are all well worth growing. 'Autumnalis Rosea' has pink flowers, and 'Pendula Rosea Plena', a weeping form with double flowers, is a real gem. All Z6–9.

Genista aetnensis (**3**), Mount Etna broom, is a tree you don't often see. Think of a broom bush growing on a trunk and with its branches weeping down. In midsummer, the whole tree looks as if it's been powdered with gold dust as the yellow pea-flowers come out, and if you get close enough, you'll find it's pleasantly scented. Not something for a cold situation, but good in a warm, sunny, sheltered, milder garden. It reaches about 25 × 25ft (7.5 × 7.5m), casts virtually no shade, and is a superb specimen on a lawn. Z9–10.

1 *Buddleja alternifolia.*
2 *Prunus* × *subhirtella* 'Autumnalis'.
3 *Genista aetnensis.*

Evergreen shrubs

Since they keep their leaves in winter, evergreens form a year-round backbone to the garden. The majority are ideal for outlining the shape of beds and borders, but some of the large-leaved kinds are architectural plants that can stand alone as specimens.

Evergreens are generally easy to grow in any reasonable garden soil, in sun or light shade, though some kinds, such as camellias and rhododendrons, need lime-free, or acidic, soil. They don't need regular pruning, but if they do become too big, then simply cut out a few complete branches in early spring to improve the shape – avoid snipping little bits all over the place. Don't plant too many evergreens in your garden. If you do, the scene will become unchanging and a little like a cemetery. That said, evergreens are available in lots of colors other than deep funereal green.

Some shrubs, especially evergreens such as camellias and rhododendrons, are difficult to root from cuttings, so if you want to raise new plants, layering is the most reliable means of doing it. It's also a good way to beef up a sparse specimen quickly; instead of severing the rooted layers to dig up and plant elsewhere, just leave them where they are, around the edge of the parent plant, so that it looks thicker. Layering can be done at any time in autumn or spring as long as it's not too hot and dry.

Layering a shrub

Choose healthy young shoots growing around the edge of the plant that can easily be bent down to the ground. Fork plenty of organic matter in to improve the soil at the point the chosen shoots touch the ground; work in some gritty sand if the ground is heavy clay.

Use a knife to make a shallow sloping cut 1–2in (2.5–5cm) long, no more than a third of the way through the stem, and about 4–6in (10–15cm) from the tip. Dust the cut surfaces with hormone rooting powder and twist the stem slightly so the wound stays open, or else lodge a matchstick in it. Bend the shoot down to the ground, lay the wounded part flat into a shallow (1in /2.5cm) deep trench in the improved soil. Hold it down with wire hoops, pressing one over the stem either side of the wound.

Bury the stem, but leave at least 2in (5cm) of the tip of the shoot above ground. Water the layer, and repeat in dry spells. Layers should be rooted a year later, but leave them where they are until the young plant has started to grow new shoots before cutting its "umbilical cord." Then wait another few months before moving it. The best times to dig up and move rooted layers of evergreens are early spring and early autumn. If you have layered deciduous shrubs, move them in late winter or midautumn.

Architectural evergreens

Any of these can be grown in a border, but they are also good specimens if you want year-round character in a special spot.

Phormium tenax (**1**), New Zealand flax, is valuable for its modernistic, spiky shape, strappy leaves, and (in some cultivars) loud color schemes – purple, pink, or peach stripes. Don't just think of them for contemporary gardens; they look good in mixed borders and in pot, too. They need a sunny spot with reasonable drainage. Phormiums grow slowly to make clumps about 6ft (2m) high and 4–6ft (1.2–2m) wide. Although grown for foliage, mature plants produce spikes of waxy cream bells in a hot summer. If hammered by a bad winter, they usually regrow from the base. Z9–10.

Fatsia japonica (**2**) is one of the best-known architectural evergreens, especially with flower arrangers. It's a bushy shrub that grows into a 5–6ft (1.5–2m) mound, with shiny, almost starlike leaves that, on a big specimen can be almost 30cm (1ft) across. Although foliage is the main reason for growing it, fatsia flowers in late autumn, with clusters of cream flowers followed by black berries, very like those of ivy. Late insects love it, and so do the birds that live on them. Z8–10.

Viburnum rhytidophyllum (**3**) has dark green, wrinkly, long, oval leaves with felty beige backs and, in winter, the entire plant is dotted with clusters of matching beige-felted buds that open in spring to tiny white flowers. Given time, it grows into a huge, mound-shaped plant 15 × 15ft (4.5 × 4.5m), but you can keep it smaller by pruning. Z5–8.

1 *Phormium* 'Sundowner'.
2 *Fatsia japonica.*
3 *Viburnum rhytidophyllum.*

Large flowering evergreens

Flowering evergreens are dual-purpose shrubs, with good flowers
of their own, but the larger kinds also make a good background
for other plants when they are planted at the back of a border.

4
5
6

Mahonias (4) are essential evergreens, not just for architectural
foliage but for the winter or early spring flowers that, in some, are
scented of lily-of-the-valley. If I could have only one, it would be
Mahonia × media 'Lionel Fortescue', Z8–9. It flowers in mild spells
from autumn through spring, it's well scented, and it makes a
rather upright, spiky shape, about 7 × 3ft (2.1 × 1m) in five years.
It can get much bigger, but when it develops middle-aged spread,
you can prune to keep it a suitable size, just after flowering. Cut it
back quite hard to around knee height, and it will regrow happily.

Arbutus unedo (5), the strawberry tree, is an architectural gem.
It has warm, red-brown, self-shredding bark and clusters of white,
urn-shaped flowers in autumn. It fruits at the same time – the fruits
are from last year's flowers. The round, red "strawberries" actually
look more like lychees and, yes, you can eat them, but they're totally
tasteless, so I wouldn't bother. *A. unedo* makes a big, bushy shrub
or small tree, depending whether it's grown on one or several stems.
It reaches 8 × 5ft (2.4 × 1.5m) in ten years, more eventually. Z7–9.

Ceanothus (6) are among the most spectacular flowering evergreens
and are well known for their fluffy blue flowers in spring or
summer. But *Ceanothus* 'Autumnal Blue' flowers constantly from
midsummer to autumn. The flowers are the color of a deep blue
summer sky. It's a rather upright shrub, growing about 10 × 6ft
(3 × 2m), and needs a warm, sunny spot with good drainage. In a
border, don't put anything too tall in front of it to cut out the light.
Alternatively, plant it on a sunny, south-facing wall and clip it
lightly each spring to keep it flat. Zone 9–10.

4 *Mahonia lomariifolia.*
5 *Arbutus unedo* f. *rubra.*
6 *Ceanothus* 'Autumnal Blue'.

Small flowering evergreens

The small flowering evergreens are useful for the front of a border. Alternate them with perennials or deciduous shrubs, and the area doesn't suddenly turn totally bare when winter comes around. Pop a few clumps of short-growing spring bulbs in between them in autumn, and you have the basis of a good all-year-round feature.

Sarcococca hookeriana* var. *digyna (1), Christmas box, is less upfront, but more unusual. The name is a bit misleading, because it doesn't usually flower till late winter or early spring, and then what you notice first is the scent. The flowers are spindly and fragile-looking, white with a hint of mauve, and lined up along the stems. The plant looks like a series of 3ft (1m) suckers that spread out slowly. Okay, not the most spectacular plant, but it does its stuff at a sparse time of year, and it's a lot better than it sounds. Z6–9.

Cistus (2), the sun rose, flowers all summer and has large, single flowers like crumpled poppies in white or shades of pink. All cistus need lots of sun and well-drained soil. *Cistus × hybridus*, with white flowers, and the aptly named 'Silver Pink' grow into neat mounds, 3 × 3ft (1 × 1m), and are the best for rock or gravel gardens, banks, and the front of sunny borders. Other species grow into 6ft (2m) mounds; they tend to be messy, so I'd stick to the shorter, more squat jobs myself. Z8–10.

Hebes (3) have fluffy spikes of bottlebrush flowers and a very long season, from summer to midautumn. They need similar conditions to the sun rose, and the two look good together. *Hebe* 'Autumn Glory' (violet-purple) will make dome-shaped bushes about 4ft (1.2m) tall and across, and *H. pinguifolia* 'Sutherlandii' makes upright, gray-leafed domes topped with white flowers in summer. Mostly Z8–10.

1 *Sarcococca hookeriana* var. *digyna*.
2 *Cistus × hybridus*.
3 *Hebe pinguifolia* 'Sutherlandii'.

Acidic soil-loving evergreens

If you garden on acidic soil, then you can go in for all the acidic soil-lovingshrubs that, elsewhere, the rest of us can only grow in pots of acidic soil mix. Rhododendrons, camellias, and pieris are the "big three." They all like dappled shade or weak sun and a sheltered site with plenty of organic matter in the ground so it doesn't dry out badly in summer. I always like to see them growing with "bark trees,"such as birches, *Acer griseum*, and *Arbutus unedo*, and character shrubs, such as Japanese maples, all of which are happy in rhododendron-growing conditions as well as in normal gardens.

Rhododendrons (4) flower mostly in midspring, and there are choices for Zones 3 through 11. They range in size from the tiny ones that aren't much bigger than the indoor azaleas that you buy in pots in winter, to real whoppers that are big trees in the wild. For most gardens, the bushy hybrids that reach about 6 × 8ft (2 × 2.4m) in ten years are the ones to go for. They come in many colors. Some of the best for small gardens or pots are *Rhododendron yakushimanum* hybrids (Z5–9), such as 'Sneezy' (pink) and 'Grumpy' (creamy pink); they make tight, dome shapes 4 × 4ft (1.2 × 1.2m).

Camellias (5) flower on either end of winter, with pink or white flowers, some of which look almost like waterlilies. They'll put up with near-neutral soil, though it's a good idea to give them a shot of fertilizer containing sequestered iron each spring so the leaves don't go yellow. There are dozens of popular cultivars; the semidouble pink *Camellia* × *williamsii* 'Donation' is still one of the best. Flowers tend to fall as they fade, rather than staying on the bush and turning brown, as is the case with varieties of *C. japonica*. Camellias need shelter to protect the fragile flowers, and east-facing sites should be avoided. Give those with white flowers extra shelter; the petals turn brown at the least excuse if exposed to bad weather. Z7–8.

Pieris (6) is the plant people often think of as an outdoor poinsettia. The dome-shaped plants have strings of white bells at the tips of some shoots in spring, and the rest have bright red or pink new foliage; the two don't always coincide. For the rest of the year, they look a tad ordinary unless you grow a variegated one, such as *P.* 'Flaming Silver', which has white-edged leaves. Most are slow growing and, at ten years of age, have usually reached about 6 × 4ft (2 × 1.2m) or thereabouts. Given enough time, in acidic woodland, where conditions suit them perfectly, they can get quite big. If you need to prune them, do so after the flowers are over and the spring leaf colors have faded back to green. They need shelter from drying winds and frost, which turn new growth brown. Z5–9.

4 *Rhododendron yakushimanum* 'Ken Janeck'.
5 *Camellia* × *williamsii* 'Donation'.
6 *Pieris japonica* 'Pink Delight'.

Deciduous shrubs

Flowering deciduous shrubs add seasonal highlights to a border; most kinds are only at their best for about six weeks of the year, so you need to achieve a balance between these and the plants that provide all-year-round interest, particularly as these plants lose their leaves in winter. Many of them are faster growing than evergreens, and some need regular pruning to keep them neat.

Unless specific growing conditions are stated, you can safely assume that woody plants are happy in any reasonable garden soil that has been properly prepared, enriched with a reasonable amount of organic matter, and isn't waterlogged in winter.

Spring in the shade garden at Barleywood, where deciduous shrubs such as viburnum and amelanchier come into their own before the leaf canopy of the oak is at its summer density.

Shrubs for spring flowers

Spring is the peak season for the most popular shrubs: barberries, viburnums, forsythia, kerria, and *Daphne mezereum*, but if you want three real troupers, these are the ones I wouldn't be without.

Ribes sanguineum (1), the flowering currant, is an old-fashioned, cottage-garden shrub with a bushy, upright shape, at around 5 × 5ft (1.5 × 1.5m), and with deep pink, bunch-of-grapes flowers in April. Z 6–8. The buffalo currant (*Ribes odoratum*) is bigger, 6 × 5ft (2 × 1.5m), with scented yellow flowers and leaves that take on purple autumn tints. Z5–8. Both are good for sun or light shade.

Magnolia stellata (2), the star magnolia, is the one with the white, waterlily-like flowers that open just ahead of the leaves. It makes a rounded bush about 5 × 5ft (1.5 × 1.5m). Grow it in a bed or border, or as a stand-alone shrub in the lawn. Very similar, but bigger all around and with pale pink flowers is *Magnolia × loebneri* 'Leonard Messel'. Both Z5–9. They need a sheltered site in sun or light shade, but, unlike the bigger tree magnolias, they aren't fussy about the soil as long as it's reasonably well drained. Don't disturb the thick, fleshy roots at planting time; you'll slow down establishment.

Spiraeas (3) that are spring-flowering have a foam of tiny white flowers all over the plants. They're good for separating colors that clash in a border and look great with evergreen foliage and carpets of spring bulbs. *Spiraea* 'Arguta', bridal wreath (Z5–8), is an old favorite – a slightly unkempt, bushy dome, 6 × 6ft (2 × 2m), flowering in April. It's indispensable for flower arrangers. In smaller gardens, go for *S. nipponica* 'Snowmound' – a compact 3-ft (1-m) dome with arching sprays of closely packed white flowers in June. Z4–8.

1 *Ribes sanguineum* 'Porky Pink'.
2 *Magnolia stellata*.
3 *Spiraea* 'Arguta'.

Shrubs for summer flowers

Most gardeners turn to border perennials for summer color, forgetting that there are plenty of good flowering shrubs that will add brightness farther back in the border.

Hydrangeas (1), the *macrophylla* selections, are old stalwarts, good anywhere where the soil is reasonably moist, in sun or in light shade under trees. The dome-shaped bushes average out around 4–5ft (1.2–1.5m) tall by as much across, though they'll grow bigger in the right spot. The hefty, rounded heads of pink, white, or blue flowers are at their best in late summer, then dry out on the plant and fade attractively. The flowers come in two types – mopheads, whose domed heads are filled with flowers, and lacecaps, which have a fringe of flowers round an open center. Don't deadhead hydrangeas when the flowers are over; leave the flowers on for added interest in autumn and winter. But if you are going to prune hydrangeas, do it properly – so many people don't and wonder why they never have flowers. It's one of the most regular problems that crops up in my mailbox. Z6–9.

Kolkwitzia amabilis (2), the beauty bush, looks its best in late spring, when it is covered in yellow-spotted, pink, foxglovelike flowers. You'll need plenty of room for it; it grows into a loose, twiggy, dome shape about 8 × 8ft (2.4 × 2.4m). When buying, ask for the cultivar 'Pink Cloud', and, if possible, buy it in flower. A lot of people are disappointed when they end up with a poor-flowering form. This is an excellent shrub through which to grow a late-flowering clematis; it's big enough to take one, and it does need a little color later in the year. Z5–9.

Pruning hydrangeas

You don't need to prune hydrangeas at all, but it's a good way of giving them a spring cleanup and deadhead all in one operation. Young plants rarely need anything more than light deadheading, taking off no more than the remains of the old flower.

Large, elderly hydrangeas often need thinning out. Start by cutting out one or two of the oldest stems completely, as low down in the plant as you can. Then take out any long or ungainly looking stems that stick out and spoil the symmetrical shape.

Finally, go over the whole plant deadheading it, only instead of just removing the dead head, follow the stem down to the next nonflowered side shoot and cut just above it. If the dead heads have disappeared during the winter, you can usually see where they have been by the bare bit of shoot at the top of the stem. Shoots with leaves right to the tip have not flowered and, if you cut those back, you will be removing the coming year's flower buds.

1 *Hydrangea* 'Nigra'.
2 *Kolkwitzia amabilis*.
3 *Lavatera*.
4 *Hibiscus syriacus* 'Diana'.

Blue hydrangeas

To get the truest colors, blue hydrangeas need acidic soil, pH 4–5; and pink or red ones need a soil pH of 6–7; get it wrong, and most change to a washed-out mauve. White ones stay whitest at pH 6.5–7.5. Check with a soil-testing kit to see which colors will grow best for you. If you don't have the right soil for blue cultivars, you can fertilize the plants with iron or aluminum sulphate to acidify the soil, though you need to keep treating them regularly. You can improve red or pink flower colors by watering them several times a year with a handful of garden lime dissolved in a watering can full of water. Otherwise, grow blue hydrangeas in pots of acidic soil mix, and they will show their true colors.

Lavatera (3) is excellent for the back of a sunny, well-drained border. It looks like a hollyhock with 6ft (2m) stems, grayish leaves, and large, rose-pink flowers. 'Barnsley' has paler pink flowers with a red "eye." The plants will flower from midsummer to autumn, but they aren't long lived and quickly look ratty. The secret is to cut the entire plant back hard in spring to get rid of the old stems and encourage some new, young, free-flowering ones. Replace older, worn out plants from cuttings every two or three years. Z7–9.

Hibiscus syriacus (4), a hardy hibiscus, is a spectacular shrub. All it needs is a sunny, sheltered spot with well-drained soil. It grows steadily to make an upright shape, 5 × 3ft (1.5 × 1m) or more, and throughout late summer and early autumn, it is covered in flowers like those of the familiar subtropical hibiscus, but not quite so big, about 3in (8cm) across. 'Oiseau Bleu' (pale blue) and 'Woodbridge' (mauve-pink) are the most popular. 'Diana' is the best white-flowered single. I'd give the double-flowered cultivars a miss, unless you grow them in pots in the conservatory – they sound attractive, but the flowers get bashed to bits outside. Z5–9.

5 *Potentilla* 'Limelight'.
6 *Buddleja davidii* 'Black Knight'.

Potentillas (5) are superb fillers for the front of a border, or grow them on a bank, in a rock garden, or in pots. They are neat, dome-shaped plants with ferny foliage studded with masses of small flowers in orange, red, yellow, or pink. They have an incredibly long flowering season, from midsping to midfall, and although they like sun, they'll do in light shade between bigger shrubs – red-flowered cultivars are actually best grown in light shade,since it helps prevent the flower color from fading. Z3–7.

Buddleja davidii (6), the butterfly bush, is easily identified, as from midsummer to autumn, its cone-shaped, purple, mauve, or bluish flowers are covered with butterflies. There is a variegated cultivar, 'Harlequin', which you either love or hate, but the old favorite is the deep purple-flowered 'Black Knight'. Buddleias usually grow about $10–12 \times 8$ft ($3–3.6 \times 2.4$m). If that's too big for you, look for 'Nanho Petite Indigo'; it reaches only 6×4ft (2×1.2m). Z6–9.

Pruning buddleias

The butterfly bush (*Buddleja davidii*) grows at an alarming rate, and if you don't prune it each year it becomes tall and leggy and looks very scruffy. Prune it in two stages each year.

In autumn, after the last flowers are over, cut off the top third of the shrub. Don't worry about pruning above a bud, because all you are doing is "shortening the sail" so the thing won't get too badly bashed about in the wind – buddleias are quite brittle.

The real pruning is done in late winter. Simply cut back last year's cane-like stems to within 1in (2.5cm) of their base, just above where they grow from the trunk. To tame an overgrown buddleia, cut the entire shrub back to a stump about 2ft (60cm) above ground in late winter New shoots will grow even out of quite thick, old trunks, so you won't kill it.

Shrubs for autumn color

By the time summer is over, borders are often left with an end-of-term feeling, so it's worth looking out for a few slightly unusual shrubs to add a splash of late color to your garden palette.

***Callicarpa bodinieri* var. *giraldii* 'Profusion'** (**1**), beautyberry, has great autumn color. The leaves turn pink, red, and purple before they fall, leaving the shrub thickly clad in clusters of small violet berries that you probably missed earlier. It will grow to about 6 × 6ft (2 × 2m), which may make it a bit big for a lot of gardens where an "autumn special" is a bit of a luxury, but do grow it if you can. Z6–8.

Hydrangea quercifolia is the oak-leaved hydrangea, which has large white cones of lacecap flowers in late summer, and oakleaf-shaped leaves that turn bronze-red in autumn. It grows about 5 × 5ft (1.5 × 1.5m). Prune it the same as for other hydrangeas (see page 416). Z5–9. If you like the oak-leaved hydrangea, you'll probably like cultivars of other hydrangea species, such as *H. paniculata* 'Grandiflora' (Z4–8) and *H. arborescens* 'Annabelle' (**2**) (Z4–9). Both flower in summer with massive white flowerheads that keep going well into autumn, when the leaves turn golden yellow.

Clerodendrum trichotomum* var. *fargesii (**3**) is an unusual large shrub or small tree, about 8 × 8ft (2.4 × 2.4m), which saves its whole show for the back end of the year. It flowers in late summer, with sprays of maroon buds that open to a starburst of small, white flowers. Soon after, the maroon calyces part to reveal the bright turquoise berries that they enclose. The foliage has a slightly acrid scent when bruised, so it's best put where you won't touch it – it needs lots of sun, shelter, and well-drained soil. You might need to seek it out, but it really is worth the effort. Z6–9.

1 *Callicarpa bodinieri* var. *giraldii* 'Profusion'.
2 *Hydrangea arborescens* 'Annabelle'.
3 *Clerodendrum trichotomum* var. *fargesii*.

Shrubs for winter interest

Once winter comes around, there are very few shrubs worth getting excited about, so don't miss out on the few that are.

***Cornus alba* 'Sibirica'** (**1**), the red-stemmed dogwood, is a plant you can't take your eyes off in winter. The bare stems are that shade they used to call sealing-wax red. Z2–8. Those of *Cornus sanguinea* 'Midwinter Fire' are a stunning mix of cochineal red and orange. Z5–7. These dogwoods are excellent for a boggy or even wet spot but are equally happy in normal garden conditions, in sun or light shade, and grow about 5 × 4ft (1.5 × 1.2m). Cut out the oldest stems annually in March to trigger lots of young shoots, which have the brightest-colored bark. Manure them well to keep up their strength.

Hamamelis* × *intermedia (**2**), the witch hazels, come top of my winter must-have list. They are rather upright then spreading, open bushes that grow 8 × 6ft (2.4 × 2m), and flower in mild spells from leaf-fall in autumn until early spring. There are hybrids with red, orange, or yellow flowers, but the one I'd recommend is *H.* × *intermedia* 'Pallida', which has the biggest, pale yellow, spidery flowers of any of them, coupled with golden autumn foliage tints. The flowers are strongly perfumed on a warm winter day, but if the weather is cold, blow on them, and you'll fool them into releasing their scent. If you fancy a witch hazel but don't have room, try one in a pot – I've had one for several years, and it's still doing beautifully. The yellow-flowered ones have golden autumn color, and the orange and red ones have ruddy leaf tints. Nifty. Z5–9.

1 *Cornus alba* 'Sibirica'.
2 *Hamamelis* × *intermedia* 'Pallida'.
3 *Corylus avellana* 'Contorta'.
4 *Daphne cneorum*.
5 *Philadelphus*.
6 *Viburnum farreri*.

***Corylus avellana* 'Contorta'** (**3**) is a real winter stunner. It has wildly twisted stems that you see properly only when the leaves have fallen. In early spring, there are long yellow catkins dangling from them. Slow growing, it gets to about 8 × 8ft (2.4 × 2.4m). Z3–9.

Scented shrubs

Shrubs with scented flowers add oomph to whatever else is looking good at the time. Plant them in a sheltered spot so that the fragrance doesn't blow away; the warmer and more still the air is, the more powerfully the scent will build up.

Daphne cneorum (**4**) is a low-growing evergreen shrub with oval leaves that smothers itself in rose-pink flowers in late spring. The delightful fragrance will stop you in your tracks. Plant it on a bank or a traditional rock garden where it can tumble down the slope. It is happy in any well-drained soil, even those that are alkaline. The variety 'Eximia' is particularly fine. Size 6in (15cm) by 3ft (1m). Z5–7.

Philadelphus (**5**), the mock orange, has very fragrant white flowers in late spring and early summer. They come as small as the 30in × 5ft (75cm × 1.5m) 'Manteau d'Hermine', with strongly scented double flowers, but P. 'Belle Etoile', at 4 × 5ft (1.2 × 1.5m), and P. *coronarius*, which comes in at 8 × 6ft (2.4 × 2m) are arguably the strongest scented. If you want a mock orange that looks good when the flowers are over, the ones you want are P. *coronarius* 'Variegatus', with cream and green leaves, or the acid yellow-leaved P. *coronarius* 'Aureus'. Don't give this one too sun-baked a spot, or it will scorch. Z5–8.

Viburnums (**6**) with good scent come in two waves. The early batch includes *Viburnum farreri* (white to palest pink, Z6–8) and *V. × bodnantense* 'Dawn' (bright pink, Z7–8), which bloom from autumn, through mild spells in winter, to early spring. *V. carlesii* 'Aurora' (pale pink, Z5–8), *V. × juddii* (very pale pink, Z5–9), and *V. × carlcephalum* (white, Z6–8) all flower from mid- to late spring. Most grow to about 6 × 6ft (2 × 2m) and have attractive autumn leaf tints – they're good all-arounders.

4

5

6

Filling in the fine detail

Trees, evergreens, and flowering shrubs provide the background to the garden and some seasonal highlights, but what makes the ever-changing tapestry of colors are the flowers – roses, herbaceous perennials, bulbs, annuals, alpines, and exotics.

Making plant associations

The smaller flowers are the next plants to add as your planting develops, but it's no good just picking your favorites and hoping they'll look good together, because they probably won't. You need to create plant associations – attractive groups – so that each plant shows its own best points but also brings out the best in its neighbors. The one thing I'd always do if you are buying plants for a particular bed is to stand them in a group at the garden center or nursery to see how they look together. At home, stand them in position on the actual spot and rearrange them as necessary until you hit the winning combination. Making good plant combinations is an art that grows on you with practice, but a few tips come in very handy for starters. It takes me ages to get it right, sometimes – but I still get a lot of pleasure out of doing it.

Contrast, contrast, contrast

Designers don't see things the same way as gardeners. Where we see a good plant, what they see is texture, height, shape, size, and color. When you make plant associations, try to think more like a designer, and leave your horticultural appreciation for later.

The aim is to put plants together that contrast well. Go for contrasts of shape and texture first. A tall, upright, bony-looking plant, such as bamboo, looks good with a large, prickly, horizontal leaf, such as those of gunnera. Strappy-leaved phormium looks

Tall, spire-forming perennials such as delphiniums change the scale and form of the border as they grow – contrasting well with lower, fluffy plants.

great with a low, creeping carpet at its feet. Contrast shiny evergreens with rough-textured trunks or prickly stems. Big, round flower shapes, like those of the ornamental alliums, stand out well against a background of small, frothy, filler flowers and upright spikes.

Think triangles

Keep thinking about making triangles. Choose one star plant, and a couple of less exciting but useful extras – even the most hard-bitten plantsperson won't believe how good it makes your best plants look. Try one spire-shaped plant with one bushy and one low, spreading type if you want a "recipe."

When you are grouping plants, odd numbers always look better than even ones – go for groups of three or five. The effect is bolder and less spotty than a mass of singletons. Arrange your threes and fives in triangle shapes, and, if you find it too daunting to plan an entire bed, you can compromise. Make lots of three-and-five plant triangles, then link them with a carpet of something neutral, such as *Alchemilla mollis,* that runs through the entire bed.

Colors and color schemes

It isn't luck that makes certain colors work well together. Make your mind up whether you want a hot scheme based on red, orange, and yellow, or a pastel scheme that majors in pink, mauve, blue, and purple – it's a heck of a lot easier not to mix the two together.

If you want a border of opposite colors, then purple and yellow, red and green, or blue and orange contrast well. Don't overdo it: you'll soon get fed up with the visual argument. Try graduating colors in a border rather like a rainbow – from reds and oranges, through yellows and greens, to blues and violets.

If you want a border of many colors, try planning plant triangles each based on one set of complementary colors, and then plant plenty of neutral-colored foliage between them to give a sense of unity.

Contrasting strappy fountains of phormium (New Zealand flax) are offset well against the fluffy flowers and foliage of blue brachyscome and felicia and yellow bidens.

The same patch of ground can play host to plants that flower at different times of year, so tulips (*left*) can be followed by summer annuals (*center*), such as nigella (love-in-a-mist), then autumn crocuses erupt at the end of the year (*right*).

Pinch ideas

Some of the best ideas you'll ever find are other people's, which is why avid gardeners spend so long taking photos and making notes when they visit flower shows and gardens. As soon as you need a bright idea for plants that go well together, there you are – a folder full of them.

Less is more

A traditional plant arrangement relies heavily on sheer numbers for impact, but if you are making a contemporary look, then you want only a tenth of the number of plants, so each one needs to have ten times the charisma.

Three-dimensional chess

Yes, I know what you're thinking. It's all very well, but you'll end up with plants that all look their best at the same time. Well, you need to build in the seasonal factor. It's easy to add spring and summer bulbs or annuals into the gaps between shrubs. If you can't wing it, make several tracing-paper overlays of the same bed, then mark in what's up and what's underground, what's in flower and what's evergreen. That way you'll cover the entire year and can see where the gaps are and think of ways to fill them.

Last word

If you get it wrong, *don't worry*! Beds and borders are not cast in concrete – plants can always be moved – and I have yet to visit a garden where every bed and border works. They are always being developed and changed. The important thing to do is to enjoy the journey – not turn it into a voyage to hell!

Roses

Unless you have a formal garden, you probably won't want traditional rose beds, but roses still have a place even in today's "outdoor living rooms." Bush roses cohabit well in mixed borders with shrubs and perennials, groundcover roses are good for covering banks, and patio roses pack as much flower power into containers as bedding plants but are much less bother.

Consider scent as well as color (which varies in its power) and also disease resistance, which will save you from spraying regularly.

Here I've just chosen a few of my favorite roses – and even that's a hard call. My favorites won't necessarily be yours, so get yourself out there with a notebook and investigate some more – there are literally hundreds to choose from!

Learning the lingo – rose terminology

Hybrid teas (HTs)

HTs have 1–3 large flowers at the end of each stem, and they are repeat-flowering (remontant) roses. Nowadays we're supposed to call them large-flowered bush roses, which is how you may see them described in catalogs. The Botanical Police will probably turn a blind eye if you call them hybrid teas in the privacy of your own rose bed.

Floribundas

These are also repeat-flowering roses, with a large cluster of many flowers at the tips of their stems. They are now correctly called cluster-flowered bush roses.

Shrub roses

This is a loose umbrella term for a group that includes old-fashioned roses, cultivated cousins of the rose species, and sometimes the more garden-worthy wild species themselves. Unlike modern bush roses, some shrub roses don't flower continuously all summer. For the ones that don't repeat, the main flush is late spring/early summer.

Groundcover roses

These are a modern invention. Some cultivars trail out over the ground while others are bushy and dense and grow wider than they are tall. Many of them flower all summer.

Patio roses

These are small bush roses (dwarf cluster-flowered bush is the modern way of putting it) that look and behave just like floribundas but on a smaller scale, usually 12–18in (30–45cm) high. They aren't the same as miniature roses, which are smaller still, and, frankly, aren't as good as patio roses.

Bush roses

For me, a rose without scent is only half a rose. It's good to see old-fashioned fragrance being bred back into many of the new cultivars that come out each year. Some of them are very good indeed, but a lot of the older cultivars are still tried-and-tested winners. Go for the more disease-resistant kinds if you don't want to do a lot of spraying. All Z5–9.

Whisky Mac (**1**) appeals to some people because of the name, but it's really quite descriptive because the flower is a warm, bright, amber shade of single malt that's seldom found in roses. It's a hybrid tea, which on paper doesn't sound too clever, since the disease resistance isn't all that special, but if you can live with that, it's well worth growing for the scent – which is rosy rather than whisky. It grows to a bushy 30in (75cm).

Margaret Merril (**2**) would be my bush rose of choice if I could have only one. A pure white floribunda with a perfume that knocks your socks off, she's vigorous, stands a shade over 3ft (90cm) high and has reasonable disease resistance.

1 *Rosa* Whisky Mac.
2 *R.* Margaret Merril.
3 *R.* 'Deep Secret'.
4 *R.* Fragrant Cloud.
5 *R.* 'Just Joey'.
6 *R.* 'Fragrant Delight'.

'**Deep Secret**' (3) is a hybrid tea for closet romantics who want a dark, black-red rose with a really rich scent. Unlike most roses of this much-sought-after color, this one is quite a good do-er, strong and disease resistant, and about 3ft (90cm) tall.

Fragrant Cloud (4) is an old favorite hybrid tea, rather a loud coral red, and one of the strongest scents going. It's what they always used to call a bedding rose, which means it grows neat and compact – suitable for growing in blocks in formal rose beds. It can be kept to about 30in (75cm) tall and, like most bush roses, is good for cutting. Not in the first rank for disease resistance, but not so weak that it becomes a martyr. If you want the classic, highly scented, fat-flowered hybrid tea, this is it!

'**Just Joey**' (5) is another distinctive hybrid tea with scented, coppery orange flowers that are slightly wavy around the edges. It looks good grown with coppery pink shades as well as more amber or yellow colors. It's a good bedding rose at 30in (75cm) tall and has stood the test of time.

'**Fragrant Delight**' (6) is a highly scented floribunda with large, coppery pink flowers flushed yellow toward the center. It has good disease resistance and makes a slightly more upright shape than some. It grows to about 30in (75cm).

Roses need not be confined to rose gardens; nowadays, they are often used in mixed border settings. Here *Rosa* 'Geoff Hamilton', a shrub rose, is planted with a variety of colorful shrubs and climbers.

1 *Rosa* 'Geranium'.

2 *R.* Getrude Jekyll.
3 *R.* Graham Thomas.
4 *R.* 'Nevada'.
5 *R.* 'Roseraie de l'Hay'.

Shrub roses

Shrub roses are great for growing in mixed borders, and some make good rose hedges. I've included a couple of species roses here, too.

Rosa moyesii **'Geranium'** (**1**) is a selection of the species with small, single, sealing-wax red "wild rose" flowers. It is also grown for its large scarlet, bottle-shaped hips. Excellent for the back of a big border or wild garden, because it grows to 8 × 6ft (2.4 × 2m) and is very disease resistant. Honeybees love it. Z4–9.

Gertrude Jekyll (**2**) is an English rose bred to combine the long flowering season of modern bush roses with the scent and quaint flower shape of old-fashioned roses. It's rich pink, slightly ruffled, and well scented, growing roughly 5 × 3ft (1.5 × 1m). Like most of the modern English roses raised by David Austin, Gertrude Jekyll is especially good if planted 2ft (60cm) apart in groups of three so that the branches intertwine, making a dense thicket of flowers. Z5–9.

Graham Thomas (**3**) is another real winner among the English roses, The flowers are the color of a free-range egg yolk, with a tea rose scent and a shape that is close to a peony. Irresistible. About 4ft (1.2m) tall and disease resistant. Z5–9.

'Nevada' (**4**) is a real classic, and in late spring has enormous single, cream-colored flowers with golden stamens clustered in the center. It's elegant, but it does need a lot of room – it grows to 6 × 6ft (2 × 2m). It can succumb to blackspot – but I love it! Z4–9.

'Roseraie de l'Hay' (**5**) has bright green, crêpe-paper leaves that never fall victim to mildew or black spot, and the fragrant, double magenta flowers appear right through the summer. It's a waist-high bush if you prune it back in spring; otherwise, it will get to 6ft (2m) or more. Z4–9.

Patio and groundcover roses

These are the roses to plant in 12–15in (30–38cm) pots of soil-based mix on your patio, though they'll be just as happy at the front of a mixed border. There are lots of different cultivars and new ones come out every year; this is a very small selection of my favorites. They are hot on color but less impressive on the nose. All Z5–9.

Pruning patio and groundcover roses

• Groundcover roses don't need any special pruning at all; just take out any dead or broken stems whenever you see them. You can also prune out any badly mildewed shoot tips as an alternative to spraying.

• Prune patio roses the same way as full-sized bush roses, but on a smaller scale. Don't cut them back lower than 6in (15cm) from the ground.

Magic Carpet (5) is a prostrate groundcover rose that's also good for hanging baskets; the flowers are semi-double and lavender-pink with a faint scent. In the open ground, it'll cover a circle with a 4ft (1.2m) radius and about 1ft (30cm) deep.

Gingernut (6) is good for pots – a neat, bushy patio rose with lots of gingery orange flowers produced all summer. It grows to about 18 × 15in (45 × 38cm). Very disease resistant but has little scent.

Sweet Dream (7) is very similar but with pale peach flowers; again good for disease resistance, but not much scent.

'Bright Smile' (8) is a small bush rose that grows to a width and height of about 18in (45cm). Throughout summer and autumn it bears clusters of lightly scented, double yellow flowers.

5 *R.* Magic Carpet.
6 *R.* Gingernut.
7 *R.* Sweet Dream.
8 *R.* 'Bright Smile'.

Perennials

Whether grown for foliage or flowers, perennials are the flesh on the bones of any garden.

Unless you go whole hog and plan a herbaceous border consisting of nothing but perennial flowers, the usual way of growing them is in gaps between shrubs in a mixed border to provide seasonal highlights. Perennials are, of course, plants that die down to an overwintering rootstock each autumn and grow up again the following spring.

Perennials perform best if you keep them happy by dividing them. Do this in spring if you garden on wet or heavy clay soil, and for all delicate perennials, or those with thick or fleshy roots. Autumn is okay for the more indestructible plants with fibrous roots as long as you have light, freely draining soil – otherwise, the damaged roots can't heal and the plants rot.

But don't divide the plants until you need to; wait until they are obviously dying out in the center or they have spread too far. The most vigorous perennials may need dividing every 2–3 years; slow spreaders may not need doing more than every 6–7 years, if then.

Most of the perennials I've described are happy in any ordinary garden soil with reasonable drainage and some organic matter. They like nonscorching sun, or the kind of light shade cast by surrounding plants in an uncrowded border. If they like something different, I've said so. Otherwise, take it as read that they like standard conditions. Here's the cast in order of appearance.

Perennials for spring

Spring-flowering perennials are among the most welcome of all – partly because they show that the garden is coming to life again, and partly because they can be easily seen at a time when a lot of plants are not yet ready to emerge from dormancy. Many of them are good for shady borders, because they flower before the leaf canopy on the trees is fully developed.

Dicentra spectabilis (1) is called bleeding heart because of the locket-shaped, pink-and-white flowers that hang down in rows from its arching, ferny-looking stems. It forms clumps about 18 × 18in (45 × 45cm). It dies down quite early unless grown in rather moist soil and with shade from the afternoon sun, so you'll need plants nearby to fill the gap later in the summer. Z3–9.

Omphalodes cappadocica (2) flowers looks just like a posy of long-stemmed forget-me-nots growing from the center of a bouquet of nearly heart-shaped leaves. It grows to about 1 × 1ft (30 × 30cm). 'Starry Eyes' has flowers edged with paler blue. Z6–8.

Helleborus x hybridus (3) is the Lenten rose – quite a connoisseur's plant these days. To get your favorite colors, buy them in pots when they're in flower from late winter well into spring . The spotted ones and the greenish or deep mauve-purple cultivars are especially sought after. They'll make evergreen clumps, 18 × 24in (45 × 60cm). Once established, hellebores hate being moved, but they do self-seed – move the offspring while they are small. Z6–9

Polygonatum multiflorum (4), Solomon's seal, sends fat buds poking up through the ground that quickly grow into 2ft (60cm) tall arching stems with small bunches of white bell flowers dangling down between the pairs of leaves in May. Plants spread slowly for 2–3ft (60cm–90cm), but it's easy enough to dig up any that come up where you don't want them. Z4–8.

Pulmonaria 'Lewis Palmer' (5) is a clump-forming lungwort with oval leaves that are spotted with greenish white. Its flowers open pink and then turn blue, which is why the English know it as "soldiers and sailors," after their uniforms. 12 × 18in (30 × 45cm). Z5–8.

1 *Dicentra spectabilis.*
2 *Omphalodes cappadocica* 'Starry Eyes'.
3 *Helleborus × hybridus.*
4 *Polygonatum multiflorum.*
5 *Pulmonaria* 'Lewis Palmer'.

Tall, summer-flowering perennials

These are the big boys of the summer border, but don't assume they always need to be in the back row. They make great high points in your triangular set pieces, too, and some of them make really fabulous specimen plants.

In summer, the herbaceous border comes into its own – a patchwork quilt of flowers that looks cheery, even on cloudy days.

Acanthus spinosus (**1**) is positively architectural; big and striking with great, thistly-looking leaves and 5ft (1.5m) stems topped with tall spikes of dusky mauve and pink, white-lipped flowers. These appear in early summer but dry out on the plants and look good for most of the summer. Acanthus is happy in very well-drained and dry gardens in plenty of sun, but it doesn't like being disturbed once it's established, taking a few years to settle in. Grow it as a big specimen on its own, or team it with other drought-tolerant plants. Z5–9.

Salvia uliginosa (**2**) is nothing like the red bedding salvia. This has sky blue flowers in loose spikes at the top of rather wiry stems in late summer and early autumn. It makes a slightly unkempt, bushy shape, maybe 5 × 2½ft (1.5m × 75cm). It isn't the hardiest of plants, but cuttings root easily. Take a few when you take geranium cuttings, and overwinter young plants under cover. Z8–10.

Phlox paniculata (**3**) is a traditional herbaceous border favorite that can be relied upon to put on a good show whatever the weather. Phlox have huge, domed heads of scented flowers through much of summer at the tops of stems 2½–3½ft (75cm–1.1m) tall, depending on the cultivar, and they come in clear, strong colors – violet, pink, orange, red, white, and purple. Clumps slowly spread to 3ft (1m) before they die out in the middle and need dividing. Z4–8.

Achillea filipendulina **'Gold Plate'** (4) is also a sun-lover, but it's fine for a bright spot in a well-drained border with a little temporary shade. It's more spectacular than the average achillea – everything is about twice the usual size. The flat, bright yellow flowerheads are 6in (15cm) across, on 4ft (1.2m), ferny-leaved stems. The clumps spread slowly to maybe 3ft (1m) across. Z3–9.

Euphorbia characias **subsp.** *wulfenii* (5) takes as much sun as you can give it and needs well-drained soil, so it's good for a dry garden. The large, rounded heads of bright lime green flowers appear in spring but last until summer. It's evergreen and very architectural, forming a dome 4 × 4ft (1.2 × 1.2m). As with all euphorbias, the sap is irritant, so take care when you cut out the old stems. You will need to cut them close to the base when the flowers are past in mid-summer to make room for the new stems and next year's flowers. Z7–10.

Geraniums (6) include so many excellent hardy cranesbills. 'Mrs Kendall Clark' (Z4–8) has pale blue flowers with dark blue veins, and at 3ft (1m) tall, likes a bit of support. 'Wargrave Pink' (Z4–8) is low and restrained with lots of pink flowers, and the magenta-flowered *G. psilostemon* (Z5–8) makes 4ft (1.2m) high mounds.

1 *Acanthus spinosus.*
2 *Salvia uliginosa.*
3 *Phlox paniculata.*
4 *Achillea filipendulina*
  'Gold Plate'.
5 *Euphorbia characias*
  subsp. *wulfenii.*
6 *Geranium psilostemon.*

433

Not-so-tall, summer-flowering perennials

Most of these are front-of-the-border plants, and, one way or another, they put on a great show for most of summer.

Dianthus (**1**), pinks, especially the modern ones such as 'Doris', flower abundantly, and many have clove-scented flowers. They are mat-forming evergreens, 6 × 24in (15 × 60cm), for dry, sunny spots. They're short lived, so take cuttings to replace the old clumps after 2–3 years. Z5–10.

Hemerocallis (**2**), daylilies, make clumps of strap-shaped leaves, some of which are evergreen or nearly so, with straight stems topped by large, lilylike flowers in a wide range of colors and patterns. Each flower only lasts a day, but most clumps keep flowering for several weeks. Most grow to 18–36in (45–90cm) tall by as much across, depending on the cultivar. Shorter kinds are good at the front of the border – tall kinds are great fillers farther back. One of my "must-have" border perennnials. Z3–10.

Agapanthus (**3**) have strap-shaped leaves and long-stemmed spheres of blue or white flowers from July to September. Most reach 30in (75cm), but dwarf ones, half as tall, include the stunning 'Midnight Blue'. Great in a sunny, well-drained border, or in large pots in cold areas, which can be moved under glass in winter. Most aren't that hardy (Z7–10), but the Headbourne Hybrids (Z6–9) are pretty tough and will usually come through the winter in well-drained soil if given a protective mulch.

1 *Dianthus* 'Gran's Favourite'.
2 *Hemerocallis*.
3 *Agapanthus* 'Underway'.
4 *Heuchera*.

Heucheras (**4**) have good foliage – colored, marbled, or metallic – and they flower well, too, in summer, with sprays of tiny pink, green, or white bells. They like sun or shade and reach 1 × 1ft (30 × 30cm). Z3–8.

Perennials for late summer and autumn flowers

I hate coming home from my summer vacation to find the garden going over, so I make sure there are plenty of late starters ready to pick up the baton.

Sedum spectabile (5) is what we used to call the ice plant; it's second only to buddleia for attracting butterflies. It makes a 18 × 18in (45 × 45cm) cluster of waxy, blue-green leaves with flat-topped pink or white flowers perched on short, fat stems. Being semi-succulent, a well-drained, sunny spot is essential; otherwise, it just rots off in winter. Z4–9.

Anemone × hybrida (6), Japanese anemone, flowers for weeksr. The clumps do spread after a few years, so you might need to dig them up and divide them regularly to keep them in check. They grow to 3 × 3ft (1 × 1m), and the upright stems are topped by pink or white, single or semi-double flowers. They take a while to settle in – be patient. Z4–8.

Schizostylis (7) is such a reliable late bloomer, I'm amazed everyone doesn't know it. *S. coccinea* 'Major' has strappy leaves and loose spikes of rosy-red flowers. It flowers for weeks, and even longer in mild autumns. There are pink ones – 'Mrs. Hegarty' and 'Sunrise' – and *S. coccinea* f. *alba* has white flowers. Give them moist, rich soil in sun or light shade. Z7–9.

Aster novae-angliae (8), the New England aster, is the relatively mildew-free alternative to the New York asters. They look the same – big sprays of pink or mauve daisies – and late butterflies love them. For shorter ones, 30in (75cm) tall, a few twigs pushed into the clumps in late spring give enough support; the tall ones, at 4ft (1.2m), need a grow-through support from spring onward. Z4–8.

5 *Sedum spectabile* 'Brilliant'.
6 *Anemone × hybrida* 'Honorine Jobert'.
7 *Schizostylis coccinea* 'Sunrise'.
8 *Aster novae-angliae* 'Herbstschnee'.

5
6
7
8

Grasses

Grasses and grass look-alikes, such as sedges, make good partners for perennials, because their linear forms and elegant seedheads contrast well with all sorts of leaves and flowers. On a breezy day, grasses ripple – just like a field of grain – and it looks as though waves are running through the border.

Grasses are treated like most other perennials; clumps slowly increase in diameter and can be dug up and divided in spring when they outgrow their space or start balding in the middle. Cut herbaceous grasses down close to the ground in spring, so the dead rubbish is out of the way before new growth comes through; otherwise, they look like a mess.

In winter, grass seedheads, evergreen leaves, and dead stems of herbaceous plants look magical outlined in frost, so don't be in too much of a hurry to neaten them. Although evergreen grasses don't need cutting back, it's worth pulling out dead leaves in spring, and if they look scruffy. It won't harm to give them a complete haircut – fresh growth will soon have them looking as good as new again.

Grasses really earn their keep – they have wonderful foliage, spectacular seedheads, and many look good even when they have dried out in winter.

Grasses for foliage

Some of the most eye-catching grasses are those with brightly colored leaves or bold variegation; these are good for containers as well as for special places in borders.

1 *Hakonechloa macra* 'Aureola'.
2 *Imperata cylindrica* 'Rubra'.
3 *Helictotrichon sempervirens*.

***Hakonechloa macra* 'Aureola'** (1) is a choice, deciduous grass for borders – good for pots, too, if it's kept well watered. The leaves are lemon with lime green stripes. It likes sun and fertile soil that drains well but never dries completely. The clumps, 8in (20cm) tall, form elegant, waving carpets, 12in (30cm) across. Z5–9. Good at the border front, and magic with creeping *Lysimachia nummularia* 'Aurea' (Z4–8), with mats of round, golden leaves 2in (5cm) high.

***Imperata cylindrica* 'Rubra'** (2), Japanese blood grass, has bright red, semi-translucent leaves; with the sun behind them they look as if they are on fire. It's deciduous, about 15in (38cm) high, and grows slowly to make clumps 12in (30cm) across. It's fussier than some and likes a sunny site with fertile, moist but well-drained soil, which means plenty of organic matter and watering in hot weather. Z4–9.

Helictotrichon sempervirens (3) is a steel blue, evergreen grass that forms architectural tussocks and, when it's grown alone, looks like a big pincushion, 18 × 24in (45 × 60cm), punctuated by 3ft (1m) long seedheads. It needs good drainage and lots of sun and is fairly drought tolerant, making it a good plant for a gravel garden. Z4–9.

Grasses for glamorous seedheads

Whatever you do, don't let the flower arranger in your family pinch all the best seedheads. They look good in the garden, even after they become a bit battered.

Stipa tenuissima (1) grows into thick clumps of fine, green, thread-like leaves and feathery seedheads. Clumps grow to roughly 2 × 2ft (60 × 60cm). A very good grass for placing between perennial flowers toward the front of a border, and it's especially beautiful when animated by the breeze. Z7–10.

Miscanthus sinensis **cultivars** (2) include some very elegant tall, fountain-shaped plants with big, buff-colored, feathery seedheads and colored or variegated leaves. They are magnificent in the middle of borders in between perennials, since they make good contrasts without taking up too much room. *M. sinensis* 'Morning Light' is one of the best of the variegated forms, with very narrow, gray-green and white-striped leaves, 4ft (1.2m) tall (if you include the seedheads) and 2ft (60cm) across. *M. sinensis* 'China' has a slightly reddish tinge to the leaves and red flowers that turn pinkish buff as the seeds form. Z4–9.

Pennisetum villosum (3), feathertop, is aptly named. It has perhaps the most spectacular seedheads of all – big, fat, and fluffy, outstanding for the front of a border – clumps grow 18 × 24in (45 × 60cm). It needs good, fertile, well-drained soil that isn't wet in winter. . It is rather tender (Z9–10), so it won't survive a cold, wet winter unless you move them into a frost-free greenhouse. *P. alopecuroides*, fountain grass, is about the same size and even more sensational-looking, with great bristly, silvery green bottlebrush flowers that turn to feathery, purple-flushed buff seedheads when they mature. Z6–9.

1 *Stipa tenuissima.*
2 *Miscanthus sinensis* 'Undine'.
3 *Pennisetum alopecuroides* 'Woodside'.

Evergreen grasses

Evergreen grasses and sedges are good for year-round gardens, giving structure when other plants have died back as well as looking beautiful when covered in frost or seen against snow. The smaller grasses are especially good in pots if you are worried about them being lost in the garden.

Festucas (4) are the grasses to choose if you want a small, drought-tolerant tussock with true-blue foliage. Go for a good named cultivar, such as *Festuca valesiaca* 'Silbersee' (Z5–9), *F. glauca* 'Blaufuchs', or *F. glauca* 'Elijah Blue' (both Z4–8) if you want the very best color. They are all good for rock features, seaside gardens, gravel gardens, and pots, and they grow slowly to about 1 × 1ft (30 × 30cm). They have delicate, feathery seedheads. Try a small plantation of them – half a dozen or more – mulched with pieces of bluestone. The color combination is stunning.

Carex buchananii (5) is a rather upright, clump-forming, evergreen sedge with stiff, reddish brown, threadlike leaves that have coppery highlights and unusually curly tips. Growing to 2 × 1ft (60 × 30cm), it is good for pots or for the fronts of borders with good, well-drained soil containing plenty of organic matter. It does best in sun, although it doesn't want scorching conditions. Plant one specimen in a contrasting container, or mix a few in a prairie-style border. It looks especially good planted among orange flowers. Z6–9.

***Carex oshimensis* 'Evergold'** (6) makes a shaggy, green-and-gold-striped mound, 8 × 12in (20 × 30cm); again, it's a good plant for pots or the front of a border. It likes a cool, not-too-dry spot in light shade – the color fades a bit in strong sun. One plant makes a focal point, several together make an eye-catching groundcover under taller shrubs and perennials. Z6–9.

4 *Festuca glauca* 'Elijah Blue'.
5 *Carex buchananii*.
6 *Carex oshimensis* 'Evergold'.

Groundcovers

From a design point of view, groundcovers create carpets of flowers or foliage. Groundcovers can be used beneath trees or shrubs, or to help to pull everything together in a border, and they make great backdrops for spring bulbs. There is a practical angle, too, since they help to suppress weeds, so they're useful on banks or other places that are hard to weed. Mulching between the plants in spring holds back weeds and gives them extra nutrition, but give them some general-purpose organic fertilizer as well. They don't need a lot of attention, but they do need to be cleaned up once a year. Prune woody kinds lightly to keep them in shape, in spring if they flower after midsummer, and just after flowering if they flower in spring. Herbaceous kinds die down for the winter, and the dead stems need clearing away in autumn or spring.

Woody groundcovers

If you use low-growing evergreen shrubs as a groundcover, then you can be assured that they will do their job all year round.

Heaths and heathers (1) make a good evergreen groundcover for sunny sites with acidic, well-drained soil containing plenty of organic matter. They include *Erica carnea*, *Calluna vulgaris* (both Z5–7), *Daboecia cantabrica* (Z6–8), and their cultivars, growing, on average, 10 × 24in (25 × 60cm). If you choose all three, you'll have flowers almost year-round in shades of pink, purple, and white; some have gold, red, or orange leaves for extra color. Clip them lightly with shears when the flowers fade.

Cotoneaster dammeri (2) really hugs the ground as though it feels it might float away if it let go. Its leaves are dark green, oval, and deeply veined, and in winter the bright red berries stand out well. In shady spots below trees and shrubs this is a really useful plant, and although it grows little more than 6in (15cm) high, it can spread sideways for a good couple of yards (2m). Z6–8.

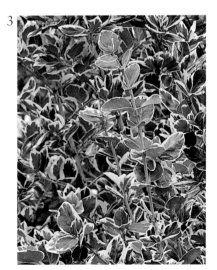

Euonymus **'Emerald Gaiety'** (3) is a more subtle alternative to the brighter 'Emerald 'n' Gold'. Where the latter's evergreen leaves are a confection of green and yellow, in 'Emerald Gaiety' they are green and creamy white, but nonetheless eye catching. Both will also climb up a wall if planted against vertical brickwork, and when planted as a groundcover they may sometimes send a shoot or two up through a shrub, but this is nothing that cannot be kept in check with a light trim in spring. Both Z5–9.

Perennial groundcovers

You could argue that there is little point in groundcovers that are not in evidence all the year round. In that case, stick to the woody evergreens. But if you want a thick mat of growth that emerges afresh each spring and disappears in winter, then these are the plants for you. Over time the clumps will expand to fill all the avilable ground, so that as well as the leaves smothering out weeds, the thick crowns will do the same.

Ajuga reptans (4), bugle, remains evergreen if conditions are kind; otherwise, it ducks down for the winter and reappears in spring. In spring, spikes of blue flowers appear, but the leaves can be green and white ('Variegata'), purplish-red ('Atropurpurea') or cream, green, and bronze ('Burgundy Glow'). Happy in sun or shade, it's not fussy about soil and grows to 3 × 24in (8 × 60cm), with 6in (15cm) flower spikes. Z3–9.

Tiarella cordifolia (5) is a useful little plant that is aptly named the foam flower. I say aptly because the domes of downy, maple-shaped leaves are covered with 1-ft (30-cm) high spires of tiny white flowers in summer, and they really do look frothy. Great in shade in any half-decent soil, spreading into 1–2-ft (30–60-cm) clumps. Z3–7.

Brunnera macrophylla (6) is like a large-flowered forget-me-not. It's a perennial that gives a welcome splash of color in early spring, making dense clumps, 1 × 2ft (30 × 60cm), of kidney-shaped leaves with sprays of delicate blue flowers floating above them. Over time it grows to carpet the ground with its attractive combination of long-stalked leaves and deep mats of flowers. Z3–7.

1 *Erica carnea* 'Springwood Pink' and *Erica × darleyensis* 'Arthur Johnson'.
2 *Cotoneaster dammeri*.
3 *Euonymus fortunei* 'Emerald Gaiety'.
4 *Ajuga reptans* 'Catlin's Giant'.
5 *Tiarella cordifolia*.
6 *Brunnera macrophylla*.

4

5

6

Bulbs

Bulbs emphasize the changing seasons, and they are a good way of packing even more plants into a limited space. Use them as carpets or clumps. Most bulbs need deep, well-drained soil. Spring bulbs are good naturalized in grass (allowed to remain undisturbed), or under shrubs where they won't be watered in summer, enjoying the dry conditions they need when they are dormant. In wet conditions, they can rot. Summer-flowering bulbs are dormant in winter. Corms and tubers also tend to be loosely referred to as bulbs, although they are really different structures botanically.

Plant hardy kinds, such as lilies, in spring or autumn; they need good drainage and rich, fertile soil. Plant frost-tender summer bulbs, such as gladioli, once the ground begins to warm up a bit, so frosts are over before the shoots appear above ground. They need digging up, drying off, and storing under cover in much the same way as dahlias. Plant spring-flowering bulbs in autumn. As a rule of thumb, plant them three to five times as deep as the height of the bulb.

Dividing snowdrops

Snowdrops have a very short dormant season, and they transplant best if they are moved while they still have their leaves – a condition known as "in-the-green." Dig up the complete clump of snowdrops. Tease them apart with your fingers. Don't use a knife or spade, or you'll damage the bulbs; if cut, they rot. Each new clump can have three to ten bulbs. Prepare the soil in the same way as for planting perennials, then plant clumps of snowdrops about 6–8in (15–20cm) apart, to the same depth that they were planted previously. Firm them in lightly and water well.

Winter- and spring-flowering bulbs

These are bravest of all our garden plants and therefore the most welcome. The real heralds of spring, everyone should grow them.

Snowdrops (1) are usually the first flowers to put in an appearance. There are many varieties with single or double flowers, and they are best naturalized under shrubs or in grass so that they can come up year after year. Clumps increase in size but can easily be divided. Z3–9.

Crocuses (2) are wonderful in shallow pots (called "pans"), which can add early spring color. Species like C. *tommasinianus* can be naturalized in grass or in beds and borders, where the amethyst spears of flowers can be enjoyed in ever increasing numbers. Z3–9.

Anemone blanda (3) produces those short white, pink, or blue, star-shaped flowers you sometimes see carpeting the ground under shrub borders in spring, and that is probably the best way to use them. They grow about 6 × 4in (15 × 10cm), and, if left to naturalize, they slowly spread and produce a thicker carpet. Add clumps of taller or more sophisticated spring bulbs for contrast. Z4–8.

Narcissus (4) species and cultivars come in a huge range. The term "daffodil" is sometimes applied only to the tall, large-trumpet ones. All the rest may be referred to as narcissi. Some of the most useful are the dwarf hybrids, such as 'Tête-à-Tête', 'February Gold' and 'Jetfire' which grow about 8–12in (20–30cm) tall. They flower earlier than large hybrid daffs, but the flowers are small and tough enough not to get battered by spring weather, and the foliage is compact, so it doesn't create the usual eyesore – it is short enough to get swallowed up by summer perennials growing up around it. I reckon they are the best for garden planting, but they are also good for spring containers. Z3–9.

Tulips (5) are much more formal-looking flowers that were always used for spring bedding, containers, and other smart settings, but small groups of large, fringed parrot tulips or elegant lily-flowered tulips – the ones with the wasp waists – look good tucked into a carpet of *Anemone blanda* or when filling niches between shrubs. All tulips need a sunny spot with well-drained soil, but most of the species (the so-called botanical tulips) are choice kinds that need particularly fast drainage and lots of sun. Where tulip bulbs are prone to soil pests that bore holes in them, allowing rot to set in, they are best dug up when the foliage dies down and stored in a cool, airy place for the summer. Plant bulbs in October or November; they don't root until then and may rot if planted earlier in wet soil. Z4–7.

5 *Tulipa* 'Ballerina' planted among forget-me-nots.

1 *Galanthus* 'Ketton'.
2 *Crocus tommasinianus*.
3 *Anemone blanda*.
4 *Narcissus* 'Tête-à-tête'.

Summer- and autumn-flowering bulbs

Gardeners who think that flowering bulbs are simply for spring miss half the fun. Summer-flowering bulbs are even more spectacular and just as indispensable.

Lilium (1), the lilies, are treated more like clump-forming perennials that happen to have bulbs instead of fibrous roots. Plant three to five of the same cultivar in a group at three to five times their own depth, then leave them alone until the clump needs dividing – do this fall. Most like well-drained, rich, fertile, neutral to acidic soil and a spot where their flowers are in sun but the ground is shaded. If you want strong scent, the best to go for are the Oriental hybrids, such as 'Star Gazer', with deep red flowers edged in white and grows about 4ft (1.2m) high; 'Casa Blanca' is pure white. The tiger lily (*L. lancifolium*) is the old favorite with black-spotted orange flowers whose petals curl back toward the center – it has no scent, but it doesn't mind light dappled shade. Tall and robust, it grows to 4–5ft (1.2–1.5m) high. I prefer to grow lilies in pots and stand them in beds and borders when they come into bud – that way I can protect them from slugs and snails, and from my misplaced hoe! They'll be happy in the same pots for three years if well fertilized. Z3–8.

1 *Lilium* 'Star Gazer'.
2 *Dahlia* 'Kenora Sunset'.
3 *Nerine bowdenii*.
4 *Allium hollandicum* 'Purple Sensation'.
5 *Gladiolus byzantinus*.

Dahlias (2) can be loud, but I have a soft spot for them because they are so obliging. At last, they are coming back into fashion. They are not hardy, so unless you live in a mild area and are prepared to risk leaving the tubers in the ground (which needs to be well drained and thickly mulched with manure or compost), dig them up and store them in a frost-free place in winter. Z8–10.

Storing dahlias

Leave dahlia plants in the ground until the leaves start turning black, showing they've been exposed to a frost – don't worry, it won't have been enough to harm the tubers underground.

Cut the plants down to about 6in (15cm) above the ground, then dig up the tubers and wash of the soil. Leave them out in the sun to dry. Store them in nets, or in stacking trays no more than one layer deep, in a frost-free place where there is plenty of air circulation. Don't store them in a warm place, or you'll prompt them to make early growth long before it's safe to replant them.

Nerine bowdenii (3) needs a hot, dry, sunny spot, perhaps at the base of a south-facing wall. The spidery pink, lilylike flowers appear in late summer or autumn, but the leaves don't appear until later, and they stand through spring. The bulbs are summer dormant, when they want hot, dry soil to prepare them for flowering. Plant them 1ft (30cm) apart and leave them undisturbed. Z8–10.

Alliums (4) are wonderful bulbs to pepper through a border where their drumstick flowers will explode like fireworks. I particularly love 'Purple Sensation', which produces lilac-purple orbs on 3-ft (1-m) high stems in summer. Plant the bulbs in fall, in curving little group that will link other groups of flowers together. The bulbs will happily push up among them. Z2–10.

Gladioli (5) are the one flower that I do have a bit of a problem with. Well, they are so stiff and starchy. Grow them on the vegetable patch if you like them for cutting, or grow the much more graceful *Gladiolus byzantinus* in your beds and borders. This deep magenta gladiolus is the one gladiolus I would plant in my garden! The large-flowered types (grow them if you want to – don't listen to me!) need to be planted 4in (10cm) deep and 1ft (30cm) apart in spring, staked when they flower, and dug up and over-wintered in a garage. *G. byzantinus* can be naturalized 2in (5cm) deep and 6in (15cm) apart in sunny, well-drained soil. Z8–10.

1 *Musa basjoo.*

Exotics

Exotic plants give you a great excuse to exercise your design skills to create a tropical look for the summer, but whether you grow them in pots on the patio or plant them out, the tender kinds are only temporary residents – when frost threatens, they need the protection of a frost-free greenhouse or conservatory.

Musa (1) is the botanical name for bananas. In the wild, bananas grow into short, squat trees with huge leaves. In the Caribbean, the leaves are tattered by the wind, but in average gardens we can have them them with their leaves whole. *Musa basjoo*, Japanese banana, is a hardier one (Z8–10), which means that it is hardy in milder parts of the country, though it may dies back to ground level in winter, so you seldom see a specimen much more than 4ft (1.2m) tall. If you can't find *M. basjoo*, then just put any banana plant you can find in the garden for the summer and move it indoors in winter. It will come as no surprise that you won't be picking huge crops of bananas, but do enjoy those squeaky leaves.

Cannas (2) were once used as "dot plants" for adding height to carpet-bedding displays, and they've made a comeback lately, thanks to the exotics craze. They grow 6–8ft (2–2.4m) tall, and have big, loud, orchidlike flowers on straight, leafy stems. Cannas come in a range of red-hot reds, oranges, and yellows, and there are some that also have colored leaves, such as 'Australia' with dark red leaves, and 'Roi Humbert' with royal purple ones. In winter they die down to big rhizomes that don't stand freezing, so they need lifting and storing under cover. Unlike dahlia tubers, they must not dry out completely, so it's best to pot them and leave them covered with potting mix that stays barely moist. Alternatively, you can grow them in big pots on the patio, where they won't grow quite so big. Z8–11.

Hedychium (3), the ginger lily, comes into the same bracket as cannas – spectacular – but not so well known or widely available. It makes large, 5–6ft (1.5–2m) clumps of straight stems with banana-like leaves and spectacular flowers with long, wispy stamens sticking out all around. Then it dies back to a rhizome that needs treating the same as an overwintering canna. *H. coccineum* 'Tara' (Z8–10) has orange flowers with red stamens. and *H. gardnerianum* (Z9–10) is lemon yellow, again with red stamens. Where marginallyhardy, leave ginger lilies in well-drained ground, but mulch them thickly to insulate the roots.

Plectranthus argentatus (4) is a loose, mound-shaped shrub, 1 × 3ft (30 × 90cm) with large, oval, silver-felty leaves that have scalloped edges. It does flower – in summer, with clusters of pale blue to off-white flowers – but it's the leaves that I grow it for. Min. 50°F (10°C).

Dicksonia antarctica (5), Tasmanian tree fern, is just about hardy outside all year round in mild, sheltered gardens; I have a small grove of them at home that has survived for several years, but instead of being evergreen, as they are back home in New Zealand, the leaves turn brown with severe cold, and the tops of the plants need protection in winter. We put inverted, lamp-shade-shaped cones of wire netting around the crowns in October and stuff them with straw. These are nailed on with metal staples and stay in place until the middle of April. Tree ferns aren't cheap plants, so if you don't want the risk, grow them in pots and put them in the greenhouse for the winter. Z9–10.

2

3

2 *Canna indica* 'Purpurea'.
3 *Hedychium coccineum* 'Tara'.
4 *Plectranthus argentatus*.
5 *Dicksonia antarctica*.

4

5

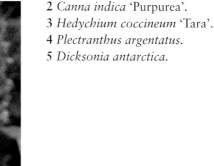

Eschscholzia californica, the California poppy, is a cheerful annual that will romp through your garden and provide a fabulous carpet of bright, sunny color.

Annuals and biennials

Forget about the small bedding plants that are used in containers or formal bedding designs (see page 384): the ones I'm thinking about are the taller, more unusual annuals and biennials for filling gaps around the garden while you are waiting for slower shrubs to grow, and for providing splashes of seasonal color in mixed borders.

Remember that annuals are the plants that will grow from seed, flower, and die within twelve months, whereas biennials grow from seed in their first year and flower and die in their second.

Hardy annuals

Handy gap-fillers for a mixed border, these have summer-long flowers. Sow them outdoors in early spring where you want them to flower if you have light, weed-free ground, or better still, sow them in pots or trays of "cells" in an unheated greenhouse or cold fram, then plant them out when they are big enough.

***Cerinthe major* 'Purpurascens' (1)** is a relative newcomer, with striking silvery blue, often silver-spotted leaves and tubular, purple-blue flowers. It makes an open spreading clump about 1 × 1ft (30 × 30cm), so plant 3–5 in a group to beef each other up. Once established they self-seed, so transplant or thin them out to leave just those you want.

***Eschscholzia californica* (2)**, California poppy, is irrepressibly cheerful; it grows quickly and easily from seed and makes a 1ft (30cm) high carpet of large, silky flowers in warm, bright colors from early summer to early autumn. It self-seeds readily (rather too readily at times), but the seedlings are easily pulled out – don't bother trying to transplant them because, typically, like most poppies, they don't like disturbance. If it's not practical to sow the seeds where you want the plants to flower, sow small pinches in fiber pots and plant out pot and all as a ready-made clump before the roots grow out through the sides.

***Helianthus annuus* (3)**, sunflowers, come in several sorts. There are giants with single stems up to 15ft (4.5m) – good for competitions, or grown up against the wall of the house. There are also modern ones that are shorter and bushier, around 3 × 3ft (90 × 90cm), with multiple stems and lots of flowers. There are also sunflowers in velvety reds, mahogany, and orange shades, as well as traditional yellow, and there are some with double flowers. They are all good for cutting and last an amazingly long time in water.

Half-hardy annuals

The taller half-hardy annuals are a bit neglected but include some real show-stoppers. Sow seeds in a indoors in early spring and raise young plants in a heated greenhouse. They can't be planted out until after the last frost. Give them a warm, sunny site with well-drained soil, and water them until established.

Cleome spinosa (4) has heads of elegant, spidery flowers with narrow, curving petals in white, pink, or magenta. It grows to 4ft (1.2m) tall. For great teamwork, grow it with cosmos.

Cosmos (5) has light, ferny foliage topped by fragile-looking, slightly wavy flowers with a yellow center. The tallest are 'Purity' (white) and 'Sensation Mixed' (various colors) at 4ft (1.2m), but there are shorter kinds at 30in (75cm), if that's more in proportion to the spot you have in mind.

Tithonia rotundifolia (6) has chunky orange or yellow daisies on strong, upright stems. 'Torch' reaches 4ft (1.2m) but there are shorter ones, such as 'Goldfinger', at 30in (75cm).

1 *Cerinthe major* 'Purpurascens'.
2 *Eschscholzia californica*.
3 *Helianthus annuus*.
4 *Cleome spinosa*.
5 *Cosmos bipinnatus* 'Purity'.
6 *Tithonia rotundifolia*.

Biennials

Biennials are old-fashioned, but some kinds are creeping back into vogue. Many will self-seed, so once you've grown one batch, it's just a case of transplanting self-sown seedlings from then on. Start the ball rolling by sowing seeds in late spring or early summer, then transplant young plants to the flowering positions in early autumn.

Campanula medium (**1**) is the Canterbury bell, which – yes – is an old-fashioned flower, but it flowers in that awkward gap between spring and summer, when you are glad of something to fill the gap between the spring bulbs and the summer perennials. The double ones, at 3 × 2ft (90 × 60cm), are particularly unusual-looking, though there are smaller cultivars and the more usual ones with single flowers in white or shades of blue and pink. Z5–8.

Dianthus barbatus (**2**), sweet Williams, certainly have old-fashioned charm, but if you can't find room for them in the garden – and my favorite spot is under roses – then they are something to grow in a row on your vegetable patch and use for cutting. That's what my grandad did. The clove scent reminds you of supercharged carnations. They grow to 1 × 1ft (30 × 30cm) or thereabouts. Z3–9.

Verbena bonariensis (**3**) is a definite must for mixed borders. You don't really see the candelabra of the stems, because they're so upright and wiry with narrow leaves. All you notice are the tufts of airy, purple, gypsophila-like flowers that look as if they are suspended in space among shrubs and tall perennials. They go with anything and look good wafting through an entire border. Plants sometimes come up for a couple of years, and they self-seed where happy. Transplant small plants in late summer to wherever you want them to flower the following year. Plants can be potted in autumn, overwintered in a greenhouse, and used for cuttings. Z7–11.

1 *Campanula medium.*
2 *Dianthus barbatus* 'Oeschberg'.
3 *Verbena bonariensis.*

Rock plants

Rock plants are little gems: tiny mat- or mound-shaped plants to enjoy close up. Raised beds and rock features, or containers, are the best places to enjoy them. When planting, water new plants in well; rock plants in containers and raised beds need watering in hot, dry weather, even after they are established. Once planted, they can stay put for years, but do protect them from slugs and snails and weed rock features regularly, since small plants are soon swamped. Clear fallen leaves from rock features in autumn, and regularly pick plants over to remove dead flowers, dead leaves, and old stems of those that die down for winter.

Spring-flowering alpines
Rock features usually look their best in the springtime, sinc this is when all the dwarf bulbs and the majority of popular rock plants are in flower.

Phlox subulata (4) grows into small spreading mats, 4 × 15in (10 × 38cm) and is smothered in late spring with red, pink, or blue flowers similar to, but much smaller than, those of the border phlox. Z3–8.

Mossy saxifrages (5) are the group of saxifrages that look exactly like patches of moss, 1 × 6in (2.5 × 15cm), and are covered with small pink or red flowers like upturned bells. *Saxifraga* 'Cloth of Gold' (Z5–7) is especially pretty; the foliage is bright yellow and lacy textured. It produces clouds of tiny white flowers.

Pulsatilla vulgaris (6), Pasque flower, makes small, upright clumps of silky foliage with large, single violet flowers. It needs alkaline soil. Allow 4 × 8in (10 × 20cm). Z5–7.

4 *Phlox subulata*
  'Alexander's Surprise'.
5 *Saxifraga exarata*.
6 *Pulsatilla vulgaris*.

Alpines for summer color

Summer is the time a lot of rock features start loosing their oomph, unless you make a point of finding plants that are at their best then.

The traditional rock garden still has a lot going for it – provided you can fit it into your own style of gardening.

1 *Campanula cochleariifolia* 'Elizabeth Oliver'.
2 *Helianthemum* 'Rhodanthe Carneum'.
3 *Lithodora*.

***Campanula cochleariifolia* 'Elizabeth Oliver'** (**1**) makes ground-hugging mats of foliage, 2 × 12in (5 × 30cm) that can spread quite a distance and pop up to start a new colony, but it's not invasive. The carpets of double, pale blue bellflowers are very welcome. Z5–7.

Helianthemum (**2**), the rock rose, is a ground-coverer with masses of papery flowers that may be white, yellow, orange, pink, or red, with a central boss of golden stamens. It grows no more than 1ft (30cm) high but a good 3–6ft (1–2m) across. Z6–8.

Lithodora (**3**), previously called Lithospermum, are old rock garden classics, with deep blue flowers on spreading, mat-shaped plants, 4 × 18in (10 × 45cm). *Lithodora diffusa* 'Grace Ward' and 'Heavenly Blue' are two good ones for Z6–8; both have star-shaped flowers from early summer to early autumn and prefer acidic, organic soil.

Evergreen alpines

Any rock feature needs its share of evergreens for year-round interest.

Sisyrinchiums (4) look like mini iris plants with stiff, upright, evergreen leaves and star-shaped flowers all summer; most of them grow to about 8 × 8in (20 × 20cm) and have purple-blue flowers. The *Sisyrinchium californicum* Brachypus Group, which has dark-veined yellow flowers, grows to only 4in (10cm). All of the sisyrinchiums are fairly drought tolerant. Z8–9.

Saxifrages (5) that are referred to as "encrusted" saxifrages are a group of species with rosettes of evergreen leaves covered in a chalky white exudation. They produce airy sprays of delicate white flowers in spring. The most spectacular is *Saxifraga* 'Tumbling Waters' (Z6–7), which makes a single, large silvery rosette, 8in (20cm) across. The plant takes several years to produce the trademark waterfall of white flowers, and then it dies.

Kabschia saxifrages make neat, tightly packed leafy mounds and flower prolifically each spring; *S.* 'Jenkinsiae' (Z6–7) is a reliable favorite with large, round, pale pink flowers in early spring. Individual plants are about 1in (2.5cm) across, but they multiply slowly to make small mounds.

Sempervivums (6), alias hen and chickens, were once grown on the roof for luck. They can survive heat, drought, and need next to no soil, but, when properly planted in a container or bed, they'll grow into much better-looking specimens. Plants are round and spiky and pile up into knobby, succulent clumps, 6 × 8in (15 × 20cm) or more across. Fat, hefty spikes of flowers emerge in June. Lots of different cultivars are available, with green or red leaves, plain or shiny. Z4–10. There is also *S. arachnoideum*, the one to grow for the cobweb effect – the rosettes are decorated with spun silk. Z5–8.

4 *Sisyrinchium* 'Californian Skies'.
5 *Saxifraga* 'Tumbling Waters'.
6 *Sempervivum* 'Raspberry Ripple'.

13 WATER FEATURES

Design considerations

When you are planning a water feature, you need to bear in mind most of the things you'd take into account if you were making a new flower bed. Think about the shape and style that is going to suit you and your type of garden – will it be formal, informal, natural, or contemporary?

A natural pond made alongside a contemporary deck to provide the best of both worlds.

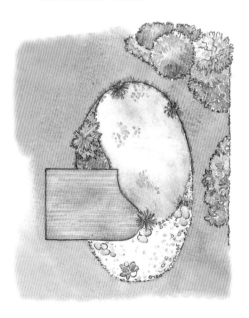

Ask yourself whether you want the main emphasis to be the water plants, fish, wildlife, or moving water itself. How much maintenance are you prepared for? If child safety is an issue, you probably won't want anything with open, standing water, even if it's only a few inches deep. Once you have organized your thoughts, choose the place that is both right for you and for whatever is likely to live in the water.

Siting ponds

A pond is incredibly hypnotic, so you'll want to put it somewhere you can sit and "switch off." The patio is a good place, or you might want to put it in a quiet spot farther down the garden where there's room for a garden bench opposite. It'll soon become your favorite outdoor retreat, where you can listen to the sound of running water and watch dragonflies, fish, and wildlife. It makes you feel drowsy just thinking about it.

A sunny spot may be pleasant for anyone water-watching, but it's absolutely essential for the well-being of the pond's complex

Water world

Water plants need sunlight to photosynthesize, which is how they oxygenate the water. You can often see tiny bubbles coming up from them on a sunny day – and that's what enables fish and other water wildlife to survive. Oxygen is also crucial for all sorts of minute pond life that clean the pond, right down to the friendly bacteria that clean up after everybody else.

Don't panic if your pond looks murky (*top*), and don't add tap water in the hope of clearing it; you will only make matters worse. The pond water will clear itself once it corrects its natural balance (*below*). Remove any leaves that might fall on the surface of the pond, but otherwise leave the pond undisturbed for a few weeks, and you will start to see a difference.

ecosystem. Keep your pond well away from big trees and shrubs, even though they may seem to be an obvious background. Given half a chance, the roots can grow through the lining of a pond and make it leak, and repairing a pond liner is no joke. The leaves will also fill it up in autumn and foul the water.

Allow yourself enough space for a pond. You'll always need more room than you think. A very small, shallow pond isn't suitable for fish; the water will heat up too much in summer and can freeze solid in winter, which wrecks your water plants, too. As a rule of thumb, don't make a pond any smaller than 2ft (60cm) deep, and at least 3 × 5ft (1 × 1.5m) across – preferably 2ft (60cm) or so bigger. Don't imagine you can cram it into a corner of your property, either. You need to leave enough room all around it for reaching in to do essential maintenance. End of lecture.

Both the movement and sound of water can be enjoyed in this simple feature. Water is pumped up through a central aperture in the stone column and then falls into a hidden tank, from which it is recirculated.

Small water features

If you choose a wall fountain or a pebble pool with nothing living in the water, then you can construct them in sun or shade. These features are a good way to add a sparkling focal point to a shady part of the garden – but you'll still find them easier to keep clean, and the pumps will run more smoothly if they don't get clogged up with fallen leaves.

If you are worried about small children using the garden, these are safe water features since they don't contain standing water, but you'll need to put them close to an electricity supply to power the pump. Otherwise, go for a very basic type of water feature; a wide plant container without any drainage holes in the bottom, and a floating solar fountain, or a few temporary floating plants, such as water hyacinth (*Eichhornia crassipes*), on the top, which you just stand outside for the summer.

Ponds

There are all sorts of ponds to choose from to suit any garden style. Formal ponds have a geometrical shape, usually a circle or a rectangle, and normally have vertical sides. They are used mostly for waterlilies and goldfish, with a few oxygenating plants under the water surface to keep things healthy. Informal ponds have an

Where there's a bit of space to spare, a large sheet of water, a board bridge, and swaths of planting are nothing short of spectacular.

irregular, more natural-looking shape that suits the average family garden much better. This type will have planting shelves around several sides, on which to stand baskets of marginal plants. They should have a sloping pebble "beach" so that birds can get in to bathe safely, and frogs and other critters (who will drop by for a drink) can climb out.

Wildlife ponds are more natural still; here, *all* of the sides are gently sloping. You don't tend to find the same formally ornamental marginal plants growing around the sides, but bog plants will be at home in the soggy margins, and a few deep-water or floating aquatics are happy in the middle. Instead of putting in fish, which will feed on naturally occurring water creatures, most wildlife gardeners prefer to wait for tadpoles and newts to turn up.

Pond care calendar

Don't just dig it, fill it, and leave it. With a little regular maintenance, your pond will be good to look at all the year round.

Spring
Anticipate that the pond water will turn green in spring; it should clear itself naturally after a few months, though a brand-new pond may stay green for the whole of its first year. Be patient.

Pull out blanketweed – those clumps of stringy green slime suspended in the water – with a wire-toothed rake, taking care not to puncture the liner. Always leave it on the pool side overnight, so that any pond creatures within it can escape back into the water, then consign it to the compost pile. Fish out duckweed with a fine-mesh net. Try to avoid using chemical "cures" for algae or blanketweed, and instead use one of the biological treatments that won't harm wildlife or pond plants. They work by increasing the numbers of naturally occurring, beneficial, water-cleaning bacteria.

Summer
Feed fish between May and September. Once the pond is established, the fish will also eat snails' eggs, mosquito larvae, and other wild food for themselves. If you want a natural wildlife pool, fish are best left out altogether. Pull out handfuls of oxygenators regularly if the pond looks too full of them.

Autumn
When the pond has been there several years, you'll need to remove the excess deposits of silt that form naturally on the bottom. Don't empty the pond of water; just bale out as much as you can with a small plastic bowl, taking care not to perforate the liner. Don't be too thorough – leave a good 1in (2.5cm) layer of muck in the bottom for water plants to root into.

With the exception of the evergreen oxygenator *Lagarosiphon*, most aquatics are perennials that die down in winter. To prevent debris buildup, remove free-floating plants once they are killed by cold, cut down marginals flush with the surface of the water, and pull out decaying lily leaves. Keep autumn leaves off the pond with a net.

Winter
Little or no pond maintenance is needed during the winter. If you have fish in the pond, however, place a section of log or large plastic ball on the surface. Either helps to absorb the force of ice forming on the surface; also, if there's just a little ice, you can pour hot water over the ball or log to open up a breathing hole for fish.

Dealing with excavated soil

Use the soil removed when excavating a pond to make a raised bed, bank, or rock garden somewhere else in the garden – not right behind the pool; it will always look like a spoil heap. Alternatively, if the topsoil is good, use it in beds and borders around the garden. Nasty, heavy clay is best disposed of in the footings for a path or paving, or have it taken away.

How to... build a pond

You'll see ready-made plastic or fiberglass ponds for sale in garden centers, but it's a lot cheaper and easier to do it yourself by digging a hole the shape and size that you want and then lining it with flexible butyl rubber or plastic sheeting to make it hold water.

Design your pond first, choosing a shape that fits easily into a rectangle based on the size of the lining material available, so you don't have to order special sizes, which are more expensive. Avoid having tight, fussy curves or acute angles; they are difficult to fit the liner around and can create weak banks that easily cave in.

Calculating how much liner you need

Measure the pond length, multiply the depth at the deepest point by two, and add the two together. Add 20in (50cm) for overlap at the edges. Then do the same thing with the width. Those two figures tell you what size sheet you need, with enough spare to tuck in around the sides.

What you need

- *spade*
- *level*
- *bottle of dry sand for marking out*
- *board long enough to reach right over the pond*
- *soft building sand to cushion the liner from sharp stones*
- *sheet of butyl pond liner*
- *pool liner underlay, wooden pegs, and craft knife*
- *paving or sod for edging*
- *hose*

1 Clear the site to leave the soil bare and reasonably flat. Mark out the shape of the pond by trickling dry sand from a bottle.

2 Dig it out. Make the bottom of the pond firm, flat, and stone-free. Dig at least a third of the area 2ft (60cm) deep for fish and deep-water plants. The rest can be 18in (45cm) deep for most other aquatics. If you want marginal plants, make flat "shelves" at the sides, 6in (15cm) wide and 8in (20cm) below the surface. Make very gently sloping edges where you want "beaches."

3 Lay the board over the hole and rest a level on top. The top of the pond sides must be level; otherwise, the water will look as if it's all run down to one end. If they're not level, shift some soil to even it out – it must be right. Check the levels from front to back and from side to side.

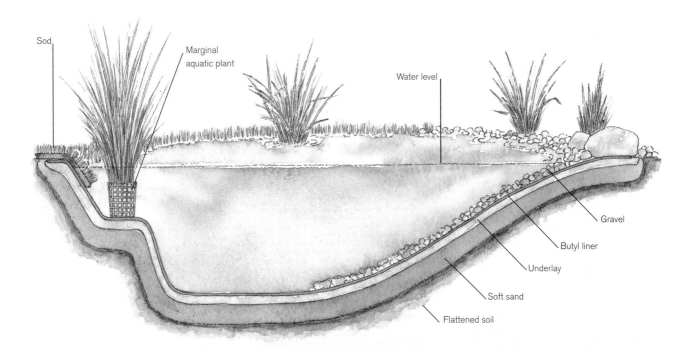

Sod

Marginal
aquatic plant

Water level

Gravel

Butyl liner

Underlay

Soft sand

Flattened soil

4 Spread a 1in (2.5cm) layer of soft sand over the base, shelves, and slopes. Then cover the whole area in pond underlay. Peg this into place. With one person at each end, lift the folded liner over the pond, position it centrally, and carefully unfold it. Don't drag the liner about too much or walk on it. Put a few bricks on the edge of the liner to prevent it from blowing around.

5 Start filling the pond with water by leaving a hose running. As the increasing volume of water weighs the liner down into the hole, tug the folds of the liner so that they cling around the curves in small, neat folds. When the pond is full, trim the liner to a 1ft (30cm) overlap.

6 Laying paving stones at the rim of the pool will hide the liner, which could decompose if exposed to the sun. Alternatively, for a natural-looking wildlife pond, lay sod so that it overlaps the rim and runs down into the water. It will be quite happy and makes a nice edging. Lower the plants into place, and allow oxygenating plants six weeks to establish before introducing fish.

Water features

You can create all sorts of water features by starting with a basic pebble-pool kit, which you can buy at most garden centers, and a pump that you have to buy separately. The kit consists of a reservoir container that you sink into the ground (with the pump inside), and a lid that covers it. The water outlet spout on top of the pump pokes out through the middle of the lid. When it's been installed, you lay a carpet of pebbles over the top, and the water appears to just run away – it's actually going back into the hidden reservoir container and being endlessly recycled.

Decorative detail

There's a lot you can do with a basic pebble pool, depending on how you finish it. Like an iceberg, nine-tenths of it is underground, so all you see is the decorative bit on top. You can pile a heap of pebbles around the water outlet from the top of the pump, so that the water runs over the stones and looks like a small natural spring. If you want something more elaborate, either fit a nozzle on the top so the water sprays out as a fountain, or fit an ornament or a millstone over the top of the spout for the water to run over. All sorts of ornaments are sold especially for use with water features – such as terracotta jugs, seashells, or what have you – and they've had a hole drilled through them for the water to run into or out of. The choice is up to you.

If you fit anything over the top of the water outlet, make sure there's a good seal between the outlet and your ornament; otherwise, the water will leak out there instead of being forced to come out where you want it. Put everything together and make sure it is working properly before you cover the lid of the fountain with pebbles.

Care of water features

Top up the water once a week in spring and summer, because there are bound to be some losses from evaporation.

The only way to prevent algae from forming on the pebbles and anything else that stays wet all the time the pump is running is to add a chemical algicide to the water.

In cold areas, where there may be a risk of the water in the reservoir or pipework freezing in winter, dismantle the water feature and clean and store the pump indoors to avoid damage. Generally speaking, though, the pump is best kept running for as much of the year as possible.

Pumping power

A pebble pool needs a power supply to run the pump, so it must be located close enough to a socket for the cord to reach. It can be plugged in indoors, if you drill through the wall close to a socket and allow room for the transformer. If you have power in a shed or conservatory, you could also plug in there. You must always connect the pump to a circuit breaker for safety. Employ a qualified electrician if electricity is a mystery to you.

How to... **build a water feature**

It's the perfect job for the weekend – not too strenuous, and capable of being constructed in the smallest corner of the garden. But if you plan on using heavy lumps of rock, enlist the help of a friend, and if you are hazy when it comes to the use of electricity, then get a competent electrician to lay the cabling for you. If you are not sure about which sort of pump you need, or indeed which size, explain to someone at your local garden center what you are planning to build, and they will be able to advise you what equipment will best meet your needs.

What you need

- *plastic reservoir*
- *submersible pump*
- *drilled rock or monolith*
- *wire grid and netting*
- *length of hose and silicone sealant*
- *screwdriver and craft knife*
- *pebbles or shale*
- *electricity supply*
- *spade and level*

1 Dig a hole large enough to take the reservoir. Remember that the larger the reservoir, the less frequently you will need to refill it. Sink the reservoir into the ground and check that it is level. Pack it with soil or sand so that it is stable. The pump needs to be attached to the electric cable by an electrician, and then placed in the bottom of the reservoir. Fasten a length of hose to the pump outlet so that it can be fed through the stone. Add the water, and check that the pump is functioning.

2 In order to stabilize the monolith, the wire grid with finer netting over the top is now put in place, the hose threaded through it, and the mesh then covered with shale. The hose is then fed up through the monolith, which is maneuvered into the upright position and checked for stability. The flat cut top of the monolith needs to be checked to make sure that it is level, so that the water will flow evenly down all faces of the rock.

3 It is important that the hose is sealed into position at the top using silicone. This ensures that the water runs down the face of the rock rather than down the inside of the aperture. The protruding piece of hose is cut off with a craft knife and the silicone allowed to dry for at least a couple of hours before the fountain is switched on.

Water plants

Plants are essential in ponds. They offer bed and breakfast facilities and act as shelters for the pond's various inhabitants, and they provide vital services like air conditioning and waste disposal. This is all very necessary, because each year a substantial layer of fish manure and decomposing plant material is deposited at the bottom of a pond.

Once a pond has grown into the landscape it will look as though it has always been there.

Plants also look good, providing foliage and flowers all summer. There are four types of water plants – deep-water aquatics, marginals, submerged oxygenators, and free-floaters. For a pond to function properly, you need to include a few plants from each of the first three groups. Free-floaters are an optional extra.

Marginals, as the name suggests, are happiest at the margins of a pool, whereas the others prefer their roots to be in the water. Water plants tend to be grown in large, net-sided pots or plastic planting baskets, which stand on the planting shelves or floor of the pond. They prevent plants from spreading too fast and make them easier to lift out when dividing them. Plants are sold in small pots and should be potted on into baskets about 10in (25cm) or more for the pond.

Water plants have evolved to live in low-nutrient environments, so use special aquatic soil mix for potting them. Don't use garden soil; it may pollute the water if it contains traces of garden products. And don't use ordinary potting mix; it contains nutrients that encourage algae to grow in the water and turn it green. If fertilizer gets into the pond – for instance, if it's washed out of surrounding beds by rain – it will encourage a green algal bloom.

Even the nitrates present in tap water can be enough to cause an algal or blanketweed problem; use rainwater to top up ponds if you can. Each time you remove excess water weeds, blanketweed, or overgrown plants from the pond, you're removing a source of nutrients from the water.

Pond life is sensitive to chemicals of any kind, so take great care not to use pesticides or weedkillers anywhere near a pond. If you use chemical water treatments for pond problems, always check that they're safe for wildlife, fish, and the plants in your pond. Many products are suitable only for water features where nothing lives. I'd rather spend my time getting the balance right.

Dividing water plants

Like dry-land perennials, marginals and other water plants need dividing when the clumps get too big. Divide them in early spring, but don't do it unless you really need to; they're ready to split if they stop flowering or the leaves start growing vertically instead of horizontally. Fast-growing native plants, such as flowering rush (*Butomus umbellatus*), may need splitting every two years; water irises and dwarf cattail (*Typha minima*) within 3–4 years, and waterlilies only after 5–7 years.

Lift the basket out of the pond, taking care not to tear the liner, and swirl it around to let tadpoles and other creatures back into the water. Tip the plant out or, if the roots have grown through the sides of the basket, cut the container to release it. Split the clump with a sharp spade, as you would with a border perennial. Choose a strong piece with healthy young shoots to replant, then dump the rest on the compost pile. Replant into a basket of aquatic soil mix. Top with gravel to hold the soil mix in place and to prevent fish from disturbing it. When repotting waterlilies, bury only the roots – the rhizomes should sit on the surface of the soil mox. Sink the baskets slowly back into the pond. Don't worry if the water goes cloudy – it'll soon clear.

> ### Planting depth
>
> *The one thing you must do when you buy a new plant is to give it the right depth of water to grow in – and when plant labels and reference books talk about depth, they mean the depth of water over the top of the roots, not the depth of water you ought to stand the pot in. Yes, it can be confusing until you get the hang of it.*

Sometimes it's possible to pry out part of an overcrowded aquatic plant with an old knife, removing a good portion of the roots as well as some shoots. The parent plant can be topdressed and put back in the water, while the youngster is potted up in its own basket of aquatic soil mix, top-dressed with gravel, and returned to the pond to grow on its own.

Marginal plants

These are plants that grow in shallow water around the edge of the pond. Besides looking good, they do all sorts of good work for the pond community. Their vertical stems provide footholds for dragonfly nymphs to climb out of the water when it's time for them to turn into adult dragonflies, and their roots use up a lot of minerals in the water that would otherwise feed algae, so, like other water plants, they behave rather like vegetable water-filters.

Renovating an overgrown pond

If a pond gets completely overcrowded and messy, it's time for a complete renovation job. Spring is the time to do it. You'll be up to your armpits in mucky water for hours, but it'll look a lot better when you've finished.

Take out all the plants, including the submerged aquatics, clear out as much silt as you can, all except about 1in (2.5cm) of it anyway, leaving the original "dirty" water behind. It's much better than new tap water, with its load of chlorine and nitrates. And this way, you can leave fish and frogs alone and don't need to worry about tadpoles.

Sort out your plants. Some will be worth dividing and replanting, but those that aren't up to much are best tossed on the compost pile so you can start again with new ones.

The water should settle within a few days. Take the time to neaten up around the edges, freshen up the surrounding planting, whip out any weeds, and top-dress the ground with more pebbles or gravel.

Butomus umbellatus (**1**), flowering rush, has no leaves, just green, reedlike stems, 30in (75cm) tall, which, in late summer, are topped by 3ft (90cm) stems of pink flowers. It grows in mud or in up to 5in (13cm) of water. Best in a medium to large pond. Z5–11.

Sagittaria sagittifolia (**2**), arrowhead, is a potentially invasive plant, but if you weed out the self-sown seedlings from the sludge in the bottom of the pond each spring, it's controllable. It grows 18in (45cm) high, with arrowhead-shaped leaves and three-cornered white flowers arranged in loose tiers up each spike in August. If you like this but want more cultivated looks and less of a spreader, go for 'Flore Pleno' – double flowers, so no seedlings. It grows a bit taller but more slowly. For 3–6in (8–15cm) of water. Z6–11.

Typha minima (**3**) is the one to go for if you have a soft spot for cattails. The dwarf cattail is only 15in (38cm) tall, with nearly round, brown "tails" impaled near the tops of some of the stems. It's well behaved and good for a small natural pond, as well as the garden kind, growing in 1–4in (2.5–10cm) of water. Z3–11.

Cotula coronopifolia (4), brass buttons, is good in small ponds. It's a self-seeding annual, so once you have it, new plants reappear in the same spot each year. A neat clump, 16in (5cm) high, with flowers like petal-less daisies – just the yellow boss in the middle. Z7–9.

Iris laevigata (5), Japanese water iris, flowers throughout erly summer with large, single to semi-double blue or white flowers. The rest of the time, clumps of upright, 18in (45cm) long, sword-shaped leaves make a background for the later flowers of other plants. Grow them in mud or in up to 3in (8cm) of water. Z4–9.

Lobelia cardinalis (6), the cardinal flower, is a wet-loving version of the well-known bedding plant; but it's nothing like it. This grows to 3 × 2ft (90 × 60cm), with spikes of cardinal red flowers in summer. Z3–9. The cultivar 'Queen Victoria' (Z4–9) is similar, but 2ft (60cm) taller and proportionately wider, with dark red flowers and beet red leaves – there aren't many pond plants this colorful. Grow them in mud or in up to 3in (8cm) of water, and be prepared to watch plenty of seedlings appear.

1 *Butomus umbellatus.*
2 *Sagittaria sagittifolia.*
3 *Typha minima.*
4 *Cotula coronopifolia.*
5 *Iris laevigata.*
6 *Lobelia* 'Queen Victoria'.

Deep-water aquatics

These are plants that grow in much deeper water, so stand their baskets on the bottom of the pond a little way out from the banks. Some deep-water plants grow up out of the water, but others have leaves that float on the surface.

Aponogeton distachyos (**1**), water hawthorn, has long, oval leaves, like stretched waterlily pads that float on the water, and odd-shaped clusters of white flowers that stick up just above the surface and look like mouthfuls of pearly-white sharks' teeth – a sort of friendly "Jaws." Water hawthorn is a suerb all-around water plant; it's the first to start flowering each year and the last to stop. It's in business from spring to autumn, and it's also scented – the flowers have a strong scent of hawthorn that, on still summer evenings, is strong enough to carry past the edge of the pond and fill the air with fragrance. At about 2ft (60cm) across, water hawthorn is small enough for even the tiniest ponds as long as there's at least 1ft (30cm) of water. Don't submerge it more than 2ft (60cm) deep. Z9–10.

Orontium aquaticum (**2**), golden club, looks like a plant that can't quite make up its mind whether to lie flat on the water or stick out, so some leaves do one thing and the rest do the other. The flowers look like gold-tipped, white birthday-cake candles poking up out of the water in spring. The leaves grow in a circle about 18in (45cm) in diameter. Give it 1ft (30cm) of water to grow in. Z6–11.

***Zantedeschia aethiopica* 'Crowborough'** (**3**) is the best of the calla lilies for growing outdoors; it's hardier than most. When it's grown in a pond, it can be left outside all year in many areas, since 6in (15cm) of water is enough to insulate it from cold. It has large, arrowhead-shaped leaves and big white spathes that appear through-out summer. It grows about 24 × 18in (60 × 45cm). Z (7?)8–10.

1 *Aponogeton distachyos.*
2 *Orontium aquaticum.*
3 *Zantedeschia aethiopica* 'Crowborough'.

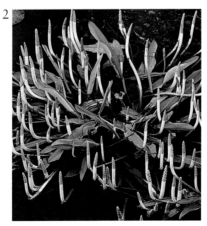

Waterlilies

Waterlilies are just another type of deep-water aquatic, with floating leaves and roots growing in a planting basket on the bottom of the pond, but because they are so popular, there is a huge choice. If you've ever read *The Tales of Beatrix Potter*, you'll have a soft spot for waterlilies. I still can't look at a lily pad without thinking of Mr. Jeremy Fisher.

The things to check before buying a waterlily are the spread and the planting depth, or you might have a problem. Many waterlilies were bred about a century ago, when people had large lakes to accommodate them – cramped into a modern garden pond, they'd be crawling up the walls after a couple of years. If yours is a small pond, 4 × 6ft (1.2 × 2m) or less, with 2ft (60cm) of water to stand a waterlily in, these would be my top three. Don't get carried away; in a pond that size, one waterlily is all you'll have room for. If you want a white one – and I would – that's a problem. Most grow too big for a small pond, and the dwarf white *N. pygmaea* 'Helvola' is probably too small. About 18in (45cm) across, it's free- flowering and has attractively marbled leaves. If you have a spot where it won't be swamped by more vigorous plants and where there'll be 6–10in (15–25cm) of water over the crown, try it. All Z4–11.

Nymphaea **'James Brydon'** (**4**) has purple-splashed leaves and double, bright orange-red flowers, and it's one of the most prolific you can find for a small pond, making a circle of leaves 3ft (90cm) across.

Nymphaea **'Froebelii'** (**5**) has darker red flowers that are more bowl-shaped, and it also grows to 3ft (90cm) across.

Nymphaea **'Laydekeri Liliacea'** (**6**) has pale pink flowers and bronze-marbled leaves; it'll spread about 2ft (60cm) across and has slightly smaller flowers than the other two.

The right spot for waterlilies

Waterlilies are quite fussy plants. They won't grow under the spray from a fountain or in moving water, so forget about combining them with fountains and waterfalls – it just won't work. And if you try to grow them somewhere they aren't in full sun all day, they won't flower well – but get it right, and you are on to a winner, because a decent waterlily will flower all summer once it's had a year or two to become properly established.

4 *Nymphaea* 'James Brydon'.
5 *N.* 'Froebelii'.
6 *N.* 'Laydekeri Liliacea'.

If you have a large expanse of water, you can really pack in the plants and still see the water beneath.

1 *Eleocharis acicularis.*
2 *Ranunculus aquatilis.*
3 *Eichhornia crassipes.*
4 *Hydrocharis morsus-ranae.*
5 *Stratiotes aloides.*

Oxygenators

Oxygenators are plants that live under the water, and their job is to provide the oxygen that is needed by fish and other pond life, who also use the ferny stems of "water-weeds," as they are sometimes called, to hide and breed in.

Some oxygenators are far too vigorous for a small pond and fill it with slippery stems that you then need to weed out regularly in summer. Really and truly, the most common one, *Lagarosiphon major*, comes into this category, but it's the one that is sold everywhere. It's evergreen, so instead of dying down in winter, like most of the others, it stays put and provides valuable hiding places for fish. It's also one of the first to get its feet under the table when you set up a new pond, so I'd bear with it. Just drop two or three of the weighted bundles they sell at pond centers into the water, and they'll root just as they are. It's also called *Elodea crispa*, but for heaven's sake, don't be tricked into the Canadian pond weed, *E. canadensis* – it really is a monster.

Eleocharis acicularis (1), hair grass, is exceptionally well behaved. Grow it in small pots or in the silt on the bottom of a pond. It looks just like tufts of green hair, 6in (15cm) high and spreads slowly, to maybe 1ft (30cm) across, so you can leave it ticking away without having to worry about underwater weeding. In water 6–12in (15–30cm) deep, it's just about evergreen in winter. Z7–11.

Ranunculus aquatilis (2), water crowfoot, is a much better-looking oxygenator, because its working parts, which look like swirling green threads, are under the water. On the surface, it grows as a buttercup-like plant with branching stems, floating leaves, and single, white, yellow-centered flowers in late spring and early summer. It's not a big plant, maybe 2–3ft (60–90cm) across, so you shouldn't have problems with it in your average small pond. Z5–8.

1

2

Floating plants

Free-floating plants are a good way of providing instant shade for the surface of a new pond, before newly planted waterlilies and water hawthorn have had time to fill out and cover their rightful area. Some floating plants are not hardy and die off completely in winter, but some duck down in winter then reappear each spring. They all look fascinating, but don't be surprised if they all end up at the far end of the pond when it's windy, since they don't have any anchors.

Eichhornia crassipes (3), water hyacinth, is a tropical plant that is killed by frost, so it's no good putting it out until after frost, since cold weather tends to blacken the edges. In a warm summer, its leaf rosettes make small knobby clumps rather like leafy rafts, but don't expect to see any flowers unless you have hot summers. Should that put you off growing it? No; it's a fun plant, and children will love dissecting its foam-packed floatation chambers. Min. 34°F (1°C)

Hydrocharis morsus-ranae (4), frogbit, looks just like a minute waterlily, with leaves 1in (2.5cm) across and white, three-petaled flowers that are about the same size as the leaves. By midsummer, the original plants have produced "pups," which grow strung together by fine strands. They spend winter as resting buds in the silt on the floor of the pond, then reappear late next spring. Z6–11.

Stratiotes aloides (5), water soldier, makes big spiky tufts, which are its chief attraction. Again a novelty that sinks to the bottom of the pond in winter and gradually rises to the surface once more as the water warms up in spring. Z5–11.

How many plants?

Plants with floating leaves help keep the water cool and provide some cover for pond-life, which is vital for keeping the ecology of the entire pond in balance.

You need to plant enough of these so that by the time they have had a couple of years to establish themselves, they cover between a third and a half of the pond's surface with foliage by midsummer. Use the sizes given here to help calculate how many you need for a pond of any size.

3

4

5

Bog gardens

Out in the countryside, natural ponds are often surrounded by boggy areas, where drifts of water-loving wildflowers form a natural backdrop to the water. At home, it instinctively feels right to make a bog garden next to a pond. A bog garden is also the answer to landscaping trouble spots, such as natural hollows where water gathers and other places where the soil always stays wet.

A bog garden has a lushness about it that few other parts of the garden can match.

Making a bog garden on wet ground

When you have a patch of ground that never really dries out, the easiest way to tackle it is to turn it into a bog garden. All you do is dig in lots of well-rotted compost, manure, or some bags of composted bark to improve the soil and make it more fertile. Then, you put in plants that are natural moisture-lovers. Maintenance is simple. Mulch heavily each spring with more compost or bark. This replenishes nutrients and helps prevent the ground from drying out in summer, when the water table will be at its lowest. Sprinkle a spot of organic general fertilizer around at the same time. That's all there is to it.

Since most bog plants are perennials, it's not difficult to have a bog garden that looks wonderful in spring, summer, and early autumn, but there won't be much to see in winter unless you add a bit of window dressing. Chunky tree stumps, white birch logs, and other boggy paraphenalia all help. If space permits, I'd strongly suggest putting in a framework of water-loving shrubs that will look their best in winter, such as red-stemmed dogwood (*Cornus alba* 'Sibirica') and scarlet willow (*Salix alba* subsp. vitellina 'Britzensis').

Around the edge of a sunken bog garden, it's worth planting resilient shrubs, such as birches, cultivated elders, (try *Sambucus nigra* f. *laciniata*, with cut leaves and great autumn color), or shallow-rooted evergreens. They'll make a bit more of a background and emphasize the amphitheater feel.

Where the ground is slightly higher, it'll also be better drained and a tad drier, so you don't need to worry about sticking to real bog plants around the rim – just don't go for plants that actually need sharp drainage.

Making a bog garden where it's not boggy

When you want to make a bog garden where the ground is not naturally wet, it takes a lot more effort.

For a start, you need to treat the project a bit like making a pond, except you don't need to be quite as fussy. Dig a hole 2ft (60cm) deep and 3–4ft (1–1.2m) across, with sloping sides. Then line it. There's no need to buy a proper pond liner – any old pliable plastic will do. It doesn't even matter if there are the few odd holes in it – if you use a good sheet of new plastic, you need to stab a few drainage holes in it with a knife anyway. It's easiest to do when the liner is in place; just stand inside and make a dozen holes in a band all around and just above the bottom, so that water sits in the bottom of the hole but can leak out if it gets too deep.

On normal soil, you don't even need enough plastic to reach right up the sides of the hole, but if you have very free-draining, light, sandy soil, it's worth doing to reduce sideways movement of water, which will soon drain your "bog" in dry weather.

When you've dug your hole, refill it after mixing lots of organic matter with the soil you originally took out. Then plant with moisture-lovers and mulch as before.

Making a bog garden next to a pond

If you are making a bog garden right next to a pond, there's one thing you *must* do, and that is keep the two features separate. There's one big difference between bog garden and pond conditions – bog plants need fertile soil, while the very last thing a pond wants is nutrients in the water.

Construct your bog garden 1ft (30cm) or more away from the pond. Make sure that the edge of the bog garden is a little bit lower than the rim of the pond – that way, in case of heavy rain, the pond overflows into the bog and not vice versa.

If you have enough room and it suits the layout of that part of the garden, then separate the two with a path. You'll find it very handy for getting at both bog and pond when you're working on them, and without stepping in either.

Bog plants

"Bog plants" is simply a term for herbaceous perennials that are happy growing in permanently wet or damp soil.

You can often get away with growing the sort of marginal pond plants that will put up with growing in mud – which is what the plant labels mean when they say 0in/0cm of water – as long as you reserve the very wettest spots for them. But most moisture-loving perennials can be grown in both a proper bog garden and a damp border, just as long as the ground doesn't dry out badly in summer.

Always check plant sizes before you buy, since a lot of bog plants grow enormous and, even if you are making a big bog garden, do include some smaller plants toward the front; otherwise, all you'll see is a sea of stalks.

Small bog plants

These are the ones to go for in small bog gardens and at the edges of larger ones, especially if they're close to a pond; you don't want lots of leaves and dead flowers falling in to pollute the pond water.

Mimulus cardinalis (1) has orange-red, mask-shaped flowers that cover upright, 18in (45cm) tall clumps from midsummer to autumn. You could think of it as moisture-loving bedding – if it survives winter, it's a bonus. The original plants creep slightly, but it'll also self-seed gently, so you don't usually lose it entirely. Z6–9.

Lysimachia nummularia ‘Aurea’ (2), golden creeping Jenny, looks like rows of gold coins strung together and laid on the ground. It has golden yellow flowers all summer. It'll cover an area roughly 2ft (60cm) across in summer, and it's only 2in (5cm) high. The foliage color is brightest in some sun; in light shade, it's lime green. Z4–8.

1 *Mimulus cardinalis*.
2 *Lysimachia nummularia* ‘Aurea’.
3 *Hosta* ‘Gold Standard’.
4 *Houttuynia cordata* ‘Chameleon’.
5 *Primula rosea*.

Hostas (3) are grown mainly for their large, blue-green, golden green, or variegated leaves. There are dozens that grow to around the 12–18in (30–45cm) mark. The shorter kinds can be dotted evenly around as a groundcover, while clumps of larger types are good for between patches of summer-flowering perennials. The flowers of most hostas are subtle – spikes of off-white or bluish mauve bells in early summer, though in some they are quite handsome. They are excellent plants for growing in light dappled shade, but as long as the ground stays quite moist, they'll also tolerate a fair bit of sun.

Hostas are slow to spread, so you don't usually need to divide them for 5–6 years. It often takes them a year or two to settle down afterward, so don't do it until you really need to. The things you must worry about when you grow hostas are slugs and snails; given half a chance, they can reduce the plants to lace doilies and Swiss cheese overnight. Z3–8.

***Houttuynia cordata* 'Chameleon'** (4) is a 6in (15cm) high scrambler with ivy-shaped leaves variegated in cream, red, and green. It doesn't appear above ground until early summer but soon spreads to make a ground-covering mat, 3ft (90cm) or more across. The flowers, in midsummer, are single and white with a yellow cone in the middle, but there aren't many of them, and they're not the main attraction. It creeps by underground stems, so it's an easy plant to divide. Z6–11.

Primula rosea (5) is one of the very early-flowering bog plants, with shocking pink flowers, but that early in the season you are grateful for anything with that much punch. It's a tiny plant about 6in (15cm) high, so plant it in groups for impact. The leaves are soon swallowed up by neighboring plants and it disappears in summer; mark the spot so you don't hoe it out. Z3–8.

3

4

5

Medium-sized bog plants

Plants in the 2–3ft (60–90cm) range aren't usually too big or spreading to rule them out for smaller bog gardens, where one of each is going to be enough. In a big bog garden, grow them in groups so that they'll make a bigger splash.

Astilbes (**1**) enjoy the same conditions as hostas, and the two contrast well with each other. Astilbes make rather upright clumps with ferny foliage and plumes of fluffy flowers in mauve, purple, red, pink, or white. Again sizes vary according to cultivar, but one that's always popular is 'Fanal', which grows to about 24 × 18in (60 × 45cm), with deep red flowers. Z4–9.

Lythrum salicaria **'Blush'** (**2**) is an improved form of the purple loosestrife – supposedly noninvasive, and with delicate, soft pink spikes on 3–4ft (1–1.2m) tall, bushy plants. If you don't have room for anything as big as 'Blush', then go for *Lythrum virgatum* 'The Rocket', which is a really neat upright clump, 2 × 2ft (60 × 60cm), with bolt-upright, pink flowers like candles. Both flower from early to late summer. May escape into natural wetlands. Z4–9.

1 *Astilbe × arendsii.*
2 *Lythrum salicaria* 'Blush'.
3 *Primula florindae.*
4 *Iris sibirica* 'Butter and Sugar'.
5 *Lysimachia clethroides.*

Primroses (3) are plants I'd never want to be without in a bog garden, but you need to choose the right ones. *P. florindae* (Z3–8) is the giant cowslip, growing to 2 × 2ft (60 × 60cm), which has big leaves and stems topped by a shaggy head of nodding, yellow "cowslip" flowers in July. The candelabra primroses are positively architectural, with their tiers of flowers; *P. pulverulenta* (Z4–8) has 2–3ft (60–90cm) spikes of deep red flowers in June. *P. japonica* (Z3–8) is similar, but about half the height and with crimson-red or white flowers in May. If you want a mixed bunch, the 'Harlow Carr Hybrids' (Z4–8) are a good choice – everything from glowing orange to shocking pink and rich crimson.

Iris sibirica (4) is the one to choose for bog gardens, which aren't quite wet enough for true water irises like *Iris laevigata*. It's perfectly happy where the soil is just moist. It has upright stems and narrow leaves that look like stiff grass, and flowers between late spring and early summer. I fancy 'Butter and Sugar', which has yellow and white flowers that remind me of raw cake batter. Z4–9.

Lysimachia clethroides (5) is an unusual loosestrife, growing in 3 × 2½ft (90 × 75cm) clumps, with arching, buddleia-like cones of white flowers at the top of rather upright stems, from late summer to autumn. It's just about as vigorous as its cousin, the yellow loosestrife (*L. punctata*), which is saying something. Z4–9.

Candelabra primroses of the 'Harlow Carr Hybrids' strain growing by the pond at Barleywood.

14 EDIBLE GARDENS

Growing your own

It's a real treat to wander out into the garden with a basket on Sunday morning to pick a few fresh vegetables for lunch, or to pop out after work to gather a salad for supper. It's also very convenient when you live miles from the stores, as we do.

Growing your own gives you a tremendous feeling of achievement, and, even if you are short of space, it's still worthwhile cultivating your favorites – they taste so much better when you eat them within minutes of being picked.

Home-grown vegetables need not be grown in traditional regimented rows – they can be arranged in formal patterns.

For the flavor and feel-good factor, I can't recommend organic vegetable gardening strongly enough, even if you aren't so particular elsewhere. Yes, it means getting the hang of a few new techniques, but it's not difficult – and for anyone who likes to know what's happened to their food before they eat it, it's essential.

What's worth growing yourself and what's not

Don't even think about trying to grow everything. Unless you are a total enthusiast with time on your hands and plenty of room, life's too short to be truly self-sufficient and you'd just fill the garden with everyday stuff that, frankly, you might just as well buy at the stores.

No, what's really worth growing at home are unusual crops and those that taste best picked and eaten straight from the garden. If you are short of time, don't take on more than you can manage – concentrate on a few quick, compact crops that you have time to grow well. That's much better than being forced to watch beds full of vegetables being ruined by neglect.

Won't it look awful?

Contrary to what a lot of people still think, growing things to eat doesn't mean turning the garden into a mess. Nowadays, it is fashionable to grow edible crops in ways that look good.

Even in a tiny space, you can grow worthwhile crops in pots, grow bags, or a small raised bed, or go for serious productivity in intensive deep beds. Where there's more room, a conventional vegetable patch can be as much of a feature as a flower bed – just add ornamental edging or a hint of architecture, and go for vegetables that are naturally more decorative. Most garden centers and mail-order seed catalogs stock golden zucchini (such as 'Gold Rush), purple beans (try 'Purple Teepee', 'Royalty', or 'Purple Queen'), red lettuces with fringed or oak-shaped leaves, yellow tomatoes ('Sungold' or 'Golden Sunrise'), red-leaved beets ('Detroit Crimson Globe'), and white pumpkins ('Lumina'), all of which taste as good, if not better, than the normal kinds.

Practical points

To grow vegetables, fruit, or salad greens, you need deep, rich, well-drained soil and a sunny situation. The trouble is, when you are trying to fit a plot into an existing garden, you usually need to make the most of the space available.

If the soil isn't too special, there's quite a bit you can do to improve it. On poor, light soil, dig in lots of well-rotted organic matter – a barrowful per square yard/meter isn't too much. With clay soil, add organic matter *and* work in gritty horticultural sand at about a bucketful per square yard/meter. If the ground has a few inches of fairly good soil over impenetrable clay or stones, digging is not the answer – it just brings more rubbish to the surface. Instead, pile organic matter thickly on top.

Shade isn't easy to alleviate. You can thin out surrounding trees or shrubs to let more light in, but if the only available space is shady, don't waste your time trying to produce roots or fruiting crops – they'll never do well there. Stick to leafy kinds: brassicas, lettuce, sorrel, and arugula, which will cope. Most herbs will grow in light shade, though connoisseurs say they don't develop their full flavor without sun – I don't agree. But see if there isn't somewhere sunny that you could grow a few crops, even in pots or beds.

Start thinking of vegetables as ornamental plants, and suddenly they can take on a dual role.

Little and often

The secret of good vegetable growing is to put in time little and often, so you keep on top of weeds and any problem pests and diseases. You can't catch up all in one frantic weekend, just before you expect to be picking, because the odds are that your veggies will have vanished by then. And anyway, a little light pottering is the best kind of gardening.

Deep beds enable plenty of vegetables to be packed into a small space.

Deep beds

Deep beds, popularized by my old friend, Geoff Hamilton, are a very intensive way of growing a lot in a small space by growing them much closer together than usual in deeply worked, compost-rich soil, where the roots can penetrate a long way.

Making deep beds is hard work initially, since you need to dig out one trench at a time to about two spades' depth and backfill it with a mixture of compost and topsoil, then move on until you've covered the bed – but you do it only once, and the results really pay off. You don't do much hoeing, because crops are planted closely to smother out weeds. At the end of the season, there's no digging to do – just rake off rubbish and roughly fork the surface over after spreading more organic matter over it, the same as you do when you are replanting vacant rows during the growing season.

The reason deep beds work so well is because the soil never gets compressed – you work from paths on either side. The soil stays open, and roots can burrow through it easily. Most people make deep beds 4ft (1.2m) wide, so you can work without stepping on the soil, and 10ft (3m) long, so you don't take shortcuts across the middle.

Traditional plots

The usual way to grow vegetables is in rows, at the spacing recommended on the back of the seed packets and in reference books. With this method, you leave wide soil paths between rows of crops, because you need to walk through your crops to work. There's more hoeing to do, since weeds come up on the paths, and the soil needs digging over properly at the end of the season, not just to work in more organic matter, but also to open up the soil, because the paths get seriously squashed down.

Root vegetables   Brassicas   Greens, peas, beans, onions

What about crop rotation?

If you grow vegetables the traditional way, you should practice crop rotation. The idea is to divide your patch into three and grow each of the three main groups – root crops, brassicas (the cabbage family), and salad greens, plus peas, beans, and onions – in its own area. Each year, you move everything on to the next space so that the same crop never grows in the same ground more than one year in three. This way, each type of crop receives exactly the right soil preparation, each benefits from whatever the last crop has left in the ground, and there is less risk of plants picking up root diseases from a previous crop.

Greens, peas,   Root vegetables   Brassicas
beans, onions

Crop rotation is certainly a good thing to do if you have a large-scale vegetable garden, but, it has to be said, that with today's small modern gardens, it isn't always that practical. If you don't have a plot that can conveniently be divided into three, or you don't want to grow vegetables from all three groups, then my advice would be to forget it. Just avoid growing the same type of plant in the same patch of ground two years running, and don't try to grow root crops on ground that has had a good dose of manure in the last six months, which just makes them fork. You'll be very unlucky to run into problems, and if you do, just grow something else.

Brassicas   Greens, peas,   Root vegetables
beans, onions

Getting organized

Even if you don't go in for crop rotation, it's a good idea to plan what you'll be putting in where. It helps make the best use of the space – you won't have ground that doesn't produce anything for ages then have three rows of lettuce that need eating all at once.

Divide a piece of paper into columns, one for each container, bed, or block of space, then list in each one what you want to grow there. Start at the beginning of the growing calendar, and show what will occupy each bit of ground through the season. Bear in mind that some crops, such as Brussels sprouts, take an entire growing season to mature, while others, such as lettuce, take only weeks. You don't need to follow it slavishly, but it's a start.

Routine jobs

The vegetable growing year has quite a soothing routine to it. Late autumn (usually better) or early spring is when you prepare the ground. Spring is the main sowing and planting time. Then, in summer, as you finish up fast-growing early crops, you clear away the remains and put something else into the gap as soon as you can. The last seeds or plants will be going in around July or early August, although if you have gaps between your winter brassicas and leeks in the autumn, you can plant overwintering onion sets to keep the ground fully employed – they'll be ready to eat by the following June.

The basic jobs of sowing, thinning, and transplanting are the same regardless of which vegetables you are growing.

Sow seeds thinly in shallow drills made with the tip of a stake, or the corner of a Dutch hoe, held against a taut garden line.

The soil must be really well prepared and well nourished. Cover small seeds to a depth of no more than 1/4in (6mm), and large ones, such as beans, to their own depth. On heavy clay soil, it's best to cover seeds with a sprinkling of horticultural vermiculite or sowing medium, instead of soil. They'll come up better and faster. Remember not to sow root crops in ground that has been manured within the last six months.

Thin out seedlings to 1–2in (2.5–5cm) apart when they first come up, while they are easy to handle, then thin them again to their final spacing a few weeks later. You can transplant seedlings that are to be moved elsewhere when they are big enough to handle. Don't transplant root crops – it makes the roots split or the plants run to seed prematurely, and with carrots, the aroma you release will attract carrot rust fly.

Hoe between rows regularly to prevent weeds from swamping your crops. It's easiest to do when you can barely see the weeds germinating; if you wait till they have a good hold, you need to hand-weed with a trowel, which takes a lot longer.

Water regularly in dry spells, and fertilize long-stay crops, such as brassicas, leeks, and tomatoes, several times during the growing season. You can either sprinkle general-purpose organic fertilizer between the rows and water it in, or you can use diluted liquid fertilizer that you put on with your watering can, aiming the stream at the roots. Don't get fertilizer onto leaves, since it can scorch them. If you do, wash it off with plain water.

To draw a seed drill, position a taut garden line on the soil, stand on it, and draw the corner of a Dutch hoe along it in short bursts to make a furrow of the required depth.

Gather crops frequently and while they are young and tender – there is no pleasure in eating big toughies.

Control pests and diseases organically. Pick off aphids, beetles, and caterpillars by hand any time you see them. Cover brassica and carrot plants with very fine woven mesh to screen out cabbage root fly, cabbage white butterflies, and carrot rust fly. Grow disease-resistant varieties whenever you can. 'Fly Away' or 'Sytan' are carrot varieties resitant to carrot rsut fly, 'Trixie' for clubroot-free broccoli, avoid rust in leeks with 'Toledo' or 'Porvite', and keep viruses in zucchini at bay with 'Tarmino' or 'Defender'. Encourage beneficial insects, which prey on insect pests, by planting nectar-rich flowers, such as marigold (*Tagetes patula*), poached-egg flower (*Limnanthes douglasii*), and *Phacelia tanacetifolia*.

Gather crops little and often without waiting for a whole row to be ready, or you won't be able to use them all in time, and some will go to waste. I find keeping hens a good solution to sudden gluts – they appreciate the varied diet, and it does wonders for the eggs.

Protect very early or late crops with a row of cloches, or use the economical modern equivalent – cover them over with sheets of horticultural row cover (fleece).

Traditional vegetables

There are lots of essential vegetables you might want to grow that aren't decorative enough to show off in a trendy potager or in pots on the patio; they are the ones to pack into your intensive deep bed if you want maximum output for minimum input – or just grow in a traditional patch in the back yard.

Onions and scallions (1) are easiest grown from sets, which are like tiny dry baby onions that you push down into well-prepared soil in rows, about 6in (15cm) apart, in late winter. There's no thinning out: all you do is keep them hoed. Most people who sow them from seed do so in the greenhouse and prick out the seedlings into pots to plant out in spring when they are big enough to see properly; the tiny seedlings look like grass and are easily lost in the garden. If you must, sow seed in shallow drills and thin the seedlings to 6in (15cm). Scallions are planted from sets like onions, but for regular pullings, sow every three weeks from March to July. Or be crafty and sow for dual-purpose – use the thinnings as scallions, and leave the rest 6in (15cm) or so apart to grow into autumn bulb onions.

Leeks (2) are a lot easier than onions to grow well – you are less likely to clobber them with the hoe, and they produce more food from the same area. They are good all-purpose crop for the kitchen. Real leek-lovers need to grow two varieties, one for use before winter sets in and another for afterward, since the early kinds don't stand for long without rotting, and the lates don't bulk up early. Sow in shallow rows in early spring, and transplant when big enough to handle. Foodies might like fashionable baby leeks, so sow a row of an early type and don't transplant but thin them out to 1in (2.5cm) apart – they are ready once they reach pencil thickness, from midsummer.

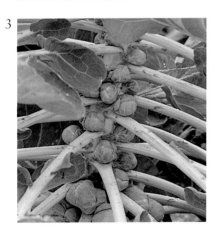

Brussels sprouts (3) are the vegetables kids love to hate, but now there are sweeter varieties without the bitter taste. As with a lot of winter crops, you need to grow two varieties – an early and a late – if you want to pick from autumn to spring. Sow sprouts in a seed-bed in early spring, thin the seedlings out to 2in (5cm) apart, then, in mid to late spring, transplant them to their final positions spacing them about 18in (45cm) apart. Sprouts need a rich, fertile soil that's been well manured, but the secret of growing hard, round, tight sprouts is to plant into very firm soil – tamp it down well. Don't plant sprouts in a newly prepared deep bed, since the soil is too fluffy at first – wait until the ground has settled. As the plants grow up, tie them to a stake so they don't blow over.

1 Onions.
2 Leeks.
3 Brussels sprouts 'Maximus'.
4 Beet.
5 Carrots 'Early Nantes'.
6 Potatoes 'Pink Fir Apple'.

Beets (4) are making a comeback. Avoid sowing them too early or they may bolt; early varieties are designed to solve this problem, so sow them first, in early spring. Sow thinly; traditional varieties have several seeds in each cluster, then thin to 4in (10cm) apart – don't try to transplant root crops, or they will 'fork'. Choose from a variety of colorful kinds.

Carrots (5) need a deep, fine, well-drained soil; they dislike thick clay or stony ground. Stick to tried-and-tested varieties for reliable bulk. If you like designer veggies, look for trendy white or yellow carrots, but if carrot rust fly is a problem grow a resistant variety; otherwise, you'll need to cover the plants with fine insect-proof mesh to eliminate egg-laying adult flies. Avoid planting in recently manured ground or they will fork. Sow the seed thinly along a shallow drill – early varieties in spring and summer for pulling as new baby carrots about 10-12 weeks later, and main-seasons in early to midspring for pulling in late summer and autumn. They keep best in the ground, but if you can't use them all before the ground freezes, they can be dug up and stored under cover.

Potatoes (6) for planting need to be proper seed potatoes bought from seed firms or the local garden center – don't plant potatoes from the supermarket, since they can carry viruses. These days, old heritage spuds and show-winning varieties are widely available; look out for modern pest- and disease- resistant varieties if you've had problems before and prefer to grow organically. Plant potatoes in deep, fertile soil, but not where you've recently dug in organic matter, or you're asking for problems with underground pests. Plant them in early spring, 5in (13cm) deep with 15in (38cm) between them in rows spaced 30in (75cm) apart. Plant early types before the later maincrops. It's not essential to let maincrop seed potatoes sprout before planting them; it's only with the earlies you need to bother with coaxing and tending the new sprouts.

Recommended varieties

Onions – 'Ailsa Craig' a large reliable favorite; 'Red Baron' red-purple skin.

Scallions – 'White Lisbon' a reliable favorite; 'Redmate' red-purple variety to grow as scallions or as bulbs.

Leeks – 'King Richard' early; 'Toledo' late rust-resistant; 'Musselburgh' a winter favorite.

Beets – 'Boltardy' round, bolt-resistant; 'Cylindra' large tubular-shaped root.

Carrots – 'Autumn King' reliable variety; 'Early Nantes' early; 'Yellowstone' yellow roots; 'Kuttiger' white roots.

Brussels sprouts – 'Peer Gynt' use until winter; 'Trafalgar' ready later; 'Icarus' child-friendly, bitterness-free variety.

Potatoes – 'Edzell Blue' blue-skinned heritage variety for roasting or mashing; 'Kerr's Pink' heavy bearer for baking or roasting; 'Sante' good pest and disease resistance, ideal for organic growing; 'Pink Fir Apple' late gourmet salad variety.

4

5

6

Ornamental vegetables

If you don't have a traditional patch, you can still grow useful amounts of mainstream crops in the garden. Try growing groups of tall veggies in borders with flowers around them, or train climbing crops up obelisks, on a trellis, or over arches. Or how about an ornamental potager, based on a circle or octagon and divided into segments with a different crop in each. Put an obelisk in the middle for climbing beans, and surround with a dwarf edging of herbs. Following William Morris's dictum, it's both useful *and* beautiful.

Climbing green and runner beans (1) do well on trellises and arches and can also be grown in a trough against the patio wall, given some netting or a trellis to climb up. The flowers are similar to sweet peas, though in fewer colors – just red, pink, or white. Runners are the beans to grow for quantity – they're very productive, and you can keep picking from the same plants all summer. Go for a stringless cultivar, or pick them when still tender, at 4–6in (10–15cm) long; don't let them grow huge. Climbing beans are usually thought to have the finer flavor, but they run out of steam at half time, so for beans all summer, make a second sowing to follow on. Neither is frost-hardy – don't put plants out until after frosts are past.

Corn (2) is another good-looking edible crop that is fun to grow, but it's no good for containers and not worth dotting around in a border. Because corn is pollinated by the wind, the only way to be certain of ears setting properly is to grow a decent-sized block of it. Still, you can grow them either in a decorative vegetable patch or potager, where it makes a good centerpiece to a geometric design, or you can grow it in a conventional vegetable patch. Raise plants in the same way as pumpkins and zucchini. Don't put them out until the soil has warmed up and dried out a bit and any risk of frost has passed.

Zucchini (3) are very easy to grow – sun, fertile soil, a bit of fertilizer, and plenty of water. These days, most are bush cultivars that make a mound of leaves with the fruit tucked away in the middle. Sow seeds in a frost-free greenhouse in midspring, and plant out after the last frost. Bush kinds can be grown in 15in (38cm) pots, or in grow bags on the patio. Those with golden fruit are more ornamental than the green ones, which are better in a vegetable patch. They are usually terrifically productive, if you keep cutting the zucchini regularly – turn your back for a day or two, and suddenly you have giant weapons. Don't despair – stuff 'em with your favorite filling.

1 Runner bean 'Painted Lady'.
2 Corn 'Sweet Nugget'.
3 Zucchini 'Ambassador'.
4 Sugar pea 'Sugar Snap'.
5 Pumpkin 'Rouge Vif d'Etamps'.
6 Black Tuscany kale.

Sugar peas (4) are peas you eat complete with their pods; 6–12 plants give a worthwhile crop from a small space. Grow them up twiggy sticks in the vegetable patch or in troughs on the patio against a not-too-hot wall with netting or a trellis for support. For an early crop, sow seed in pots in a greenhouse in late winter and plant them out during a mild spell in early spring. Or sow where you want the plants to bear in early spring. In cooler areas, several sowings between then and midsummer will keep you well supplied with peas all summer.

Pumpkins and squashes (5) look spectacular, and, if you stick to those with smaller fruit, there is no problem with letting them scramble up a trellis or wigwam, though they need tying up. Large-fruited sorts are too heavy to grow this way – they need to run along the ground, but they look good growing over a bank. Squash and pumpkin plants are fast-growing vines with spiny stems and big, prickly-backed leaves; they need regular watering and heavy fertilizing, but they are fun to grow and children love them. Sow them like zucchini. Summer squashes are ready to eat, like zucchini, when they are big enough, but winter cultivars need to ripen on the plants and are ready to pick in mid- to late autumn.

Brassicas (6) look wonderful in a potager with nasturtiums or annuals to attract beneficial insects, especially if you go for the pretty ones, such as red cabbage, purple kale, red-leaved Brussels sprouts, or the Black Tuscany kale with frilly leaves of darkest green. These taste as good as they look. Don't confuse them with ornamental cabbages and kales sold for winter bedding; they aren't worth eating. To grow your own brassicas, sow seeds in drills in well-prepared ground in spring, then transplant seedlings to their final positions when they're a good size, 6–8 weeks later.

Recommended varieties

Climbing beans – 'Hunter' flat beans; 'Cobra' pencil beans.

Runner beans – 'Desiree' white flowers, stringless; 'Sunset' pink flowers, early.

Corn – 'Honey Bantam Bicolor' supersweet yellow and white kernels; 'Sundance' good for cool summers.

Zucchini – green 'All Green Bush'; golden – 'Gold Rush'.

Sugar peas – 'Oregon Sugar Pod'; 'Sugar Snap'.

Pumpkins – 'Atlantic Giant' for size; *Summer squashes* – 'Patty Pan' greenish white; 'Sunburst' yellow; *Winter squashes* – 'Butternut' tubular beige squash.

Red cabbage – 'Red Drumhead'; 'Red Jewel'; 'Red Winner'; *Purple kale* – 'Redbor' crinkly; *Red sprouts* – 'Falstaff'; 'Red Delicious'.

4

5

6

Salad greens

If you never grow any other edibles, a salad bed is one thing you shouldn't be without. From an area no more than 6 × 2ft (2m × 60cm), you can pick enough to keep a small family well stocked for most of the season. If you don't have a patch, make a small raised bed, or use a packing crate as a large container.

How and what to grow

Fertile ground and constant moisture are essential for greens to grow quickly and stay succulent and tasty. If they run short of water or suffer a check, they'll bolt or fail to heart up properly and be tough and bitter to eat. Sow salad greens in short rows and thin seedlings, first to 1in (2.5cm) apart, and later to the final spacing. Use the small plants you pull out as salad greens. Clear the ground when you've cut the whole row, remove debris, and work in a little organic fertiizer. Then sow or plant the next batch right away to keep the ground fully occupied. To extend the growing season, cover early spring and late autumn crops with horticultural fleece or cloches to protect them from the weather.

Lamb's lettuce (1), or corn salad, are small plants, like compact 2in (5cm) lettuces. The flavor is like a very superior lettuce. Sow it in early spring, and again later in summer or even early autumn for late crops. It's small and fast growing, so it's ready in weeks – cut the whole rosette. The thinnings also make a very good salad.

Chicory and endive (2) can be tricky to grow – they don't heart up as reliably as lettuce. Different types vary in sowing times, so check the back of the packet – most are sown in early summer for eating in autumn. Thin or transplant to leave the plants about 8in (20cm) apart. Non-forcing types of chicory should form a heart naturally toward the end of their growing season. Endive makes a loose, open head rather than a tight heart, and it tastes bitter unless you blanch it. Cover each plant with an upturned bucket for a week or two before cutting. Watch out for snails; they enjoy blanched endive, too.

Arugula (3) has a hot, peppery taste. Sow a short row any time from midspring to midsummer, thin to 3in (8cm) apart, and pick a few leaves when they're big enough, leaving the plant to grow on. You can pick from the same plants all summer, but, after flowering begins, arugula won't grow new leaves; that's the time to sow again.

Recommended varieties

Red lettuce – 'Lollo Rosso' very frilly; 'Blush' small iceberg type tinged red-bronze; 'Oakleaf' long, decorative, indented leaves; 'Cerize' red; 'Cocarde' red/yellow tinged, looseleaf; 'Funly' green frilly, red and green; 'Salad Bowl'; pick a few leaves and leave the rest to grow.

Cos lettuce – 'Little Gem' and 'Sherwood', both exceptionally well-flavored mini cos; no need to tie up as you do the large cos lettuces.

Chicory – 'Sugar Loaf' green-hearting non-forcing winter-hardy; 'Pallo Rosso' round red radicchio; 'Rosso di Treviso' pointed red radicchio.

Endive – 'Frisee' finely divided and curly.

Lettuce (4) is the staple salad leaf for many, and many types can be sown from early spring to late summer. The different types include: red; oak-leaved; the conventional green, hearting kind; looseleaf lettuce that doesn't form a heart – just pick a few leaves at a time and leave the rest of the plant to keep growing – and the upright cos lettuce. 'Little Gem' is easier to grow than full-sized cos, which need tying up with raffia to make them heart up properly. To keep a constant supply all season, sow part of a row each time you thin the last batch. It works better than sowing every 2–3 weeks; lettuces grow faster in warm weather, so regular sowings catch up with each other. Space 8–12in (20–30cm) apart, depending on cultivar.

Oriental greens (5) are dual-purpose plants, used cooked in stir-fries and raw as salad leaves. Sow them in summer. Use the thinnings for stir-fries or salads; the rest mature 6–8 weeks later. Chinese cabbages need time to form a heart – space them 10–12in (25–30cm) apart. Space the quicker-growing pak choi 6in (15cm) apart. The large, loose-leaf oriental greens, such as mizuna and mibuna, need 12–15in (30–38cm) of space. Watch out for slugs, snails, and flea beetle; they're all fond of Oriental greens.

1

2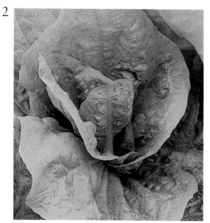

1 Lamb's lettuce.
2 Chicory.
3 Arugula.
4 Lettuce 'Little Gem'.
5 Oriental greens.

3

4

5

Growing in containers

Growing vegetables in containers is just like growing bedding plants – treat them exactly the same way. Yes, really!

Choose good-looking and highly productive plants such as herbs, strawberries, climbing or runner beans, tomatoes, zucchini, or salad greens. Hardier crops, such as strawberries and lettuce, can be planted in spring, but leave the tender kinds, such as tomatoes and green beans, until after the last frost.

Use any good brand of multipurpose soil mix to fill the containers. After planting, water the plants to settle them in, and from then on, water often enough to keep the soil mix moist. This will probably mean every day when the weather is warm, but do the finger test if you want to be sure. A quick prod reveals all. Damp as a freshly wrung-out washcloth? It's fine. A touch dusty? Water it. Four weeks after planting, the nutrients in the soil mix will have been used up, so start using liquid fertilizer once a week at first, rising to twice weekly as the crops grow bigger and fill the pots. As salad greens become big enough to eat, pick little and often, so you don't denude the display in one fell swoop.

Provided the container is of adequate dimensions, most vegetables will be happy growing in a restricted space. Just make sure they do not go short of fertilizer and water.

How to... **plant an edible hanging basket**

Hanging baskets make good use of space, and they are a great way to prevent slugs and snails from swiping your crops. They'll look good and be productive too, which is very satisfying. Put them in an open spot with good light, but with some shelter from wind. You will need to fertilize and water a hanging basket regularly, since it contains only a limited amount of soil mix. And don't forget that hanging baskets dry out more quickly than ground-level pots because they're more exposed to the air, and evaporation will be greater – water-retaining gel crystals help here. But because the basket is suspended, it will probably have better access to light all around than it would at ground level – and you don't even need to bend over to pick. You could also try tumbling outdoor tomatoes in a hanging basket.

1 Position the basket on an empty flowerpot so that it is stable. Put the liner in place and tuck its folds neatly together. All kinds of liner are available – from plastic to jute and organic matting materials. Think twice about using sphagnum moss which, like peat, needs to be conserved. The purpose of the liner is to prevent the soil mix from falling through the mesh but also to help keep roots cool.

2 Add a little multipurpose soil mix conbined with water-retaining granules to the bottom of the basket. Water the plants well, then tap them out of their pots and position them so that their shoots emerge through the upper sides of the basket – you can push them through from the outside, squeezing the rootball, or the inside, carefully feeding the shoots through – whichever is easiest.

Add more soil mix, and then plant the center of the basket with more herbs and the trailing tomato plant or the cucumber. A small depression in the center of the basket will allow for easier watering. Check the basket for its water needs at least once a day, and fertilize once a week with dilute liquid tomato fertilizer during summer.

Patio crops

Quite a few of the bushier vegetables make attractive patio plants; if you didn't know that they were edible crops, you'd think they were something exotic.

Colorful crops

Cucumbers, tomatoes, and peppers occupy their pots all summer, but it's also worth considering shorter-term crops for the patio. Dwarf beans can be planted out from midspring to midsummer – purple-podded ones are particularly attractive. They're about 1ft (30cm) high, and you'll fit a dozen in a 12in (30cm) pot, or fifteen in a 15in (38cm) pot. Fertilize and water like bedding plants. When you've picked all the beans, pull out the old and put in some more.

New potatoes (**1**) are a good early crop in a 15in (38cm) pot. Plant tubers in early spring in a frost-free greenhouse, then put them out on the patio after the last frost. Or plant them outside in early to midspring, 6in (15cm) deep. Kept fertilized and watered, they'll be ready to harvest in early summer – grow some mint to go with them.

Chilli peppers and other tender vegetables enjoy the hot and sheltered conditions of a sunny patio, which will help them ripen their fruits.

Cucumbers (2) also enjoy patio conditions, and they are fast-growing and productive, so you should be picking a couple of cucumbers per plant from early summer onward. You won't need to be bothered with long, running vines if you plant one pf the semi-bush types. However, on the patio, cucumber plants look more decorative rambling over a trellis or tied up to an obelisk standing in the middle of their pot, sideshoots and all. That way they grow more, smaller, cucumbers, which are usually a lot more welcome than an occasional whopper. Fertilize and water cucumber plants the same as tomatoes and peppers.

Pepper and chilli pepper (3) plants are very decorative, but all of them have green fruit at first – it's not until they ripen in late summer that they turn yellow, red, or purple. Treat them exactly the same as bush tomatoes. They are a bit slower growing and need lots of sun and warmth, the kind of weather that much of the country experiences in summer. If you live in a cooler area, grow these in containers in a protected spot, such as a sunny corner patio, instead of in the open ground. The same applies to eggplant.

Tomatoes (4) were originally considere decorative fruiting plants that nobody in their right minds thought of eating. Now, you can get tomatoes with pink, gold, or white fruits that are as tasty as the familiar red kinds, so they make a really colorful addition to the patio. They are easy to grow, and, like other frost-tender crops, tomatoes benefit from lots of warmth and sunshine, although there are some kinds that are adapted to cooler areas. Keep them well-watered, and fertilize them once or twice a week with liquid tomato fertilizer. Don't overdo it on either score, or you'll spoil the flavor and they'll make soft growth, which is more susceptible to foliar and fruit diseases.

1 New potatoes.
2 Cucumber 'Burpless Tasty Green'.
3 Pepper.
4 Tomato 'Gardeners' Delight'.

How to... **grow outdoor tomatoes in pots**

Tomatoes are such a popular crop that you'll probably find lots of different cultivars on sale in the garden center – and that's a lot easier than growing your own from seed. They come in two kinds: upright or vine tomatoes for growing on a single stem, and the far more popular bush tomatoes, which are – well – bushy. The bush ones are much easier to grow and need no special training – and the tomatoes keep appearing from midsummer until frost if you treat them right.

What you need

- *12–15in (30–38cm) pots*
- *potting mix, preferably soil-based*
- *4ft (1.2m) stakes and soft twine*
- *tomato plants – try to find ones that stay small*
- *liquid tomato fertilizer*

1 After the last frosts, around the end of May, stand the pots in a sunny, sheltered spot. Fill with soil mix and plant a tomato plant in the middle of each. Push a stake in behind the plant, 2in (5cm) away from the stem, and tie it loosely up to it with soft garden twine. Water the plant in, and keep the soil mix slightly on the dry side for the first two weeks or until the first cluster of flowers opens – it helps to persuade plants to concentrate on flowering and fruiting instead of growing overly leafy.

2 Give a dilute liquid fertilizer once or twice a week – as much as it takes to wet the soil mix thoroughly.
As the plants grow, keep tying the stem to the stake. Bush cultivars don't need trimming or training, but use several stakes to support the stems, so they don't break under the weight of fruit. Train upright varieties as a single stem; nip out sideshoots as soon as you see them, but take care not to break off the flower clusters. Nip the growing tips out after 3–4 clusters of fruit have formed.

3 Because you reduce the fruit clusters on upright varieties, the fruit will swell and ripen fast, and you won't be left with a lot of half-grown green fruit at the end of the season. Expect tomatoes to start ripening in midsummer; they'll continue until cold autumn weather stops any further growth, then the plants will be killed by the first frost, so pick any remaining green fruits to ripen indoors in a warm place.

Fruit

Contrary to what a lot of people think, you don't need to have a huge garden with an orchard to grow fruit. Nowadays, there are all sorts of dwarf fruit trees, but even in a tiny garden you can grow apples in tubs, strawberries in pots, and fruit bushes trained flat against a wall, all of which look good and produce very worthwhile crops.

Practical stuff

To grow any kind of fruit, you need deep, fertile, well-drained soil and a sheltered site with plenty of sun. Avoid an east-facing spot like the plague, because most fruit flowers early, and if frozen flowers thaw out fast in the early morning sun they'll be killed, which means no fruit for a year. If you don't have the right spot, frankly, you'd be better off growing something else and buying fruit at the stores. You'll get so little return that it just won't be worth the space.

Yes, you can improve less than ideal conditions, as long as they aren't too awful. For example, you could plant a windbreak to protect an exposed site, improve shallow or poorly drained soil by adding lots of compost (and very coarse sand, in the case of clay), or prune overhanging trees to let in more light. But it's often easier just to grow a small amount of fruit on sunny walls or in containers on the patio.

The easiest fruits to fit into a small garden are strawberries – cultivated with the minimum of effort in a modest-sized bed.

You can even grow strawberries in a hanging basket outside the back door.

Planting and aftercare

Autumn or spring are the very best times to start growing fruit, though plants that are sold growing in pots can be put in at any time of year, as long as the soil is workable. Prepare the ground well, with lots of organic matter, and plant them just like normal trees or shrubs. Fruit trees need to be staked. Leave a 3ft (1m) circle of bare soil around them if you are planting them in grass so that there's less competition for food and water.

Each spring, mulch all fruit generously with well-rotted manure and provide a general-purpose organic fertilizer. If the weather turns dry when the fruit is swelling, keep the plants watered – otherwise, you'll have small fruit at best, and at worst, it'll all fall off prematurely. It's a good idea to get into the habit of sprinkling a handful of organic rose fertilizer to each square yard/meter of soil around the plants in August, and watering it in – it helps encourage the current year's growth to mature and promotes good flowering next year, which bodes well for the next fruit-picking season.

Choosing fruit

There are lots of different cultivars of most popular fruits available in garden centers, and even more if you look to see what specialized nurseries offer in their catalogs. So how do you decide which to choose? Taste is the first thing to go for. Go to an apple tasting event (advertised in the gardening press and local newspapers in late summer), or try fruit from a friend's garden, and ask the name of those you enjoyed eating. But important though it is, taste is not the only thing you need to take into account.

Most fruit trees need a pollinator – another cultivar of the same type of plant – to produce fruit, so you actually need two plants. Clearly any old two won't do – they both need to flower at the same time and must be sexually compatible. I'm not joking – some fruit tree pollen just does not mix happily, so check before buying.

If space is tight, stick to self-fertile cultivars. They produce fruits when fertilized with their own pollen. Alternatively, buy a family apple tree – they have several compatible individuals grafted onto one trunk. You can have a couple of different eating apples and a cooker all growing on the same tree. You don't have this problem with bush and cane fruit; all the popular types are self-fertile.

Then there's the question of flowering time. In a cold area or exposed situation, choose a late-flowering cultivar to avoid frost damage to the flowers, which wrecks your chances of a crop of fruit. If you are growing several different cultivars of the same type of fruit, it's worth choosing a mixture of early, intermediate, and late-ripening kinds to stretch your harvest.

How to... **plant a strawberry jar**

A strawberry jar is the ultimate solution for gardeners who think their patch is too small for fruit. Alright, you won't become self-sufficient, but the pleasure of picking a fresh strawberry or two for your morning cornflakes is well worth the space taken up by a single flowerpot. You'll be surprised just how much fruit a single pot can produce – and some strawberry jars are very large. That said, avoid the massive ones, since they contain a huge amount of soil mix that can become cold, soggy, and inhospitable to plants. A pot up to 12in (30cm) in diameter and 18in (45cm) deep is plenty large enough, and shallower half pots or pans are also suitable.

After fruiting, cut the plants back to within 2in (5cm) and give dilute liquid tomato fertilizer once a week until September. Reduce watering in winter and stand the pots by the house (or take tem under cover) for shelter. Start fertilizing again in April and the plants will produce a second crop.

What you need

- *suitable jar with wide rim or planting pockets up the sides*
- *potting mix, preferably soil-based*
- *liquid tomato fertilizer*
- *strawberry plants*
- *horticultural fleece (row cover)*

1 Spring is the time to plant your strawberries. Put in sufficient soil mix to bring the level up to the first planting hole. (You can also plant strawberries in a hanging basket if you have a sheltered spot in which to hang it.)

2 Water the young plants well, then squeeze the rootballs and ease them through the planting holes and into the soil mix. Lightly firm the soil mix around them. A strawberry jar has the advantage of keeping developing fruits clear of the ground so that there is no need to protect them with mats or straw. Slugs and snails are also likely to be less of a problem (though they will not be absent altogether).

3 Plant up the top of the pot, water the container well, and stand it in a sunny, sheltered spot. If frost threatens when the plants are in flower, wrap the pot with horticultural fleece and remove it when the danger passes. Frosted flowers turn black in the center, and no fruits are produced. Use netting to protect the ripening fruits from birds if necessary.

Soft fruit

Soft fruits are the ones that grow on canes, on bushes, or, in the case of strawberries, on herbaceous perennial plants.

Gooseberries and redcurrants (**1**) are usually grown as bushes on a "leg" – a short trunk – that makes it easier to get a hoe or a mower beneath the branches. Both can be trained as cordons (grown on a single stem) to grow flat against a wall, which saves space, and gooseberries also make very good standard plants, trained in the same way as standard fuchsias. Whichever method you prefer, plants need pruning regularly – tackle them both in the same way. Just after the fruit has been picked in summer, shorten all the sideshoots that have grown in the current season back to about five leaves from their base. In winter, when the leaves have fallen, shorten the leaders (main shoots) by about half their length. Not that difficult to master, really. Z3–8.

Blackcurrants (**2**) are big bushes whose shoots all grow out from below ground level, and they don't take to being pruned into fancy shapes. If you don't have room for one, and they usually reach 5 × 5ft (1.5 × 1.5m), you are best doing without. They are one of the few fruits that doesn't mind wet or heavy soil, but they are also very greedy plants that need a good mulch of manure each spring. With these, you prune in winter – thin the bush out by cutting out a few of the oldest and woodiest stems close to the ground, and trim back fruited stems to just above a strong sideshoot. Alternatively, if you find it easier, instead of picking the fruit as usual, cut the whole stem to take indoors and pick in comfort, and that acts as combined picking and pruning for the year. Z3–8.

Raspberries (**3**) are many people's favorite soft fruit, but, unless you have lots of room, I'd give the summer-fruiting kind a miss. Go for autumn-fruiting cultivars instead. They are ready to pick from late summer and go on until the first serious frost of autumn.
The plants are about 3ft (1m) tall, and you don't need to put up post-and-wire supports or tie them up. And instead of worrying about which canes to cut off and which to keep, as you do with the summer sort, you just chop the lot down to about 2in (5cm) above the ground every spring. You don't even need to grow them in rows – a raspberry thicket in a small bed will provide all you can eat without making very much work at all. The very best thing about autumn raspberries is that although they taste as good as the summer sort, birds may not be as interested. Yes, you'll lose a few, but unless you protect summer raspberries under nets or a fruit cage, you'll lose the lot. Z3–9.

Strawberries (4), being small plants, are often the most convenient fruit to grow in today's gardens. Buy young plants in pots in spring. Plant them in well-prepared soil in a sheltered sunny situation, spaced 18in (45cm) apart in rows 3ft (90cm) apart. At flowering time, spread straw all over the soil, tucking it well under the plants, or fit special strawberry mats round them, so that the fruits don't get splashed with mud each time it rains and go moldy. As soon as small green fruits have set, cover the plants with bird netting. After all the fruits have been picked, go over the plants with shears and cut them down close to the ground – you can afford to be quite rough with them – then rake up the rubbish and put it on the compost pile. Sprinkle organic rose fertilizer (which is high in potassium) all over the strawberry bed at a couple of handfuls per square yard/meter and water it well in; the old leaves are soon replaced by healthy, strong young growth ready for next year. Replace old plants every 3–4 years, using runners produced from a few parent plants that aren't cut back after fruiting. Z3–10.

Individual information

All the information you need about pollination, flowering, and ripening times should be found on the label, in the nursery catalog, or in the adverts in gardening magazines at about the time you are making up your mind about which fruit to buy. New cultivars are constantly coming along and, with fruit, new ones often offer significant advantages over the old ones.

1 Gooseberry 'Whinham's Industry'.
2 Blackcurrant 'Boskoop Giant'.
3 Raspberry 'Leo'.
4 Strawberry 'Pandora'.

Fruit and vegetables mix well in a cottage garden.

Tree fruit

If you like the easy life, the best way to grow fruit such as apples and pears is to grow standard trees. Buy one with a good branching shape in the first place, and you won't need to do much pruning for years. You don't really need to prune them at all, but if you thin out the growth slightly, you'll have better quality fruit – bigger and better colored – though in smaller quantities.

Apples, pears, plums, and cherries can all be grown as standard trees, and, as long as you choose cultivars grown on dwarfing rootstocks, they'll stay fairly small and compact.

All apple cultivars are grafted on to rootstocks that control their vigor – dwarfing rootstocks have been developed to make the trees suitable for small gardens.

More vigorous rootstocks produce taller trees that are better suited to commercial orchards. You can grow dwarf fruit trees instead of ornamental trees in a small garden; the blossoms are every bit as attractive as that of flowering cherries and crabapples, and you have the bonus of a delicious crop of fruit.

Apples (**1**) can be bought on very dwarfing rootstocks, which produce fruit within the first year or two after planting. These rootstock produce a tree that grows only to 6 × 6ft (2.4 × 2.4m). A few self-fertile apples are available, such as 'Greensleeves'. Z3–9.

Peaches, nectarines, and apricots (**2**) would be my first choice for a warm, sunny wall. They can be fan trained, and you only need one since they are self-fertile. You'll be able to pick an incredible amount of fruit, and it's easily protected from birds by draping a net over it. Buy a fan-trained tree and tie the main branches to horizontal wires at 18in (45cm) intervals up the wall. Each year, in late spring-early summer, cut out any shoots that grow out from the wall or in toward it, and tie in all the rest to increase the bearing area. There are naturally dwarf varieties of nectarine and peach that are small enough to grow in large pots. Z5–9.

Cherries and plums (**3**) are worth growing if you have room; there are dwarfing rootstocks for sweet and sour (pie) cherries, which produce slower-growing trees about 5 × 4ft (1.5 × 1.2m), but nothing for plums that gives a tree less than two-thirds normal size – too big for most small gardens. 'Morello' and 'Stella' cherries are self-fertile, as is the plum 'Victoria'. There are lots of different kinds of plum: American, Asian, American-Asain hybrids, prune plums, bullaces, and gages. You can grow fan-trained forms against a wall, which makes it easier to protect ripening fruit from birds. Cherries Z4–9, plums Z4–10.

Pears (**4**) are best trained against a sunny wall as espaliers (with several horizontal tiers of branches). The fruit ripens far better in a warm spot, and it's a good way of controlling vigor; no very dwarfing rootstocks are available yet for pears. 'Conference' is self-fertile. 'Doyenne du Comice' is the fattest and juiciest. Z4–9.

1 Ballerina apple.
2 *Prunus persica* 'Flat China'.
3 Plum.
4 Pear 'Doyenne du Comice'.

Herbs

No cook wants to be without herbs for the pot, and no gardener wants to be without them for fragrance. Many of them are perennial, they can be squeezed into pockets on the patio or corners of borders, and a little of most kinds of herb goes a long way. Any reasonable soil and a sunny spot is all they require.

Herb gardens

Formal herb gardens are traditionally round or square, often with a clipped, dwarf evergreen hedge around the outside as a year-round outline, something architectural (such as a sundial or container) in the middle, and a tapestry of herbs filling the remaining space. Alternatively, you can design something more complicated, based on a knot garden, with gravel paths in between the beds, and clipped rosemary or lavender making the scented outlines of the knot's pattern.

In an informal herb garden, you can make mixed borders using woody, perennial, and annual herbs, just as with ornamental shrubs and flowers. Don't limit yourself to culinary herbs, which can look terribly green – add medieval medicinal plants, such as lavender, foxglove, and the apothecary's rose (*Rosa gallica* var. *officinalis*) to give the garden a bit more color. You could also bring in other useful plants – those that attract butterflies, bees, or beneficial insects – without losing the thread of your herbal theme.

Herbs are also good for contemporary gardens; they look as much at home growing in containers made of stainless steel or other nontraditional materials, surrounded by pebbles or glass nuggets, as they do in traditional terracotta. The strong green shapes of herbs, combined with their scent and, in some cases, clippability, make them a good foil for way-out designs and unusual surroundings. So long as the growing conditions are right, they'll be quite happy.

The majority of herbs, and especially the culinary ones and the aromatic herbs, such as lavender and rosemary, are natives of the Mediterranean and grow best in warm, sunny conditions with very well-drained soil. It doesn't need to be particularly fertile, but I would recommend adding lots of coarse sand to keep the drainage up to snuff. These herbs really don't like too much winter moisture standing around their roots.

There are lots, though, that are quite hardy and that thrive in wetter soils, and some that even tolerate some shade – most of the mints and sorrel come into this category.

A formal herb garden with sundial surrounded by chamomile is only one way of growing herbs.

Herb care

Herbs are some of the very easiest edible crops to look after.
Mediterranean-style herbs such as bay, rosemary, thyme, and sage
must have a warm, sunny spot with very well-drained soil, and
basil is very fussy about warmth and shelter, but it doesn't like hot,
searing sun – it's best grown in pots of soilless potting mix in semi-
shade. Other herbs, such as tarragon, parsley, sorrel, and mint are
happiest in normal garden conditions in sun or light shade with
soil that holds moisture but where they won't have wet feet.

Plant perennial herbs in spring and frost-tender herbs in
summer, shortly after the last frost, so you have the longest season
in which to use them.

Remove flowers from short-lived leafy herbs such as basil and
chervil to keep them going longer, also from cilantro and dill if you
want them for leaves rather than seeds. But there's no need to
bother taking flowers off of the perennials.

Enthusiasts claim herbs have more flavor if they are kept short
of water and not fertilized so they must struggle, but I suggest you
treat them more kindly – water lightly when the soil dries out, and
use a general purpose liquid fertilizer regularly every 2–3 weeks for
herbs in containers. Only big loutish perennial herbs like mint need
lots of water and heavy fertilizing; when you grow mint in pots,
you can hardly be too generous.

Herbs also lend themselves to being
grown in a contemporary setting
and in sleek containers.

Cottage gardens are the natural home of herbs, and here culinary and ornamental varieties are most easily combined.

Evergreen herbs

These are the Mediterranean herbs that put up with any amount of heat and drought once they are established, which makes them particularly good for growing in containers, gravel gardens, and in gaps between paving. They are also good for courtyard gardens and patios where there is a lot of reflected heat and light. Wherever you grow them, good drainage, not-too-rich soil, and plenty of sun are the essentials.

Rosemary (*Rosmarinus officinalis*) (**1**) makes a spiky, piney-scented bush about 3 × 3ft (90 × 90cm) with lots of tiny, pale blue lipped flowers in spring. There are various named cultivars, such as 'Sissinghurst Blue', tall and columnar with rich blue flowers; 'Majorca Pink', which is compact and has pink flowers; and 'Severn Sea', which is short and squat with flowers of bright blue. Z7–10.

French lavender (*Lavandula stoechas*) (**2**) is the one to grow for culinary use – the flowers are dried, rubbed from the stems, and cooked with lamb, if you are feeling experimental, or mixed with other dried Mediterranean herbs. French lavender has a pair of long purple "flags" waving from the top of the flowerhead, like streamers, and the foliage is narrower and more needlelike than other lavenders. It is not so hardy as the likes of 'Hidcote', though the similar *Lavandula* 'Helmsdale' is quite tough. Z8–9.

Bay (*Laurus nobilis*) (**3**) can eventually grow into a large evergreen bush or tree, up to 20 × 10ft (6 × 3m), but in an herb garden, it is usually kept pruned to size or grown in a large pot or tub, which acts like a corset. It can be trained into a standard and grown in a pot, used as the centerpiece of a formal herb garden, or stood on a doorstep or on the patio. In a pot, it's not good at coping with a long, cold winter in the open, so move it under cover. Z8–10.

Culinary sage (*Salvia officinalis*) (**4**) has thick, wrinkled leaves and grows a bushy 30 × 24in (75 × 60cm) or thereabouts, with a strong turkey-stuffing scent and flavor, but its colored forms – purple sage (*S. officinalis* 'Purpurascens'), golden sage (*S. officinalis* 'Icterina') and tricolor sage (*S. officinalis* 'Tricolor') – look a lot more decorative. They are slightly smaller, with more delicate leaves that "mummify" on the plants in winter instead of remaining evergreen, and, although they aren't so strongly scented, they're still good for cooking. Z5–8.

Thymes (**5**) come in two basic types. The creeping ones run to about 2 × 24in (5 × 60cm), and the upright thymes usually come in at about 12 × 12in (30 × 30cm). All of them have pink or mauve flowers around midsummer and tiny, strongly scented leaves. Some, such as 'Doone Valley' (creeping, Z6–9) have gold-variegated foliage, and several, such as *Thymus serphyllum* 'Lemon Curd' (creeping, Z4–9) have citrus-scented foliage. 'Fragrantissimus' is orange scented. *T. herba-barona* (Z6–9) has a caraway scent and was traditionally put under a cut of beef while it roasted. Try it!

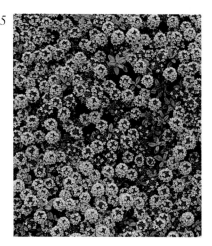

1 Rosemary (*Rosmarinus officinalis* 'Sissinghurst Blue').
2 Lavender (*Lavandula stoechas*).
3 Bay (*Laurus nobilis*).
4 Sage (*Salvia officinalis* 'Purpurascens').
5 Thyme (*Thymus pulegioides* 'Bertram Anderson').

Herbaceous herbs

Perennial herbs that die down each winter and come up again each spring are happiest in normal garden soil, and though they want sun, they don't like scorching-hot conditions. Treat them just like herbaceous flowers, and cut the plants down close to the ground in autumn when they die down naturally.

1 Herbs like chives, with its lilac pompoms, are spectacular when in flower.

Chives (*Allium schoenoprasum*) (**1**) grows in 10 × 6in (25 × 15cm) clumps like bunches of slim scallions; the hollow leaves have a mild oniony flavor. If you are serious about your chives, cut the plants almost down to ground level periodically during the summer to get rid of old or yellowing leaves, and "force" a new crop of strong young leaves for cutting. If you don't bother, the clumps will have tufts of spiky mauve flowers that are as good as ornamental alliums any day, and bees love them. Z3–9.

Sorrel (*Rumex acetosa*) (**2**) looks like weedy dock but on a smaller and more refined scale. It reaches 12 × 12in (30 × 30cm) with flower stems 3ft (90cm) high. Pick the small young leaves to use in salads or omelettes, or to cook like spinach. The larger leaves are handy to use as home-grown "foil" for wrapping meat you are baking or barbecuing. Sorrel will grow in light shade. Z4–8.

Mint (3) is a real thug if you let it spread, so most people grow it in a large plastic pot sunk to the rim in the ground. It likes plenty of moisture and it's a greedy plant, so when it's grown in a pot, give it liquid fertilizer every few weeks. In the ground, mulch it heavily each spring with rich compost and dose it with general-purpose organic fertilizer. Dig up a few roots to start a new mint patch every 2–3 years, since it soon exhausts the ground. If you want fresh mint in winter, pot up a few roots in autumn to keep on a windowsill indoors.

There are several kinds of mint to choose from: spearmint, *Mentha spicata* (Z3–7), is the best for mint sauce, but the furry, round-leaved "Bowles mint" (*M.* × *villosa* var. *alopecuroides*, Z5–8) is the one to put in the pan with your home-grown new potatoes. For something prettier for containers, try gold-variegated ginger mint (*M.* × *gracilis* 'Variegata', Z6–9), or white-edged pineapple mint (*M. suaveolens* 'Variegata', Z6–9), in pots by the back door. Or try them mixed with bedding plants, such as *Mimulus*, which enjoy similar conditions.

Fennel (*Foeniculum vulgare*) (4) has feathery, anise-flavored leaves that are used mostly for cooking with fish – don't confuse the herb fennel with the fat, swollen Florence fennel that is used as a vegetable. Bronze fennel (*F. vulgare* 'Purpureum') looks prettier, if it's a more ornamental effect you want, and the foliage can be used for cooking in the same way as the plain green sort. The flat yellow flower heads look pretty, but if you let fennel run to seed – which it does naturally after midsummer, making a plant 4ft (1.2m) tall and 2ft (60cm) across by then – you can anticipate a whole lot of self-sown seedlings next year. Z4–9.

2 Sorrel (*Rumex acetosa*)
3 Mint (*Mentha suaveolens* 'Variegata').
4 Fennel (*Foeniculum vulgare* 'Purpureum').

2

3

4

Annual herbs

Think of annual herbs as culinary bedding plants – they'll do best in richer soil, with a degree of shelter and plenty of fertilizer and water. If you want to produce industrial quantities for drying or freezing, then grow them in rows in the vegetable patch. If you only need a few, grow them in a multistory planter by the kitchen door, team them with annual flowers in pots and hanging baskets, or plant them in a potager with other crops. For best results, sow annual herbs in pots in a greenhouse or on a windowsill indoors in spring, then plant them out when the soil warms up a bit.

Parsley (1) comes in flat-leaved and curled-leaved cultivars; the flat-leaved sorts are considered to have the better flavor; the curled looks better as garnish. Seed germinates best at 70°F (21°C) and even though it will come up outside, it is very slow. Sow it thinly in small pots indoors and plant out the whole potful without disturbing the roots – seedlings don't like being pricked out. In any case, a potful grows quickly into a thick clump, 9 × 9in (23 × 23cm), that produces much more parsley than a single plant. Parsley is biennial, so although it comes up again in its second year, it only does so in order to flower. It then goes to seed right away, so you need to sow a new batch each spring.

Basil (2) is indispensable, and specialized seed producers and herb farms offer a range of cultivars, from the large lettuce-leaved to the highly perfumed Genovese basil, including types with fringed leaves or purple foliage. Basil is a real lover of warmth, whose seedlings do best at warm temperatures – don't plant them out for a couple of weeks after the last frost to be on the safe side. Most basils grow about 12 × 6–12in (30 × 15–30cm); nip out the tips regularly to keep plants leafy instead of going to seed. Even so, you'll still need to sow 2–3 lots of basil over the growing season, because plants lose the urge to grow bushier once they reach flowering stage. Most people love them with tomatoes and mozzarella cheese, but try them on buttered carrots, too. Wow!

Cilantro (3) has leaves that look very similar to flat-leaved parsley, but the flavor is slightly peppery – add a few to salads or to home-made curries just before you serve them. Like basil, it's popular as a leafy herb, but unless you sow a named cultivar that is bred specially for leaf production, it will try to go to seed. The seeds, if left on the plants to ripen, are the source of coriander spice that is used in curries and other sauces. Grind your own in a peppermill – used right away it has much more flavor than the already-ground stuff you buy.

Chervil (4) has fine ferny leaves with a delicate, anise-like flavor, but it is quite a short-lived annual, 6 × 6in (15 × 25cm), that runs to seed within a few months. Pick all the leaves you can use before it flowers, then pull it out and sow some more.

Dill (5) is like fennel that's been on a diet; it has the same feathery leaves and similar upright, bushy shape, and if you let it go to seed you'll recognize the family resemblance in the flat heads of yellow flowers. If you are growing dill for the leaves, keep it closely cut to delay flowering, but if you want it for seed, then avoid cutting the leaves – it'll reach 3 × 1ft (90 × 30cm). Let the seed ripen naturally on the plant, then complete the drying process by hanging the heads upside down in paper bags in a cool, airy shed.

Borage (6) is pretty rather than terribly useful, but essential if you want an herb garden that attracts bees. The prickly oval leaves make a rosette at first then send up a thick succulent stem hanging with blue flowers, which are pretty when included in cold drinks. If you want to be very fancy, freeze the flowers in an ice tray and add them to other summer drinks, too.

1 Flat-leaved parsley.
2 Sweet basil (*Ocimum basilicum*).
3 Cilantro.
4 Chervil.
5 Dill.
6 Borage (*Borago officinalis*).

15 WILDLIFE GARDENS

Gardens and wildlife

The last fifty years have seen a gradual role reversal. Nowadays, it's often the countryside that is highly manicured, and it's gardens that wildlife rely on for a living.

The popularity of garden ponds has meant a huge increase in the numbers of newts and frogs; many butterflies that are now scarce in the country find everything they need in gardens, and several once-common countryside birds now rely on gardens for food supplies, especially in winter. At Barleywood, we have thriving colonies of long-tailed tits, wrens, tree creepers, and woodpeckers, which, years ago, you'd never have seen.

Much of the difference is due to the far lower usage of pesticides in gardens than on farmland, even among people who don't go completely organic, but a lot of gardens are also being designed and managed with wildlife much more in mind. It's a good thing for all concerned, even if it does mean learning a slightly new way of gardening.

Once the garden has been designed and planted up, leave it alone as much as possible – the less disturbance it gets, the better your chances of attracting scarce creatures such as newts and stag beetles. Don't clear away old perennial flower stems until spring; spiders and other beneficial insects use the dead plants to hibernate in during the winter.

But don't give up gardening – even in a wild garden, you still need to clear out brambles, nuisance weeds, and unwanted tree saplings before they become established. Mulch woodland corners in spring with leaf mold, chopped-up leaves, or bark chips, and in autumn, allow fallen leaves to pile up naturally. Cut down pond-side plants and wild flowers in late autumn, after they've shed their seeds, or leave them until early next spring, just before the new growth starts.

What's in it for you?

A little wildlife adds a lot to the garden. There's always something to watch – a mother robin teaching her babies how to tug worms out of the lawn, or frogs gathering for their ritual get-together in the pond each spring. There's a background of natural sounds from the dawn chorus, croaking and buzzing, to territorial calls of birds and, if you're lucky, owls high in the trees on calm nights. There are butterflies, birds, and bees, and strange insects to identify, and with something to interest the whole family, the garden can become – dare I say it – educational.

Garden ponds have become a stronghold for frogs (*top*), whose natural habitats are vanishing. Frogs are great slug eaters, too. Flowers with plenty of nectar, such as sedum, will attract butterflies (*bottom*).

From an ecological standpoint, all those different kinds of creatures interreact with each other in some way, and that can be a very good thing for the gardener, because in time a natural balance establishes itself. The "good" wildlife cancels out the "bad" wildlife and will take care of garden pests automatically. Well, partially at least.

By doing something as simple as not spraying the aphids on your roses, all sorts of creatures, such as lacewings, hoverflies, and song birds, will turn up to feed on them. Once insects take up residence in gardens, larger creatures such as birds and bats drop in to feed on them, and they all do their bit to help.

Nature is an intricately balanced and interdependent network of organisms, from insects to birds and mammals, and any interference by the gardener is bound to upset things. The trick is to try and go along with everything and just tweak here and there, rather than barge in with a sledgehammer.

In time, predators and pests achieve a natural balance, and, although you never get rid of your pest problem entirely, there won't be enough pests to do much damage – if pest numbers rise, then predators will increase in proportion to mop them up before there's a problem. It's biological control at its best – effortless and free and, above all, natural.

How to start the ball rolling

The first step in natural gardening is to quit the chemical habit. If you've been a chemical user for a long time, you'll have eradicated most of the beneficial creatures from the garden, and it will take them a while to find their way back. They won't put in an appearance until there's a supply of food to attract them, so you can anticipate a "difficult" gardening season or two when you first stop using chemicals. The ubiquitous pests, such as aphids and slugs, will inevitably build up before the good guys move in – but stick with it.

Anything you can do to make the garden more wildlife-friendly will help, even if you don't create a special wildlife garden – just incorporate a few of its features around your existing garden. Leave uncleared patches of old plant stems and long grass at the back of borders or around the edges of the garden, where beneficial insects can overwinter; then they'll be ready to go back to work right away in spring.

You don't fancy giving up on chemicals? Well, more and more garden chemicals are being withdrawn from the market every year on safety grounds. That gives you food for thought, doesn't it? You might just as well look to sensible alternatives before there are none left at all.

Caterpillar food plants

Attracting adult butterflies is one thing, but any responsible wildlife gardener gives them somewhere to lay their eggs and provides food for their caterpillars. Most of the carrot family provides food for species of swallowtails, and milkweed and butterfly weed are favored by monarch caterpillars. Fritillaries (the insects, not the bulbous plants) feed on violets and their relatives, and the comma and question mark butterflies' larvae will show up on elms and hackberries. Many moths lay eggs on apple, willow, hawthorn, or poplar trees.

Hang feeders for birds in autumn to sustain them through the winter.

Making a wildlife garden

It makes sense to design a garden so that the features you use most, like a patio and the lawn, are closest to the house, with your best flower beds forming a view from the living-room windows, leaving the more natural-looking area elsewhere in the garden.

It's the most practical arrangement – this way, you avoid bringing mud indoors; it helps the garden blend in to surrounding fields if you live out in the countryside, and wildlife won't be disturbed because you won't need to walk through "their" patch

This wildlife area is positioned at the far end of a long, narrow garden. Although cultivated, it takes its inspiration from the lines of the natural landscape.

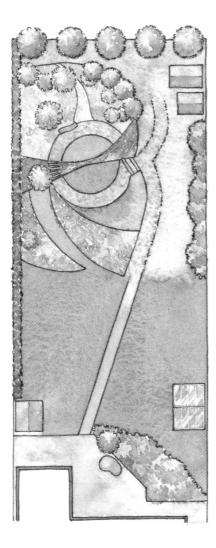

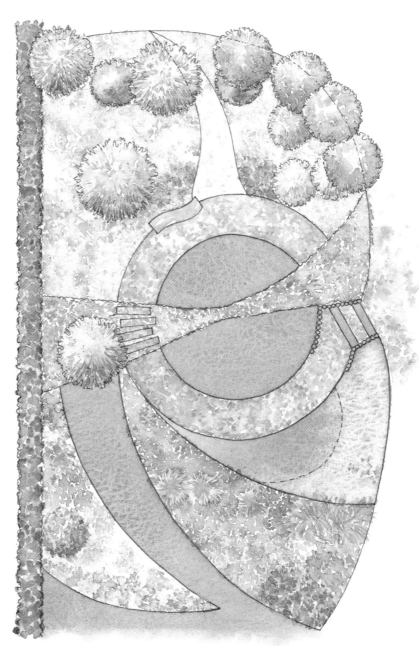

every time you sit out on the patio or go to the shed. Even quite shy creatures will be attracted, in time.

That's the way I've planned Barleywood – when you go out the back door, there's a paved courtyard garden, followed by several different flower gardens, but the higher up the hill you go, the more natural the garden becomes, until you reach the top, when it levels out into a wildflower meadow surrounded by woods.

But don't go away with the idea that you must live in the country to have a wildlife garden – far from it. In a small town garden you can dedicate a special wild area, but if you have space to make a separate wildlife garden room, screened off behind fences, hedges, or shrub borders, it's as good as having the countryside right on your doorstep.

Making it happen

To attract wildlife, the garden needs to provide certain basic facilities. A supply of food is essential – both naturally occurring food, such as insects and thistleheads, and food you put out specially, such as bird seed. Water is vital for drinking, but birds also need to bathe, and amphibians need larger areas of water to breed in, so think about making a pond. All wildlife needs shelter and security, so they'll feel more at home given patches of long grass, dense shrubs, ivy on walls, trees for birds to perch, roost, and nest in, stacks of logs, dead leaves, old plant stems and rotting vegetation.

The challenge of a wildlife garden is to put together all these ingredients, which are usually left out of "polite" gardens, in a way that looks attractive to humans as well.

My ideal small wildlife patch would contain one good-sized tree, a few fruiting or berrying shrubs, some long grass with a short path mowed through it, and banks of wildflowers. A mixed hedge would provide food and shelter for birds, insects, and mammals, and a pile of logs held together with soil would suit the creepy-crawlies. Remember that 40 percent of woodland wildlife lives in rotting wood.

Give yourself a bench or a fallen log to sit on, and position it in front of a pond – the sort with shallow edges, so it makes a natural bathing beach. If you don't have room for them all, simply select your favorites, but the more features you can fit in, and the greater the diversity of plants you include, the more types of wildlife your garden will attract.

How to encourage birds

Birds will visit the garden out of curiosity, but the more they like it, the more you'll see of them. There are several things you can do to make your garden into a mini bird sanctuary.

Bats

Night-flowering plants, such as the 3ft (90cm) tall, white flowering tobacco (Nicotiana sylvestris) *and wild thornapple* (Datura stramonium), *attract moths that also draw in bats, which feed on night-flying insects. Moths will also be attracted by a light left on in the garden at night. Now that modern houses don't have the easy access to roof spaces that old buildings once did, you might think about putting bat boxes up in tall trees – they look like nest boxes for birds, but with long, narrow slots instead of the usual round entrance holes.*

Grow plants that provide them with natural food – seeds of ornamental and wild grasses, berries, and fruits, sunflowers, and thistlelike plants, such as teasels. Put out bird seed, suet, bits of cheese, and dried fruit – especially in winter, when there's not much natural food around, and in spring, when they have chicks to feed. Peanuts are fine in winter, but don't put them out in spring, because baby birds can choke on them. Real enthusiasts have live mealworms delivered to put out for insect-eaters in spring.

A shallow bowl of water is always popular for bathing in, if you don't have a pond with shelving edges for birds to use, but many birds enjoy giving themselves dust baths, so a border with fine powdery soil that stays dry in summer becomes a popular stop-over. Otherwise, spread some fine sand in a small hollow in a garden bed, which birds will soon find.

Trees and large shrubs are essential for birds; they need cover to get away from predators. Birds always feel happier about feeding where there's a thicket nearby that they can escape to when they feel threatened. A tall tree with a pointed top, or a bare horizontal branch sticking out, always makes a popular place for male birds to sing their territorial songs to warn off other males in the area. The more perching and roosting places the better, but you need quite dense foliage for birds to stop and nest.

Creating a wildflower lawn

If you have a wildflower meadow, cut it once in early spring then leave it long until August, mowing short grass paths through it to allow access. Use a scythe or line trimmer to cut it, rake up the "hay," and cart it away. If your grass is a more normal lawn that contains short-growing wildflowers, such as primroses, violets, and bird's-foot trefoil (see page 528), cut it once a month or so with the blades set high so that they pass safely over the flowers.

Bird feeders (*above*) bring life to any garden, while plug plants (*below*) can be established in existing grassy areas more easily than wildflower seeds. Even cowslips (*right*) can be encouraged to grow in profusion within a couple of years.

Ten widely cultivated flowers for butterflies and bees

Sedum spectabile
ice plant, 24 × 18in
(60 × 45cm); chunky
succulent stems
topped by flat
clusters of pink
flowers are very
sought after by
butterflies and bees
in late summer and
autumn.

Helenium
30 × 24in
(75 × 60cm); orange
or yellow daisies in
late summer that are
very popular with
butterflies and bees.

Lavender
24 × 36in
(60 × 90cm); mauve
or purple scented
flowers in summer,
much loved by bees.

Marjoram
12 × 18in
(30 × 45cm); sprays
of pink flowers on
aromatic plants in
summer attract a
good variety of
butterflies as well
as bees.

Mint
36 × 36in
(90 × 90cm); short
spikes of mauve
flowers in summer
attract butterflies
and bees. Buddleia
mint has the biggest
spikes of flowers
and attracts most
insects, including
beneficial kinds.

Achillea
milfoil, 30 × 18in
(75 × 45cm); flat-
topped summer
flowers in red, pink,
or yellow that attract
butterflies, bees, and
beetles.

Centranthus ruber
valerian, 36 × 24in
(90 × 60cm); clusters
of small red, pink, or
white flowers at the
tips of the stems in
summer attract
butterflies and bees.

Solidago
goldenrod, 36 × 36in
(90 × 90cm); spires
of yellow flowers
from mid- to late
summer attract bees
and butterflies. They
are not responsible
for causing or aggra-
vating hay fever.

Scabiosa
scabious, 30 × 18in
(75 × 45cm); large
pincushion blue or
white flowers,
irresistible to
butterflies.

Aster novae-angliae
New England aster,
42 × 30in
(105 × 75cm); sprays
of small autumn
daisies in pink,
mauve, purple, and
blue shades on tall
stems, good for
butterflies and bees.

1 *Crataegus persimilis* 'Prunifolia'.

Wildlife-friendly trees

Wildlife-friendly trees are the sort that provide fruit or berries for birds to eat and provide them with good cover from predators. They'll also be ideal places for birds to perch during the day, roost at night, or make nests. Nearly all trees house an insect population, too, another food source for the birds.

Tree species that have attractive blossoms are doubly valuable in the garden – all those I've listed here are suitable for a fairly small garden, and they look good enough to grow in a normal garden as well as in the wildlife kind.

Hawthorns (**1**) are all good wildlife trees (Z4–9), but *Crataegus persimilis* 'Prunifolia' (Z6–7) has everything; white blossoms in spring, large, red oval berries in late summer and autumn that persist well into winter, and maybe the best autumn color of all the hawthorns. The berries of this and many other hawthorns are a great favorite with waxwings. It reaches 15 × 8ft (4.5 × 2.4m).

Elderberries (*Sambucus nigra*) (**2**) make bushy trees, around 12 × 8ft (3.6 × 2.4m) with corky bark and a naturally craggy shape. The bark is a great insect refuge, and the flat-topped clusters of white flowers in midsummer are followed by purple-black berries that birds enjoy. Wild elderberries can be pruned to shape or cut back to a stump in early spring – you can cut them as hard as you like; they'll still grow back but won't flower that year. Cultivated forms of *S. nigra* have finely cut, colored or variegated leaves, some of them with great autumn color. They also carry bird-friendly fruit, though not in such large quantities as the wild species. Z6–8.

Holly (*Ilex* species and varieties, Z5–9) (**3**) have berries that are often left untouched fora long time. Male and female flowers are carried on different plants, and usually only the females that have been fertilized by male pollen will carry berries, so you need at least one of each sex. However, *Ilex aquifolium* 'J.C. van Tol' (Z7–9) is a female sort that does not require cross-fertilization to fruit.

Crabapples (**4**) are more decorative than culinary apples and equally appreciated by wildlife. They have attractive white or pale pink spring blossoms and large crops of small red, orange, purple, or yellow apple-shaped fruit. They are often little larger than big berries and usually vanish by early winter. Some cultivars have fruits that hang for a long time on the trees, providing useful late winter food for birds; if that's your main requirement, go for *Malus* 'Red Jade' (small red fruit) and 'Golden Hornet' (lots of yellow fruit). Anticipate roughly 15 × 10ft (4.5 × 3m). Z4–8.

Cotoneaster (5) (Z5–9) berries are great favorites with birds and are usually taken as soon as they ripen in late summer, but a big tree cotoneaster, such as *Cotoneaster frigidus* 'Cornubia' (Z7–8), at 18 × 18ft (5.4 × 5.4m) makes a spectacular focal point in a garden. It provides so much bird food that the berries last quite a long time before they're all gone.

Shadblows (*Amelanchier*) (6) have clusters of beautiful and delicate white spring blossoms that appear just about the same time as the young foliage is opening out to pale bronze. Small red berries ripen to purple or black in summer, when the branches are full of birds in search of a meal, well before most other berries are at the eatable stage. Most shadblows also color well in the autumn – a bonus for the humans. Allow about 15 × 15ft (4.5 × 4.5m). Z3–9.

Apple trees (7) provide valuable perching places for birds and are also inclined to attract aphids and other insects for them to feed on; in late summer and autumn, windfall apples are eaten by all sorts of birds and mammals. A standard apple tree on a semi-dwarfing rootstock will occupy a space of about 12–15ft (3–4.5m). Z3–9.

2 *Sambucus nigra*
  'Guincho Purple'.
3 *Ilex* 'J.C. van Tol'.
4 *Malus* 'Golden Hornet'.
5 *Cotoneaster* 'Coral Beauty'.
6 *Amelanchier lamarckii*.
7 *Apple* 'Winston'.

Shrubs to attract wildlife

These are plants to grow in a mixed hedge or windbreak; you can also plant them in a border with decorative shrubs or grow them in groups in a wildlife garden.

Buckthorns (*Rhamnus*) (**1**) are deciduous shrubs with bright red autumn leaves, and red berries that turn black when ripe in summer. Allow about 8 × 8ft (2.4 × 2.4m). They grow in grim conditions, including boggy, acidic soil, but are also happy in normal garden soil. Some are considered invasive, however. Z3–9.

Guelder rose (*Viburnum opulus*) (**2**) bears clusters of white flowers, followed in late summer by bunches of red berries; it is a tall, upright, bushy shrub, about 8 × 4ft (2.4 × 1.2m). It's good for wet, heavy clay soil and very tolerant of poor conditions in general. You need two plants for a good crop of fruits, so put both into the same hole when you plant if you don't have much room. Z4–8.

Privet (*Ligustrum*) (**3**) might not appear a natural choice for wildlife, but a hedge of it is an apartment complex for a wide range of birds. If you don't want a hedge, grow one as a shrub. Unclipped privets have white flowers that attract insects and insect-eating birds, and the flowers are followed by black berries. Z3–10.

Firethorn (*Pyracantha*) (**4**) makes a good, predator-proof hedge, and if you don't have room for a large, free-standing shrub roughly 8 × 8ft (2.4 × 2.4m), it's also very attractive trained flat against a wall. Besides making a safe place for birds to perch and nest, the berries are in great demand in winter and are usually left until after cotoneaster berries, which birds generally prefer. Z5–9.

Butterfly bush (*Buddleja davidii*) (**5**) is well known for attracting butterflies into gardens, but wild seedlings turn up all around railroad tracks, so it's quite acceptable in a wildlife garden. The cone-shaped purple, mauve, blue, or white flower heads appear from mid- to late summer and attract several species of butterflies with their abundant nectar. Z6–9.

Barberries (**6**) of all sorts offer thorny shelter and berries, though for a wildlife garden, the large and prickliest evergreens with the biggest crops of berries are probably better than the smaller and more polite garden kinds – they have orange or yellow flowers in early summer. Among the best are *Berberis darwinii* (Z7–9), *Berberis julianae* (Z6–9), and *B. × stenophylla* (Z6–9), both about 10 × 10ft (3 × 3m), with black berries.

1 *Rhamnus frangula.*
2 *Viburnum opulus.*

Roses (7) that produce hips are good specimen shrubs for a
wildlife garden, but if you want a hedge for an open, windy spot,
then the best are cultivars of *Rosa rugosa* (Z2–9), which have
wrinkled leaves and big, squashy, tomato-shaped hips. They include
'Scabrosa', 6 × 4ft (2 × 1.2m), with mauve-pink flowers, and 'Fru
Dagmar Hastrup', 3 × 3ft (1 × 1m), with pink flowers. They have
the biggest hips, and birds can go mad over them. *R. pimpinellifolia*
(Z3–9), which has ferny leaves and small black hips, is as good, but
choose cultivars with single flowers; double-flowered forms rarely
have hips. *R.* 'Geranium' (Z4–9), 8 × 6ft (2.4 × 2m) has single red
flowers that bees love, followed by scarlet bottle-shaped hips.

Rubus species (8) include several that are prickly, edible-fruited
scramblers for wildlife gardens; Japanese wineberry (*R.
phoenicolasius*, Z5–9), with handsome, red-bristly stems, is good
for training along a fence, say 4–8ft (1.2–2.4m). Use the
strawberry-raspberry (*R. illecebrosus*, Z5–9) for covering a bank –
it'll reach about 1–6ft (30cm–2m), but it's not self-fertile, so you
need two plants. But if you have room, then cultivated blackberries
and loganberries always find a firm following with birds, and even
foxes and other mammals will take blackberries.

3 *Ligustrum vulgare.*
4 Pyracantha.
5 *Buddleja* 'Lochinch'.
6 *Berberis* 'Goldilocks'.
7 *Rosa rugosa.*
8 *Rubus* 'Loch Ness'.

There is something particularly pleasing about a patch of wildflowers – even if we do get the feeling that nature can manage perfectly well without us.

1 *Cardamine pratensis.*
2 *Caltha palustris* var. *palustris.*
3 *Menyanthes trifoliata.*

Wildflowers

Wildflowers (including non-native species with a "wild" look) are more than just decoration for a wildlife garden, they are wildlife in the vegetable sense of the word. A good range of wildflowers is vital to attract insects and feed their larvae. To grow your own, sow seeds in pots or cell-trays – annuals in spring, perennials in autumn – then plant them out into soil that has been forked over but *not* fertilized.

Mix grassland species with grass seed, then sow them as you'd sow a new lawn – without the fertilizer. Better still, plant young plants into short grass; cut out a plug of sod and plant into the gap in autumn. Sprinkling wildflower seed into existing grass doesn't work.

Wildflowers for damp ground and around ponds

Some are happiest with their feet in water, or at least in mud. They make a perfect bridge between pond and garden.

Lady's smock (*Cardamine pratensis*) (**1**) is a slender, 24 × 6in (60 × 15cm) plant with watercress-like leaves, from which 6in (15cm) spikes of lilac-pink flowers emerge in spring. Good for moist, sunny places, including short grass, or beside ponds. Z5–8.

Marsh marigold (*Caltha palustris*) (**2**) or kingcup, makes a rounded, 2 × 2ft (60 × 60cm) clump of heart-shaped leaves; it flowers from March to June with yellow flowers that look like large, single buttercups. It grows in boggy ground and in shallow water. Z3–7.

Bog bean (*Menyanthes trifoliata*) (**3**) is a water plant that's ideal for boggy ground or at the edges of a wildlife pond. The leaves run out over the water, to about 4ft (1.2m), with delicate white flowers on 6in (15cm) spikes sticking up above them. Z3–7.

1

2

3

Wildflowers for long grass

There are two main groups of wildflowers that live in long grass: annuals and perennials – the latter being those that will persist by self-seeding without cultivating the soil in between times.

Ox-eye daisy (*Leucanthemum vulgare*) (**4**) is like a looser version of a chrysanthemum, with yellow-centered, white-petaled daisies standing up on stems 18–24in (45–60cm) tall, in summer. It's very impressive spaced out evenly in a stand of long grass, and it's a perennial so it comes up every year. Introduce it as plugs, and you'll have it forever. Z3–8.

Field poppy (*Papaver rhoeas*) (**5**) is one of the best annuals (along with bachelor's buttons – *Centaurea cyanus* – as well as *Coreopsis*, *Gaillardia*, and *Cosmos*) for colonizing newly cleared ground. The previous species are often a major constituent of wildflower seed mixes, along with other nonnative and native species. The poppies grow to about 12in (30cm) high with a 8in (20cm) spread. After the first year, self-sown seeds will be in the soil, so they'll come up again automatically – provided that it is raked over and disturbed. Allow it to remain untouched, and the grasses will take over and the flowers will disappear. Annual.

Yellow rattle (*Rhinanthus minor*) (**6**) looks like a feeble stinging nettle, grows to 2ft (60cm) tall, but often less, with small leaves and big, pale yellow flowers. It doesn't sting and it's actually a semi-parasite of grass, so it's handy for curbing the vigor of coarse grasses that often make a meadow look out of control. The hollow seedheads rattle in the wind, or when the long grass is cut, hence the name. It's an annual or short-lived perennial that can take a while to get established, but then it persists by self-seeding. Z6–8.

4 *Leucanthemum vulgare.*
5 *Papaver rhoeas* Shirley series.
6 *Rhinanthus minor.*

Wildflowers for shade under trees

This is where you can create a little patch of woodland fringe – where many birds take shelter and the larvae of some butterflies and moths feed and pupate.

Wood anemone (*Anemone nemorosa*) (**1**) is a perennial spring flower, 6–8 × 6in (15–20 × 15cm), that grows from a slow-spreading underground stem, and dies down shortly after flowering. The flowers look fragile – white, single, and starry – growing just above delicate, buttercup-shaped foliage. It needs to be grown in carpets to make an effect, and it takes time to establish, but it's absolutely charming. It needs light shade, as in a woodland clearing – in too dense shade, it can remain dormant for years until there's more light. Z4–8.

Celandine (*Ranunculus ficaria*) (**2**) is usually a nuisance in gardens, but in damp, shady ground under trees and shrubs in a wildlife garden, it makes shining carpets of gold that really light the place up in spring. By early summer, the foliage has died down and the plants have disappeared until next year. Z4–8.

1 *Anemone nemorosa.*
2 *Ranunculus ficaria.*
3 *Geranium phaeum.*
4 *Digitalis purpurea.*
5 *Fragaria vesca.*

Dusky cranesbill (*Geranium phaeum*) (**3**), or mourning widow, has been domesticated in gardens, but once you've bought a plant, it'll self-seed gently, coming up between shrubs and among other flowers, in well-drained to dry soil, including shady places. The flowers are deep maroon, almost black, but lilac and white forms often turn up as self-sown seedlings. Z4–8.

Foxglove (*Digitalis purpurea*) (**4**) is a short-lived perennial that self-seeds, so you'll find seedlings coming up here and there, and it'll grow in light shade under trees, as well as in clearings on any soil that's not too dry. Plants can reach 6ft (2m) where they are happy, but mostly they are about 3–4ft (1–1.2m), with a basal rosette of large leaves up to 2ft (60cm) across; plants look best in groups. The spotted, mauve-purple, thimble-shaped flowers, arranged in rows up the stems, are great favorites with bumblebees. Z4–8.

Wild strawberry (*Fragaria vesca*) (**5**) looks like a miniature version of the cultivated strawberry plant, with three-lobed leaves and white flowers in summer. They are followed by red, finger-tip-sized fruits, which are tasty to eat but very fussy to pick, so they're best left to the birds. It spreads slowly by runners, making loose, open mats maybe 3 × 4ft (1 × 1.2m); good as a fruiting groundcover in damp, shady places under trees. Z5–9.

Look upon a grove of foxgloves in late spring. and admit to yourself that there are few sights as elegant or breathtaking.

Wildflowers for short grass

These are for those who can't get to grips with a full-blown meadow; just mow the grass with the blades set high enough to miss these little treasures.

Cowslips (*Primula veris*) (**1**) flower in spring, with tubular golden flowers in clusters at the top of a 8in (20cm) stalk. They prefer drier ground and more open situations than many other primroses, so while you'll find many of them in wet spots, cowslips will be the ones growing out in the drier meadow. Z3–8.

Bird's-foot trefoil (*Lotus corniculatus*) (**2**) likes dry, sunny spots and can be a lawn weed on sandy soils. The yellow pea flowers are often streaked with red. They are visited by several butterflies in search of nectar, and the leaves feed caterpillars of skippers and hairstreak butterflies. Z5–8.

Common primrose (*Primula vulgaris*) (**3**) makes 4 × 6in (10 × 15cm) clumps of pale yellow flowers in ealy spring; it'll grow in bare soil between shrubs, but it's happiest in short, damp, shady grass. Z4–8.

Violets (**4**) are plants of moist shade that make small clumps of heart-shaped leaves that are studded with typical violet flowers. Sweet violet (*Viola odorata*, Z8–9) has scented flowers from late winter into spring and spreads by runners to make low a groundcover up to 18in (45cm) wide. The dog violet (*V. riviniana*, Z5–8) flowers in late spring and early summer but is unscented and remains as clumps. Heartsease (*V. tricolor*, Z4–8) is more like a miniature pansy than a violet; the plants are upright, with 8in (20cm) stems topped by little flowers in cream, yellow, and purple. It grows in poor-quality, underfertilized lawns, but it's worth planting in a wildflower lawn, where it will self-seed but never enough to be a nuisance.

1 *Primula veris.*
2 *Lotus corniculatus.*
3 *Primula vulgaris.*
4 *Viola tricolor.*

How to... **build a birdhouse**

Of course, you can cheat and buy a ready-made birdhouse, but if you have a few odd bits of lumber kicking around, you don't need a degree in civil engineering to make your own condominium for local birds. Put up the birdhouses in autumn to give the birds a chance to check them out before they start settling into their spring nesting sites. You will also be offering year-round residents suitable roosting place for the winter months. Site birdhouses above head height, where they will present a challenge to marauding cats. Avoid facing them into the prevailing wind.

What you need

- *pieces of wood cut to size appropriate for the birds you're trying to attract (ask local experts, look in books, or go online for specific dimemensions)*
- *nails and screws*
- *hammer and screwdriver*
- *roofing felt or reinforcing wooden strips*

1 Make the birdhouse from pieces of wood cut to the sizes you've chosen for a given species. You can use weatherproof plywood or old floorboards (although the latter might have a more limited life). It's a good idea for the roof to slope just a bit. Nail the bottom, back, and side sections together.

2 The roof can be more elaborate, either with reinforcing ridges (made from semicircular wooden rods), or with a piece of roofing felt to make it more weatherproof. The front of the box should have a hole cut to the diameter preferred by the species you are attempting to attract; some species don't want a hole a prefer a large "window" instead.

3 Cut a channel through the lower edge of the front, then screw the section in place about 2in (5cm) from the top edge. Hammer a headless nail through the channel and bend it over to act as a fastening. At the end of the winter, swivel the headless nail and swing open the front so that you can remove old nests and clean out the inside. A clean box is more likely to attract new occupants.

16 COVERED GARDENS

Greenhouse gardening

In gardening terms, glass is what you might call a luxury. You can get by without it, but if you take the plunge and invest in a greenhouse or conservatory, you'll never regret it. Gardening under cover opens up so many new opportunities – new plants to grow, more propagation techniques to try – and, it has to be said, it's great fun. Under glass, you are in your own little world where you can get away from it all, forget everything else, and just potter about with plants – whatever the weather.

A greenhouse can be used for practical or decorative purposes – most folk use theirs for a bit of both. If you incline toward the decorative, you'll probably want to use it for plants that are too delicate to put out in the garden, or a collection of specialized plants for which you need complete control over the growing environment. If you fall into the practical camp and live in an area with coolish summers, you could raise indoor tomatoes, peppers, and melons, which produce far heavier yields in a greenhouse than in the open. You'll also be able to propagate plants on a much bigger scale than you could manage on the windowsills indoors.

Greenhouses are rather like boats – the smaller the size, the greater the pleasure.

If you're buying a new greenhouse, it's worth the extra expense of putting in some heating. You'll not only be able to add frost-tender plants to your collection and keep tender patio perennials through the winter, you'll also have a winter retreat where you can garden all the year around. But it's not worth heating a whole greenhouse just for a couple of geraniums – if you are going to heat it, use it to the max, and fill it up with exciting plants that justify the expense.

Where do I put it?

When you start with an empty garden, it's no trouble to find a spot for a greenhouse. You can pick the perfect place and just work the rest of the garden around it. Does that sound a bit drastic? The trouble is, by the time most people get around to buying one, they already have a fairly well-filled garden, so it's a case of putting it wherever you can. You may be able to dig up a patch of lawn or take a chunk out of the vegetable garden. It might mean taking down a tree to let more light in, or clearing part of a border.

You see, a greenhouse needs plenty of light, and there must be easy access for glass-cleaning and general maintenance all around. It needs to be well away from trees that cut out sunlight and that drop branches or leaves. You don't need to hide a greenhouse away down at the end of the garden; if you choose a good-looking one and fill it with displays of potted plants, it can be quite a feature of the garden, just like any other garden building. The greenhouse at Barleywood is the star of its own Mediterranean garden. But if you're going for a more functional house, to grow indoor tomatoes and raise cuttings, then it's most practical to put it close to the shed and the vegetable patch.

You also need to think about other facilities you'll need in the greenhouse. You'll need a water and electricity supply nearby, and a hard path leading up to it. These can be quite expensive to put in, so it pays to choose a spot not too far from existing services.

Types of greenhouse

The cheapest greenhouse you can buy is a standard-sized, aluminum-framed one from the home-supply stores, usually about 8 × 6ft (2.4 × 2m). But if price isn't your top priority, it's worth looking around at various greenhouse manufacturers' catalogs to see what else is available. There are various other styles and sizes that might suit you better – it just depends on how much you want to invest.

Wooden greenhouses have a traditional look and feel, and any time you want to put shading or insulation materials up inside, you can just use drawing pins instead of needing to buy special gadgets.

Plants around a greenhouse

Unlike a shed or gazebo, you can't really plant trees and shrubs to fuzz the shape of a greenhouse, because you don't want anything that'll plunge it into shade. But that doesn't mean it must stand out like a sore thumb.

You can grow a carpet of low plants around it, or go traditional and plant narrow beds of flowers for cutting around the sides. Plants like nerines, Amaryllis belladonna, *and winter-flowering* Iris unguicularis *would be fun to try; they enjoy the sun and warmth reflected by the glass but don't cast any shade.*

Otherwise, you can screen the greenhouse by planting a bed of shrubs (or a trellis with climbers) closer to the living room windows than the greenhouse, so that they mask it from view but don't block out any of the light.

533

Try to make sure that a greenhouse fits comfortably into a garden, rather than sticking out like a sore thumb.

The downside is that you need to treat the wood with preservative every year to prevent rot, and, as wooden greenhouses age, they start needing quite a bit of maintenance.

Metal greenhouses need little maintenance, and modern glazing means they are sealed against drafts, so there are fewer worries if you are heating them. If you fancy a change from the functional type, you could choose one of the mock Victorian styles, or go for a colored structure instead of bare metal – mine is this sort, in dark green. The plastic-coated alloy is virtually maintenance free.

Besides the conventional rectangular-shaped house, you can also find six-sided greenhouses, which are rather like glass gazebos – good for really tiny gardens where looks are important. You can pack them with plants, since they have staging on all sides except the one with the door. Both metal and wood models are available.

Lean-to greenhouses have rather gone out of fashion, since most people would rather have a conservatory these days. But if you have very little space, try a slim lean-to greenhouse, which is more like a glass cupboard with shelves. This can be a handy way of raising a few bedding plants, or making an indoor plant display, and it's economical to heat in winter. Overheating can be a problem in summer, though, unless you watch the ventilation; the temperature shoots up when the sun is shining on it.

Plastic tunnels don't look great, but if you can tuck one out of the way, they're a cheap alternative to a greenhouse for growing tomatoes in a cool summer. You can also use them as walk-in cold frames for out-of-season veg, bringing on young plants, or hardening off bedding. They don't need foundations like a proper greenhouse, but you do need to replace the plastic every 4–5 years; it goes brittle and tears after prolonged exposure to sun. Mine makes a valuable overflow from the greenhouse in winter, when it's bursting with plants that just need a little protection from frost.

Fitting out the greenhouse

There's no point in buying a lot of specialized greenhouse gear until you know how you'll actually use the house. If you'll be growing crops in beds in the ground, you don't need much, other than a row of paving slabs down the middle to divide the area into two soil borders, so that you can work without stepping on the soil.

If your main interest is in propagation or displaying a collection of potted plants, you'll need staging and possibly some shelves to make good use of the space, maybe a heater and propagating case too. People who want to grow a bit of everything compromise by paving half the floor area to stand staging on, leaving the other half as a soil border, which should be deeply dug, with lots of well rotted manure added.

Greenhouse jobs

There's no big mystery about gardening under glass: you simply do the same jobs you'd do outdoors – watering, fertilizing and weeding. But instead of just looking after plants, you need to control the climate as well, by heating and ventilating when necessary.

Fertilizing and watering

Most greenhouse plants are grown in containers of some kind, so fertilizing and watering will come as second nature to anyone who's ever grown houseplants or looked after pots on the patio. The big difference is that, under glass, plants dry out a lot faster in summer, because the greenhouse interior heats up so quickly when it's sunny.

The easiest way to keep greenhouse potted plants watered in summer is by standing them on capillary matting, which is like a thin, water-absorbing blanket covering the surface of the staging. If the pots are well watered initially, they'll soak up all they need as long as you use plastic pots with plenty of holes in the base and keep the capillary matting damp. Just give it a good drenching with the hose each morning when it needs it. Large containers are best watered by hand or fitted with a drip-irrigation system.

I must say, I prefer to stand my plants on staging covered with pea gravel – it keeps them stable, improves atmospheric humidity, and leaves the pleasure of watering to me. I call it gardening. Regular fertilizing, every week or ten days, is essential throughout summer, when greenhouse plants are growing fast. Liquid or soluble fertilizers are the best to use for plants in containers. If regular fertilizing isn't practical, then mix slow-release fertilizer granules into the soil mix you use to pot up the plants in spring. It should last them for the rest of the season.

When the weather is colder, in autumn and spring, plants won't be growing very fast, so they need very much less fertilizer and water than in summer, and in winter, many are barely doing anything. At this time, avoid watering any more than you need to, so that the humidity stays low. Cold, damp air encourages fungal diseases to attack resting plants.

Ventilation and shading

Keeping the greenhouse cool in summer helps prevent plants from drying out too fast and prevents other problems, such as scorched leaves, shed fruitlets, and aborted flower buds. The obvious way is to open the ventilators. Aim to do so as soon as the temperature rises above about 55°F (13°C). Fit automatic ventilator openers that can be preset to operate at a chosen temperature. That way

Remember that ventilation in summer is every bit as important as heating in winter.

Your greenhouse doesn't just need to be a functional addition to your garden (*opposite*), it can also be geared to ornamental plants and used as a conservatory.

you don't even need to think about it, and your plants won't burn up while you are away at work. It also helps to "damp down" daily by splashing water onto the greenhouse floor, which cools and humidifies the air as it evaporates.

Cutting out some of the sun is another way of preventing a greenhouse from overheating, so paint liquid shading on the outside of the glass each summer; it washes off again easily in autumn when you need the extra light. Alternatively, go for the luxury of blinds, which can be raised and lowered as necessary.

By ventilating, damping down, and shading, you keep the atmosphere inside the greenhouse much more tolerable; plants carry on growing, instead of shutting all systems down. Wilting is the first symptom of stress, but with regular watering and proper greenhouse management, you should be able to avoid it easily.

Heating and insulating

In winter, greenhouses suffer from exactly the opposite conditions; cold and excess moisture are the cause of a lot of problems. In much of the country, from September to May the greenhouse needs heating if you are going to use it for anything other than hardy plants.

The easiest way to do this is with an electric fan heater. Buy a greenhouse model, which has waterproof connections designed for use in a damp environment, although it won't stand being splashed with water. Position the heater roughly at the center of the greenhouse – low down, but not directly on the floor, since it will ingest a lot of dust and dirt, which wrecks the motor. Gas heaters that run off a cylinder or a gas line are available for greenhouses, but they are expensive. If you try to maintain temperatures higher than about 45°F (7°C), they produce a lot of water vapor that can encourage fungal diseases. Kerosene creates the same problem, but it is less often used for greenhouse heating nowadays due to the high price of the fuel and the bother of carriage and storage.

Whichever type of heating you choose, aim to keep the temperature in the greenhouse at least above freezing, around 38–40°F (3–5°C). To help reduce your heating bills, pin bubble-wrap insulation up in the roof or around the walls. Leave the ventilators free, so they can still operate normally. If it's totally sealed, the greenhouse environment will become very humid, and that really encourages fungal disease in cold, dull weather.

If you are heating the house, I'd strongly advise buying a maximum-minimum thermometer, so you can keep tabs on the overnight temperature and adjust the heater thermostat if need be. Thermostats aren't always accurate, so buying a thermometer could save you a fortune.

Greenhouse crops

There's a lot of satisfaction to be had from growing something to eat under glass. All those I've listed here are summer crops, but if you can turn on some heat in spring and autumn, they'll have a longer bearing season, which means bigger total yields.

Tomatoes (1) produce roughly 7lb (3kg) of fruit per plant under cold glass, and up to 15lb (7kg) if you plant early in a heated greenhouse. Both greenhouse and outdoor cultivars can be grown under glass, but greenhouse types really need warmth. Upright, cordon cultivars take up less room than the bush kinds. In an unheated house, plant only after the temperature remains well above freezing at night; you'll be picking ripe fruit from early July onward. If you turn the heat up to 50°F (10°C) at night, you can plant in early spring and start picking around early summer, but they'll be expensive tomatoes. It's more economical to plant later and turn on the heat to 40–45°F (5–7°C) as the nights turn cold in autumn – you could have tomatoes well into autumn.

After planting, water plants lightly to start with. Tie each plant to a 6ft (2m) stake as it grows, and remove sideshoots as they appear. After the first flower opens, water more and fertilize regularly with liquid tomato fertilizer. Leave tomatoes on the plants until they turn red, so the full flavor develops. Don't remove the bottom leaves until they turn yellow – it doesn't make the fruit ripen any faster. Nip the plants' tops out eight weeks before you want to pull them out at the end of the season; it helps partly developed tomatoes ripen, so you're not left with a lot of little green ones.

1 Greenhouse-grown tomatoes being tied up to prevent them from falling over.

Figs (2) fruit best when their roots are confined in a 15–18in (38–45cm) pot; when they are given a free root run, all they grow is masses of leaves. Plant a fig tree in spring or summer, using a soil-based potting mix. Train it into a fan shape, by nipping out misplaced shoots while they're tiny. Stand the tree flat against the greenhouse wall, where it won't take up much room. In summer, fertilize it regularly with liquid tomato fertilizer and water heavily, especially when the fruits are swelling. Prune in winter when it is dormant. Just reduce the size and improve the shape, so it doesn't get out of hand. Minimal heat is needed if you grow 'Brown Turkey' or 'Brunswick'.

Eggplant, sweet peppers, and chilli peppers (3) belong to the same family as tomatoes, and you can grow them in almost the same way (see page 537), but since the plants grow short and bushy, the only support they need is a short stake for the main stem. You won't get a huge crop of peppers, especially if you allow the fruit to turn red instead of picking them green, but one or two eggplant and chilli plants will produce enough for most households. They're a tad more tender than tomatoes, so plant 2–3 weeks later. The same goes for cucumbers and melons.

2 Fig (*Ficus carica* 'Brown Turkey').
3 Eggplant.
4 Cucumber 'Painted Serpent'.
5 Grapes.
6 Melon supported in a net.

Cucumbers (4) give incredibly high yields under glass, so a single plant is usually enough. You can expect to pick at least a couple of cucumbers each week, and 3–4 or more if you grow the short mini cucumbers. To save greenhouse space, grow one of the all-female F1 hybrid cultivars. In ordinary cultivars, if a female flower is pollinated by a male, the cucumbers become bitter. Always pinch off the chaps, the ones without a miniature cucumber behind them. Train the main stem up a tall stake, and remove all the tendrils and sideshoots. With the F1 type, the fruits grow from flowers that appear in the leaf axils, where a leaf joins the main stem.

Cucumbers can be touchy when first planted, so water them sparingly until they are 2ft (60cm) high. Then increase the supply, and fertilize them weekly with a general-purpose liquid fertilizer – they like more nitrogen than you find in tomato fertilizer. As a change from the usual kind, try lemon cucumbers, which have round, yellow, lemon-sized fruit. Grow them in exactly the same way, but *don't* remove the sideshoots; that's where the cucumbers grow from. Train them in the same way as cantaloupe plants.

Grape vines (5) take up a lot of room and create quite heavy shade, so don't try growing sunlovers, such as tomatoes, underneath. Only minimal heating is needed unless you want to grow late-ripening, specialized cultivars. Plant the roots in rich soil in a well-prepared border, and train one main stem up the back wall of the house and under the ridge. Thin out the sideshoots to 1ft (30cm) apart and train them down the glazing bars of the roof. These become your permanent framework of stems. Each year, sideshoots that grow from these will bear flowers, followed by grapes. After one or two bunches of grapes have set on each sideshoot, nip back the growing tip to a few leaves beyond the bunches. If you want big fruits, thin out the bunches when the grapes are about pea-sized, using narrow-nosed grape scissors to remove every other grape.

Keep the vine well-fertilized and watered in summer. Prune in winter when it is completely dormant, cutting all the sideshoots back to the main framework.

Cantaloupes (6) are grown just like F1 hybrid cucumber plants, apart from the training. Melons don't grow from the main stem but from sideshoots, so allow them to grow until you spot a swelling fruit and then "stop" that shoot; cut the tip off about two leaves beyond the baby melon. You should get 4–6 melons per plant over the summer, but to be sure of a crop, it's essential that the flowers are pollinated. If there aren't many bees about, hand-pollinate the flowers with a small, soft brush by dabbing it into all the fully open flowers, one after another, every couple of days.

Recommended varieties

Tomatoes – in unheated greenhouses grow any patio variety (see Chapter 6), plus beefsteak varieties such as 'Dombito' and 'Marmande'. Try medium-sized 'Marion', 'Sonato' and 'Stupice', which is very early.

Sweet peppers – grow any listed in Chapter 6 for outdoors, plus large-fruited 'Jumbo Sweet' or 'Big Bertha'; exotic 'Carnival Mixture' grows green, red, yellow, violet, and purple-black.

Chilli peppers – grow any listed in Chapter 6, but also very hot varieties such as 'Thai Dragon'.

Eggplant – 'Moneymaker' (reliable purple-black fruit); 'Red Egg' (orange egg-sized fruit ripening red); 'Chinese Ancestors' (mauve, white, striped, fat and thin fruits).

Cucumbers – 'Pepinex 69' (traditional long and green); 'Carmen' (virus and disease resistant); 'Athene' (good in cooler greenhouses).

Cantaloupes – 'Amber Nectar' (aka 'Castella'), salmon-pink flesh, superb flavor; 'Sweetheart' (scarlet flesh, good flavor, very reliable).

Grapes – 'Black Hamburgh' (sweet black grapes for an unheated house); 'Crimson Seedless' (superb red grapes).

Figs – 'White Marseilles' (ripen gold); 'Rouge de Bordeaux' (purple with deep red flesh).

Pick over ornamental plants such as pelargoniums every few days, removing faded leaves and flowers. It keeps them looking neat, and it removes a potential source of fungus disease.

Ornamental plants

Greenhouse pot plants provide seasonal color for staging and shelves. If you don't have a heated greenhouse, stick to annual, summer varieties that are thrown away at the end of their flowering season, rather than tender greenhouse perennials that need to be kept frost-free in winter.

Coleus (*Solenostemon*) (**1**) are grown for their very colorful leaves; plants are easy to raise from seed sown in a heated propagator in early spring. If you have named cultivars, then take cuttings in spring or summer. Coleus plants look good between flowering plants in a greenhouse display, and they like fairly generous fertilizing and watering in summer. Nip out the flower buds as soon as you see them; the leaves fade if the plants are allowed to flower. Coleus need a temperature of 65°F (18°C) to get them through winter, so keep cuttings in a heated propagator, take the parent plants indoors, or raise new ones from seed each spring.

Cyclamen (**2**) make a great show under glass, from autumn until late spring, given a minimum temperature of 40°F (5°C) and gentle watering and fertilizing. Cool, bright conditions are to their liking – too much heat and water and they will collapse, never to recover. Tug out dead flowers complete with their stems, and treat yellow leaves the same way. In early summer, the plants start yellowing, which indicates they are ready for their annual rest, so gradually reduce the watering until the tubers are dormant. Stand the pots outside in a cool, shady place for the summer. Repot in late July, and begin very gentle watering until the plants are growing strongly again, then move them back to a shady part of the greenhouse in September, before the first frost.

Freesias (**3**) are relatively easy to grow under glass; plant the corms, six to a 5in (12cm) pot in late summer or early autumn and, during winter, keep them very lightly watered and free from frost. As the flower spikes start appearing in spring, tie them to split stakes with raffia to keep them straight, and begin fertilizing with diluted liquid tomato fertilizer. When the flowers are over, or you've cut them to take into the house, continue fertilizing until the leaves start to turn yellow, then reduce the watering and allow the corms to dry off gradually for their summer rest. The same bulbs can flower again for many years, but grow small offsets in a "nursery" pot while they plump up, because they won't flower until they are big enough.

Fuchsias (4) are regular summer favorites. The best kinds to grow under glass all year round are those with particularly large or fragile flowers, such as the California Dreamer Series and the exotic-flowered species, which would soon be ruined by the weather if you risked them outside. They enjoy light shade. Pot up rooted cuttings or repot young plants in spring, water freely all the time they are growing well, and give half-strength tomato fertilizer every week or ten days. Reduce the watering in autumn, then keep plants almost dry and at a minimum temperature of 40°F (5°C) in winter, when they are dormant.

Achimenes (5), or hot-water plants, are sold as tiny tubercles in spring. Plant three or five to a 4in (10cm) pot, covering them to their own depth with soil mix. Water sparingly, and stand them in a heated propagator, at 50–60°F (10–15°C), until the first shoots show, then move them to a shady part of the greenhouse. The plants grow to about 12in (30cm) high and flower their socks off through summer and early autumn. Fertilize and water regularly; never let them go dry when in active growth or they will stop growing. In late autumn, reduce watering to allow the tubercles to dry off gently, and store them in their pots in a frost-free place for winter.

1 Coleus.
2 *Cyclamen persicum*.
3 *Freesia* 'Ballerina'.
4 Fuchsia.
5 *Achimenes* 'Scarlatti'.

6 *Streptocarpus* 'Falling Stars'.
7 *Primula malacoides.*
8 *Clivia miniata* yellow selection.
9 Cactus.
10 *Pelargonium* 'Fringed Aztec'.
11 Regal geranium.

Streptocarpus (6) is another very glamorous plant, flowering from midsummer to midautumn, and some of the new cultivars will bloom all year round. Repot plants in spring – a 5in (12cm) pot is the biggest they'll ever need; they have only small root systems. Keep the soil mix moist and fertilize regularly in summer, when plants need to be grown in light shade, since they scorch easily. In winter, they'll be fine at 40–45°F (5–7°C) if they're kept almost dry, but they'll be happier kept just moist and at room temperature, so move them to a windowsill indoors.

Primula malacoides (7) is a popular winter-and spring-flowering pot plant for a greenhouse that's kept at 40°–45°F (5–7°C). Grow your own from seeds sown in late spring. Keep the seedlings cool and shady in summer, then pot them into 3–5in (8–12cm) pots when they are big enough. They are usually thrown away after they finish flowering. *Primula obconica* is larger in all its parts and more robust and easier to grow, though its leaves can make some people break out in a rash. I love it and it has been a firm favorite since my Parks' Department days.

Clivia (8) is an exotic-looking, evergreen perennial with strap-shaped leaves and several stems topped with large, long-lasting, yellow-centered orange trumpet flowers in late winter or early spring. Plants need good light, but the leaves scorch easily, so keep them in medium to heavy shade during summer. Water clivias all year round, but only sparingly in winter, when they need a minimum temperature of 40°F (5°C). Begin fertilizing with half-strength liquid tomato fertilizer as soon as you see the first flower buds, and continue till late summer. Repot after flowering if necessary. Raise new plants from seed removed from the ripe fruit that sometimes follow the flowers, or split up big old plants.

Cacti and other succulents (9) are very collectable – they look good all year round, they put up with any amount of sun and heat, and many of them flower each spring. Contrary to what a lot of people think, the plants need plenty of water and occasional weak liquid fertilizing in summer. In winter, they need to be kept almost dry, in a minimum temperature of 40°F (5°C). Most are quite slow growing and need repotting only every 2–3 years in spring, using a well-drained, gritty cactus mix containing no more than 50 percent organic matter.

Zonal pelargoniums (10) are commonly known as "geraniums" and they are, for me, a must in the greenhouse. All right, so they are common bedding plants, but you can grow all kinds of beauties in a frost-free greenhouse. Try 'Appleblossom Rosebud' with its fully double rose-shaped flowers of white tipped with rose pink, or miniature varieties like 'Red-black Vesuvius' whose leaves are deep purple-gray, setting off the scarlet flowers. The 'Angel' pelargoniums are miniature versions of regals (see below), and they have a charm all their own. All demand full light and hate soggy soil mix. Given these requirements they are happy as pie.

Regal geraniums (11) are the posh relatives of the bedding sorts, with jagged-edged leaves and orchidlike flowers that are too fragile to last well outside. They need to be grown on a sunny windowsill indoors or under glass, where they flower through a cool summer and well into autumn. Pot rooted cuttings into 3in (8cm) pots, or repot young plants into 5in (12cm) pots in spring, using a soil-based potting mix. Water lightly until they fill the pot with roots. In summer, water more generously, fertilize once a week with liquid tomato fertilizer, and pick off yellow leaves and dead flower heads regularly. In autumn, slowly cut back the watering and stop fertilizing. Plants need to be kept fairly dry in winter and at 40°F (5°C). Propagate by stem-tip cuttings taken during summer.

The conservatory

A conservatory isn't just a greenhouse tacked on over the patio doors; it is part of the house – a room used by people in which plants are part of the furniture. A conservatory needs to look good, so there's no place for things like potting benches, propagators, and sprayers, and there's no place for plants that don't look their best. It's a show house, not a work place.

A traditional conservatory is a matchless addition to any period house.

Choosing and siting a conservatory

This isn't a do-it-yourself project. You need professional help. Several firms specialize in conservatory design and construction, and they'll be able to suggest a style and proportions that look right for your house, as well as undertaking the work.

Victorian-style conservatories are very popular, but in some situations, a fifties-style structure, with stained-glass window panels, a contemporary design, or one that's been designed specially for you will look much better. When it comes to construction, hardwood looks smart and needs little maintenance but if, from the looks point of view, a white-painted job will suit the situation better, then frankly I'd go for PVC. Yes, I know it's not natural, but it'll save you no end of painting and routine maintenance. And if you live near the ocean or other similarly exposed situation where painted wood deteriorates rapidly, it'll last a great deal longer.

The one thing I would insist on is washable flooring – ceramic tiles, quarry tiles, or a good quality vinyl, because there's bound to be a certain amount of water and plant mess. You'll want to be able to clean up easily, and carpet will soon look a bit jaded.

When it comes to siting a conservatory, the only practical place on a lot of houses is outside the living room, with access through French windows or sliding patio doors – but be imaginative. You could use a conservatory to link the kitchen and living room so that it becomes a garden dining room. Maybe you can knock through a passageway wall and turn what was previously wasted space at the side of the house into a summer sitting room. That's where a good firm comes in; they can show you all the possibilities.

A sunny, south-facing spot isn't essential – far from it. A conservatory built in that situation will be like an oven in summer unless you put in lots of blinds and fans. A shadier exposure will stay far more comfortable, and it also means you'll be able to grow a wider range of plants.

Managing a conservatory

A conservatory is rather like a cross between a living room and a patio, so looking after conservatory plants is the same as for any other plants in containers. They may be part of the furniture, but they need more than an occasional dusting. They need regular watering; more in summer and less in winter. Fertilize them weekly from late spring to early autumn, using quarter-strength tomato fertilizer for flowering plants and general-purpose liquid fertilizer for foliage kinds. To prevent plants from making a mess, spend some time each week picking off dead leaves and flowers – it's surprisingly therapeutic, and they look so much better afterward.

You probably won't want to use pesticide sprays in the conservatory, even if you use them elsewhere. Look for organic alternatives, but if you don't overload the conservatory with plants, you won't have half the pest problems. If you stand affected plants on the patio for the summer, most pests clear off all on their own.

The only extras you need worry about are shading and ventilating in summer, and heating in winter. Various kinds of internal blinds are available to keep things cool in summer, and roof fans will circulate the air to supplement roof vents. If you use the conservatory all year round and want to keep it at room temperature, the best way is to have extra radiators added to the central heating system. Otherwise, use electric skirting heaters along the bottom of the walls. If it's used only occasionally and you don't grow plants that need much warmth, there's no point heating it more than enough to keep it frost free, and a normal greenhouse fan heater will do that nicely.

Against a modern house you can afford to be more outlandish – and sit among the plants whatever the weather.

Conservatory plants

Stagger home with a mature bougainvillea, and the Mediterranean touch is yours.

This is where a conservatory has nothing in common with your living room, because – with few exceptions – conventional houseplants aren't all that happy in the conservatory. That's because the sunlight is a lot stronger and temperatures may fluctuate quite dramatically. Proper conservatory plants are best suited to the conditions, and – as always – a few big specimens look much better than lots of little ones. But when you are choosing plants, besides looks, the thing to check is which temperature they need to be kept at in winter.

Bougainvillea (**1**) is a large, spiky climber that's covered in pink, apricot, or purple bracts for most of the summer. It's good for training on a sunny wall. It puts up with quite high temperatures, and although it appreciates generous fertilizing and watering during the growing season, it's relatively droughtproof. Bougainvillea is a very good choice for a conservatory that's heated to between 40–55°F (5–13°C) in winter; it needs a cool, dryish spell then to initiate flower buds – if you keep it too hot when it wants to be resting, it won't flower. In early spring, prune the plant back to within a few buds of its main framework of stems to keep it neat.

Brugmansia (**2**) is what we used to call datura, or angel's trumpet. It has large, oval leaves and huge, trumpet-shaped flowers in white, yellow, or an unusual sort of burnt orange. It grows like crazy in summer, when it needs lots of fertilizer and water. It's also quite prone to aphids and whitefly, so that wants keeping an eye on. Prune it quite hard in spring, just before it starts growing, to stop it from growing too big. It's at its absolute best trained as a standard, when you need to trim up only the head, the same as for a standard fuchsia. Keep it at 40°F (5°C) or above, in winter.

Geranium maderense (**3**) is a spectacular biennial for a 12in (30cm) pot, growing leaves one year and producing flowers the next. It makes a 3–4ft (1–1.2m) tall, symmetrical arrangement of lacy leaves, and the stems are topped by mauve-pink, cranesbill-like flowers. Grow plants from seed sown in spring, and keep them at a minimum of 40°F (5°C) in winter.

Plumbago capensis (**4**) is another south-of-France special, best trained as a wall shrub in a sunny spot, where the sky blue flowers appear from midsummer well into the autumn. Give it the same treatment as bougainvillea, and you won't go far wrong.

Stephanotis (5) is the climber to choose if yours is a slightly shady conservatory and you can keep a fairly steady, living-room temperature all year round. It's evergreen, with large oval leaves and big clusters of scented white flowers in summer. Train it up an ornamental trellis or around a plant support frame stuck into its pot. It needs to be slightly potbound to flower well, so repot it only in spring when it really needs it, and then give it only a slightly bigger pot.

Oleanders (*Nerium oleander*) (6) are tender trees or large shrubs with a Mediterranean air, and clusters of waxy-looking pink or white flowers for most of the summer. Grow them in pots in a hot, sunny conservatory and stand them out on the patio in summer, if you are short of space. They like fairly generous watering and fertilizing, but in winter they like to be kept nearly dry and at a minimum of 40°F (5°C). Watch out for the sap, because it's an irritant and tends to leak out if the plant is injured.

1 *Bougainvillea glabra.*
2 *Brugmansia.*
3 *Geranium maderense.*
4 *Plumbago capensis.*
5 *Stephanotis floribunda.*
6 *Nerium oleander.*

Abutilon (7) is a rather upright, bushy shrub with large, bell-shaped flowers in apricot, yellow, or red that appear throughout summer and, in some cases, all winter as well. The dark red 'Nabob' is especially good. The leaves are large and attractive, making this a striking plant for a large pot, given a stake for support. Its only fault is that it's a bit prone to aphids and whitefly. Fertilize and water generously in summer, less in winter. It needs a minimum of 40°F (5°C). Repot, when it's needed, in early spring.

Jasmines (8) have a heady scent that percolates the entire room, and they'll twine themselves around a trellis for support. *Jasminum polyanthum* is commonly sold as a houseplant and has pink buds opening to white flowers in spring, but it'll reach 10ft (3m) and isn't much to look at when it's not in flower. You'd be much better off with *J. azoricum* from a specialized nursery; it's more compact, evergreen, and has fragrant white flowers all year round. Avoid pruning it if possible. It needs 40°F (5°C) in winter.

7 *Abutilon* 'Nabob'.
8 *Jasminum polyanthum*.
9 Citrus (× *Citrofortunella microcarpa*).
10 *Passiflora edulis*.
11 *Acacia dealbata*.
12 *Tibouchina urvilleana*.

Citrus (9) are *the* must-have conservatory plants nowadays, but to be honest, they aren't the easiest to grow. Keep them in pots barely big enough to hold the roots, and repot them in spring only when they are potbound. Use a soil-based potting mix with 25 percent potting bark or large perlite pieces added – citrus need a rich but very free-draining mix. When repotting, go only to a pot one size larger than the last. Apply a special citrus fertilizer, or use general-purpose liquid fertilizer, not tomato fertilizer, and water thoroughly when the soiol mix starts to feel dry. Don't use the "little and often" technique for citrus. In winter, they'll need a temperature of 45–50°F (7–10°C), and you can cut down on watering quite severely. I know it all sounds rather fussy, but citrus are worth all the effort once you get the hang of them – home-grown oranges and lemons score maximum brownie points when the neighbors drop in for a drink, and the blossoms smell divine.

Passionflowers (*Passiflora*) (10), in their tender forms, are becoming popular as conservatory climbers for covering a wall – although they're fast growing, they cling to a trellis using tendrils, so there's no need to tie them up. The flowers are similar to the outdoor passionflower, but often bigger and in other colors, including red. If you are going to grow a passionflower, you might just as well grow one with edible fruits as well as attractive flowers, in which case *Passiflora edulis* is probably the best. Grow it in a large pot, fertilize and water it generously in summer, and prune it in early spring, as for bougainvillea, to prevent it from growing too big. The fruits are ready to eat when they are purple and wrinkly; the proper way to eat them is just like a boiled egg – slice the top off and dive in with a spoon. Give it 40–45°F (5–7°C) or more in winter.

Acacia dealbata (11) is the florist's mimosa, the one with ferny foliage and lots of tiny, fluffy yellow balls of flowers in late winter. It makes an elegant conservatory tree that can be stood outside in summer. Treat it the same as abutilon, but start applying liquid tomato fertilizer as soon as you see buds appearing. In a mild area, you might get away with it in an unheated conservatory, but it normally needs to be frost-free.

Tibouchina urvilleana (12) looks quite exotic, though it's really quite tough; it's a naturally bushy conservatory shrub with large, oval evergreen leaves and big, velvety purple flowers all summer. Give it a large pot, fertilize it regularly in summer, and keep the soil mix moist all the time. It doesn't want to dry out completely, even in winter, when it needs a minimum temperature of 40°F (5°C).

Undercover nursery

Once you have a greenhouse, instead of just dabbling at plant production, you can really go to town. A greenhouse traps the sun's heat and acts as a natural "propagator," so summer cuttings root easily, and seeds of hardy plants germinate readily inside it. But if you want to propagate plants early in the year, or you want to take more difficult cuttings, then you'll need an electricity supply and a few extra items of equipment.

Propagators

A heated propagator looks like a big, clear plastic box that sits on a solid tray containing embedded heating cables. By combining steady bottom heat, humidity, and protection from drafts, it provides ideal conditions for rooting cuttings or raising seedlings. It needs to stand on staging inside the greenhouse, with a nearby outlet to plug into. Some models are big enough to hold four standard-sized seed trays, while others hold only two. You can simply fill the interior with small pots if you want.

Before you use the propagator, spread a 1in (2.5cm) layer of damp sand over the base, and switch it on so the inside warms up. If you use it in winter or early spring, even with background heating to keep the greenhouse frost-free, you'll probably need to set the propagator thermostat to the maximum to maintain 60–65°F (15–18°C). This is suitable for most seed germination and rooting softwood cuttings. In an unheated greenhouse, it's best to wait until spring, when the temperature is naturally warmer.

As you fill the propagator with pots or trays, push them up close together to make the best use of the space, and rewet the

After all these years, I still get a thrill watching seeds germinate. Lupines come through in a matter of days.

sand regularly to keep it damp. As well as distributing the heat evenly, this creates the humidity that sustains a good growing environment. Although it sounds like a waste of heat, keep the ventilators in the lid of the propagator open on all but cold nights to keep the air inside moving and to help avoid fungal diseases.

When you take young plants out of the propagator, remember that they've been used to perfect conditions, so don't put them directly into the garden. Grow them on in the greenhouse for a while first, and then wean them gradually to outdoor conditions.

Cold frames

A cold frame is handy if you grow a lot of frost-tender plants that need hardening off before you can plant them out in spring. You can't take frost-tender bedding plants out of a warm greenhouse and expect them to acclimatize to outdoor conditions overnight. Hardening off lets them get accustomed to moving air and fluctuating temperatures gradually.

Stand the plants out in the cold frame a couple of weeks before you expect the last frost, open the lid every morning, and shut it each night. If it's going to be cold overnight, cover the lid of the frame with burlap or several old newspapers for insulation. If you don't have a cold frame, the alternative is to move plants out of the greenhouse on fine days and move them back at night for a while weeks before it's safe to plant them out. Choose a spell of settled, mild, still weather to plant out tender plants.

A cold frame is also a good place to propagate hardy annuals and perennials from seed or to root semi-ripe cuttings taken later in summer. With its lid open, use it to grow on young plants, such as primroses, cyclamen, or winter bedding, during summer; these are plants that need intensive care but at lower temperatures than they'd have under glass. Once you have a cold frame, you'll find it invaluable for all sorts of overflows from the greenhouse.

Other handy propagating items

If you propagate plants only occasionally, you can get by just using seed trays with rigid plastic lids – unheated propagators that keep seeds and cuttings humid and protect seedlings from drafts and pests. Alternatively, make your own propagating covers by cutting the bottom off plastic bottles and sitting them over the top of flower pots – unscrew the cap for ventilation.

In the garden, you can root a lot of easy cuttings in summer in well-prepared ground in an odd corner of the garden underneath a plastic cloche – or plant out single cuttings and push a bottle-propagator into the ground over each one.

Cold frames are indispensable as a halfway house between the greenhouse and the great outdoors.

Propagation methods

The quickest way to propagate most plants is from cuttings. You can have a new plant flowering within a few months from a cutting, when to grow the same type of plant from seed might take an entire growing season. Some plants take several years to flower when they are grown from seed, but a cutting that is taken from a mature, flowering plant is already sort of mature, so it starts flowering much faster – you've just shortened the juvenile phase. Many hybrid plants do not come true from seed, but cuttings are always identical to the parent – the original clone.

Seed is useful for growing plants that don't produce good cutting material or that won't root from cuttings, and it's the best way to raise large numbers of bedding plants, which flower quickly from seed. People often get confused by all the different types of cuttings and when to take them, but it's a lot more logical than at first it seems. It's mostly down to how firm the current season's growth becomes as the season progresses – softwood cuttings come first, semi-ripe come next, with hardwood cuttings last.

You can always tell a real gardener's greenhouse by the amount of clutter it contains and by the amount of plants being grown from seeds and cuttings.

How to... **take softwood cuttings**

Softwood cuttings, also called tip or stem-tip cuttings, are taken from the tips of soft young shoots in spring and summer, before the tissue has turned woody. This type of cutting is used to propagate bushy plants that root quickly and have reasonably long stems. They are rooted in trays or pots. Use this method of taking cuttings for argyranthemums, fuchsias, osteospermums, pelargoniums, penstemons, and tender perennials and greenhouse pot plants.

Softwood cuttings of most plants will root at any time between late spring and late summer or early autumn. Midsummer is the very best time for more difficult plants; if you want to take all of your softwood cuttings at once, instead of spreading the load over the season, that's the time to do it. Cuttings of frost-tender plants should be taken in late summer so that they can be kept in a heated greenhouse through the winter and so be saved for the next year.

What you need

- *sharp penknife or craft knife with disposable blades*
- *3in (8cm) pots filled with sowing medium*
- *hormone rooting powder*
- *plastic bag or propagating lids to cover cuttings*
- *pencil or dibber*

1 Remove soft shoot tips from suitable plants with a sharp knife. The cutting should be 2–3in (5–8cm) long when prepared (see step 2), though fuchsias may only be 1in (2.5cm) long. Tricky cuttings (and there are not that many of them) can have their cut stem bases dipped in hormone rooting powder.

2 Remove the lower leaves and make a basal cut just below a leaf joint. Fill an 3in (8cm) pot with sowing or rooting medium, and tap it to settle the contents. Insert the cuttings around the edge of the pot – three cuttings will normally be happy in a pot this size. Don't bury the cuttings too deeply – the lower leaves should be clear of the medium. Water the cuttings in.

3 Either fasten a plastic bag over the pot and cuttings with an elastic band, or use a rigid, plastic transparent top sold especially for propagating. Stand the pot in a heated propagator or on a warm windowsill, not in the scorching sun. Check the pot regularly, and remove any rotting cuttings. Pot up the young plants as soon as they start to grow and when tapping them out reveals a healthy root system.

How to... **take semi-ripe cuttings**

Semi-ripe cuttings are similar to the softwood type, but they are taken later in the season – in late summer or early autumn, when this year's new growth has started to go woody at the base, where it grows out from an older stem.

You should use semi-ripe cuttings for evergreen herbs, conifers, boxwood, heathers, and many shrubs. They are usually rooted in prepared soil in a cold frame. If you have only a few, you could use pots, or prepare a patch of soil out in the garden to put the cuttings in, and cover them with cut-off beverage bottles or cloches instead.

1 In late summer and early autumn, select shoots that are young and vigorous but quite firm to the touch. They should be pliable but not sappy. Cut them off with a pair of pruners and keep them in a plastic bag while you are gathering more material. In the case of branching, bushy plants such as boxwood and yew, strip off this year's stems from older branches so that they peel away with a "heel" of old bark attached to the base.

2 Trim the base of the cuttings below a leaf joint and remove leaves from the lower two-thirds of the stem, as well as thorns from prickly plants. Pinch out any sappy shoot tips. The prepared cuttings should be about 4in (10cm) long. With heel cuttings, simply trim the heel to remove any long whiskers. Insert the cuttings 3in (8cm) apart in trays of rooting medium (multipurpose soil mix mixed with its own volume of sharp sand to improve drainage). Hormone rooting powder can be used on tricky subjects.

3 Water the cuttings in and stand the tray in a cold frame that is kept closed but can be opened a little to allow ventilation in fair weather. Most cuttings will root during winter and spring and can be potted up or planted out later in spring. Some may take longer and may need to be left until autumn.

How to... **take hardwood cuttings**

Hardwood cuttings are usually taken in midautumn, around the time the leaves naturally fall from deciduous plants, up through the time it gets quite cold.

    Hardwood cuttings should be used to propagate easy-to-root deciduous shrubs with long, straight stems, such as roses, *Cornus*, willows, fruit tree rootstocks, *Rubus*, and hazel. They are slow to root, and most kinds need to stay put until the following autumn before being moved. The big benefit is that you don't need any special facilities.

What you need

- *pruners*
- *spade*
- *coarse sand*
- *spare patch of ground in the garden*

1 Cut long shoots from the plant so that they include the woody base of this year's growth, and trim the tops off to leave them about 8in (20cm) long. If you want cuttings to grow into trees, in the case of willows for instance, leave them their full length with the top untrimmed; you can take cuttings 2–3ft (60–90cm) long with willows.

2 Remove any leaves. Dip the base of the cuttings in rooting powder – choose the strongest kind available for use especially on hardwood cuttings, since it contains more of the active ingredient. Choose a patch of bare ground in an open, sunny spot. Make a slit trench with the spade by pushing it vertically down to its full depth, then waggling it backward and forward to open up a 2in (5cm) wide V-shape, then sprinkle a 1in (2.5cm) layer of sand all along the bottom.

3 Push the base of each cutting down firmly into the slit trench, leaving only the top 2in (5cm) sticking out above the ground in the case of 8in (20cm) cuttings (more for longer ones). Continue pushing cuttings in 3in (8cm) apart until they are all in, then close the trench by firming the soil down from either side of it with your foot. Water well.

How to... **root leaf cuttings**

Leaf cuttings are used to propagate plants that don't have any stems, and they can be taken at any time during the late spring or summer. They are rooted in trays and are usually ready for potting 6–8 weeks later.

Leaf cuttings are suitable for *Streptocarpus*, *Saintpaulia* (African violet), *Begonia rex*, and many succulent plants.

What you need

- *sharp knife*
- *seed tray*
- *rooting medium*
- *transparent propagator lid*

1 *Streptocarpus* (the Cape primrose) has long, tongue-like leaves that can be chopped up to make several cuttings. Cut a healthy, rich green leaf from the parent plant. Avoid any that are pale yellow or showing signs of browning.

2 Taking care to remember which is the top and bottom of the leaf, slice it up into sections about 1½in (3cm) long. (Leaves of *Begonia rex* can actually be cut up into square sections larger than a postage stamp, but their polarity – top and bottom – is still important.)

3 Insert the cuttings into the rooting medium so that they sit up rather like gravestones. The bottom ½in (1cm) of leaf section should be buried and the rest left protruding. The cut surface which was nearest the parent plant (i.e. the bottom) should be inserted, with the top edge still visible. Keep the cuttings in a warm propagator. They can be dug up and potted individually when a new young plant has been produced at the bottom of each of them.

Many succulents can be propagated from leaf cuttings.

Variations on the leaf cuttings theme

Entire leaves of *Begonia rex* can be cut from the parent plant and laid on the surface of rooting medium in a seed tray. Secure them with wire or opened-up paper clips bent open to make U-shaped pins. Take a sharp knife and push it through the main veins to make a slit about ½in (1cm) long. Place the tray in a warm propagator, and make sure that the medium and the atmosphere do not dry out. In a couple of months' time, tiny new plants will arise from the cut tissue. When they are large enough, they can be dug up and potted on individually.

With *Saintpaulia* (African violets), cut off a whole leaf complete with 1in (2.5cm) of leaf stalk, and push the stalk into a pot of sowing medium. Keep it warm and humid, but don't cover with plastic, or it will rot. A cluster of plants will grow from the base of the stalk: pot each singly when they are big enough to handle.

Leaves of some succulents, such as the echeverias, root naturally when they drop off the plant. Choose young, whole, fully expanded leaves, and barely press the end where they were attached to the plant into a sandy rooting medium (made by mixing equal parts coarse sand and rooting medium). New roots and shoots will grow from that point.

Secret of success

Green thumbs have nothing to do with it – the trick is to stop cuttings from dehydrating or rotting before they root.

To prevent dehydration, check often to see if cuttings need watering, and aim to keep their medium just moist all the time. Cover all but hairy, felty, or succulent cuttings with a lid to keep them humid.

To prevent rot, don't overwater, and ventilate regularly to keep air circulating. Pick off dead or mildewed leaves often, and remove flowers and buds – they divert energy from root production.

Propagation tricks

When you don't have a lot of propagating materials, or you want to take a few cuttings of things that are expensive to buy but difficult to root, it's always satisfying to know that are there are tricks and shortcuts that you can use.

Softwood shrub cuttings in sun frames

A wide range of shrub cuttings can be rooted easily by taking 6–8in (15–20cm) softwood cuttings in summer and putting them outside in the ground under a "sun frame." Choose a sunny spot, and prepare the soil as for semi-ripe cuttings (see page 554).

You need a rigid plastic cloche with a square of rigid plastic to cover each end, so that it's totally enclosed. Paint the outside with greenhouse shading, so your cuttings don't scorch. Prepare softwood shrub cuttings as before (see page 553). Push them into the ground about 2in (5cm) apart. Water them in thoroughly, then cover with the cloche. Seal the ends up, and pile soil around the edges, so that humidity builds up underneath – you want to be able to see condensation forming on the inside. Lift the cloche off once a week to remove any mildewy leaves or cuttings that have gone rotten, and water the cuttings so the steam-bath effect continues. After about 6–8 weeks, start to increase the ventilation and after three months or so remove the cloche entirely. The cuttings will root slowly, and most should be ready to pot in autumn; leave the rest until next spring.

Missed the boat?

With woody shrubs, if you miss out on the chance to take softwood cuttings in midsummer, you can take semi-ripe cuttings later or hardwood cuttings right at the end of the season, so you have several bites at the cherry.

Softwood cuttings need protection from the elements, so invest in a corrugated plastic cloche to keep them safe.

Difficult cuttings

As a general rule, if a plant is more expensive than other species of a similar size at the garden center, it's usually because it is difficult to propagate. Some "problem plants," such as named cultivars of Japanese maples (*Acer palmatum*), must be grafted, but a lot of difficult plants can be easily increased by layering (see page 159). But if you have a greenhouse, it's worth trying cuttings of other hard-to-root kinds such as camellias, rhododendrons, passionflower, wisteria, and clematis in a heated propagator. Don't expect a high success rate, so take plenty more cuttings than plants you want, but if even only a few root, you can feel very pleased with yourself, and you'll know you've saved a few dollars.

Take a mixture of softwood and semi-ripe cuttings in summer to hedge your bets, and in the case of clematis, take internodal cuttings (see box below). Always use the strongest rooting powder – the stuff for hardwood cuttings if possible.

Put three cuttings in around the edge of a 3in (8cm) pot filled with rooting medium. After watering them, stand the pots on the damp sand inside the propagator and turn the heat up. Shade the propagator from the sun. Aim to keep a steady 70°F (21°C) inside, and close the propagator's ventilators to create 100 percent humidity. Water the sand to maintain a steamy atmosphere but don't overwater the cuttings, and watch out for mildew or signs of rot.

Cuttings will root at varying speeds, and none are quick. Pot up the rooted cuttings individually – any that haven't rooted or rotted at the base can go back in for a second try.

Offsets

There are some plants that are no trouble to propagate at all, because they virtually do it themselves – they are the ones that produce offsets, as many cacti, other succulents, and bromeliads do, or those that build up big clumps, such as clivias.

With offsets, simply detach as many as you need when they are big enough to grow independently at the start of the growing season in spring, then pot them up.

Spring is also the best time to divide clump-forming plants, but here you'll need to tip the parent out of its pot and work your fingers in between to separate part of the original plant, complete with its roots.

Treat a newly potted offset or division like a cutting that is only partly rooted. Give it extra care while it grows itself some more roots – keep it warm and draft-free, don't let it dry out, and don't overwater it. That said, it's the easiest way you'll ever find to propagate plants.

Clematis cuttings

To make internodal cuttings, remove a length of this year's stem and cut off the soft material from the end, leaving semi-ripe wood. Keeping the top uppermost, divide the rest of the stem into cuttings with two pairs of leaves. Cut cleanly just above the top pair, and 1–2in (2.5–5cm) below the bottom pair – it's important to keep them the right way up. Dip the base in hormone rooting powder, then push into pots as usual.

Caring for young plants

The average garden-center plant tends to be quite large so that it has a better chance of surviving the pitfalls it's likely to meet when planted in the garden, such as slugs, drought, and competition from other plants. A rooted cutting or young plant wouldn't stand a chance – it's like sending a boy out to do a man's job. No, young plants need growing on in almost nursery conditions until they are roughly the same size as you'd buy them at the garden center – only then are they ready to plant out.

Cuttings rooted in the garden

Hardwood cuttings that you've rooted outside in the garden are already quite well acclimatized, since they've been grown in the open from start to finish. Other types of cuttings that you've rooted outdoors in a cold frame, or other temporary cover, need to have the ventilation gradually increased over 6–8 weeks. That way, they slowly get used to wind and weather in easy stages before you take away their protection entirely.

The best way to grow them on is to line them out, as nurseries call it. In autumn or early spring, dig them up from their rooting place and plant them in well-prepared ground in the vegetable garden or in a special nursery bed. Plant them 12–18in (30–45cm) apart, with 2ft (60cm) between the rows. Water them in and leave until they are big enough to transplant to their final positions, any time in late autumn or early spring, when they are dormant.

If you don't have a suitable spot, or you need your plants to be portable, dig them up and put them into pots to grow them on. You'll need to water and fertilize them, so it makes more work, but some people like it better this way.

Cuttings rooted in pots or trays under cover

Plants that have rooted in pots can be potted up any time during spring, summer, or early autumn. Delicate plants that aren't big on root disturbance are best moved in spring or autumn.

Tip them carefully out of their propagating pots, and pot one cutting in the middle of a 5in (12cm) pot. If you have lots of cuttings of the same sort, plant three close together in the middle of the pot: you'll have a big, bushy plant in less than half the usual time. Stand the plants in a shady part of the greenhouse or cold frame, or put them in a plunge bed. Keep them watered and give them liquid fertizer once a week. To encourage a good shape, "stop" them once or twice by nipping out the growing tips.

Making a plunge bed

A plunge bed is like a topless cold frame, half-filled with sand. Its job is to act as a nursery bed for hardy plants in pots that need somewhere safe to keep growing until they are big enough to plant out in the garden. Although not essential, avid propagators find it very handy. If you buy a lot of plants, it comes in very useful for holding them until you are ready to plant them out. It can also be turned into a low cold frame for rooting semi-ripe cuttings, just by laying a sheet of plastic over the top as a lid.

Stand the base on loose, bare soil, half-fill it with sand, then rake it level and water well. Water the plants, then sink their pots to the rims in the damp sand so they can take up water as needed. Dampen the sand every few days: it's much quicker than watering lots of pots one at a time.

Epilogue to Part Two

Well, that's it. I hope you feel more in tune with plants and gardens than you did when we started. You'll keep making mistakes – we all do – and I'd not be telling the truth if I didn't admit to being irritated by my own errors of judgment. But at least now you might know what your intentions should be, and that's the most important thing.

I've been gardening for a living now for almost forty years, and if anything, I enjoy it now more than ever. Each spring rekindles a childish enthusiasm for sowing seeds, and the nearly mindless task of mowing becomes a safe haven for daydreams.

To some, gardening may seem like a harmless sort of pursuit that is of little real importance in a world where mightier issues grab the headlines. I don't agree. When power-crazed world leaders have long since been forgotten, foxgloves will still emerge in the shade and waterlilies open their starry flowers in the sun.

I believe passionately that gardening is the most important thing in life. Growing plants is, for me, the ultimate reality, the real thing, and something that anyone can do on the smallest patch of ground. Think of your own small garden as a patch on the larger quilt that is the entire country. If we all looked after our patches, what a quilt we would have.

Heigh-ho. Grow well, and enjoy your garden.

Raising your own plants is really the best feeling there is.

Index

ACKNOWLEDGEMENTS

How to be a Gardener has been one of the most rewarding projects I've ever undertaken, but then when something starts as a vague idea over lunch, and develops over a period of five years into two television series and two books, there is always a degree of wonder and, with any luck, a sense of fulfilment if things turn out well. If the reception granted to the television series and the book are anything to go by, that is certainly the case.

Much of that combined success is due to two talented and forbearing sets of people whose hard graft and endless good humour made things happen. In the production of the television series I have been helped tremendously by Dick Coulthurst, Helga Berry, Cassie Walkling and Rachel Malin, while Russell Jordan, Neil Woodger and Ross McInnes constructed the gardens on time and with great care.

The ever affable Jo Swift was generous with design help, and my regular cameraman Paul Hutchings and sound engineer Gordon Nightingale turned even the wettest days into something worth turning out for. Tim Shepherd again stunned us with his wonderful slow-motion footage, achieved thanks to months of patience in his studio. To the editors I owe especial thanks, for turning my disparate pieces to camera into a cohesive and inspiring whole.

Sue Thompson and the staff at the Royal Horticultural Society's gardens at Wisley were always tremendously helpful when we filmed there, and made sure we never went short of refreshments.

The National Trust staff at Hinton Ampner in Hampshire were equally welcoming.

The patient garden owners have, I hope, ended up with something better than anticipated. I most certainly have, thanks in the main to my producer Kath Moore. I am at a loss to find words that say a big enough thank you to her. Like Sam Goldwyn, she has managed to make something bigger than both of us, as well as making the journey stimulating, rewarding and a bit of a laugh.

The book has been a mammoth undertaking and could not have been accomplished without the encouragement of Nicky Copeland, the considerable editorial skills of Helena Caldon, and the design flair (and baking skills) of Isobel Gillan, who kept the patient photographer Jonathan Buckley and myself well supplied with cake and buns while trying to work out what shape each picture had to be. Jonathan deserves plaudits for making me and my gardens look so good, and for keeping his figure.

To Sue Phillips I am indebted for her unparalleled research skills, and to Lin Hawthorne for her patient checking of details. Amanda Patton has produced the clearest of artwork from my vague sketches with endless patience.

And finally I must admit that without Sue Richards and Bill Budd my garden would not be half so beautiful as it is. I owe them more than I can say.

How to be a Gardener has been a team effort, and team efforts are usually not without their trials. I can honestly say that this one was.

The photographer would like to thank the following owners and designers for kindly allowing their gardens to be photographed:

The photographer would also like to thank Helen Yemm for her assistance with this project and the following owners and designers for kindly giving permission for their gardens to be photographed:

Abbey Dore Court, Herefordshire (Charis Ward) p 130; Abbey Road, Hampshire (Fred and June Dod) pps 46 and 110; American Impressionists Garden, Giverny, France (designer: Mark Brown) p 58; Barleywood, Hampshire (Alan Titchmarsh) pps 61, 80, 89, 92, 99 (*1*), 105, 124, 138, 156, 177, 198 and 238; Beth Chatto Gardens, Essex (Beth Chatto) pps 36, 77 and 96; Church Lane, London (Paul Kelly) pps 100 and 128; Earl's Court Road, London (Camilla Shivarg) p 101 (*bottom*); Eastgrove Cottage, Worcestershire (Malcolm and Carol Skinner) pps 11 and 237; East Ruston Old Vicarage, Norfolk (Alan Gray and Graham Robeson) p 225; Glen Chantry, Essex (Sue and Wol Staines) pps 17 (*all*), 63, 94, 101 (*top*), 108, 133 and 134; Great Dixter, East Sussex (Christopher Lloyd) pps 107 (*all*) and 192; Hatfield House, Hertfordshire (Lady Salisbury) p 10; Hollington Herbs, Berkshire (Judith and Simon Hopkinson) pps 187 and 257; *Home Front* garden, Hackney (designer: Diarmuid Gavin) p 13; Ketley's, East Sussex (Helen Yemm) pps 28 and 123; Lady Farm, Somerset (Judy Pearce) p 99 (*3*); Landor Road, Warwickshire (Maurice and Wilmur Green) pps 35, 88 and 125; Merton Hall Road, London (Gay Gray) p 251; Peachings, Hampshire (Gill Siddell) pps 19, 71, 127, 164 and 173; Perch Hill, East Sussex (Sarah Raven) p 54; Roger's Rough, Kent (Richard Bird) p 99 (*2*); Rose Cottage, East Sussex (Fergus Garrett) p 114; Squires Hill Lane, Hampshire (Sarah and Andrew Coyle) p 103; Spencer Road, London (Anthony Goff) pps 86–87, 193, 197 and 241; Sticky Wicket, Dorset (Pam Lewis) p 255; St John's Road, Staffordshire (Maureen and Sid Allen) pps 29, 98 and 229; Tower Street, Hampshire (Jesse Delaney) pps 2, 27, 67 and 85; Upper Mill Cottage, Kent (David and Mavis Seeney) pps 77 (*top*) 116 and 223; Waterperry Gardens, Oxfordshire p 97; Wellhouse Road, Hampshire (Verity and Andrew Bronwitt) p 168.

BBC Gardens: Cottage Garden designed by Joe Swift & Sam Joyce for The Plant Room 256, 268, 292, 338, 377; No Space Garden designed by Joe Swift & Sam Joyce for The Plant Room 269, 304, 305, 328, 357b; No Time Garden designed by Russell Jordan 270, 374; Hot Garden designed by Joe Swift & Sam Joyce for The Plant Room 274, 288, 423, 557; Natural Garden designed by Joe Swift 261 Sam Joyce for The Plant Room 275, 282; Blank Canvas designed by Joe Swift & Sam Joyce for The Plant Room 284, 285, 297t, 307, 497; Water Garden designed by Sandy Worth 456.

Other Gardens: Barleywood, Hampshire (Alan Titchmarsh) 376, 390t, 414, 447, 498, 536; Barry Road, London (Jonathan Buckley) 389; Beth Chatto Gardens, Essex (Beth Chatto) 404, 430; Canning Road, London (Erica Hunninger) 364t; Chelsea Physic Garden, London 264; Chelsea Flower Show 2001, A Real Japanese Garden designed for the *Daily Telegraph* by Professor Masao Fukuhara 266; Chelsea Flower Show 2002 Visual Retreat designed by Wynniatt-Husey Clarke 267; Chelsea Flower Show 2002, High Fliers Haven designed by Chloe Wood & Tamsin Woodhouse 276; Chelsea Flower Show 2002, The Accenture Garden designed by Miriam Book 485; Chelsea Flower Show 2002, Kelly's Creek designed by Alison Wear & Miranda Melville 277r; Chelsea Flower Show 2002, Sanctuary designed by Steve Woodhams 278; Chelsea Flower Show 2000, Zen Inspired designed by spidergarden.com 364; Chelsea Flower Show 1999, A Chef's Garden designed by Sir Terence Conran 492; Chiltern Road, Buckinghamshire (Jo Chatterton) 340r; Church Lane, London (Paul Kelly) 334, 363; Coton Manor, Northamptonshire (Ian & Sue Pasley-Tyler) 504; Crystal Palace Road, London (Sue Hillwood Harris) 352; Culverden Road, London (Nick Ryan) 290; Grafton Park Road, London (Robin Green & Ralph Cade) 289, 291t, 379, 383t, 481, 505, 534; Great Dixter, East Sussex (Christopher Lloyd) 334t, 337, 424c, 443t, 447, 470, 520; Glen Chantry, Essex (Sue & Wol Staines) 170r, 198t, 210, 218l, 226; Eastgrove Cottage, Worcestershire (Malcolm & Carol Skinner) 424; East Ruston Old Vicarage, Norfolk (Alan Gray & Graham Robeson) 524t; Hinton Ampner House, Hampshire (The National Trust) 296, 298, 398; Hollington Herbs, Berkshire (Judith & Simon Hopkinson) 506; Ketley's, East Sussex (Helen Yemm) 280, 334, 482, 506; Ladywood, Hampshire (Sue Ward) 308, 312, 340l, 341, 399; Longstock Water Gardens, Hampshire (John Lewis Partnership) 458; Meynell Crescent, London (designed by Steve Woodhams) 381; Peachings, Hampshire (Gill Sidell) 537; Pentridge House, Dorset (Mr & Mrs King) 518r; Perch Hill, East Sussex (Sarah Raven) 448; RHS Garden Wisley, Surrey 424l; Rofford Manor, Oxfordshire (Mr & Mrs J. Mogford) 502; Sheffield Park, Sussex

(The National Trust) 265; Shepherd's Bush (Deidre Spencer) 362; Spencer Road, London (Anthony Goff) 386; Sticky Wicket, Dorset (Pam Lewis) 527; Stoneacre, Kent (The National Trust) 333; Sycamore Mews, London (designed byPenny Smith) 368; Upper Mill Cottage, Kent (David & Mavis Seeney) 372, 436; Valentine Cottage, Hampshire (Mr & Mrs Brown) 295, 313, 340r, 344, 358r, 380, 427, 518t, 532; Welcome Thatch, Dorset (Diana Guy) 281, 294t, 400, 552; West Dean Gardens, Sussex (Edward James Foundation) 494; West Green House, Hampshire (Marylyn Abbott) 314; West Green House Cottage (David Chase) 272, 287, 316t, 369.

Photographs copyright © Jonathan Buckley 2003
Except the following photographs from: A–Z Botanical 319 (5), 357 (2) photographer Anthony Seinet, 357 (3) Ian Gowland, 476 (1) BON, 476 (6) Adrian Thomas, 452 (3) J Malcolm Smith, 471 (3) Yves Tzaud, 522 (1) F Merlet, 523 (3) Chris Martin Bahr; Arcaid/MHK 545 Martine Hamilton Knight; Ardea 514T and 517 John Daniels; David Austin Roses 429(i) BBC Worldwide 316B, 383B, 422, 457 and 550 Tim Shepherd; Garden Picture Library 345 (1) Neil Homes, 349 (1) Janet Sorrell, 387 (5) Howard Rice, 437 (3) David Cavagnaro, 467 (4) and 468 (1) Howard Rice, 471 (5) Sunniva Harte, 474 (1) J S Sira, 519 TR Sunniva Harte, 542 (7) John Glover; Harpur Garden Library 353 (5), 411 (6), 475 (5), 541 (2 and 4); Andrew Lawson Photography 542 (10), 544, 547 (5 and 6); Marianne Majerus Photography 320 (4), 332 (6), 372 (3), 406 (3), 503(2), 548 (10), 548 (11); Clive Nichols Garden Pictures 334 (2), 336 (1), 410 (3), 419 (3), 426 (2); Oxford Scientific Films 470 (1) Gordon Maclean, 471 (4); Photos Horticultural 349, 357 (5), 359 (3), 408 (3), 429 (6 and 7), 451 (5), 470 (2) 541 (5).

BBC Worldwide would like to thank the above for providing photographs and for permission to reproduce copyright material. While every effort has been made to trace and acknowledge all copyright holders, we would like to apologize should there be any errors or omissions.